Finance and Investments Using *The Wall Street Journal*

Peter R. Crabb, Ph.D.
Northwest Nazarene University

McGraw-Hill
Irwin

Boston   Burr Ridge, IL   Dubuque, IA   Madison, WI   New York   San Francisco   St. Louis
Bangkok   Bogotá   Caracas   Kuala Lumpur   Lisbon   London   Madrid   Mexico City
Milan   Montreal   New Delhi   Santiago   Seoul   Singapore   Sydney   Taipei   Toronto

McGraw-Hill Irwin

FINANCE AND INVESTMENTS USING *THE WALL STREET JOURNAL*
Peter R. Crabb

1 2 3 4 5 6 7 8 9 0 CUS/CUS 0 9 8 7 6 5 4 3 2

ISBN 0-07-282936-2

www.mhhe.com

The McGraw-Hill Companies

Preface

For many years, finance professors have used *The Wall Street Journal* in their classrooms. *The Journal* continuously provides opportunities to illustrate theories and concepts put forth in finance textbooks and lectures. My students regularly evaluate the use of *The Wall Street Journal* as one of their most valuable experiences in school. This book is a formal adoption of this successful teaching methodology.

Finance and Investments Using *The Wall Street Journal* is, however, more than a study guide. The chapters that follow lead the student through traditional textbook material with real and current financial information. This book assists students with their study of finance by providing exercises that go beyond hypothetical questions on textbook theories, and by providing thought provoking questions for class discussion from actual articles.

Each of the following chapters has the same general format. The chapter begins with a list of learning objectives and key terms, followed by the written material. This presentation of the subject is not as comprehensive as that found in a general corporate finance or investments text, but the material will help students understand the important terms and concepts in finance. Throughout the chapter the student is asked to complete questions to insure their understanding of these important terms and concepts. Data for the questions are drawn from actual *Journal* articles, reports, and tables and answers to these questions are included in the appendix.

Further exercises and discussion questions are found at the end of each chapter. The student is asked to apply what they have learned by repeating some assignments from the chapter using a current edition of *The Wall Street Journal*, and a final exercise takes a more in depth look at the concepts presented in the chapter. Each chapter concludes with an article or feature column from a previous *Journal* and a series of questions for further thought and discussion in the student's study group or class meeting.

To students, I hope you find your study of finance through this book to be both interesting and rewarding. And to professors, I hope you find that using this approach makes teaching finance and investments as interesting and rewarding as it has been for me.

Acknowledgements: In all I do I give thanks to God; for from him and through him and to him are all things (Romans 11:36). I am grateful for the love and support of my wife and family during this project. My thanks to Brenda Johnson of Northwest Nazarene University for assistance editing the text and to Cody Crail, an outstanding NNU student, for assistance with the assignments, exercises, and discussion questions. Finally, I am grateful to Michele Janicek and all of the McGraw-Hill staff for making this project a success.

Peter R. Crabb, Ph.D.
Professor of Finance and Economics
School of Business and Economics
Northwest Nazarene University

Table of Contents

PART I – INTRODUCTION

PART II – ECONOMIC ANALYSIS

PART III – SECURITIES MARKETS ANALYSIS

PART IV – INVESTMENT ANALYSIS

PART V – DERIVATIVE SECURITIES

PART VI – PORTFOLIO MANAGEMENT

PART VII – CORPORATE FINANCING

PART I

INTRODUCTION

Chapter 1

Finance and Investments in
The Wall Street Journal

Objectives

1. Describe the different types of financial markets reported on in the *WSJ*.

2. Describe the different types of investments reported on in the *WSJ*.

3. Learn how to quickly navigate the sections, pages, columns, tables, and charts of financial information in the *WSJ*.

Key Terms

Financial Markets	Secondary Market	Organized Exchange
Financial Assets	Money Markets	Over-the-Counter (OTC)
Primary Market	Capital Markets	Real assets

This chapter presents an overview of the *WSJ*, and the financial markets and institutions on which the *WSJ* reports. Information from the *WSJ* is used here to describe the types of financial markets that exist and the types of investments traded in these financial markets. The chapter includes an exercise designed to help you learn where and how to find information on finance and investments in the *WSJ*.

Financial Markets

A *financial market* is a market in which financial assets (securities), such as stocks and bonds, can be purchased or sold. A *financial asset* is any contractual claim on an asset or group of assets. For example, a stock is a contractual claim on the assets of a corporation. A bond is also a legal contract in the form of a loan to a corporation. Financial markets are means of financial intermediation – the transfer of financial savings from one part of the economy, to investments in another part of the economy. Financial markets also provide investors a means to manage risk.

There are three broad classifications of financial markets: primary versus secondary markets, money versus capital markets, and organized versus over-the-counter markets. In a primary market, new securities, such as stocks or bonds, are issued by corporations. This market involves the exchange of funds for a financial claim. The financial claim may be either debt or equity. Debt instruments or debt securities are contractual obligations of a debtor (borrower) to a creditor (lender). A company that sells bonds is borrowing from the purchaser of the bond. In a primary market sale of a bond the borrower receives cash, and the lender receives a financial asset, the IOU. Equity securities or stocks are financial claims for ownership rights in a corporation as well as grants of voting rights for the management of the corporation. In a primary market sale of stock, the firm again receives cash, but this time in exchange for ownership rights.

For example, on June 14, 2002 the WSJ reported that Pacer International, Inc., a truck and rail line shipper, sold 14 million shares of stock to the public on June 13 at $15 per share. This primary market transaction raised $210 million for the company in exchange for ownership interests. News of primary market transactions are reported each day in the WSJ. Articles discussing the offerings are most often found in the Money and Investing section.

Previously issued debt or equity securities trade in the secondary market. When stocks or bonds are sold between investors no new funds are created for the issuer of the security - the corporation. Secondary markets serve an important function by providing liquidity for sellers. The more liquid a financial assets (the more easily it can be bought and sold) the less risk involved for the investor. When stock or bond markets are more liquid there are lower costs associated with finding buyers. After their sale in the primary market, all types of stocks and bonds trade in secondary markets.

The Pacer International Inc. stock discussed above began trading in the secondary market on June 13, 2002. Recall that the firm sold the shares at $15 each. On its first day of trading, the stock price rose higher, and the last trade of the day was at $15.95 per share. This secondary market activity in the stock is also found in the Money and Investing section of the WSJ. The Money and Investing Section includes trading activity for major stock transactions each business day.

Exercise 1-1

The following two headlines appeared in the *WSJ* on June 14, 2002:

"Treasury Plans Sale of $32 Billion in Short-Term Bills"

"Wal-Mart, Target Slide on Gloomy Retail Data"

1. Which headline refers to primary market transactions?

2. Which headline refers to secondary market transactions?

Money and Capital Markets

The second classification for a financial market is a money or capital market. The *money market* is a market where short-term investments, usually less than one year in length, are traded. This market is a debt market only. Since stocks are a claim on the assets of a corporation, and corporations are generally ongoing concerns, stocks represent long-term securities for the firm. The money market has only high quality issuers, including the U.S. government and low risk corporations. That is, firms that borrow in the money market are well-known companies with a strong history of meeting their obligations. The money market is very liquid (high number of buyer and sellers), but since it is short-term in nature it provides low returns on investment. The *capital market* on the other hand is long-term (greater than one year), includes both stocks and bonds, and has a range of corporations (low and high risk).

Each day the Money and Investing section of the *WSJ* includes a table entitled Money Rates. The Money Rates table includes rates for commercial paper – a money market security. Commercial paper is a short-term (less than 270 days) debt instrument issued by well-established corporations. Commercial paper is often used by other corporate financial managers wishing to earn interest on the cash flow from their business until it is needed. The Money and Investing Section also includes the Credit Markets column. The Credit Markets column covers both new (primary market) and existing (secondary market) debt securities from the U.S. Government, state and local governments, and corporations. Long-term U.S. Government securities are called Treasury notes and bonds. These capital market transactions range from 1 to 10 years in maturity.

Exercise 1-2

Refer to the two headlines in Exercise 1-1.

1. Which headline refers to money-market transactions?

2. Which headline refers to capital market transactions?

Stock and Bond Exchanges

The third classification of financial markets is based on where the market activity, buying and selling, takes place. In this respect, financial markets are either organized or over-the-counter (OTC). An *organized exchange* for financial assets has a visible marketplace, such as the New York Stock Exchange (NYSE) on Wall Street in New York City. In this marketplace, members trade securities that are "listed" on the exchange. In contrast, some markets for financial assets are traded by wired computer networks. These *over-the-counter* markets are made-up of securities dealers, and have no central or physical location. The National Association of Securities Dealers Automated Quotation System (NASDAQ) is an OTC market for stocks.

The secondary market for bonds includes organized exchanges and an OTC market. Most corporate bonds are traded in over-the-counter markets. However, many bonds from large issuers are traded on the organized exchanges, such as the NYSE and the American Stock Exchange (AMEX). The secondary market prices and current yields for these bonds are found in the U.S. Exchange Bonds table of the Money and Investing section. Also, the Markets Lineup column reports the closing value of the Dow Jones Bond Averages – an index of corporate bonds.

Exercise 1-3

CURRENCY TRADING

Key Currency Cross Rates

Late New York Trading Thursday, June 13, 2002

	Dollar	Euro	Pound	SFranc	Peso	Yen	CdnDlr
Canada	1.5394	1.4512	2.2660	0.9839	.15960	.01233	...
Japan	124.90	117.74	183.85	79.829	12.949	...	81.135
Mexico	9.6455	9.0928	14.198	6.1648	...	.07723	6.2658
Switzerland	1.5646	1.4749	2.3031	...	.16221	.01253	1.0164
U.K.	.67930	.6404	...	.4342	.07043	.00544	.44131
Euro	1.06080	...	1.5615	.67799	.10998	.00849	.68909
U.S.	...	.9427	1.4720	.63914	.10368	.00801	.64960

Source: Reuters

Exchange Rates

The New York foreign exchange mid-range rates below apply to trading among banks in amounts of $1 million and more, as quoted at 4 p.m. Eastern time by Reuters and other sources. Retail transactions provide fewer units of foreign currency per dollar.

	U.S. $ EQUIVALENT		CURRENCY PER U.S. $	
Country	Thu.	Wed.	Thu.	Wed.
Argentina (Peso)-y	.2841	.2890	3.5200	3.4600
Australia (Dollar)	.5670	.5710	1.7638	1.7512
Bahrain (Dinar)	2.6525	2.6525	.3770	.3770
Brazil (Real)	.3695	.3598	2.7065	2.7795
Britain (Pound)	1.4720	1.4712	.6793	.6797
1-month forward	1.4694	1.4686	.6805	.6809
3-months forward	1.4636	1.4627	.6832	.6837
6-months forward	1.4548	1.4540	.6874	.6878
Canada (Dollar)	.6496	.6510	1.5394	1.5360
1-month forward	.6492	.6506	1.5404	1.5370
3-months forward	.6480	.6495	1.5431	1.5397
6-months forward	.6462	.6476	1.5476	1.5441
Chile (Peso)	.001502	.001496	665.65	668.35
China (Renminbi)	.1208	.1208	8.2769	8.2769
Colombia (Peso)	.0004234	.0004249	2362.05	2353.25
Czech. Rep. (Koruna)				
Commercial rate	.03092	.03104	32.342	32.215
Denmark (Krone)	.1267	.1271	7.8931	7.8695
Ecuador (US Dollar)	1.0000	1.0000	1.0000	1.0000
Hong Kong (Dollar)	.1282	.1282	7.7999	7.8000
Hungary (Forint)	.003903	.003904	256.24	256.15
India (Rupee)	.02041	.02043	48.990	48.950
Indonesia (Rupiah)	.0001143	.0001147	8751	8715
Israel (Shekel)	.2018	.2008	4.9550	4.9800
Japan (Yen)	.008006	.007954	124.90	125.73
1-month forward	.008019	.007966	124.71	125.54
3-months forward	.008044	.007991	124.32	125.14
6-months forward	.008086	.008033	123.67	124.48
Jordan (Dinar)	1.4184	1.4184	.7050	.7050

	U.S. $ EQUIVALENT		CURRENCY PER U.S. $	
Country	Thu.	Wed.	Thu.	Wed.
Kuwait (Dinar)	3.2895	3.2862	.3040	.3043
Lebanon (Pound)	.0006606	.0006607	1513.88	1513.50
Malaysia (Ringgit)-b	.2632	.2632	3.8001	3.8000
Malta (Lira)	2.2989	2.2999	.4350	.4348
Mexico (Peso)				
Floating rate	.1037	.1033	9.6455	9.6790
New Zealand (Dollar)	.4885	.4917	2.0471	2.0338
Norway (Krone)	.1271	.1271	7.8688	7.8650
Pakistan (Rupee)	.01663	.01663	60.125	60.125
Peru (new Sol)	.2889	.2881	3.4618	3.4713
Philippines (Peso)	.01982	.01982	50.445	50.445
Poland (Zloty)	.2485	.2486	4.0248	4.0220
Russia (Ruble)-a	.03182	.03181	31.425	31.435
Saudi Arabia (Riyal)	.2666	.2666	3.7505	3.7504
Singapore (Dollar)	.5598	.5599	1.7865	1.7860
Slovak Rep. (Koruna)	.02121	.02117	47.158	47.242
South Africa (Rand)	.0969	.0986	10.3200	10.1455
South Korea (Won)	.0008173	.0008173	1223.60	1223.60
Sweden (Krona)	.1030	.1030	9.7073	9.7052
Switzerland (Franc)	.6391	.6390	1.5646	1.5650
1-month forward	.6395	.6393	1.5638	1.5642
3-months forward	.6401	.6400	1.5623	1.5626
6-months forward	.6409	.6408	1.5602	1.5605
Taiwan (Dollar)	.02944	.02944	33.970	33.970
Thailand (Baht)	.02368	.02363	42.225	42.315
Turkey (Lira)	.00000065	.00000064	1534500	1553500
United Arab (Dirham)	.2723	.2723	3.6730	3.6730
Uruguay (Peso)				
Financial	.05789	.05789	17.275	17.275
Venezuela (Bolivar)	.000837	.000851	1194.50	1175.50
SDR	1.2900	1.2925	.7752	.7737
Euro	.9427	.9428	1.0608	1.0607

Special Drawing Rights (SDR) are based on exchange rates for the U.S., British, and Japanese currencies. Source: International Monetary Fund.

a-Russian Central Bank rate. b-Government rate. y-Floating rate.

Use the above table which lists rates of exchange for the U.S. dollar relative to foreign currencies to answer the following questions.

1. According to the text accompanying the table, where does trading in foreign currencies occur?

2. According to the text accompanying the table, between what parties did this trading occur?

3. Is this an over-the-counter or organized exchange?

Investments

Investors have many different opportunities in which to invest their funds. Financial assets such as stocks and bonds can be held by investors in both direct and indirect forms. Investors can buy and sell stocks and bonds directly through financial markets, or indirectly by pooling their funds with other investors. Mutual funds are investment vehicles that pool the money of many small investors and invest it in shares of companies, bonds, or other assets. A mutual fund is a company itself, with a board of directors that hires the fund's managers. A key advantage of mutual funds is that you can invest small amounts and your money automatically buys a share in the in many different companies. The Mutual Funds tables of the Money and Investing section include the pricing and return information for thousands of stock and bond funds. The tables also include a report called the Mutual-Fund Scorecard which tracks the best and worst performing funds in a variety of different sectors.

Information on the investment value of financial assets is easily found in the *WSJ*. A good summary of financial market activity is the Markets Lineup page, found each day in the *WSJ* on the second page of the Money and Investing section. This full page table reports secondary market activity for stocks, bonds, and mutual funds. The Stocks section of this table includes price changes in many different sectors of the U.S. financial markets. The Interest Rates & Bonds portion of this table includes listings of interest rates for corporate borrowers and a listing of Consumer Rates. Consumer rates include money market accounts and certificates of deposits.

To this point our discussion has focused on the markets for financial assets, or financial securities. These assets are only one type of investment. Other investment opportunities exist in the market for real assets. Just like with financial assets, investors seek capital gains or current income from real assets. A *real asset* is any tangible piece of property – an item that can be seen and felt. Two common investment choices for real assets are real estate and commodities, such as gold and diamonds. Investors can purchase real estate (land, houses, office buildings, or apartments) either directly or indirectly. Real estate can be purchased directly from the seller or investors can pool their money in real estate funds. Similarly, investments in commodities can be bought directly, or indirectly through stocks and mutual funds. Information is available in the *WSJ* for many types of commodities and real estate. For example, the Futures tables found in the Money and Investing section of the *WSJ* includes prices for gold coins such as the American Eagle.

Exercise 1-4

Markets Diary/ *Trading for Monday, June 24, 2002*

Stocks

Dow Jones Industrial Average   9281.82   ▲ +28.03

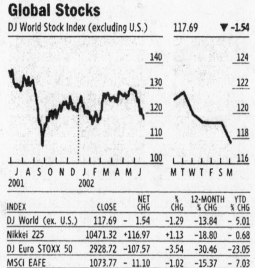

INDEX	CLOSE	NET CHG	% CHG	12-MONTH % CHG	YTD % CHG
DJIA	9281.82	+28.03	+0.30	−11.64	− 7.38
Nasdaq Comp.	1460.34	+19.38	+1.34	−28.79	−25.13
S&P 500	992.72	+ 3.58	+0.36	−18.54	−13.53
Russell 2000	459.09	− 1.98	−0.43	− 5.18	− 6.02

Global Stocks

DJ World Stock Index (excluding U.S.)   117.69   ▼ −1.54

INDEX	CLOSE	NET CHG	% CHG	12-MONTH % CHG	YTD % CHG
DJ World (ex. U.S.)	117.69	− 1.54	−1.29	−13.84	− 5.01
Nikkei 225	10471.32	+116.97	+1.13	−18.80	− 0.68
DJ Euro STOXX 50	2928.72	−107.57	−3.54	−30.46	−23.05
MSCI EAFE	1073.77	− 11.10	−1.02	−15.37	− 7.03

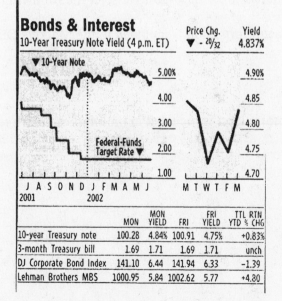

Bonds & Interest

10-Year Treasury Note Yield (4 p.m. ET)   Price Chg. ▼ − $^{20}/_{32}$ Yield 4.837%

	MON	MON YIELD	FRI	FRI YIELD	TTL RTN YTD % CHG
10-year Treasury note	100.28	4.84%	100.91	4.75%	+0.83%
3-month Treasury bill	1.69	1.71	1.69	1.71	unch
DJ Corporate Bond Index	141.10	6.44	141.94	6.33	−1.39
Lehman Brothers MBS	1000.95	5.84	1002.62	5.77	+4.80

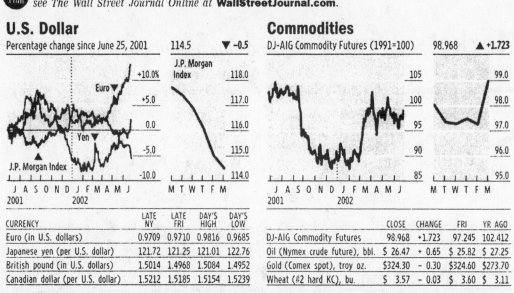

U.S. Dollar

Percentage change since June 25, 2001   114.5   ▼ –0.5

CURRENCY	LATE NY	LATE FRI	DAY'S HIGH	DAY'S LOW
Euro (in U.S. dollars)	0.9709	0.9710	0.9816	0.9685
Japanese yen (per U.S. dollar)	121.72	121.25	121.01	122.76
British pound (in U.S. dollars)	1.5014	1.4968	1.5084	1.4952
Canadian dollar (per U.S. dollar)	1.5212	1.5185	1.5154	1.5239

Commodities

DJ-AIG Commodity Futures (1991=100)   98.968   ▲ +1.723

	CLOSE	CHANGE	FRI	YR AGO
DJ-AIG Commodity Futures	98.968	+1.723	97.245	102.412
Oil (Nymex crude future), bbl.	$ 26.47	+ 0.65	$ 25.82	$ 27.25
Gold (Comex spot), troy oz.	$324.30	– 0.30	$324.60	$273.70
Wheat (#2 hard KC), bu.	$ 3.57	– 0.03	$ 3.60	$ 3.11

Source: *The Wall Street Journal*, June 25, 2002. Reprinted by permission of Dow Jones & Company, Inc. (c) 2002 Dow Jones & Company, Inc. All Rights Reserved Worldwide.

Use the above charts and tables from the *WSJ* to answer the following questions.

1. What financial asset information is included in the Markets Diary report?

2. What real asset information is included in the Markets Diary report?

Project 1-1

Repeat Exercises 1-1 and 1-2 using a recent edition of the *WSJ*.

1. Find a headline that refers to primary market transactions?

   Date _____

2. Find a headline that refers to secondary market transactions?

   Date _____

3. Find a headline that refers to money-market transactions?

   Date _____

4. Find a headline that refers to capital market transactions?

   Date _____

Project 1-2

To answer the questions below, review a recent copy of the *WSJ*. Take a look at each of the first three sections – section A, or "First" section, section B, "Marketplace", and section C, "Money and Investing".   You can also learn how to navigate the pages of the *WSJ* by taking an on-line tour. Go to http://tour.wsj.com. This web site will take you through each of the three main sections of the newspaper. The topics discussed below can be found by clicking on the section title and scrolling through the drop-down menu.

1. Under what heading and in what section of the WSJ will you find the latest news of inflation, unemployment, and Federal Reserve policy?

    _____

2. Under what heading and in what section of the WSJ will you find reports that describe trends, issues and legislation affecting small businesses?

    _____

3. Under what heading and in what section of the WSJ will you find the closing price and net change for stocks traded in Canada or Africa?

    _____

4. Under what heading and in what section of the WSJ will you find announcements of quarterly and annual financial figures from corporations?

    _____

5. Under what heading and in what section of the WSJ will you find a digest of the latest news developments from around the world?

    _____

Discussion Questions

Number of Millionaires Rose 3% in 2001 Despite Downturn

By JANE J. KIM
Dow Jones Newswires

NEW YORK—The number of millionaires last year grew the most in countries where they diversified their wealth away from stocks, according to the World Wealth Report released by Merrill Lynch & Co. and Cap Gemini Ernst & Young.

Despite the economic downturn, the number of high net-worth individuals world-wide—defined as those with financial assets of at least $1 million, excluding real estate—rose to 7.1 million in 2001, up 3% from the previous year. Meanwhile, their combined wealth edged higher to $26.2 trillion.

The 3% growth in 2001—roughly half of the 6% growth recorded in 2000 and a significant decline from the 18% gain in 1999—indicates that a "significant minority" of high net-worth individuals remained heavily invested in equities, especially "growth" stocks, according to the report, which published its first edition in 1997. Slower economic growth and falling stock markets were the strongest dampers on the portfolios of high net-worth investors.

Many rich investors, however, were successful in expanding their worth. Besides shifting away from stocks, those who were successful rebalanced their remaining equities away from technology and growth stocks toward value and blue-chip names. They also sought out alternative investments such as hedge funds and structured products, and relied more heavily on help from their financial advisers. Many high net-worth individuals started moving their money toward hard assets such as real estate, fixed income and alternative investments near the end of 2000, said Alvi Abuaf, vice president, global financial services at Cap Gemini Ernst & Young.

1. According to the article, what did "successful" investors do in 2001?

2. List and describe some of the financial assets mentioned in the article.

3. List and describe some of the real assets mentioned in the article.

4. What region of the world is most heavily invested in equities (stocks)? Why do you think this is so?

PART II

ECONOMIC ANALYSIS

Chapter 2

Economic Analysis

Objectives

1. Describe the economic data regularly reported in the *WSJ*.

2. Learn to use economic reports and economic principles to analyze financial market activity

3. Understand how inflation effects financial markets and the economy.

4. Understand the government's role in the economy.

Key Terms

Gross Domestic Product (GDP)	Leading Economic Indicators	Monetary Policy
Real GDP	Consumer Price Index (CPI)	Federal Funds
Unemployment Rate	Producer Price Index (PPI)	Fiscal Policy

All companies are affected to some degree by the overall level of economic activity. For this reason, investors and managers alike track the economy using economic data available from both private and government sources. The *WSJ* reports all the latest news on the economy and includes data for most economic releases. In this chapter we will explore economic reports on inflation, unemployment, and economic activity at all levels. This information is valuable when analyzing financial markets. The ability to understand economic data also helps us to understand the nature of the business cycle, the ebb and flow of economic activity, and the government's role in the economy.

Economic Activity

Inside the first section of the *WSJ* you will find the Economy column. The articles in this section of the paper cover all the latest news on economic activity, including economic data reports and economic policies. With regard to economic data, let's start at the top. The broadest measure of overall economic activity is ***gross domestic product (GDP)***. GDP is the most closely watched of all economic variables because it is arguably the best measure of society's income, or its well-being. Just as a company is said to be 'doing well' if its net income is up, a society with a growing GDP will be better off; consumers will have more to spend on goods and services. When society is better off business activity improves, improving profits and raising stock prices. GDP measures the market value of all the final goods and services produced in the economy. Including only the final output avoids the measurement of economic activity twice. For example, steel is used in the production of automobiles, but the final purchase price of the automobile includes the cost of the component steel.

The U.S. Department of Commerce measures and releases quarterly estimates of GDP, expressed at seasonally adjusted annual rates. The *WSJ* reports the latest announcement of GDP data, and follows with any subsequent revisions to the data. The first Department of Commerce report, released one month following the end of the quarter, is an estimate that is frequently subject to revision when more data is collect. The *WSJ* article on GDP announcements includes a statistical summary of the data; breaking down the major components of GDP – personal consumption (the personal spending of consumers), investment (both residential and non-residential investments by businesses and individuals), net exports (total exports – total imports), and government purchases.

As an example, on April 29, 2002 the *WSJ* reported the most recent GDP announcement – 5.8% annualized real GDP growth in the first quarter of 2002. The article points out that more than half this growth was due to business non-residential investment. In the first quarter of the year businesses were primarily replenishing inventories rather than producing for new sales. This is an addition to the second component of GDP- investment. Investments in inventories, however, is not as permanent as investments in new buildings or equipment; suggesting the strong growth in GDP may be only temporary.

To measure the change in income for the economy without including the impact of changing prices, GDP is reported on a constant-dollar, or real, basis. ***Real GDP*** is the market value of all final output of goods and services using prices for a given base year (currently 1996). Thus, the current output is calculated using the base year prices as opposed to current prices. Since real GDP is not affected by changes in prices, any change in its value reflects only changes in actual production. Current-dollar, or nominal, GDP reflects changes in production as well as prices. Nominal GDP may increase or decrease simply because of changes in the selling price of goods, and not because of any actual change in the quantity of goods and services sold. To breakout this affect of prices, the U.S. Department of Commerce also publishes a measure of the price level known as the implicit price deflator (IPD), which is calculated as the ratio of current-dollar value to the corresponding constant-dollar value, multiplied by 100. The annual rate of change in the IPD is included in the summary report following the *WSJ* article on GDP.

When a society keeps its workers employed it will produce a higher level of GDP than would be possible if many workers were without a job. Therefore, another good measure of the economy's well being is the percentage of its labor force that is currently unemployed, or the ***unemployment rate.*** The unemployment rate is calculated as the number of unemployed workers divided by the total labor force and multiplied by 100. Every month the U.S. Department of Labor reports on the level of unemployment and other labor statistics. These statistics are based on the Labor Department's regular survey of thousands of U.S. households. The *WSJ* reports the latest announcement of the unemployment rate and includes a statistical summary of the data; breaking out some important demographics such as men and women, teen-agers, and minority unemployment rates. Another important statistical release with this report is the average weekly hours for the month. The number of regular hours worked and the level of overtime work generally expand with an improving economy.

Real GDP and the unemployment rate are good measures of overall economic activity, but they both lack one important feature that investors and business managers need to make sound decisions. Each of these statistics is backward looking rather than forward looking. Investors and managers need economic information that will help them forecast business activity in the future. No economic indicator is going to be 100% accurate at predicting the future, but some indicators are likely to rise or fall in advance of an economic upturn. Therefore, economists have created an index of variables from a wide variety of economic activity that generally rises in advance of an overall economic upturn. The index of ***leading economic indicators*** is compiled by the Conference Board, a private research group, and is designed to predict economic activity six to nine months in advance. A three to four month sustained decline in the index consistently precedes a decline in overall economic activity (GDP). The average weekly hours worked data, previously discussed as part of the unemployment report, is one of the ten leading economic indicators. The other nine are stock prices (500 common stocks), interest rate spread, index of consumer expectations (survey), vendor performance (time to delivery), manufacturers' new orders for consumer goods and materials, building permits, average weekly initial claims for unemployment insurance (inverted), real money supply, and manufacturers' new orders for non-defense capital goods. Note that average weekly initial claims for unemployment insurance is inverted (1 over the average weekly initial claims) to reflect its relation to economic growth – a decline in unemployment insurance claims reflects an improving economy.

As an example, the Conference Board announced on April 18, 2002 that the U.S. leading index increased by 0.1 percent in March, to 112.3 (the base year being 1996, with a value of 100). For this reporting month, six of the ten indicators rose while four declined. The gains in the index would have been larger if it had not been for very weak levels of building permits and high claims for unemployment insurance. The *WSJ* reported that this small change in the index suggests that the economy should grow in the coming months, but the level of growth is likely to be small. It is important to note that stock prices, probably the most accurate and reliable indicator of future economic activity, were one of the six rising indicators in this report. This presents a problem for investors using the leading index as a gauge of future stock market activity – any future economic gains or loses may already be reflected in current stock prices. For this reason, reports on the index of economic leading may not be much help to investors trying to forecast future stock prices.

Exercise 2-1

EMPLOYMENT

Here are excerpts from the Labor Department's employment report. The figures are seasonally adjusted.

	April 2002	March 2002
	Millions of persons	
Civilian labor force	142.57	142.01
Civilian employment	133.98	133.89
Unemployment	8.59	8.11
Payroll employment	131.23	131.19
Unemployment:	% of labor force	
All civilian workers	6.0	5.7
Adult men	5.4	5.2
Adult women	5.4	5.0
Teen-agers	16.8	16.4
White	5.3	5.0
Black	11.2	10.7
Black teen-agers	35.4	31.0
Hispanic	7.9	7.3
Average weekly hours:	Hours of work	
Total private nonfarm	34.1	34.2
Manufacturing	41.0	41.0
Factory overtime	4.3	4.2

Source: *The Wall Street Journal*, May 6, 2002. Reprinted by permission of Dow Jones & Company, Inc. (c) 2002 Dow Jones & Company, Inc. All Rights Reserved Worldwide.

Use the above summary table from the *WSJ* to answer the following questions.

1. Verify the current month's unemployment rate by dividing the number of unemployed by the total work force?

2. Did the unemployment rate increase or decrease for the current month? Did the number of unemployed rise? Did the size of the workforce increase or decrease?

3. What was the change, if any, in the average weekly hours for all private, non-farm workers? What does this change suggest for the economy?

Inflation

Equally important to a society's standard of living is a society's cost of living. It is one thing to know the quantity of output in goods and services, but it is also useful to measure changes in purchasing power. A rise in the overall level of prices in the economy, or inflation, increases the cost of living for consumers. That is, inflation reduces consumer purchasing power. If consumer incomes fail to keep up with rising prices, consumers will quickly become discouraged, buying less goods and services. Therefore, financial markets and business managers closely monitor indicators of inflation. Furthermore, if lenders believe future prices will be higher they will require higher rates of interest on their loans; further discouraging consumers and businesses that borrow.

The *WSJ* includes monthly reports on inflation at both the consumer and wholesale level. The U.S. Department of Labor reports the **Consumer Price Index (CPI)**. The CPI is an inflation gauge that measures changes in the prices of consumer goods- a list of specific goods and services purchased in urban areas. This list, or "market basket" of goods, includes food, clothing, shelter, and other typical purchases, each weighted by its relative importance to the monthly household budget. The list of budget items in the CPI includes food, housing, and travel expenses. Because the way consumers spend their income is constantly changing, the CPI basket of goods, and the weights for each, are subject to revision. The Department of Labor has been criticized in the past for not promptly making these revisions to reflect changing consumer preferences. Current CPI announcements include any changes in the weights or other aspects of the index.

The Department of Labor also reports price level activity at the wholesale level. The **Producer Price Index (PPI)** is an index tracking commodities that won't undergo further processing and are ready for sale to the ultimate user, but are sold at the wholesale, not retail, level. The Department of Labor PPI report also includes a measure of intermediate and crude level prices. Just as with the CPI report, a statistical summary of the data often accompanies the *WSJ* article.

On April 17, 2002, the *WSJ* reported on the most recent announcement of the Labor Department's Consumer Price Index from the previous day. The CPI rose 0.3% in the month of March. The index was 1.5% higher than one year earlier. This annual rate was relatively low. The average rate of change was 2.4% for the previous seven years. For the same month, the *WSJ* reported that the PPI declined 1.4% over the previous twelve months. Taken together, the two reports suggest low inflation in the future – current consumer prices are rising slowly and wholesale prices are declining. Historically, as inflation declines, real GDP rises – consumers spend more and save less if prices are stable. The low inflation indicated in these reports suggests a possible rise in economic output in the near future.

Tracking inflation is important for both investors and business managers. The reason is that the real rate of return earned on any investment will be affected by the level of inflation in the future. For example, if the interest rate currently offered on a bond is five percent for the next five years, but inflation runs at a six percent annual rate, the real rate of return on this investment is negative. Thus, investors require that their investments return enough to cover the expected future inflation as well as provide some positive real rate of return. When investors and business managers expect inflation to rise they require higher rates of return on their investments. Therefore, there is a generally positive relationship between inflation and interest rates- when inflation rises, interests rates also rise.

Exercise 2-2

PRODUCER PRICES

Here are the Labor Department's producer price indexes (1982=100) for April 2002, before seasonal adjustment, and the percentage changes from April 2001.

	Index	% Chg.
Finished goods	139.0	-2.0
Less food & energy	150.5	0.4
Intermediate goods	127.6	-2.4
Crude goods	107.9	-18.9

Source: *The Wall Street Journal*, May 13, 2002. by permission of Dow Jones & Company, Inc. (c) 2002 Dow Jones & Company, Inc. All Rights Reserved Worldwide.

Use the above summary table from the *WSJ* to answer the following questions.

1. Have wholesale prices for finished goods increased or decreased over the past twelve months? Have wholesale prices for crude goods increased or decreased over the past twelve months?

2. What is the base year for the index?

3. What has been the total rate of change in prices since the base year? What has been the average annual change in the index for finished goods since the base year?

Monetary Policy

Investors and managers are not the only parties interested in the economy. The U.S. Government is very interested in growing the society's standard of living (GDP) and controlling its cost of living (inflation). The government plays an important role in the economy through both monetary and fiscal policy. First, let's look at *monetary policy* – the determination of the supply of money in the economy by the nation's central bank. In 1913, Congress established a central bank called the Federal Reserve System and charged its governing body, the Federal Reserve Board of Governors (the Fed) with maintaining a sound and stable financial system. Initially the Fed was simply a lender of last resort. Member banks of the Federal Reserve System are required to keep deposits, or reserves, with the Fed, creating a large pool of funds not being used in the economy. Historically, when banks got into trouble, say by not having enough cash flow from their loans to pay their depositors, the Fed would use reserves to lend the troubled banks money until their cash flow improved. The FED quickly learned that it could control banking activity, and therefore economic activity, by controlling the level of reserves. The Fed can encourage banks to lend more money, which in turn increases economic activity, by increasing the bank's reserve deposits. If a bank is required to hold more deposits on reserve, it can increase the amount of money it lends out. Similarly, the Fed can discourage lending, decreasing economic activity, by decreasing the bank's reserves. By increasing (decreasing) the amount of money on reserve, the Fed increases (decreases) the amount of money in the economy – the money supply.

The Fed changes the money supply by buying and selling securities. When the Fed buys securities, the buyer will deposit the proceeds in the bank account, increasing bank deposits and therefore bank reserves. When the Fed sells securities, the buyers reduce their bank deposits in order to pay the Fed for the securities, reducing deposits and therefore bank reserves. By tracking these reserves and bank lending, the Fed can track the money supply. There are three primary measures of the money supply. First is M-1, the sum of all currency and demand deposits held by consumers and businesses. Second is M-2, which is M-1 plus all savings accounts, time deposits (e.g., certificates of deposit), and smaller money-market accounts. Third, M-3 is M-2 plus large-denomination time deposits held by corporations and financial institutions and money-market funds held by financial institutions.

The *WSJ* closely follows all the Fed's activity. Federal Reserve Data is reported each Friday in the *WSJ,* including changes in bank reserves and the three aggregate measures of money. Also important to investors and managers are the levels of interest rates. The price of money is the interest rate, and like any good or service, the price of money is determined by supply and demand. When the Fed increases the money supply, the interest rate falls. When the supply of money decreases, interest rates rise. Money rates are reported daily in the *WSJ*. The Money Rates table includes the Fed's primary interest rate target, the federal funds rate. The ***federal funds*** rate is the rate of interest that banks charge each other. When the Fed wants to increase economic activity by increasing reserves, it can decrease the federal funds rate. When banks can borrow more cheaply, they can also lend more cheaply, encouraging more borrowing and therefore business activity.

As an example of monetary policy activity, the *WSJ* reported on May 8, 2002 that the Fed had decided to keep interest rates unchanged. The Fed left its federal funds target rate at 1.75%. This means that the Fed will continue to buy and sell securities in order to maintain the price of money, in this bank lending market, at a rate of 1.75% annually. This rate is much lower than the 6.5% rate that existed less than two years prior. According to this report, the Fed has been increasing the money supply, keeping interest rates low, in order to encourage business lending and overall economic activity. However, even with these previous actions the economy was not showing particularly strong growth, and the Fed, therefore decided to keep rates low for the time being.

Exercise 2-3

Federal Reserve Data

MONETARY AGGREGATES
(daily average in billions)

	1 WEEK ENDED:	
	May 20	May 13
Money supply (M1) sa	1179.4	1166.8
Money supply (M1) nsa	1174.7	1153.1
Money supply (M2) sa	5545.3	5535.4
Money supply (M2) nsa	5529.8	5531.1
Money supply (M3) sa	8129.6	8134.6
Money supply (M3) nsa	8127.6	8135.0
	4 WEEKS ENDED:	
	May 20	Apr. 22
Money supply (M1) sa	1176.0	1173.2
Money supply (M1) nsa	1174.0	1188.9
Money supply (M2) sa	5524.0	5476.6
Money supply (M2) nsa	5518.9	5575.4
Money supply (M3) sa	8112.8	8042.7
Money supply (M3) nsa	8113.6	8162.0
	MONTH	
	Apr.	Mar.
Money supply (M1) sa	1174.1	1185.6
Money supply (M2) sa	5480.1	5498.8
Money supply (M3) sa	8054.2	8065.2

nsa-Not seasonally adjusted. sa-Seasonally adjusted.

MEMBER BANK RESERVE CHANGES

Changes in weekly averages of reserves and related items during the week and year ended May 29, 2002 were as follows (in millions of dollars)

	May 29 2002	CHG FROM May 22 2002	WK END May 30 2001
Reserve bank credit:			
U.S. Gov't securities:			
Bought outright	587,669	+2,547	+58,501
Held under repurch agreemt	...	...	...
Federal agency issues:			
Bought outright	10	...	...
Held under repurch agreemt	...	...	...
Acceptances			
Borrowings from Fed:			
Adjustment credit	7	-5	-15
Seasonal borrowings	129	+24	+43
Extended credit	...	...	...
Float	-180	+568	+327
Other Federal Reserve Assets	37,009	+588	+1,750
Total Reserve Bank Credit	655,848	+12,034	+65,276
Gold Stock	11,044	...	-2
SDR certificates	2,200	...	...
Treasury currency outstanding	33,717	+14	+1,184
Total	702,808	+12,047	+66,458
Currency in circulation	653,948	+5,197	+58,978
Treasury cash holdings	412	+1	-98
Treasury dpts with F.R. Bnks	5,012	+98	-136
Foreign dpts with F.R. Bnks	109	+33	-39
Other dpts with F.R. Bnks	207	-10	-87
Service related balances, adj	10,159	...	+3,281
Other F.R. liabilities & capital	19,701	+241	+1,741
Total	689,548	+5,562	+63,640

RESERVE AGGREGATES
(daily average in millions)

	2 WEEKS ENDED:	
	May 29	May 15
Total Reserves (sa)	39,342	38,816
Nonborrowed Reserves (sa)	39,216	38,716
Required Reserves (sa)	37,985	37,629
Excess Reserves (nsa)	1,358	1,187
Borrowings from Fed (nsa)-a	127	100
Free Reserves (nsa)	1,231	1,087
Monetary Base (sa)	664,090	656,175

a-Excluding extended credit. nsa-Not seasonally adjusted. sa-Seasonally adjusted

Use the table from the *WSJ* to answer the following questions.

1. According to the data, what has been the change in the money supply (use M1 – sa, seasonally adjusted) over the past week? Over the past month?

2. What has been the change, if any, in the daily average of total reserves over the past two weeks? Given this change, is the Fed trying to encourage or discourage economic activity?

Source: *The Wall Street Journal*, May 31, 2002. by permission of Dow Jones & Company, Inc.
(c) 2002 Dow Jones & Company, Inc. All Rights Reserved Worldwide.

Fiscal Policy

The second government role in the economy comes through taxing and spending policies. *Fiscal policy* is the government's decisions on taxation and spending practices. A government that wishes to encourage economic activity can lower taxes, freeing up more funds for purchases and investment, or it can increase spending, creating jobs through government programs or giving cash credits to consumers and businesses. If the government spends more than it receives it creates a budget deficit. To cover this deficit, the government must borrow money. Thus, if the government wants to increase economic activity through spending on programs such as national defense and education, it must increase its borrowing which will increase market rates of interest. Sometimes the Fed will intervene in this situation in order to keep market rates low, but this can only have a short term effect. Thus, investors and managers monitor the government's budget to assess its impact on market interest rates.

The *WSJ* reports on the U.S. Federal Government budget each month. The Treasury Department reports the year-to-date total outlays and receipts, as well as the interest expense for the period. These figures are listed with the comparable figures for the previous year. For example, the *WSJ* reported on April 19, 2002 that the U.S. budget deficit for the month of March was $64.24 billion. This was much higher then the $24.8 billion deficit in March of the previous year. Since the monthly data is not seasonally adjusted (tax receipts are much higher in the early part of the year), the year-to-date figure is much better for analyzing the trend in fiscal policy. The increased deficit in this report suggests increased borrowing by the federal government. Such additional borrowing should raise market rates unless the Fed increases the money supply at the same time.

The *WSJ* follows all activity surrounding government policy. In the Politics and Policy columns of the first section you can find articles on all levels of government – federal, state, and local. These articles explore the latest issues in taxation and spending. As new proposals are put forward for reduced taxes or new government programs, the articles in this column discuss the pros and cons of each. For example, on Monday, May 13, 2002 the *WSJ* reported on a new federal trade bill that would increase payments to workers that lose their jobs to foreign competition. The article reviews the positions of both the bill's proponents and opponents.

Exercise 2-4

U.S. BUDGET

Here is a summary of the Treasury's report. Figures in billions of dollars, through the end of April 2002.

	Fiscal Ytd	Comparable Previous
Outlays..	$1,182.85	$1,088.56
Receipts	1,116.37	1,253.56
Surplus/Deficit........................	-66.48	165.00
Net Interest.............................	181.19	201.85

April Surplus: 67.17

Source: *The Wall Street Journal*, May 21, 2002. by permission of Dow Jones & Company, Inc. (c) 2002 Dow Jones & Company, Inc. All Rights Reserved Worldwide.

Use the above table from the *WSJ* to answer the following questions.

1. According to the data, calculate the percent change in U.S. federal government outlays and receipts for the current fiscal year-to-date?

2. Is the current fiscal deficit higher or lower than the previous year? Is this change due primarily to changes in outlays or receipts?

3. Has the interest expense of the federal government increased or decreased since the past fiscal year? Do you think this change is due to changes in market interest rates or changes in the level of government debt?

Project 2-1

Repeat Exercises 2-1 and 2-2 using a recent edition of the *WSJ*.

Date of Unemployment Report _____

1. Verify the current month's unemployment rate by dividing the number of unemployed by the total work force?

2. Did the unemployment rate increase or decrease for the current month? Did the number of unemployed rise? Did the size of the workforce increase or decrease?

3. What was the change, if any, in the average weekly hours for all private, non-farm workers? What does this change suggest for the economy?

Date of Inflation (CPI or PPI) Report _____

4. Have prices increased or decreased over the month? Over the past twelve months?

5. What is the base year for the index? What has been the total rate of change in prices since the base year?

6. What has been the average annual change in the index for finished goods since the base year?

Project 2-2

Each Monday the *WSJ* includes a table entitled 'Tracking the Economy'. This table lists the important economic data releases for the upcoming week. For each data report, the table lists the reporting period for the data, the day of release during the week, the level or change reported for the last period, and the consensus forecast for this report (from a survey of economists conducted by Dow Jones). Locate a recent Tracking the Economy table and write five of the indicators in the following table. For each economic indicator, indicate whether the consensus forecast suggests a positive or negative impact on economic activity. That is, does the consensus forecast for this economic variable suggests a strengthening economy (rising GDP) or a falling economy (falling GDP)? (Hint: to determine whether GDP will rise or fall, consider the economic indicator's affect on one of the four GDP components discussed in this chapter.)

Economic Indicator	Previous Actual	Consensus Forecast	Impact (+ or -)

Discussion Questions

Capital Spending Could Be Back, Boosting Optimism

By Patrick Barta

The long-awaited rebound in capital spending could be at hand, according to a business-investment index watched by a growing number of economists. But the economic recovery still faces challenges, new data from the Conference Board and others suggest.

The business-spending index, compiled by G7 Group Inc., a New York economic- and political-consulting firm, indicates that the economy's steep, five-quarter slide in business investment has likely come to an end. The group's preliminary index, which measures business investment in the second quarter, registered a minus five, a 62-point increase over the previous quarter. Any number less than minus 35 indicates contraction in investment. An index between zero and minus 35 indicates growth, but at lower levels than the historical average of 5% as measured in the U.S. Commerce Department's national income accounts. Results greater than zero indicate above-average business investment.

If the index is right, it would mean that the tentative economic rebound now under way has a good shot of evolving into a strong and sustained recovery as the year progresses. So far, the recovery has been led by consumers, who keep spending despite a weak job market. Business spending, by contrast, has been a no-show. If companies don't start investing again soon, the recovery could stagnate.

"The question is, will [business investment] come back fast enough" to prevent a recurrence of last year's recession, says former Federal Reserve Vice Chair-man Alan Blinder. He is a principal in the G7 Group and one of creators of the index, which, according to the firm, has had a good record of foreshadowing changes in business spending. The latest index reading suggests the answer is "yes, yes in spades," Mr. Blinder says.

But that optimism was tempered by a separate report released yesterday by the Conference Board, a New York business research group. It said that its monthly index of leading indicators fell in April for the first time since September, dropping 0.4%. Composed of 10 economic indicators, the index is generally regarded as a precursor of economic activity. Five of the survey's indicators declined last month, led by falling stock prices and a contraction in the money supply. Three rose and two remained unchanged.

Conference Board economist Ken Goldstein says the latest index doesn't necessarily mean business investment isn't recovering, but it does suggest the rebound could take a while to solidify. Though it is still possible the second half of the year will be stronger than the first, "it's going to be a bumpy road from here to there," Mr. Goldstein says.

That conclusion was consistent with another report released yesterday by the Manufacturers Alliance/MAPI, an Arlington, Va., business research group. Its first-quarter report of business activity found that only eight of the 28 industries it examines had inflation-adjusted increases in new orders compared with a year ago. But that is better than the six that experienced positive growth in the previous report.

LEADING INDICATORS

Here are the net contributions of the components of the Conference Board's index of leading indicators. The index decreased by 0.4% in April and now stands at 111.7.

	April 2002-p	March 2002-r
Workweek	0.00	0.13
Unemployment claims	-0.07	-0.20
Orders for consumer goods	0.00	0.03
Slower deliveries	0.03	0.04
Plant and equipment orders	0.01	-0.04
Building permits	0.01	-0.15
Stock prices	-0.11	0.15
Money supply	-0.17	-0.10
Interest-rate spread	-0.03	0.13
Consumer expectations	-0.07	0.11

The seasonally adjusted index numbers (1996=100) for April, and the changes from March, are:

Index of leading indicators	111.70	-0.40
Index of coincident indicators	116.00	0.20
Index of lagging indicators	100.60	-0.40

The ratio of coincident to lagging indicators was 115.3 in April, up from 114.7 in March.

p-Preliminary. r-Revised.

1. What is the business-spending index? Who complies the index?

2. How does the business-spending index compare to the other two economic statistics reported in the article?

3. Which of the statistical releases are government sponsored and which are private?

4. According to the article, what is the key benefit of the business-spending index?

Chapter 3

Industry Analysis

Objectives

1. Compare and contrast different stages in the life cycle of an industry.

2. Understand market structure and its effect on corporate strategy.

3. Describe the various Dow Jones Economic Sectors.

4. Describe the various Dow Jones Market Sectors.

Key Terms

Industry Life Cycle	Large Cap	Perfect Competition
Growth Industries	Small Cap	Cyclical
Mature Industries	Monopoly	Noncyclical
Industry Structure	Oligopolies	

In the last chapter we looked at the significant amount of data published on economic activity and its use by investors and managers. Equally important to understanding the effect of overall economic activity on financial markets, is an understanding of industry activity. Knowing the structure of an industry and the current trends within the industry helps investors and managers make sound business decisions. The *WSJ* reports the latest news on many different industries and tracks stock market activity by industry. In this chapter we will study this information to learn how industries change over time, how size and other structural characteristics affect market performance, and how business strategies differ across industries.

Industry Life Cycles

To begin an analysis of an industry consider the industry's age. Not necessarily its age in terms of years, but its age in terms of product. New technologies are often developed to advance an existing product and industry, but sometimes whole new industries arise when technological advancements lead to new products. The product stage of an industry is important for assessing the industry's prospects for market demand, earnings growth, and dividend payments. ***Industry Life Cycles*** arise from the different levels of growth in availability of resources, level of competition, and earnings potential. The stages in a industry life cycle often include development, growth, expansion, maturity, and decline. We will focus on just two of these stages: growth and maturity.

    Growth companies are companies in a position to achieve high levels of earnings and stock performance. An industry or company that is in the growth stage of its life cycle has reached a point where its business and product is established. The product is no longer in development, it is out on the market and has reached some amount of consumer acceptance. However, any profits in this market may still be small and needed for further investment to expand market share and continue product development. An example of a growth company would be Palm, Inc.- a provider of handheld computing devices. As of early 2002, the Santa Clara, California company had more than 1,000 employees and more than $1 billion in annual sales. However, its earnings were very volatile and the company has never paid a dividend to its shareholders. A young company like Palm is more likely to reinvest in its business than to part with any of its cash from operations. Thus, growth companies have low dividend yields – a low ratio of cash dividends to stock price. Investors in growth stage companies are more interested in the future possibility of high earnings than in the current income they could receive from cash dividends. Therefore, growth company stocks will trade at market prices that are many times the company's current earnings. This relationship is known as the PE, or price-earnings, ratio. The PE is found by dividing the stocks current price by the company's earnings per share for the previous 12 months. Growth company stocks have high PE ratios.

    Mature companies are companies with consistent profits, but likely to grow only has much as the economy as a whole. An industry in the mature stage of its life cycle has reached a point where its operations generate a steady and sufficient cash flow. The product is well known and the prospects for any future expansion are small. Companies in this stage have significant investments in plant and equipment and ample access to financial resources, either from their own cash flow or outside financing sources. Companies in a mature industry are likely to grow their earnings at or near the rate of growth in the overall economy. Investors in mature industry companies can usually count on a good level of current income from dividends. Since these companies have good cash flow and little expansion needs, they can pay out much of their earnings as cash dividends; sometimes as high as 50 percent. Since investors do not expect growth, mature company stocks will likely trade at low PE ratios. In summary, growth industry companies have high PE ratios and lower dividend yields, while mature industry companies have low PE ratios and higher dividend yields.

The Dow Jones Industrial Average (the Dow) is an index, or composite, of 30 large companies from primarily mature industries. It includes such long-standing and widely known names as IBM, McDonald's and WalMart. Although some companies in the index will have greater growth prospects than others, each company in the index has shown consistent profits and currently only one firm (Microsoft) fails to pay a dividend. Other market indexes are composed of more growth oriented companies. The NASDAQ Composite and the NASDAQ 100 indexes include many companies that are also widely known, but most of these firms compete in new technology industries; reinvesting most of their earnings so as to keep ahead of their rapidly changing competitors. The Russell 2000 index includes the smallest, as measured by the total value of their stock outstanding, of the 3000 largest companies in the U.S. These 2000 companies represent a wide variety of industries, but are also more likely to have greater growth opportunities and greater need for cash then their 1000 counterparts. Trading information for each of these four market indexes are highlighted each day in the *WSJ* under the Market Lineup section on page C2.

Exercise 3-1

MARKETS LINEUP

Trading for June 17, 2002

=[**STOCKS**]=

Dow Jones Industrial Average

Daily High-Low and Close, and 90-Day Moving Average

Close: 9687.42 ▲ +213.21
Divisor: 0.14445222
Market Cap: $3.086 trillion

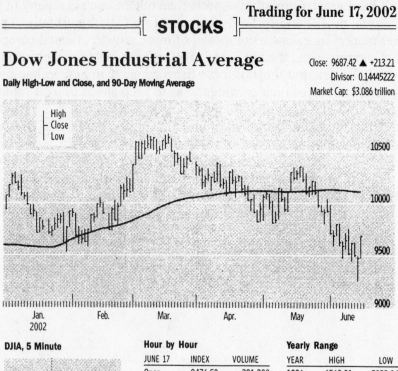

DJIA, 5 Minute

9:30 / 9:30 / 4:00
Jun. 14 / Jun. 17

Hour by Hour

JUNE 17	INDEX	VOLUME
Open	9476.50	391,200
10 a.m.	9527.09	32,550,100
11 a.m.	9611.83	78,979,100
12 noon	9646.93	113,285,700
1 p.m.	9644.02	137,905,200
2 p.m.	9642.43	158,990,100
3 p.m.	9676.21	188,555,800
Close	9687.42	240,633,300
Change	+213.21	
% Change	+ 2.25	

	THEORETICAL	ACTUAL
High	9741.77	9687.77
Low	9462.30	9476.50

Yearly Range

YEAR	HIGH	LOW
1996	6560.91	5032.94
1997	8259.31	6391.69
1998	9374.27	7539.07
1999	11497.12	9120.67
2000	11722.98	9796.03
2001	11337.92	8235.81
YTD	10635.25	9474.21

P/E Ratio[†] and Yield

	P/E RATIO	DIV YIELD
6/17/02	26.27	1.91
Year ago	22.60	1.69

Dow 30 Components Primary market net point change

AT&T	+0.12	CocaCola	+0.40	GenMotor	+1.28	IntPaper	+1.02	PhlpMor	−0.20
Alcoa	+0.21	Disney	+0.50	HewlttPk-x	+0.46	JohnsJohns	+0.63	ProctGam	+2.35
AmExprss	+2.24	DuPont	+1.54	HomeDpt	+1.52	JPMorgChas	+2.48	SBC Comm	+1.07
Boeing	+1.47	EKodak	+1.06	Honeywell	+1.39	McDonalds	+0.70	3M	+1.05
Caterpillar	−0.86	ExxnMobl	+0.88	IBM	+0.97	Merck	+0.86	UtdTch	+1.23
CitiGp	+2.63	GenElec	+0.81	Intel*	+1.28	Microsoft*	+0.43	WalMart	+1.36

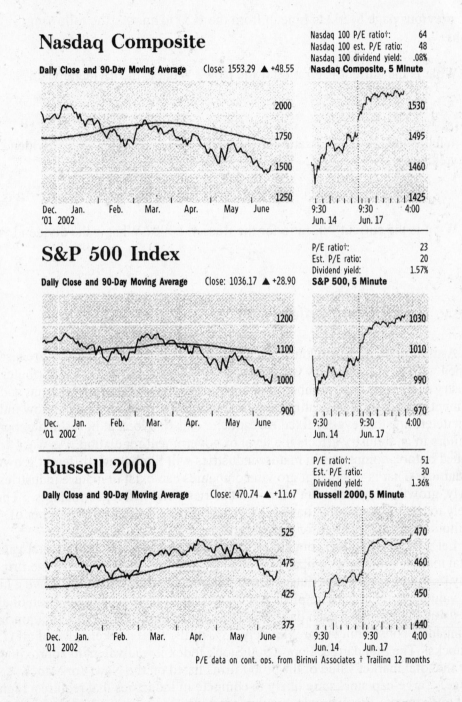

Nasdaq Composite

Daily Close and 90-Day Moving Average Close: 1553.29 ▲ +48.55

Nasdaq 100 P/E ratio†	64
Nasdaq 100 est. P/E ratio	48
Nasdaq 100 dividend yield	.08%

Nasdaq Composite, 5 Minute

S&P 500 Index

Daily Close and 90-Day Moving Average Close: 1036.17 ▲ +28.90

P/E ratio†	23
Est. P/E ratio	20
Dividend yield	1.57%

S&P 500, 5 Minute

Russell 2000

Daily Close and 90-Day Moving Average Close: 470.74 ▲ +11.67

P/E ratio†	51
Est. P/E ratio	30
Dividend yield	1.36%

Russell 2000, 5 Minute

P/E data on cont. ops. from Birinyi Associates † Trailing 12 months

Use the previous page Markets Lineup from the *WSJ* to answer the following questions.

1. What is the current P/E ratio for the Dow? What is the dividend yield?

2. What is the current P/E ratio for the NASDAQ 100? What is the dividend yield?

3. What is the current P/E ratio for the Russell 2000? What is the dividend yield?

Large v. Small Companies

As important as it is to know what stage an industry is in, analysts are also concerned with how an industry is structured. *Industry structure* is the attributes of an industry such as its size, number of competitors, level of fixed investment, and government regulation. These attributes are interrelated. We will look at how industry size can determine the level of fixed investment, and also look at how the number of competitors in an industry affects the level of government regulation. As was mentioned before, companies in mature industries will likely have different growth opportunities. That is to say that growth companies can exist in mature industries. Similarly, growth companies can exist in industries with different structures. There are likely to be companies that have growing earnings despite a large number of competitors or a small market for their product.

Let's first distinguish companies by their size in terms of total market value. The total market value of a company is found by multiplying the price of the firm's stock by the number of shares outstanding. *Large Capitalization* stocks have a high market value. As their name implies, large-cap stocks make up a big portion of all the market value that is traded each day. The Dow Jones Large-Cap index is comprised of 195 companies constituting approximately 73% of the total market value of all U.S. listed stocks. The Standard & Poor's 500 Stock Index is equivalent to approximately 75% of the total market value of the 3,000 firms listed on the New York stock exchange. Large-cap stocks are likely to compete in industries that require a high level of investment. For example, making automobiles requires a high level of investment in plant and equipment. Ford and GM are large cap stocks; their combined total market value as of December 31, 2001 was over $67 Billion. Companies such as these face different competitive threats. For example, large companies are less concerned with entry from new competitors than small companies, and large companies have more bargaining power with their suppliers. At the same time, large companies must be concerned with the competitive threat of substitute products and competing technologies.

Small Capitalization stocks have small market value. These firms constitute a small portion of the total value traded in the stock market each day. The previously mentioned Russell 2000 index is a widely watched composite of these companies. The Dow Jones Small-Cap index is another composite of smaller firms that constitutes only about 7% of the total U.S. stock market value. It is possible for a small firm to operate in a mature industry, but it is more likely that small firms are competing in industries with tremendous growth opportunities. Since the market for their product is still small, the level of investment in plant and equipment by small cap stocks will be similarly smaller. Small companies face different competitive threats than large companies. Small companies are very concerned with entry from new competitors, big and small. As smaller buyers, small companies have less bargaining with their suppliers. At the same time, small companies may be less concerned with the threat of substitute products since they are likely to be using new technologies.

The *WSJ* reports trading activity for different size companies. Each day in the Money and Investing section you can find price data for the different composite indexes based on market capitalization. The Markets Lineup section includes pricing data for the Russell 2000 index; the Dow Jones US Large-Cap, US Mid-Cap, and US Small-Cap indexes; as well as the Standard & Poor 500, 400 Mid Cap, and 600 Small-Cap indexes. Each index uses different classification schemes, but the data provides a good description of investor's assessments of the growth opportunities for the different segments of the economy. The Small Stock Focus column is also found in the Money and Investing section each day. This column reviews the previous day's trading activity with a focus on the significant moves in the prices of small companies from many different industries. For example, on Tuesday May 14, 2002, the Small Stock Focus column reported on the lagging performance of small cap stocks for the previous trading day. The broader market gained, but these gains were concentrated in the price of large , not small, stocks.

Exercise 3-2

Major Stock Indexes

Dow Jones Averages	DAILY HIGH	LOW	CLOSE	NET CHG	% CHG	52-WEEK HIGH	LOW	% CHG	YTD % CHG
30 Industrials	10118.51	9961.86	9981.58	-122.68	-1.21	11175.84	8235.81	- 9.58	- 0.40
20 Transportations	2749.01	2700.49	2728.13	- 15.54	-0.57	3049.96	2033.86	- 6.61	+ 3.34
15 Utilities	299.51	296.50	297.81	- 1.70	-0.57	393.22	273.64	-23.21	+ 1.32
65 Composite	2944.75	2904.11	2914.25	- 27.61	-0.94	3320.61	2489.27	-11.92	+ 0.76
Dow Jones Indexes									
US Total Market	253.18	249.54	250.64	- 1.98	-0.78	298.25	222.35	-14.77	- 6.03
US Large-Cap	240.10	236.54	237.52	- 2.09	-0.87	294.00	218.90	-18.18	- 8.14
US Mid-Cap	280.37	276.50	277.95	- 1.69	-0.60	302.73	226.88	- 6.71	- 0.73
US Small-Cap	305.03	300.30	302.62	- 1.37	-0.45	320.03	233.12	- 1.11	+ 0.40
US Growth	995.75	973.33	981.54	- 10.43	-1.05	1384.80	889.71	-27.76	-14.81
US Value	1292.88	1279.19	1282.15	- 8.66	-0.67	1382.03	1134.22	- 5.86	- 1.11
Global Titans 50	183.13	180.24	180.69	- 1.68	-0.92	223.32	168.34	-18.60	- 9.52
Asian Titans 50	106.78	105.79	106.63	+ 0.29	+0.16	128.96	86.94	-17.32	+11.10
STOXX 50	3459.16	3381.96	3385.95	- 47.17	-1.37	4315.21	2915.64	-21.22	- 8.66
Nasdaq Stock Market									
Composite	1671.35	1632.75	1652.17	- 9.32	-0.56	2264.00	1423.19	-24.06	-15.29
Nasdaq 100	1264.86	1226.28	1244.82	- 8.21	-0.66	1963.31	1126.95	-33.56	-21.07
Biotech	613.85	593.68	613.74	+ 14.32	+2.39	1088.58	574.12	-38.87	-32.47
Computer	791.54	767.97	777.81	- 8.87	-1.13	1138.47	653.13	-27.93	-20.67
Telecommunications	138.43	135.14	136.52	- 0.94	-0.68	353.40	130.78	-61.37	-42.31
Standard & Poor's Indexes									
500 Index	1085.83	1070.35	1074.55	- 9.27	-0.86	1283.57	965.80	-15.25	- 6.40
400 Mid-Cap	535.63	527.22	531.43	- 2.66	-0.50	550.38	404.34	+ 1.12	+ 4.55
600 Small-Cap	247.79	243.61	246.12	- 1.01	-0.41	257.81	181.09	+ 8.04	+ 6.00
1500 Index	240.01	236.54	237.58	- 1.95	-0.81	278.27	209.52	-13.45	- 5.21
New York Stock Exchange									
Composite	578.06	570.90	572.58	- 4.58	-0.79	652.03	504.21	-11.24	- 2.92
Industrials	719.66	710.44	712.18	- 6.64	-0.92	809.59	620.11	-10.90	- 3.20
Finance	606.06	597.42	599.59	- 5.07	-0.84	636.14	494.41	- 4.36	+ 0.99
Others									
Russell 2000	495.22	487.43	492.41	- 1.23	-0.25	522.95	378.90	- 1.98	+ 0.80
Wilshire 5000	10273.05	10130.58	10177.06	- 73.58	-0.72	11902.89	8900.45	-13.23	- 4.96
Value Line	361.61	356.04	358.55	- 1.88	-0.52	415.18	294.60	-12.28	- 2.98
Amex Composite	965.01	956.52	958.73	- 3.96	-0.41	962.69	780.46	+ 2.58	+13.11

Russell 2000/DJ U.S. Total Market

Reindexed to 100 on base date.

- ■ Russell 2000
- ■ DJ U.S. Total Market

Use the table and chart on previous page from the *WSJ* to answer the following questions.

1. What was the daily return on the Dow Jones US Large-Cap Index? The year-to-date return?

2. What was the daily return on the Dow Jones US Small-Cap Index? The year-to-date return?

3. Based on the chart, what has been the trend for small stocks, as measured by the Russell 2000 index, versus the overall market?

Economic Structure

The competitive threats that companies face are determined not only by the size of their competitors, but also by the economics of their industry. There are basically only three choices when considering the number of competitors in an industry – no competitors, a few competitors , or many competitors. A *monopoly* is an industry where only one firm operates. There are very few monopolies in the United States, but in some instances the government grants a firm the right to operate as a monopoly in some mature industries. Public utilities and national defense contractors are two examples. Of course a firm that operates as a government granted monopoly faces intense government regulation. Accordingly, there are limits to the potential earnings growth of these companies.

A much more common economic industry structure is the case of just a few competitors. *Oligopolies* occur when few firms compete in an industry. This type of competition is widespread in the U.S. and occurs amongst primarily large companies in mature industries. For example, the airline and automobile industries are often considered oligopolies. These firms may compete aggressively from time to time, but often don't, choosing not to compete directly with the few other firms in their industry. For example, United Airlines is unlikely to enter markets where American Airlines currently offers service; choosing instead to increase its presence in areas served by smaller rivals.

Prefect competition occurs when there are many sellers of an identical product. In a perfectly competitive industry price is usually the only differentiating factor between one company's product and that of its competitor. This level of competition is unlikely to occur in many industries since most companies are able to differentiate their product in some manner, such as quality or delivery service. Crude level materials and agricultural goods are often considered industries with high levels of competition. Some mining industries, such as gold, can compete only on price, but the high investment costs of these industries discourage many competitors from entering the market.

Exercise 3-3

Market by the Slice

Performance of DJ U.S. Economic Sectors

May 29, 2002 4 p.m. ET

Ranked by % change

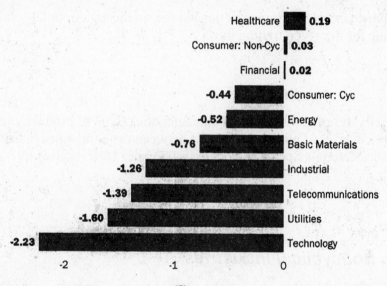

SECTOR	INDEX/PRICE	CHG	% CHG	YTD % CHG	SECTOR	INDEX/PRICE	CHG	% CHG	YTD % CHG
Basic Materials	165.49	-1.27	-0.76	+8.01	**Healthcare**	279.72	+0.54	+0.19	-9.99
DowChem	32.65	-1.15	-3.40	-3.35	Merck	57.13	+1.09	+1.95	-2.84
NewmtMin	31.24	-0.76	-2.38	+63.47	Pfizer	35.09	+0.30	+0.86	-11.94
Consumer: Cyc	273.82	-1.22	-0.44	-1.57	**Industrial**	220.85	-2.81	-1.26	-9.91
HomeDpt	40.95	-0.59	-1.42	-19.72	GenElec	31.35	-0.70	-2.18	-21.78
WalMart	54.53	-0.26	-0.47	-5.25	TycoInt	21.13	-1.07	-4.82	-64.13
Consumer: Non-Cyc	237.29	+0.08	+0.03	+8.87	**Technology**	421.66	-9.61	-2.23	-21.32
PhlpMor	56.01	+0.91	+1.65	+22.16	Intel	27.27	-1.08	-3.81	-13.29
KftFoods	42.25	+0.54	+1.29	+24.16	CiscoSys	15.65	-0.73	-4.46	-13.58
Energy	240.38	-1.26	-0.52	+1.54	**Telecommunications**	133.80	-1.89	-1.39	-25.92
ElPaso	27.01	-8.26	-23.42	-39.45	Verizon	43.89	-0.76	-1.70	-7.52
WillmsCos	15.47	-1.64	-9.59	-39.38	AT&T	12.01	-0.40	-3.22	-33.79
Financial	409.55	+0.06	+0.02	+1.25	**Utilities**	124.98	-2.04	-1.60	-1.62
Wachovia	38.65	+0.73	+1.93	+23.25	DukeEngy	33.51	-1.08	-3.12	-14.65
AmExpress	42.36	+0.68	+1.63	+18.69	AEP	43.98	-1.02	-2.27	+1.03

indexes.dowjones.com

The Dow Jones Indexes are classified by 10 economic sectors, 18 market sectors, and 51 industry groups. Use the above Market by the Slice chart and table from the *WSJ* to answer the following questions.

1. What economic sectors experienced the greatest gain, or smallest loss, in value for the given trading day?

2. What economic sectors experienced the smallest gain, or largest loss, in value for the given trading day?

3. Briefly describe the different characteristics (type of product, method of service, level of competition, etc.) between the companies listed under Basic Materials Sector and those listed under Utilities Sector?

Cyclical v. Noncyclical industries

In the previous chapter we reviewed the economic data used to measure the overall economy and discussed its cyclical nature – the tendency of GDP and unemployment to rise and fall. The business conditions, product demand, sales, and earnings, of many companies are dependent on the level of overall demand in the economy. When GDP rises, their earnings rise; when GDP falls their earnings fall. Other companies compete in industries that are far less dependent on the economy's GDP. Sales and earnings for these firms will be relatively steady even when the overall economy is faltering.

Cyclical industries are industries where the level of sales is highly correlated with the level of GDP. For example, the automobile industry is cyclical in nature. Consumers often delay the purchase of new cars when times are bad – GDP is lower and unemployment is high. *Noncyclical* industries are industries where the level of sales is uncorrelated with the level of GDP. Industries that are less cyclical in nature will generally experience a higher level of competition. For example, food processing and other agricultural related industries experience a relatively constant level of demand. Consumers do not often change their food budget when the economy grows or declines strongly.

Exercise 3-4

Best and Worst Performing DJ Global Sectors

Ranked by % change, in U.S. dollars

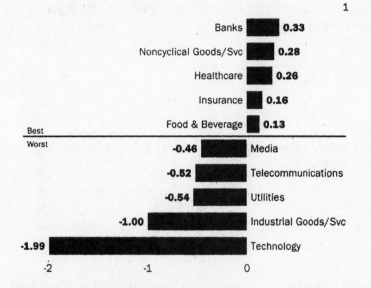

Dow Jones Global Sector Titans

May 29, 2002

SECTOR	INDEX/PRICE	% CHG	SECTOR	INDEX/PRICE	% CHG
Automobile	235.43	-0.41	**Healthcare**	279.32	+0.49
GenMotor(US)	63.00	-1.56	Merck(US)	57.13	+1.95
NissanMotor(JP)	953.00	-1.55	GlaxoWellcome(UK)	14.90	+0.88
Banks	102.09	+0.45	**Industrial Goods/Svc**	178.26	-1.08
BancoBilbao(SP)	13.13	+1.55	TycoInt(US)	21.13	-4.82
BankAm(US)	76.27	+0.74	GenElec(US)	31.35	-2.18
Basic Resources	122.21	-0.39	**Insurance**	228.58	+0.17
BarrickGold(CA)	34.30	-3.35	AFLAC(US)	31.85	+2.61
BHP(AU)	10.90	-2.33	ZurichFin(SZ)	369.00	+0.96
Chemicals	169.57	-0.17	**Media**	261.14	-0.60
DowChem(US)	32.65	-3.40	Comcast spA(US)	28.15	-3.10
ShinEtsuChem(JP)	5200.00	-1.70	Disney(US)	23.05	-2.08
Construction	101.41	-0.08	**Noncyclical Goods/Svc**	264.97	+0.26
Masco(US)	26.67	-1.15	PhilipMorris(US)	56.01	+1.65
CementosMex(MX)	58.25	-1.10	Tesco(UK)	2.50	+1.52
Cyclical Goods/Svc	188.56	-0.08	**Retail**	235.44	-0.23
FujiPhoto(JP)	3980.00	-1.97	HomeDepot(US)	40.95	-1.42
Sony Cp(JP)	7210.00	-0.96	Target(US)	40.00	-1.19
Energy	226.89	-0.68	**Technology**	387.57	-2.22
ElPaso(US)	27.01	-23.42	CiscoSys(US)	15.65	-4.46
WilliamsCos(US)	15.47	-9.59	Intel(US)	27.27	-3.81
Financial Services	285.68	+0.10	**Telecommunications**	169.35	-0.73
Fortis(NV)	25.26	+3.57	AT&T(US)	12.01	-3.22
AmExpress(US)	42.36	+1.63	Verizon(US)	43.89	-1.70
Food & Beverage	208.62	+0.29	**Utilities**	90.10	-0.56
Diageo(UK)	8.60	+0.47	DukeEngy(US)	33.51	-3.12
Unilever(NV)	70.05	+0.36	E.ON(GR)	56.83	+0.25

The Dow Jones Indexes are classified by 10 economic sectors, 18 market sectors, and 51 industry groups. Use the previous page DJ Global Sectors chart and table from the *WSJ* to answer the following questions.

1. What sector experienced the greatest gain, or smallest loss, in value for the given trading day?

2. What sector experienced the smallest gain, or largest loss, in value for the given trading day?

3. Briefly describe the different characteristics (type of product, method service, etc.) between the companies listed under Cyclical Goods & Services Sector and those listed under Noncyclical Goods Services Sector?

Project 3-1

Repeat Exercises 3-1 and 3-2 using a recent edition of the *WSJ*.

Date _____

1. What is the current P/E ratio for the Dow? What is the dividend yield?

2. What is the current P/E ratio for the NASDAQ 100? What is the dividend yield?

3. What is the current P/E ratio for the Russell 2000? What is the dividend yield?

4. What was the daily return on the Dow Jones US Large-Cap Index? The year-to-date return?

5. What was the daily return on the Dow Jones US Small-Cap Index? The year-to-date return?

6. Based on the chart, what has been the trend for small stocks, as measured by the Russell 2000 index, versus the overall market?

Project 3-2

Each day, the Industry of Corporate Focus column of the *WSJ* includes a detailed look at a specific industry or corporation. These articles identify industry trends, competitive situations, and corporate strategies? The reporting found in these stories is useful for assessing an industry's or corporation's potential for future success. Use a recent Industry or Corporate Focus column to complete the following exercises and questions.

Name of Corporation or Industry _____

If an Industry, list the companies within that industry mentioned in the article.

_____

_____

If a Corporation, list any companies mentioned in the article as competitors.

_____

_____

Using information in the article and your own knowledge of the industry, answer the following questions:

1. Is this industry characterized by large, mid-size, or small companies? What competitive threats arise because of the size of these companies?

_____

_____

_____

2. Would you characterize this industry as an oligopoly or a perfectly competitive industry? Why?

_____

_____

_____

3. Is this industry cyclical or noncyclical? Why?

_____

_____

Discussion Questions

Tougher Laws to Fight Gasoline Shortages Sought

By STEPHENIE STEITZER

WASHINGTON—Attorneys general from three states urged Congress to tighten antitrust laws and mandate increased inventories for the nation's petroleum refiners to combat gasoline shortages that lead to higher pump prices.

Those recommendations were part of a series of steps the attorneys general urged a Senate Government Affairs subcommittee to take to deter market manipulation in an increasingly concentrated industry. A subcommittee report released this week found that frequent price increases plague motorists in some areas of the country where a few refiners dominate, such as California and the Great Lakes region.

"We should take appropriate steps—and I emphasize the word appropriate but I also emphasize the word take—to reinvigorate competition in highly concentrated areas," said Sen. Carl Levin (D., Mich.), the panel's chairman.

Michigan Attorney General Richard Blumenthal suggested legislation placing the burden of proof on oil companies to demonstrate that consumers would benefit from a given merger. He also said that in a highly concentrated market, proof that prices are being set based on those of competitors should be considered evidence of an antitrust violation. Mr. Blumenthal suggested banning zone pricing, a practice oil companies use to group retail outlets into small geographic areas and charge dealers in different areas different prices for the same products. "Zone pricing," he said, "is really not a competitive measure, in fact it is anticompetitive."

Tom Greene, California's senior assistant attorney general, said Congress should establish a new strategic-fuels reserve that could be tapped when prices begin rising. The reserve could cushion the price shock until supplies grow. Mr. Greene said California is considering such a reserve for the state, and consultants have estimated it would have saved state residents as much as $1 billion when prices jumped in 1999.

The attorneys general also proposed: a one-year moratorium on major oil-company mergers in concentrated areas; supplying the Federal Trade Commission with more information and resources so it can better review proposed mergers; and reviewing whether pipelines are charging fair and reasonable rates. Four industry experts, on the other hand, urged the committee to steer clear of modifying antitrust laws, banning zone pricing and establishing strategic-fuels reserves.

Preston McAfee, a University of Texas economics professor, said price volatility isn't necessarily a problem that needs to be solved with regulations. "Stabilizing prices at a high level, such as the Canadian policy, is much worse than allowing fluctuations where sometimes you get the benefits of low prices," he said.

Instead, Mr. McAfee said the number of boutique fuels—special blends of gasoline designed to comply with various federal, state and local environmental regulations—should be reduced to eliminate the need for micromarkets. He also suggested easing Environmental Protection Agency rules to allow more pipelines to transport gasoline. "We should not let a few problems deflect us from our market economy or send us back to the miserable regulated environment of the 1970s," Mr. McAfee said.

1. What is meant by the term "concentrated industry"? How does this characteristic of an industry affect the level of competition?

2. What is zone pricing? How is this practice "anticompetitive"?

3. Why would stabilizing prices at a high level be worse than high volatility in the market?

4. According to the article, what current government regulations may be leading to high prices in this market?

Chapter 4

International Economics and Markets

Objectives

1. Discuss the economic data on U.S. international activity reported in the *WSJ*.

2. Review the globalization trends and the growth of world financial markets.

3. Describe the differences between developed and emerging financial markets.

4. Use the *WSJ* to identify the methods of investing in international financial markets.

Key Terms

Current Account	Diversification	Exchange Traded Funds
Balance of Trade	Developed Countries	American Depository
Globalization	Emerging Markets	Receipts
Closed-end funds		

Investors and managers are concerned not only with the economic situation in their country and industry, but also with the economic situation across the globe. Economic conditions in other countries affect the businesses and financial markets in the U.S. Also, financial markets outside the U.S. provide both opportunities and risks for personal and corporate investments. This chapter reviews the extensive information on international economic and financial activity found in the *WSJ*. To begin, the extent of U.S. international trade and its affect on financial markets is discussed, followed by a description of the interrelations between economies across the world and the growth of world equity markets. Next, the differences between investments in developed markets versus developing markets are reviewed. The chapter concludes with a discussion of the information found in the *WSJ* on world financial markets and different methods available for international investing.

U.S. International Trade and Investments

In Chapter 2 we reviewed the broadest measure of overall economic activity, gross domestic product (GDP). Recall that GDP includes four components - personal consumption, investment (both residential and non-residential), net exports (total exports – total imports), and government purchases. Net exports reflect the current state of international trade in an economy. An economy with positive net exports currently sells more goods to other countries than it buys; an economy with negative net exports currently sells less goods to other countries than it buys. Households and businesses must balance their cash inflows with their cash outflows; if they spend more than they take in they must borrow the difference. In the same manner, a country must balance its cash flows to all other countries with its cash inflows from all other countries. The U.S. International Account is a record of this balance. The *WSJ* regularly reports two important figures in the international account – the quarterly current account and the monthly balance of trade.

The U.S. International Account is a balanced book with two main accounts – the current account and the capital account. The ***Current Account*** is the broadest measure of U.S. trade, including trade in both goods and services between the U.S. and all its trading partners, as well as income earned on foreign investments by U.S. citizens and companies. As foreign consumers and businesses buy U.S. goods, the current account increases; as U.S. consumers and businesses buy foreign goods, the current account decreases. The same holds true for purchases and sales of services. In total, if the U.S. buys more than it sells, and earns less on investments overseas than it returns on investments to foreigners, it will run a current account deficit. Remember, however, that the inflows and outflows must balance. Thus, if the current account is in a deficit, the capital account must be in surplus. For example, if the U.S. buys $10 billion more than it sells (a $10 billion current account deficit) than the rest of the world must have $10 billion sitting around. Of course, the rest of the world will not leave this money burning a hole in its pockets, it will invest the money. Since this 10 billion is U.S. dollars, it must be invested in U.S. investments. The capital account reflects this investment. As foreign citizens and businesses invest in the U.S. (directly in plants and equipment or indirectly through financial markets), the capital account increases; as U.S. citizens and businesses invest in foreign markets, the capital account decreases.

On Friday March 15, 2002 the *WSJ* reported the most recent current account data from the U.S. Department of Commerce. The report indicated that the current account of the U.S. for the fourth quarter of 2001 widened slightly to $98.8 Billion from $98.5 Billion in the third quarter. However, for all of 2001 the current account declined for the first time in six years. For many of the previous five years, the U.S. economy was growing strongly, providing consumers opportunity to purchase many foreign goods and services (creating a current account deficit), while also providing foreign investors a good place to invest (creating a capital account surplus).

The ***Balance Of Trade***, reported monthly by the U.S. Department of Commerce, is an estimate of the gap between foreign purchases and foreign sales of both merchandise (goods) and services. This report is most often referred to as the trade report. On April 18, 2002 the *WSJ* reported the latest trade balance numbers. For the month of February, a 4% rise in imports increased the U.S. trade deficit to $31.51 billion from $28.25 billion in January. The large jump in imports overshadowed a respectable 1.2% rise in exports. The article points out that this increase may be reflective of strengthening overall economy. The strong demand for imports was partly due to businesses replenishing inventories of foreign parts and supplies in expectation of an increase in consumer demand for products.

Exercise 4-1

TRADE

Here are the Commerce Department's monthly trade figures, in billions of dollars.

	Jan. 2002	Dec. 2001-r
Total Exports	77.97	78.04
Goods	54.84	54.95
Services	23.13	23.09
Total Imports	106.49	102.76
Goods	88.92	85.94
Services	17.57	16.82
Overall trade balance	−28.52	−24.71
Goods	−34.08	−30.98
Services	5.56	6.27

r-Revised

REGIONAL TRADE BALANCES

U.S. merchandise trade balances by region: in billions of U.S. dollars, not seasonally adjusted.

	Jan. 2002	Dec. 2001	Jan. 2001
Japan	− 4.75	− 5.02	− 5.87
China	− 6.86	− 5.49	− 7.23
Canada	− 4.43	− 3.83	− 5.88
Western Europe	− 4.98	− 4.05	− 5.62
Mexico	− 2.27	− 2.00	− 2.10
NICS*	− 2.11	− 1.39	− 2.59
South/Central America	− 1.08	− 0.47	− 1.82

*-Newly industrialized countries: Singapore, Hong Kong, Taiwan, South Korea.
r-Revised
Source: Commerce Department

Source: *The Wall Street Journal*, May 20, 2002. Reprinted by permission of Dow Jones & Company, Inc. (c) 2002 Dow Jones & Company, Inc. All Rights Reserved Worldwide.

Use the above summary table from the *WSJ* to answer the following questions:

1. Verify the month's balance of trade in goods, services, and overall by subtracting imports from exports.

2. What was the percentage change in the overall trade balance for the month?

3. Calculate the percent change in exports and imports. For the month, which item had the greatest impact on the change in the overall trade balance?

4. According to the Regional Trade Balance, which country had the largest trade surplus with the U.S.? For which country or region was the change in the trade balance the greatest over the past year?

Globalization

A front page article in the March 18, 2002 issue of the *WSJ* discusses many of the linkages tying economies across the world together. Since the early 1980s, the links through trade and financial capital flows between countries has increased significantly. This trend has been termed globalization. *Globalization* refers to the increasing connectivity between economies and markets. Today, more domestic economic activity is affected by economic activity in other parts of the world and more local financial market trends are influenced by activity in global financial markets. As the article points out, this era of globalization is nothing new. In the early 1900s, considered a golden age of globalization, there were large cross-border flows of labor (human migration), transportation (shipping) costs were falling, and some of the first multinational corporations were established. Today, rather than labor crossing borders, capital investment dollars are flowing from one market to another at an increasing rate, in large part due to advances in communication technology. Both individual and corporate investment dollars leave low return markets and seek out high returns in markets around the world. As a result, a slowdown in one market may quickly cause a slowdown in another market. That is to say, that since capital moves so quickly today, investment returns are more quickly equalized around the world.

Although the potential equalization of returns across markets exists, it is likely that all markets will not move up and down in the same manner every period. This is one of the key benefits of global investing. *Diversification*, the process of holding a portfolio of investments from many different countries, can benefit investors through lower volatility and potentially higher returns. Just as risk is reduced by holding more than one stock, holding stocks from different countries can also decrease volatility and may also increase return if one market benefits from economic condition more than another. For example, the *WSJ* reported on January 2, 2002 that although Finland's stock market declined 37.83% in U.S. Dollar terms during 2001, South Korea's market was up 45.29%. The previous year was a different story. In the year 2000,

Finland's stock market was also down that year, declining 15.27%, but South Korea's market was down a whopping 58.84%. An investor holding equal positions in both markets for the two years would have much less volatility and a better total return than if each market was held separately.

With or without globalization, anyone interested in local economic and financial market activity to should watch global economic and financial trends. The *WSJ* contains many reports to help investors and managers follow developments in world markets. First, the World Watch section in the International columns of the *WSJ's* first section contains reports on all major economic data released in countries outside the U.S. For example, on May 17, 2002 the *WSJ* reported on China's balance of trade. For the first four months of the year, China's trade surplus was $8.24 Billion (exports exceeded imports by this amount) and foreign direct investment in China increased. Trends in world trade and investment such as these can have significant impacts on U.S. businesses. Second, the *WSJ* reports world financial market activity each day. The Dow Jones Country Indexes (DJCI) are representative composites of stock markets from 34 countries throughout the world. Each index is designed to represent at least 95% of the total market value of all companies trading in the given country's stock markets. The daily activity in these markets can be found in the International Stocks and Indexes table of the Money and Investing section. The index's current value, change, percent change, and year-to-date percent change for the DJCI are listed in U.S. Dollar terms. That is, the index value and change in value incorporate both the value of the stocks in the index as well as the value of the U.S. Dollar relative to the local currency. Also listed in this section is individual stock activity for 26 different markets, including Brazil, Italy, Singapore, and New Zealand.

Exercise 4-2

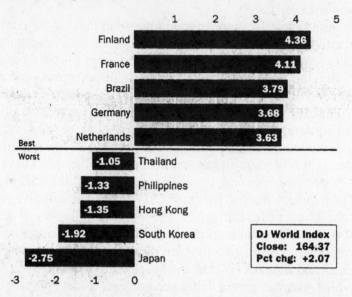

Best and Worst Performing DJ Country Indexes

Ranked by % change, on a U.S. dollar basis

Country	% change
Finland	4.36
France	4.11
Brazil	3.79
Germany	3.68
Netherlands	3.63
Thailand	-1.05
Philippines	-1.33
Hong Kong	-1.35
South Korea	-1.92
Japan	-2.75

DJ World Index
Close: 164.37
Pct chg: +2.07

Dow Jones Country Indexes

June 17, 2002 5:15 p.m. ET

In U.S. dollar terms

COUNTRY	INDEX	CHG	% CHG	YTD % CHG	COUNTRY	INDEX	CHG	% CHG	YTD % CHG
Australia	163.33	-0.29	-0.18	+5.97	Mexico	159.84	+2.24	+1.42	+1.53
Austria	101.00	-0.48	-0.47	+17.24	Netherlands	246.77	+8.65	+3.63	-4.06
Belgium	177.24	+5.19	+3.02	+3.95	New Zealand	120.36	+0.87	+0.73	+17.14
Brazil	209.39	+7.65	+3.79	-17.09	Norway	133.68	+3.29	+2.52	+6.96
Canada	177.74	+2.66	+1.52	-1.34	Philippines	56.57	-0.76	-1.33	+5.90
Chile	127.73	+1.48	+1.17	-7.14	Portugal	127.25	+1.98	+1.58	-8.57
Denmark	183.62	+2.31	+1.27	-1.96	Singapore	113.44	-0.57	-0.50	+4.67
Finland	622.88	+26.01	+4.36	-34.78	South Africa	88.48	-0.77	-0.86	+25.32
France	181.58	+7.17	+4.11	-6.10	South Korea	98.21	-1.92	-1.92	+27.21
Germany	153.18	+5.44	+3.68	-7.59	Spain	156.24	+4.27	+2.81	-6.62
Greece	103.64	-0.33	-0.32	-10.90	Sweden	190.34	+3.34	+1.79	-19.37
Hong Kong	189.18	-2.59	-1.35	-3.07	Switzerland	301.82	+8.05	+2.74	+2.69
Indonesia	44.86	-0.17	-0.38	+76.30	Taiwan	106.47	-0.55	-0.51	-0.42
Ireland	271.19	+0.56	+0.21	-9.91	Thailand	39.48	-0.42	-1.05	+38.80
Italy	135.42	+3.98	+3.03	-1.72	U.K.	155.08	+4.09	+2.71	-6.97
Japan	65.44	-1.85	-2.75	+5.07	U.S.	241.05	+6.61	+2.82	-9.62
Malaysia	101.74	-0.38	-0.37	+11.06	Venezuela	26.17	-0.04	-0.15	-24.17

Use the above chart and table from the *WSJ* to answer the following questions:

1. For the given day, what market had the greatest percentage increase? What market had the greatest percentage loss?

2. Compare these two markets to the percentage change in the DJ World Index. Was the percentage change in the best market significantly greater than the percentage change in the world markets?

3. Each of the Dow Jones Country indexes has a base value of 100 as of January 1, 1992. Which market has had the greatest overall gain since January 1, 1992? Which market has had the greatest overall loss since January 1, 1992?

Emerging Markets

Another source of diversification benefits comes from differing rates of returns available on investments in markets of poor versus wealthy nations. Poor nations have higher potential growth, but greater risk of loss; wealthy nations have less growth potential and lower risks. **Developed countries**, nations with high levels of real income, have established financial markets with high liquidity and steady long-term growth. **Emerging Markets** are financial markets in less developed, or developing, nations. These nations have low levels of real income, and their financial markets are characterized by low liquidity and volatile prices.

The Dow Jones World Developed Index includes 95% of the market capitalization in the world's developed countries. The nations in this index include Canada and the United States, the Asian nations of Japan and Singapore, the Hong Kong market, and sixteen European nations (Austria, Belgium, Denmark, Finland, France, Germany, Greece, Ireland, Italy, Norway, Portugal, Spain, Sweden, Switzerland, Netherlands, and the United Kingdom). The Dow Jones World Emerging Index includes 11 nations: Brazil, Chile, Indonesia, Malaysia, Mexico, Philippines, South Africa, South Korea, Taiwan, Thailand, and Venezuela. In the 1990s, the U.S. stock market saw gains well above the historical averages, while many smaller markets eked out only small returns. The cumulative total return for the Dow Jones World Developed Index from 1992 through 2000 was 156.25%. Meanwhile, over the same period the Dow Jones World Emerging Index returned only 13.96%. However, emerging markets could top the U.S. and other developed markets in the years ahead, making diversification across international markets worthwhile.

Many differences exist between the financial markets of developed and emerging markets. Different countries and cultures have different preferences for investments. In many cultures the willingness to take the risks associated with equity investments are less than those of other countries. Also, the accounting rules and the level of government regulation differ significantly across both developed and emerging markets. These and other differences lead to different valuations of stocks across markets. For some markets, the level of dividend payments are higher. Dividend yields, the ratio of dividend payments to stock price, varies significantly across international markets. For example, as of April 30, 2002 the dividend yield for the Dow Jones U.S. Country Index was 1.45% while the Dow Jones Australia Country Index was 3.16%.[†]

Returns and valuations of both developed and emerging markets can be tracked in the *WSJ* by following the trading data of international index funds. Like the Dow Jones Country Indexes discussed above, Morgan Stanley Capital International (MSCI) has indexes for many countries around the world. Some of the MSCI country indexes can be bought and sold as **Exchange Traded Funds** (ETFs). ETFs are shares of a portfolio designed to track the performance of a market index. The Exchange-Traded Portfolios column of the *WSJ* reports price and trading information for country and other indexes, and is found each day in the Money and Investing Section.

[†] All Dow Jones Index data Source: http://indexes.dowjones.com. (retrieved May, 2002).

Exercise 4-3

EXCHANGE-TRADED PORTFOLIOS

Includes Exchange-Traded Funds and HOLDRs
Wednesday, May 29, 2002

AMEX

YTD %CHG	52 WEEKS HI	LO	STOCK (SYM)	DIV	YLD %	PE	VOL 100s	CLOSE	NET CHG
-0.5	112.18	79.50	Diamond DIA	1.59e	1.6		27597	99.35	-0.79
-13.7	104.85	83.70	MLPharm HLDRs PPH	1.43e	1.7		1478	85	0.42
7.3	124.37	95	ML Req HLDRs RKH	3.30e	2.7		11652	120.40	0.55
-31.6	7.26	2.41	MerLynB2B BHH	.26e	7.4		333	3.51	...
-26.4	144.69	88.82	MerLynBiotch BBH	.03e			10686	97.20	-2.50
-34.1	27.50	10.06	BrdBnd HOLDRs BDH	.03e	.3		363	10.87	-0.33
-15.0	79.65	48.80	Europe HOLDRs EKH	1.35e	2.4		67	55.45	-0.52
-23.9	49.50	26.30	IntArc HOLDRs IAH	.14e	.5		76	29.18	-0.36
-21.9	47.79	23.90	Intrnt HOLDRs HHH	...			75	27.01	-0.09
-51.4	14.50	2.55	IntInfr HOLDRs IIH	...			49	3.04	-0.10
-13.4	71.80	51.28	Mkt2k HLDRs MKH	.93e	1.8		1037	52.67	-0.33
17.7	91.30	41.81	OilSvc HOLDRs OIH	.45e	.6		9306	71.79	0.18
-2.7	102.23	70	Retail HOLDRs RTH	.51e	.5		2074	94.02	-0.40
-7.2	53.37	27.31	Semi HOLDRs SMH	.05e	.1		46293	38.85	-1.34
-31.6	58.46	28.15	Sftwre HOLDRs SWH	.04e	.1		6160	30.90	-0.55
-22.4	52.30	30.85	Telcom HOLDRs TTH	.92e	2.7		2449	33.64	-0.62
-3.6	114.89	82.87	MerLynUt Tr UTH	3.42p			374	87.73	-2.43
-30.6	70.20	37.91	Wrls HOLDRs WMH	.51e	1.2		116	40.84	-0.62
6.1	46.85	32.19	iShrDJUSChm IYD	.84e	1.9		55	44.80	-0.35
0.5	57.40	40.41	iShrDJUSEn IYE	.64e	1.3		101	47.94	-0.32
8.4	42.99	30	iShrDJUSBM IYM	.53e	1.3		176	41.72	-0.28
-1.7	62.60	41.40	iShDJUSCCy IYC	.05e	.1		221	54.70	-0.06
9.3	49.23	39.27	iShrDJUSCNC IYK	.54e	1.1		185	47.66	0.13
1.3	99.50	73.15	iShrDJUSFin IYG	1.18e	1.3		73	92.95	-0.21
-9.9	65.40	54.75	iShrDJUSHlth IYH	.27e	.5		149	55.98	0.33
-9.2	56.10	37.40	iShrDJUSInd IYJ	.30e	.7		51	45.85	-0.35
9.3	89.39	73.40	iShrDJUSRE IYR	4.96e	5.7		650	87.25	0.75
-6.7	60.04	43.25	iShrDJUSTot IYY	.57e	1.1		81	49.96	-0.42
-1.2	84.60	58.60	iShrDJUSUtil IDU	1.84e	2.9		160	63.22	-0.78
0.9	86.69	65	iShrDJUSFi IYF	1.08e	1.3		34	81.19	0.09
-32.5	22.65	8.23	iShrDJInt IYV	e			181	9.80	...
-28.2	38.35	21.03	iShrDJUSTc IYZ	.28e	1.2		155	22.63	-0.32
-21.5	66.45	36.45	iShrDJTch IYW	...			1158	41.78	-1.10
8.4	102.20	72.70	iShrSP400V IJJ	1.06e	1.1		943	98.11	-0.88
0.4	77.43	60.90	iShrRu3000V IWW	1.22e	1.7		297	72.02	-0.28
-1.4	64.10	43.30	iShrMSEMU EZU	.67e	1.2		49	55.20	-0.15
-9.6	65.85	41	iShrRu2000G IWO	.10e	.2		1911	51.89	-1.15
9.8	148.10	102.90	iShrRu2000V IWN	2.13e	1.5		1660	140.60	-1.33
-12.9	47.36	32.65	iShrRu3000G IWZ	.11e	.3		66	35.60	-0.44
0.3	67.44	45.52	iShrSPEu350 IEV	.84e	1.4		447	59.28	0.09
-0.1	82.42	58.50	iShrSP600G IJT	.09e	.1		189	76.86	-1.18
10.5	99.67	66.35	iShrSP600V IJS	.60e	.6		997	94.30	-0.96
10.6	10.43	7.50	iShrMSAusy EWA	.23e	2.2		1653	10.45	0.03
26.1	9.16	6.69	iShrMSAus EWO	.14e	1.5		90	9.18	0.12
7.7	12.82	9.05	iShrMSBlg EWK	.30e	2.5		93	11.85	0.24
-3.6	15.30	8.40	iShrMSBra EWZ	.64e	5.2		862	12.24	0.14
7.5	12.55	8.70	iShrMSCan EWC	.09e	.8		1588	11.42	...
0.8	21.48	14.50	iShrMSFra EWQ	.05e	.3		452	18.90	-0.03
-0.9	17.18	10.35	iShrMSGer EWG	.19e	1.3		533	14.96	-0.13
4.3	10.99	6.85	iShrMSHK EWH	.23e	2.4		1243	9.56	-0.14
4.8	19.20	12.25	iShrMSIta EWI	.31e	1.8		192	16.87	0.12
16.0	11.12	6.71	iShrMSJpn EWJ	e			15899	8.94	-0.06
33.6	24.60	10.32	iShrMSSK EWY	.10e	.4		458	23.66	-0.42
16.0	6.44	3.96	iShrMSMay EWM	.08e	1.3		2259	6.03	0.04
8.1	18.40	11	iShrMSMex EWW	.18e	1.1		2229	16.41	-0.51
5.6	20.40	13.20	iShrMSNth EWN	.32e	1.8		218	17.92	-0.25
8.9	5.91	3.81	iShrMSSng EWS	.07e	1.3		424	5.52	-0.10
1.9	23	16	iShrMSEsp EWP	.16e	.8		73	21.06	0.11
11.7	14.40	10.55	iShrMSSwi EWL	.10e	.7		313	14.01	-0.02

YTD %CHG	52 WEEKS HI	LO	STOCK (SYM)	DIV	YLD %	PE	VOL 100s	CLOSE	NET CHG
-1.2	16.54	11.90	iShrMSUK EWU	.48e	3.3		1359	14.52	-0.03
10.3	60.19	49.70	iSHRS MSCI Pac EPP	.27p			77	59.74	0.05
-10.9	15.35	8.85	iShrMSSwe EWD	.05e	.4		248	12.21	-0.14
0.9	12.56	6.51	iShrMSTaiwn EWT	e			7878	10.88	-0.19
-33.4	40.10	19.10	iShrsGS Netwkng IGN	...			104	20.45	-0.40
-34.2	52.55	28.45	iShrGS Sftwr IGV	...			6254	29.95	-0.83
5.3	105.29	88.55	iShrs GldSach IGE	.64e	.6		3	100.70	-0.95
-8.9	79.95	44.89	iShrGS Smcdtor IGW	...			128	60.56	-1.89
-21.7	62.70	34.75	iShrGSchsTch IGM	...			89	39.70	-0.78
3.8	128.85	98	iShrsMSCI EAFE EFA	.25e	.2		3403	123.78	-0.12
-34.9	109.30	56.81	iShrsNasBioTch IBB	...			3508	59.30	-2.08
-6.7	68.17	49.55	iShrRu1000 IWB	.69e	1.2		531	56.90	-0.39
0.1	61.13	47.30	iShrRu1000V IWD	.89e	1.6		1474	55.98	-0.21
-9.9	73.95	52.80	iShrRuMidGrth IWP	.02e			82	64.75	-0.78
0.5	61.55	47.50	iShrRuMid IWR	.40e	.7		52	59.20	-0.17
6.5	84.93	64.52	iShrRuMidVlu IWS	.92e	1.1		53	83	-0.33
-12.8	59.35	40.25	iShrRu1000G IWF	.16e	.4		1109	44.42	-0.57
0.5	71.23	51.80	iShrRu3000 IWV	.64e	1.0		1061	59.96	-0.34
0.5	104.75	73.50	iShrRu2000 IWM	.96e	1.0		9751	96.87	-1.25
15.6	82.05	62	iShrs S&P/Tpx ITF	...			6	80.60	-0.13
4.2	110.87	79.10	iShrsSP400 IJH	.75e	.7		1371	105.40	-1.01
1.7	49.80	38.10	iShSPTSE6U IKC	.40e	.9		1	45	-0.20
-9.7	63.98	48	iShrsSP500G IVW	.41e	.8		231	53.53	-0.50
-3.5	65	46.30	iShrSP500V IVE	.84e	1.6		889	53.34	-0.34
-6.2	50.86	46	iShrsSPGbl Hlthcr IXJ	.01e			178	46.43	...
-1.5	124.18	85.25	iShrSP400G IJK	.14e	.1		319	112.20	-1.27
-6.2	129.23	94.25	iShrsSP500 IVV	1.38e	1.3		9250	107.20	-0.79
8.0	55.59	45.70	iShrsSPGbl GE IXC	.07e	.1		12	53.44	-0.06
-21.7	53.63	37.95	iShrsSPGbl Tele IXP	.02p			3	40.45	-0.19
5.8	128.70	88.25	iShrsSP600 IJR	.57e	.5		1690	120.98	-1.27
0.5	54.74	40.50	iShrs Tr 40 ILF	.27e			4	47.92	-1.07
9.1	94.54	77.75	iShrsCohen&St ICF	5.18e	5.6		98	92.01	1.02
-11.9	10.48	8.14	MerLynBiotch nts BPN	...			106	8.60	0.09
-22.2	49.49	27.20	Nasdaq 100 QQQ	...			712318	30.28	-0.82
-6.1	129.23	93.80	SPDR SPY	1.44e	1.3		146083	107.30	-0.80
4.3	101.67	71.50	SPDR Mid MDY	.72e	.7		11346	96.79	-0.67
11.1	24.44	17.05	SPDR BscInd XLB	.42e	1.8		3760	23.79	-0.16
10.1	30.51	21	SPDR ConSvc XLV	.20e	.3		158	29.66	-0.02
-2.2	26.50	23.20	SPDR ConStpl XLP	.32e	1.3		304	24.83	0.08
0.7	30.82	20	SPDR CycTrn XLY	.20e	.7		265	28.80	-0.06
3.0	34.03	22.37	SPDR Engy XLE	.49e	1.8		1101	27.50	-0.26
0.7	29.18	21.15	SPDR Fncl XLF	.40e	1.5		5380	26.48	-0.01
-8.4	31.49	20.40	SPDR Indu XLI	.34e	1.3		2391	25.37	-0.29
-23.4	29.69	17.27	SPDR Tch XLK	...			10001	18.38	-0.35
-4.7	33.03	25.35	SPDR Utils XLU	.89e	3.3		194	26.70	-0.45
-10.1	74.75	55.30	sTrackDJGITitn DGT	.63e	1.0		39	60.15	-0.29
-17.1	65	40	sTrackDJLCapG ELG	...	.3		47	58.55	-0.43
-4.7	135.12	109.37	sTrackDJLCapV ELV	2.18e	1.8		13	120.60	-0.26
-18.3	81.05	51.20	sTrackDJSCapG DSG	...			74	59.95	-1.06
10.2	145.20	106.03	sTrackDJSCapV DSV	7.79e	5.6		49	140.10	-0.45
-5.8	91.10	68.30	sTrackFort500 FFF	1.01e	1.3		96	77.21	-0.39
-27.6	43.90	23.10	sTrackFort e50 FEF	...			73	24.60	-0.26
-23.1	61.85	34.96	sTrackMSHTch35 MTK	...			1	39.28	-0.35
-35.3	21.65	7.55	sTrackMSInt MII	...			210	8.72	-0.32
8.5	132.50	109.70	sTrackWIshREIT	5.81e	4.5		25	128.79	1.15
-2.8	63.38	56.85◆	VanguardVipers VXF	...			12	60.49	-0.01
-4.9	118	86.80◆	VanguardTot VTI	1.29e	1.3		472	100.23	-0.56

NYSE

YTD %CHG	52 WEEKS HI	LO	STOCK (SYM)	DIV	YLD %	PE	VOL 100s	CLOSE	NET CHG
-9.3	66.63	48.20	iShrSP100Gbl IOO	.53e	1.0		15	53.53	-0.26

CBOE

YTD %CHG	52 WEEKS HI	LO	STOCK (SYM)	DIV	YLD %	PE	VOL 100s	CLOSE	NET CHG
-9.0	66.52	47.72	iShrsSP100 CBOE OEF	e			71	53.48	-0.08

Use the above table from *WSJ* to compare the dividend yield for developed and emerging markets.

1. Find the dividend yields for the France (ishrMSFra), Australia (ishrMSAusy), and Germany (ishrMSGer) exchange traded funds. Calculate the average dividend yield for these three developed countries.

2. Find the dividend yields for the Brazil (ishrMSBra), South Korea (ishrMSSK), and Malaysia (ishrMSMay) exchange traded funds. Calculate the average dividend yield for these three emerging markets.

3. Compare the year-to-date (YTD) percent change in each of the of the above countries. Which markets, developed or emerging, performed better during the given year?

International Investing

Earlier we discussed the *WSJ* article on globalization. A key reason for globalization is the increased opportunities for, and the lower costs of, international investing. There are now more ways for investors to add foreign securities to their portfolios. In this section, we will review three methods of investing in foreign markets that are regularly reported on in the *WSJ*.

The first method of adding foreign securities to an investment portfolio is direct purchase. Investors can buy shares in foreign corporations by purchasing their stocks that trade on foreign markets either through the branch office of a U.S. brokerage firm or through the foreign brokerage. The International Stocks and Indexes column of the *WSJ* reports on trading activity from Canada, Latin America, Europe, Africa, and Asia. The closing price (in local currency) and net change in the widely traded stocks of the major stock markets in these regions are reported each day. Also listed are the major stock indexes for these markets and their year-to-date returns. This section of the paper also includes the World Markets column that reports the major stock market news from around the world.

A less costly way for investors to directly purchase shares in foreign corporations is to purchase shares in foreign companies that list their stocks on U.S. exchanges. For example, the German corporation Daimler Chrysler trades on the New

York Stock Exchange. Investors can purchase this stock just as they would purchase shares in an American company. However, most shares of foreign corporations that trade in the U.S. are listed as ***American Depository Receipts*** (ADR). (These securities may also be referred to as American Depository Shares, or ADS). ADRs are securities that acknowledge ownership in a foreign company's stock that is being held on deposit with a trustee, usually an American bank with an office in the company's home country. Although these are not direct shares, ADRs trade just like regular shares. The pricing and trading information is identical. ADRs are included in the regular stock tables of the *WSJ*.

A third, and very popular, method for international investing is through investment management companies, or mutual funds. A mutual fund is a pool of investment dollars by individuals managed by professional money managers. There are many mutual funds with the express directive of investing only in markets outside the U.S. Mutual funds may be either open-end or closed-end. An open-end fund sells or redeems investors' shares in the fund at any time. A ***Closed-End Fund*** sells a limited number of shares to the public. These shares trade just like stocks on both organized and over-the-counter exchanges. The fund does not redeem shares directly, investors wishing to sells shares must do so with other investors. Many Closed-end funds have the express directive of investing only in a specific country. For example, the India Growth Fund, Inc. trades on the New York Stock Exchange and has as its objective to seek long term capital appreciation through investment primarily in equity securities of Indian companies. Closed-end fund prices and trading data is found each day in the Money and Investing Section of the *WSJ*. Each Monday, the *WSJ* contains extensive reporting data on Closed-end funds, including the previous annual return on the fund, its latest dividend, and the relationship between the price of the fund and the value of its assets. Closed-end funds may trade at or below the actually trading value of the stocks within its portfolio. The Monday report on Closed-end Funds includes the premium or discount to net asset value for the fund.

Exercise 4-4

ADRS

Wednesday, May 29, 2002			
AngloAm ADS **AAUK**	8733	18.40	-0.55
Daiei g **DAIEY**	16	1.56	0.06
✦DankaBus **DANKY**	3406	3.80	0.32
DigiTel ADS **DTAGY**	4	3.31	-0.39
FujiPhoto ADS g **FUJIY**	162	32	-0.15
Ftrmdia **FMDAY**	364	0.12	...
Instrmentarm ADS **INMRY**	3	26.71	1.08
JapanAir **JAPNY**	4	6.17	0.02
KirinBrew ADS **KNBWY**	4	84.73	...
NewTel ADS **NWLL**	24	0.94	-0.01
Nissan ADS g **NSANY**	1157	15.35	-0.06
RankGp ADS **RANKY**	38	8	0.24
Santos ADS **STOSY**	21	14.20	...
Sanyo ADS **SANYY**	8	23.40	0.25
Sasol **SASOY**	238	11.33	-0.32
Senetek ADS **SNTK**	392	0.85	...
SoPacPete ADS **SPPTY**	150	14.61	1.11
TelefMex **TFONY**	71	34.25	-1.78
TrintyBio **TRIB**	262	1.45	0.03
Wacoal ADS **WACLY**	3	41.25	1.00

Source: *The Wall Street Journal*, May 30, 2002. Reprinted by permission of Dow Jones & Company, Inc. (c) 2002 Dow Jones & Company, Inc. All Rights Reserved Worldwide.

Some less frequently traded ADRs on the NASDAQ exchange are listed each day in the *WSJ* under the NASDAQ Small Cap Issues column of the Money and Investing Section. This listing includes volume, price, and the change in price from the previous trading day. Use the above table from the *WSJ* to answer the following questions.

1. Find the closing price and trading volume for Nissan Motor Corporation, the Japanese automobile manufacturer.

2. Find the closing price and trading volume of Telefonos de Mexico, the Mexican telecommunications company.

3. Find the closing price and trading volume of Rank Group, Plc., a U.K. Real Estate management company.

Project 4-1

Repeat Exercise 4-1 using a recent edition of the *WSJ*.

Date of recent Balance of Trade report _____

1. Verify the month's balance of trade in goods, services, and overall by subtracting imports from exports.

2. What was the percentage change in the overall trade balance for the month?

3. Calculate the percent change in exports and imports. For the month, which item had the greatest impact on the change in the overall trade balance?

4. According to the Regional Trade Balance (if included), which country had the largest trade surplus with the U.S.? For which country or region was the change in the trade balance the greatest over the past year?

Project 4-2

Use a Monday edition of the *WSJ* to complete the following table on Closed-end funds for foreign markets. For each group, calculate the premium or discount to net asset value (NAV) and 52-week percent return. The NAV is the current value of the investment fund. It is calculated as the ratio of total assets minus total liabilities to total shares outstanding.

World Equity Funds			
Developed Markets			
Name of Fund	NAV	Premium/Discount	52 Wk Mkt Return
Germany Fund			
Spain Fund			
Italy Fund			
Japan Equity			
Singapore Fund			
Average			
Emerging Markets			
Name of Fund	NAV	Premium/Discount	52 Wk Mkt Return
China Fund			
Thai Fund			
Malaysia Fund			
Chile Fund			
Brazil Fund			
Average			

1. Which group had the largest return on average for the previous twelve months?

2. Which group currently has on average the largest discount, or smallest premium, to net asset value?

3. In your opinion, which group represents the best investment value/ Why?

Discussion Questions

Economists Aren't Sure if Drop In Dollar Is Good, Bad, or Both

*Manufacturing-Led Growth
Will Benefit, but Inflation
And Interest Rates May Rise*

By Jon E. Hilsenrath

NEW YORK—For years, economists have argued that the mighty U.S. dollar was primed for a fall. Now that it is starting to slip, economists are providing a mixed message about what a weaker dollar means for the economy.

Just a year ago, the U.S. dollar rose even as the economy absorbed the blows of recession and a terrorist attack. Since February, however, creeping concerns about the recovery and the stock market appear to be taking their toll.

During the past three months, the dollar has fallen by 6% against the euro and 7% against the Japanese yen. In late foreign-exchange trading yesterday, for example, it took 124 yen and 1.08 euros to

Why Japan Is Worried

Tokyo's intervention to push down the value of the yen, and the government's evident fears for the currency, show how fragile the underpinnings of Japan's nascent economic recovery may be, page A14.

buy one dollar, compared with 134 yen and 1.15 euros three months ago. When weighed against a broad basket of currencies, including top trading partners like Canada, Mexico, China and the United Kingdom, the dollar is at its lowest level since December.

In the short term, a modest decline in the dollar can help lift economic growth. That's because a weaker dollar makes U.S. exports more competitive in international markets as prices of everything from U.S.-made autos to airplanes decline relative to prices of products made else-

where. As U.S. companies pick up market share overseas, their profits are translated into more dollars back home.

For manufacturers that have complained for years that a strong dollar has undercut their competitive position, the latest moves in the dollar—if sustained—could provide welcome relief. "Our German competitors have had a bonanza," says William Weiller, chief executive of Purafil Inc., an Atlanta maker of air-purification equipment. Mr. Weiller says he has had to discount prices by as much as 25% to some customers to make up for the pricing advantage that overseas competitors hold over him. The result is that revenue, after growing just below 20% annually for much of the 1990s, is now down from a year ago.

For some other manufacturers, the current level of the dollar has started to help the bottom line. David Littmann, an economist at Comerica Bank Co. in Detroit, says he already is hearing some manufacturing companies discuss the possibility of raising prices.

But what's good for some manufacturing concerns isn't necessarily good news for the rest of the U.S. Some economists, for example, worry about the important side effects that come with a weaker currency: inflation and higher interest rates. Others worry that a precipitous drop—something far more significant than the single-digit decline registered since February—could cause stock and bond prices to drop sharply as foreign investors pull additional money out of the U.S.

At first glance, the weakening of the dollar might seem a little odd. After all, the U.S. is rebounding from recession faster, and more robustly, than most other major economies. Gross domestic product, the value of the nation's output adjusted for inflation, grew 5.8% at an annual rate in the first quarter, and while few expect such a strong showing in the current quarter, most economists agree that a recovery remains intact.

Weaker Greenback

Since the beginning of the year, the dollar has slid against the euro and the yen.

Source: Thomson Datastream

Furthermore, the economy registered 8.6% productivity growth in the first quarter, the strongest showing in nearly 20 years and an important underpinning to future investment.

Ethan Harris, chief U.S. economist for Lehman Brothers, says there are several reasons for the latest weakness that are converging at the same time. The main reason is the twin American deficits. The trade deficit in goods and services, which stood at $92 billion during the first three months of the year, is near record highs. That deficit has been a source of concern to economists for some time, but the burgeoning federal budget deficit is a new source of concern. The surprising 28.5% drop in April tax receipts has heightened concerns that budget deficits are once again a long-term problem.

Add to that continuing concerns about corporate accounting, an uninspiring earnings season, and heightened concerns about terrorist threats, and economists say that foreign investors are finding fewer reasons to pour their money in the U.S., where they have consistently put money for years. Indeed, foreigners bought less than $11 billion in U.S. stocks during the first two months of 2002, down sharply from the $33 billion in purchases during the same period in 2001.

"There are questions about the sustainability of this expansion," says Peter Hooper, chief U.S. economist for Deutsche Bank AG.

For the Bush administration, the dollar's market-driven decline may offer some relief from the steady stream of demands from manufacturers, farmers and labor unions for a government-steered devaluation of the American currency. Since taking office just over a year ago, Treasury Secretary Paul O'Neill has repeatedly rebuffed those demands.

Mr. O'Neill, traveling in Africa this week, hasn't commented on the dollar's recent steady decline. "There's no change in our strong-dollar policy," Mr. O'Neill's spokeswoman, Michele Davis, said in an interview. Mr. O'Neill's public comments since taking office demonstrate a strong skepticism about intervention, suggesting he will be just as reluctant to act against the dollar's fall as he was against its ascent.

But elsewhere in the world, officials are taking notice. The Bank of Japan on Wednesday bought dollars to push down the value of the yen and warned it may intervene again, following days of official grousing that the yen might be getting too strong too fast. Japanese officials consider a weak yen imperative to an economic recovery, because it helps Japan's massive export sector.

—Jacob Schlesinger in Washington contributed to this article.

1. According to the article, how can a weakening dollar help the U.S. economy?

2. According to the article, how can a weakening dollar hurt the U.S. economy?

3. What would a weaker dollar mean for the foreign investments held by U.S. investors?

4. If the federal budget deficit continues to increase, what must action must the federal government take? How can this action lower the value of the dollar?

PART III

SECURITIES MARKETS ANALYSIS

Chapter 5

Time Value of Money

Objectives

1. Calculate future values using compound interest rate data from the *WSJ*.

2. Calculate present values using compound interest rate data from the *WSJ*.

3. Describe how a series of cash flows can be defined as a perpetuity or an annuity, and how this definition affects the present value of the cash flows.

4. Use the *WSJ* to find information on long-term rates for annuities.

Key Terms

Cash Flow	Periodic Rate	Perpetuity
Future Value	Present Value	Annuity
Compound Interest	Discount Rate	Annuity Factor

This chapter introduces the time value of money concept. This concept is the fundamental principle behind all financial markets. In the discussion and exercises below you will use financial information from the *WSJ* to learn how time and money are related.

Future Value

Suppose you are asked to participate in an auction. The item up for bid is $100 cash. The cash will be delivered one year from now. How much would you be willing to pay for this cash today? More or less than $100? Your answer should certainly be less than $100 because, human nature being what it is, a dollar received today is worth more than a dollar received tomorrow. This principle is called the time value of money. We will use this principle throughout this section of the book to value financial assets. Financial assets are any contracts for cash to be received or paid at future dates. The time value of money principle is used to show the different value of present, versus future, cash flows. The principle also shows us the power of compound interest. Time value of money concepts can be used to describe the different value of cash flows received forever, a perpetuity, or for a specific period of time, an annuity. We will also look at how inflation affects the value of money. Information on all of these issues - compound interest, annuities, and inflation - is readily available in the *WSJ*.

Since you are not likely to bid $100 for the right to receive $100 one year from now it must be that this cash payment, or **cash flow**, is not equal in value to cash received today. Cash flows occurring in different time periods are not comparable unless they are adjusted for time value. To do this we must look at the rate of interest which can be earned on the cash between payments. Instead of paying $100 now for $100 to be received in the future I can invest my cash and receive interest.

My investment will grow to some **future value**. The future value is the amount to which an investment will grow after earning interest. This value is calculated by adding the initial investment to the investment multiplied by the rate of interest, *r*.

Future value = investment + (investment · r)

This expression can be simplified to read

Future value = investment(1+ r)

The expression (1+r) is the interest factor. If I leave my investment in place to continue earning interest after the first interest payment is made I will once again earn the interest factor 1+r.

Future value = investment(1+ r)(1+r)

Extending this idea out for any number of interest payments (*t*) gives the following expression for the future value of any investment at rate *r,* for *t* periods:

$$FV = investment(1+r)^t$$

The expression, $(1+r)^t$, refers to **compound interest**, or interest earned on interest at the rate, *r,* for *t* periods.

Compounding interest payment on interest payment increases the power of the return on any investment. For example, if my $100 investment earned 6 percent simple interest for five years, or annual interest on the original investment, the sum of the original $100 plus accumulated simple interest would be $100 x .06 x five years = $30.00. However, with compound interest an additional $3.82 is earned in the five year period. Compounding increased the power of my investment 12.7% ($3.82/$30.00).

Not all investments compound annually. Interest on some investments, particularly bank certificate of deposits (CDs), is calculated and paid frequently. If this is the case, the per-period, or *periodic rate* of interest on our investment is different. For example, if my $100 investment will again earn 6 percent annual interest, but the interest will be calculated and paid daily (365 days per year), the periodic rate is 0.01644 (0.0001644). In five years, interest on this investment will have been calculated and paid 1,825 times (365 x 5). The future value (FV) of this investment is $100 (1 + 0.0001644)^{1825}$, or $134.99.

Exercise 5-1

BANXQUOTE® Money Markets

Tuesday, June 18, 2002

Average Yields of Major Banks

		MMI°	1 MO	2 MOS	3 MOS	6 MOS	1 YR	2 YRS	5 YRS
NEW YORK									
	Savings	1.15%			1.42%	1.56%	2.11%	3.07%	4.08%
	Jumbos	1.70%	1.25%	1.16%	1.32%	1.52%	2.11%	3.13%	4.28%
CALIFORNIA									
	Savings	1.50%			1.40%	1.65%	2.29%	3.08%	4.57%
	Jumbos	1.89%	1.43%	1.42%	1.58%	1.88%	2.35%	3.22%	4.67%
PENNSYLVANIA									
	Savings	1.60%			1.35%	1.43%	1.76%	3.05%	4.50%
	Jumbos	2.21%	1.88%		1.59%	1.75%	2.11%	3.13%	4.48%
ILLINOIS									
	Savings	1.12%			1.27%	1.44%	1.80%	2.74%	4.37%
	Jumbos	1.73%	1.52%	1.52%	1.57%	1.77%	2.19%	3.31%	4.69%
TEXAS									
	Savings	1.07%			1.27%	1.45%	1.90%	2.82%	3.95%
	Jumbos	1.63%	1.35%	1.35%	1.37%	1.53%	1.99%	2.97%	4.20%
FLORIDA									
	Savings	1.61%			1.43%	1.68%	2.15%	3.03%	4.37%
	Jumbos	1.86%	1.27%	1.38%	1.50%	1.77%	2.25%	3.22%	4.57%
U.S. BANK AVERAGE									
	Savings	1.30%			1.36%	1.56%	1.99%	2.92%	4.28%
	Jumbos	1.65%	1.36%	1.36%	1.48%	1.69%	2.15%	3.05%	4.40%
WEEKLY CHANGE (in percentage points)									
	Savings	+0.03	...		−0.02	−0.02	−0.01	...	−0.03
	Jumbos	+0.03	...	−0.01	−0.02	−0.02	−0.01	−0.02	−0.10

Savings CD Yields Offered Through Leading Brokers

	3 MOS	6 MOS	1 YR	2 YRS	5 YRS
BROKER AVERAGE	1.70%	2.02%	2.51%	3.29%	4.50%
WEEKLY CHANGE	+0.01	....	−0.12	−0.23	−0.26

*Money Market Investments include MMDA, NOW, savings deposits, passbook and other liquid accounts.
Each depositor is insured by the Federal Deposit Insurance Corp. (FDIC) up to $100,000 per issuing institution.
COMPOUND METHODS: c-Continuously. d-Daily.
w-Wkly. m-Mthly. q-Qrtly. s-Semi-annually. a-Annually.
SIMPLE INTEREST: si-Paid Monthly. e-Paid Semi-annually.
n-Paid Annually. y-Paid at Maturity.
OTHER SYMBOLS: APY-Annual percentage yield. F-Floating

rate P-Prime CD. T-T-Bill CD.BD-Broker-Dealer. pp-Priced below par.
DAY BASIS: A-Actual/Actual. B-30/360. C-Actual/360.The information included in this table has been obtained directly from broker-dealers, banks and savings institutions, but the accuracy and validity cannot be guaranteed. Rates are subject to change. Yields, terms and capital adequacy should be verified before investing. Only well capitalized or adequately capitalized depository institutions are quoted.

High Yield Savings

Small minimum balance/opening deposit, generally $500 to $25,000

Money Market Investments*	RATE		APY	Six Months CDs	RATE		APY
Natl InterBank, Indianapolis IN	3.01%	dA	3.06%	Legacy Bank, Hinton OK	2.86%	mA	2.90%
ZionsBank.com, Salt Lake City UT	3.00%	dA	3.05%	Giantbank.com, Ft. Lauderdale FL	2.72%	dA	2.76%
Commercial Capital, Irvine CA	2.96%	dA	3.00%	First Capital Bank, Norcross GA	2.73%	siA	2.75%
ING DIRECT, Wilmington DE	2.96%	mA	3.00%	StonebridgeBank, West Chester PA	2.72%	mA	2.75%
UmbrellaBank.com, Summit IL	2.91%	dA	2.95%	interState Net Bank, Cherry Hill NJ	2.70%	dA	2.74%

One Month CDs	RATE		APY	One Year CDs	RATE		APY
Superior Savings, Branford CT	2.32%	mA	2.34%	ING DIRECT, Wilmington DE	3.30%	yA	3.30%
Arkansas Natl, Bentonville AR	2.23%	siA	2.25%	USAccessBank.com, Louisville KY	3.22%	mA	3.27%
Beal Bank, Plano TX	2.18%	siA	2.20%	First Capital Bank, Norcross GA	3.21%	qA	3.25%
New South Federal, Irondale AL	2.10%	siA	2.12%	Legacy Bank, Hinton OK	3.20%	mA	3.25%
Bluebonnet Savings, Dallas TX	2.01%	mA	2.03%	NetBank.com, Alpharetta GA	3.16%	dA	3.21%

Two Months CDs	RATE		APY	Two Years CDs	RATE		APY
New South Federal, Irondale AL	2.20%	siA	2.22%	USAccessBank.com, Louisville KY	4.04%	mA	4.12%
Beal Bank, Plano TX	2.18%	siA	2.20%	Allstate Bank, Vernon Hills IL	4.00%	dA	4.08%
Intervest National, New York NY	2.18%	dA	2.20%	Bofi.com, San Diego CA	4.00%	dA	4.08%
Bluebonnet Savings, Dallas TX	2.06%	mA	2.08%	BankDirect.com, Dallas TX	3.92%	dA	4.00%
Guard Security Bk, Wilkes-Barre PA	2.06%	dA	2.08%	ebank.com, Atlanta GA	3.92%	dA	4.00%

Three Months CDs	RATE		APY	Five Years CDs	RATE		APY
Omni National Bk, Fayetteville NC	2.47%	dA	2.50%	Grange Bank, Columbus OH	5.21%	dA	5.35%
Resource Bank, Herndon VA	2.48%	qA	2.50%	Intervest National, New York NY	5.21%	dA	5.35%
Middlesex Savings, Natick MA	2.45%	mA	2.48%	Bofi.com, San Diego CA	5.17%	dA	5.30%
First Savings Bank, Perkasie PA	2.37%	mA	2.40%	American Bank, Allentown PA	5.16%	dA	5.30%
First Trade Union, Boston MA	2.38%	yA	2.40%	State Farm Bank, Bloomington IL	5.15%	dA	5.28%

Source: *The Wall Street Journal*, June 19, 2002. Reprinted by permission of Dow Jones & Company, Inc. (c) 2002 Dow Jones & Company, Inc. All Rights Reserved Worldwide.

Representative rates on bank CDs are regularly reported in the *WSJ*. The method or rate of compounding (continuously, daily, monthly, etc.) varies from bank to bank. For example, if the method of compounding is monthly, the time period, *t*, in our FV equation is 12. For daily compounding, the time period is 365 days.

1. Using the BANXQUOTE table, find the rate of interest for a one year CD from Legacy Bank of Hinton, OK. What is the method of compounding?

2. Using this rate, find the FV of a one-year investment of $1000.00. Be sure to use the method of compounding used by Legacy Bank and adjust the time periods and periodic rate accordingly.

Present Value

So if I am able to invest my $100 now rather than using it to bid for $100 in the future, what should be the value today of that $100 cash flow in the future? The answer is it's *present value*. The present value is the investment necessary to generate the future cash flows. To find the present value of any future cash flow we simply reverse the process for finding the future value of an investment today. That is, the present value is the reciprocal of the future value calculation.

$$PV = \frac{cashflow_t}{(1+r)^t}$$

This expression shows that present values are directly related to the future cash flows and inversely related to the discount rate, *r*, and time, *t*. The interest rate used to compute present values of future cash flows is called the *discount rate*. The expression, $1/(1+r)^t$, is called the discount factor.

Exercise 5-2

Suppose you wanted to make a $1,000 purchase five years from today. One way to save for this purchase would be to invest in a CD. The present value equation can help us find the amount we would need to deposit in order to reach our $1,000 goal.

1. Using the BANXQUOTE table from Exercise 5-1, find the rate of interest for a five-year CD from American Bank in Allentown, PA. What is the method of compounding?

2. Use this rate to determine the present value of $1,000 received five years from now. Be sure to adjust the time periods and the periodic rate by the method of compounding used by American Bank.

Compounding

Cash flows received at different times are not comparable unless adjusted for their time value. We have shown how this principle is used in many ways. The future value of an investment can be found by compounding that investment at the compound rate of interest. Future cash flows can be discounted at the discount rate to find their present value. Another useful analysis is to find the rate of return on an investment when the present value, future value of cash flows, and the time, t, are known. In the present value formula, the expression (1+r) can be found arithmetically. The calculated rate, *r,* is also known as the internal rate of return.

For example, suppose we wanted to know the rate of interest necessary to make my $100 investment double in five years (assuming annual compounding). The $200 future value $100 PV and time period ($t$=5) for this problem are known. We solve for the discount rate in the present value equation.

$$PV = FV / (1+r)^t$$

$$\$100 = \$200 / (1+r)^5$$

$$(1+r)^5 = \$200 / \$100 = 2$$

$$(1+r) = 2^{1/5} = 1.1487$$

$$r = 0.149 \text{ or } 14.9\%$$

A simple approximation of this results exists. It is called the Rule of 72. This rule states that the time it takes for an investment to double is approximately equal to 72 divided by the annual rate, r, stated as a percentage. In the above example, dividing 72 by 14.9 gives 4.83, or approximately five years.

Suppose the rate on the CD used in Exercise 5-2 remains the same for many years to come. The *Rule of 72* can be used to approximate the number of years it will take to double your investment in these CDs. The annual percentage yield (APY) given in the BANXQUOTE report adjusts the annual rate on each reported CD to reflect the method of compounding. In general the APY is equal to 1 plus the period rate raised to the number of periods (APY = $(1 + \text{period rate})^{\text{\# of periods}} - 1$). For example, a 6% rate with monthly compounding, or a 0.5% period rate, corresponds to an APY of 6.17% [$(1+0.005)^{12}-1 = 0.0617$, or 6.17%].

Exercise 5-3

Use the table in Exercise 5-1 to answer the following questions.

1. Find the APY for the American Bank CD in Exercise 5-2.

2. Use the APY and the Rule of 72 to approximate the number of years it will take to double your investment in these CDs.

Perpetuities and Annuities

To compare cash flows received in different time periods we have adjusted them by the discount rate and compared their present values. We have looked at both single cash flows with simple interest and multiple payments of interest, or compound interest. In many cases, level cash flows of payments, principal, or interest may occur at regular intervals. For example, a home loan, or mortgage requires equal level payments of both principal and interest over the life of the loan. A stream of level cash flows that never ends is called a *perpetuity*. A stream of level cash flows for a specific period, such as the home loan, is called an *annuity*.

To find the present value of a perpetuity we divide the cash payments, or cash flow, by the rate of interest.

$$PV = \frac{cashflow}{r}$$

Notice that this formula differs from the present value formula given earlier for a single cash payment. The discount rate, r, in this equation for a perpetuity equates the never ending cash payment to the present value of the asset. This equation can be rearranged to find the discount rate, or the necessary periodic cash payment for given market rates.

$$r = \frac{cashflow}{PV} \quad \text{or} \quad r \times PV = cashflow$$

For example, suppose the government agrees to pay its citizens a fixed payment forever in exchange for a $100 loan. If the prevailing market rate of interest on long term loans is 8% annually, this payment should equal $8 per year (0.08 x $100 = $8).

To value an annuity, or a limited number of fixed future payments, we find the present value of each payment and add them together.

$$PV = \frac{cashflow}{(1+r)^1} + \frac{cashflow}{(1+r)^2} + ... + \frac{cashflow}{(1+r)^t}$$

For example, if the government agreed only to make the $8 payments for 3 years and then to return the $100 loan, the value of these payments can be found by discounting at the prevailing 8% market rate of interest.

$$PV = \frac{8}{(1+.08)^1} + \frac{8}{(1+.08)^2} + \frac{8}{(1+.08)^3} + \frac{100}{(1+.08)^3}$$

In this case the present value of these cash flows exactly equals the amount of the loan, $100. What about an annuity that does not repay the principal, but makes regular equal cash payments? This type of annuity can be found by multiplying the cash payment by what is called the ***annuity factor***.

$$PV = cashflow \times \left[\frac{1}{r} - \frac{1}{r(1+r)^t} \right]$$

For example, if the government agreed to make the $8 payments for 20 years, the present value of these payments is found by multiply the $8 payment by an annuity factor of 9.82. This annuity has a present value of $78.55 ($8 x 9.82). This type of asset is often called a fixed annuity. It pays a fixed rate of interest for a specific period of time.

The annuity factor can be used to determine the amount of money needed today (the present value) in order to generate a certain level of cash flow for a specific number of periods. For example, suppose you plan to retire at age 65 and expect to live for 25 more years. How much money will you need at age 65 in order to generate $2,000 of monthly income for 25 years if market rates are 5%. The answer is $340,760 (monthly rate, r, of 0.42% for 300 months).

$$\$340,760 = \$2,000 * \left[\frac{1}{0.0042} - \frac{1}{0.0042(1+0.0042)^{300}} \right]$$

Project 5-1

Repeat Exercise 5-3 using a recent edition of the *WSJ*.

1. Find the APY for a five year CD.

2. Use the APY and the Rule of 72 to approximate the number of years it will take to double your investment in these CDs.

Project 5-2

Fixed annuities are often issued by insurance companies and pay rates similar to long-term CDs.

1. Using a recent addition of the *WSJ*, find the BANXQUOTE table. Using the current U.S. Bank Average for CDs with five years to maturity, calculate the amount of money needed today to generate monthly income of $2,000, $4,000, and $6,000.

2. Assume that you will live for 25 years after your retirement and will need monthly income to get along. The following chart will help you get an idea of how much money you will need to retire comfortably. The amount will vary by both the amount of monthly income you want and the prevailing market rates at the time of your retirement. Estimate the number of years until you retire and use the annuity factor formula to complete the table.

Market Rates				
Years to retirement:		<u>5%</u>	<u>7%</u>	<u>9%</u>
Monthly Income:	$2,000			
	$4,000			
	$6,000			

Discussion Questions

The December 27, 2000 edition of the *WSJ* included an article entitled "Why a Baseball Superstar's Megacontract Can Be Less Than It Seems"[*]. The article discusses the details of a contract signed by shortstop Alex Rodriguez with the Texas Rangers baseball club. The 10 year contract was originally reported to be worth $252 million, but the article shows why the deferred payments and other options in the contract make it worth much less. Using the time value of money principle, show why the contract is worth less than $252 million.

---

[*] The *WSJ*, December 27, 2000 Vol. 236 Issue 124, page B1.

Chapter 6

Bond Valuations

Objectives

1. Describe and define the various types of debt securities.

2. Read and use the Credit Markets data from the Money and Investing section of the WSJ.

3. Use the time value of money principles to value debt securities.

4. Understand the basic principles of the term structure of interest rates by building and analyzing a yield curve for debt securities.

Key Terms

Bonds	Corporate Bonds	Yield To Maturity
Coupon Rate	Municipal Securities	Yield Curve
Treasurys	Current Yield	Liquidity Premium

The time value of money principle states that cash received or paid in different time periods is not comparable unless adjusted for time value. The principle is used in this chapter to understand the pricing, or valuation, of debt securities. The various classifications of bond issuers are described in this chapter and the pricing information found in the Credit Markets columns of the "Money and Investing" section of *The Wall Street Journal* (*WSJ*) is described. This information is then used to construct a valuable, graphical representation of the relationship between the return on bonds and the time to maturity.

Bonds

Any debt security obligates the borrower (issuer) to make regular, periodic payments to the lender (investor). Securities of more than one year in duration are called notes or **bonds** and are classified as capital market securities. Securities of less than one year are generally classified as money market securities. The discussion that follows concerns mainly notes and bonds, although many of the same principles apply to securities of shorter duration.

The promised payment from the issuer of a bond can be separated into two parts. The periodic interest payment to the bondholder, or *coupon rate*, is made at the contract rate of interest. The second part of the payment from the issuer is the return of the original amount borrowed. This amount is called the principal, and for most bonds this payment is made at maturity.

A fixed-rate bond carries an interest rate, or coupon rate, that stays the same throughout the life of the bond. The bond's coupon rate is set at the market rate of interest at the time the bond is issued. Thereafter, the market rate may vary, but the coupon rate, which determines the periodic interest payment, stays the same.

Types of Bonds

Governments and corporations issue bonds to raise money for their operations. A governments will borrow to fund development and other projects. Corporations borrow to build new production facilities or to acquire other businesses. The bonds issued by these different organizations work basically the same way but have differing characteristics.

U.S. Government Bonds

Treasury Bonds, Notes, and Bills (T-Bills) are debt securities issued by the U.S. government with original maturities ranging from 3-months to 30 years. This market is known as the **Treasurys** market. Securities dealers regularly buy, sell, and hold in inventory these securities. The trading activity through these dealers is called the secondary market for U.S. government securities and is reported daily in the Money and Investing section of the *WSJ* under the heading "Treasury Bonds, Notes, and Bills". Treasury bonds and notes are denominated in $1,000 increments and pay interest on a semiannual (twice yearly) basis. The price quotations are given per hundred dollars of face value. The hundred price is followed by a colon and then 32nds. For example, 101:01 means 101 and 1/32, or $1010.33.

Securities in the Treasury Bonds, Notes, and Bills table are listed in chronological order by date of maturity. In the "Govt. Bonds and Notes" section of this table maturities are listed as month and year. In the Treasury Bills section, the maturity date is listed by month, day, and year. The information given includes the original interest rate, the mid-afternoon bid price, the asked price, changes in the price, and the yield on the investment. The original interest rate is the bond's coupon rate, set at the time of issue. The bid price is the price at which securities dealers are willing to buy the bond. The asked price is the price at which securities dealers are willing to sell the bond.

Exercise 6-1

Treasury Bonds, Notes and Bills

June 19, 2002

Explanatory Notes

Representative Over-the-Counter quotation based on transactions of $1 million or more. Treasury bond, note and bill quotes are as of mid-afternoon. Colons in bid-and-asked quotes represent 32nds; 101:01 means 101 1/32. Net changes in 32nds. n-Treasury note. i-Inflation-Indexed issue. Treasury bill quotes in hundredths, quoted on terms of a rate of discount. Days to maturity calculated from settlement date. All yields are to maturity and based on the asked quote. Latest 13 week and 26 week bills are boldfaced. For bonds callable prior to maturity, yields are computed to the earliest call date for issues quoted above par and to the maturity date for issues below par. *When issued.

Source: eSpeed/Cantor Fitzgerald

U.S. Treasury strips as of 3 p.m. Eastern time, also based on transactions of $1 million or more. Colons in bid and asked quotes represent 32nds; 99:01 means 99 1/32. Net changes in 32nds. Yields calculated on the asked quotation. ci-stripped coupon interest. bp-Treasury bond, stripped principal. np-Treasury note, stripped principal. For bonds callable prior to maturity, yields are computed to the earliest call date for issues quoted above par and to the maturity date for issues below par.

Source: Bear, Stearns & Co. via Street Software Technology Inc.

Government Bonds & Notes

RATE	MATURITY MO/YR	BID	ASKED	CHG	ASK YLD
6.250	Jun 02n	100:05	100:06	...	0.52
6.375	Jun 02n	100:03	100:04	-1	1.25
3.625	Jul 02i	101:07	101:08	...	0
6.000	Jul 02n	100:15	100:16	-1	1.41
6.250	Jul 02n	100:16	100:17	...	1.51
6.375	Aug 02n	100:22	100:23	-1	1.58
6.125	Aug 02n	100:26	100:27	-1	1.69
6.250	Aug 02n	100:27	100:28	...	1.73
5.875	Sep 02n	101:05	101:06	...	1.57
6.000	Sep 02n	101:06	101:07	...	1.59
5.750	Oct 02n	101:14	101:15	...	1.65
11.625	Nov 02	104:00	104:00	1	1.60
5.625	Nov 02n	101:23	101:24	1	1.66
5.750	Nov 02n	101:24	101:25	...	1.68
5.125	Dec 02n	101:24	101:25	...	1.72
5.625	Dec 02n	102:00	102:01	...	1.71
4.750	Jan 03n	101:25	101:26	1	1.76
5.500	Jan 03n	102:07	102:08	...	1.77
6.250	Feb 03n	102:27	102:28	1	1.78
10.750	Feb 03	105:25	105:26	...	1.77
4.625	Feb 03n	101:29	101:30	...	1.78
5.500	Feb 03n	102:17	102:18	1	1.77
4.250	Mar 03n	101:28	101:29	2	1.77
5.500	Mar 03n	102:26	102:27	2	1.78
4.000	Apr 03n	101:26	101:27	3	1.83
5.750	Apr 03n	103:09	103:10	2	1.84
10.750	May 03	107:29	107:30	3	1.83
4.250	May 03n	102:04	102:05	2	1.92
5.500	May 03n	103:09	103:10	2	1.93
3.875	Jun 03n	101:29	101:30	3	1.95
5.375	Jun 03n	103:14	103:15	3	1.95
3.875	Jul 03n	102:00	102:00	3	2.03
5.250	Aug 03n	103:18	103:19	4	2.08
5.750	Aug 03n	104:03	104:04	3	2.10
11.125	Aug 03	110:06	110:07	3	2.10
3.625	Aug 03n	101:23	101:24	4	2.13
2.750	Sep 03n	100:22	100:23	5	2.18
2.750	Oct 03n	100:20	100:21	5	2.26
4.250	Nov 03n	102:19	102:20	5	2.32
11.875	Nov 03	113:01	113:02	4	2.34
3.000	Nov 03n	100:28	100:29	5	2.36
3.250	Dec 03n	101:06	101:07	5	2.43
3.000	Jan 04n	100:23	100:24	5	2.52
4.750	Feb 04n	103:18	103:19	5	2.52
5.875	Feb 04n	105:11	105:12	5	2.53
3.000	Feb 04n	100:21	100:22	6	2.57
3.625	Mar 04n	101:21	101:22	6	2.65
3.375	Apr 04n	101:05	101:06	7	2.72
5.250	May 04n	104:21	104:22	7	2.70
7.250	May 04n	108:10	108:11	7	2.72
12.375	May 04	117:24	117:25	8	2.71
3.250	May 04n	100:28	100:29	7	2.77
6.000	Aug 04n	106:13	106:14	8	2.89
7.250	Aug 04n	109:00	109:00	7	2.90
13.750	Aug 04	122:15	122:16	8	2.90
5.875	Nov 04n	106:15	106:16	8	3.05
7.875	Nov 04	111:01	111:02	7	3.05
11.625	Nov 04	119:21	119:22	8	3.06
7.500	Feb 05n	110:30	110:31	9	3.15
6.500	May 05n	108:27	108:28	12	3.27
6.750	May 05n	109:13	109:14	11	3.31
12.000	May 05	123:30	123:31	12	3.27
6.500	Aug 05n	109:05	109:06	12	3.40
10.750	Aug 05	121:21	121:22	13	3.43
5.750	Nov 05n	107:02	107:03	13	3.52
5.875	Nov 05n	107:15	107:16	13	3.51

RATE	MATURITY MO/YR	BID	ASKED	CHG	ASK YLD
9.125	May 09	111:19	111:20	4	2.80
6.000	Aug 09n	109:07	109:08	24	4.47
10.375	Nov 09	116:15	116:16	9	3.18
4.250	Jan 10i	108:22	108:23	6	2.95
6.500	Feb 10n	112:14	112:15	24	4.55
11.750	Feb 10	121:09	121:10	11	3.29
10.000	May 10	117:27	117:28	11	3.46
5.750	Aug 10n	107:20	107:21	26	4.61
12.750	Nov 10	128:28	128:29	13	3.63
3.500	Jan 11i	103:21	103:22	6	3.01
5.000	Feb 11n	102:11	102:12	26	4.66
13.875	May 11	136:11	136:12	18	3.76
5.000	Aug 11n	102:04	102:05	28	4.71
14.000	Nov 11	140:13	140:14	19	3.91
3.375	Jan 12i	102:26	102:27	10	3.03
4.875	Feb 12n	101:03	101:04	27	4.73
10.375	Nov 12	129:05	129:06	21	4.26
12.000	Aug 13	140:17	140:18	24	4.40
13.250	May 14	151:15	151:16	27	4.49
12.500	Aug 14	148:01	148:02	29	4.55
11.750	Nov 14	144:16	144:17	30	4.58
11.250	Feb 15	156:24	156:25	42	5.10
10.625	Aug 15	151:21	151:22	39	5.16
9.875	Nov 15	144:25	144:26	39	5.19
9.250	Feb 16	138:25	138:26	38	5.23
7.250	May 16	119:03	119:04	33	5.29
7.500	Nov 16	121:22	121:23	35	5.32
8.750	May 17	134:27	134:28	37	5.33
8.875	Aug 17	136:12	136:13	38	5.34
9.125	May 18	139:26	139:27	40	5.37
9.000	Nov 18	138:30	138:31	40	5.39
8.875	Feb 19	137:21	137:22	40	5.41
8.125	Aug 19	129:23	129:24	39	5.44
8.500	Feb 20	134:08	134:09	40	5.45
8.750	May 20	137:13	137:14	41	5.45
8.750	Aug 20	137:20	137:21	42	5.45
7.875	Feb 21	127:20	127:21	38	5.49
8.125	May 21	130:24	130:25	38	5.49
8.125	Aug 21	130:29	130:30	39	5.49
8.000	Nov 21	129:24	129:25	39	5.48
7.250	Aug 22	120:29	120:30	36	5.51
7.625	Nov 22	125:22	125:23	38	5.51
7.125	Feb 23	119:17	119:18	37	5.52
6.250	Aug 23	108:27	108:28	34	5.53
7.500	Nov 24	125:01	125:02	38	5.53
7.625	Feb 25	126:22	126:23	39	5.54
6.875	Aug 25	117:04	117:05	37	5.55
6.000	Feb 26	105:23	105:24	33	5.56
6.750	Aug 26	115:23	115:24	37	5.56
6.500	Nov 26	112:14	112:15	36	5.56
6.625	Feb 27	114:04	114:05	36	5.56
6.375	Aug 27	110:28	110:29	35	5.56
6.125	Nov 27	107:18	107:19	34	5.56
3.625	Apr 28i	108:12	108:13	24	3.15
5.500	Aug 28	99:02	99:03	31	5.57
5.250	Nov 28	95:21	95:22	31	5.56
5.250	Feb 29	95:25	95:26	30	5.55
3.875	Apr 29i	113:03	113:04	25	3.15
6.125	Aug 29	108:01	108:02	34	5.55
6.250	May 30	110:07	110:08	35	5.52
5.375	Feb 31	99:23	99:24	32	5.39
3.375	Apr 32i	106:06	106:07	25	3.06

U.S. Treasury Strips

MATURITY	TYPE	BID	ASKED	CHG	ASK YLD
Aug 02	ci	99:25	99:25	...	1.41
Jan 05	ci	92:11	92:13	10	3.11
Feb 05	ci	91:27	91:28	10	3.22
Feb 05	np	91:29	91:30	10	3.19
May 05	ci	90:24	90:26	11	3.36
May 05	bp	90:23	90:25	12	3.37
May 05	np	90:24	90:26	12	3.36
May 05	np	90:28	90:29	12	3.31
Jul 05	ci	90:14	90:16	11	3.29
Aug 05	ci	89:28	89:29	11	3.40
Aug 05	bp	89:15	89:17	12	3.54
Aug 05	np	89:23	89:25	12	3.45
Nov 05	ci	89:11	89:13	12	3.32
Nov 05	np	88:18	88:20	13	3.59
Nov 05	np	88:19	88:21	12	3.58
Jan 06	ci	88:10	88:12	13	3.50
Feb 06	ci	87:21	87:23	13	3.62
Feb 06	bp	87:08	87:10	13	3.75
Feb 06	np	87:18	87:20	13	3.65
May 06	ci	86:17	86:19	14	3.72
May 06	np	86:09	86:11	14	3.80
Jul 06	ci	86:18	86:21	14	3.56
Jul 06	np	85:22	85:24	14	3.82
Aug 06	ci	85:29	85:31	14	3.67
Nov 06	ci	84:23	84:25	15	3.79
Feb 07	ci	83:14	83:17	17	3.91
Feb 07	np	83:03	83:06	17	4.00
May 07	ci	82:01	82:03	17	4.07
May 07	np	81:29	82:00	17	4.09
Aug 07	ci	80:19	81:11	18	4.05
Aug 07	np	80:25	80:27	17	4.17
Nov 07	ci	80:26	80:29	19	3.96
Feb 08	ci	78:17	78:20	18	4.30
Feb 08	np	78:25	78:27	18	4.25
May 08	ci	77:08	77:11	19	4.40
May 08	np	77:17	77:20	19	4.34
Aug 08	ci	76:16	76:19	20	4.38
Nov 08	ci	75:17	75:20	20	4.41
Nov 08	np	75:16	75:20	20	4.42
Feb 09	ci	74:00	74:03	20	4.56
May 09	ci	72:29	73:00	21	4.61
May 09	np	73:09	73:12	20	4.53
Aug 09	ci	72:03	72:06	21	4.61
Aug 09	np	72:03	72:06	20	4.61
Nov 09	ci	71:00	71:04	22	4.66
Nov 09	bp	69:22	69:25	21	4.92
Feb 10	ci	69:16	69:20	21	4.79
Feb 10	np	70:00	70:03	20	4.70
May 10	ci	68:13	68:16	21	4.84
Aug 10	ci	67:19	67:23	22	4.84
Aug 10	np	68:03	68:07	21	4.75
Nov 10	ci	66:29	67:01	22	4.82
Feb 11	ci	65:11	65:14	22	4.96
Feb 11	np	66:11	66:14	23	4.78
May 11	ci	64:10	64:12	22	5.01
Aug 11	ci	63:19	63:20	23	5.00
Nov 11	ci	62:22	62:24	23	5.02

Treasury Bills

MATURITY	DAYS TO MAT	BID	ASKED	CHG	ASK YLD
Jun 27 02	7	1.65	1.64	-0.03	1.66
Jul 05 02	15	1.66	1.65	-0.04	1.67
Jul 11 02	21	1.64	1.63	-0.03	1.65
Jul 18 02	28	1.66	1.65	-0.03	1.68
Jul 25 02	35	1.61	1.60	-0.04	1.62
Aug 01 02	42	1.62	1.61	-0.03	1.64
Aug 08 02	49	1.62	1.61	-0.05	1.64
Aug 15 02	56	1.62	1.61	-0.04	1.64
Aug 22 02	63	1.66	1.65	-0.02	1.68
Aug 29 02	70	1.66	1.65	-0.02	1.68
Sep 05 02	77	1.66	1.65	-0.03	1.68
Sep 12 02	84	1.67	1.66	-0.02	1.69
Sep 19 02	**91**	**1.67**	**1.66**	**-0.03**	**1.69**
Sep 26 02	98	1.67	1.66	-0.03	1.69
Oct 03 02	105	1.67	1.66	-0.03	1.69
Oct 10 02	112	1.67	1.66	-0.02	1.69
Oct 17 02	119	1.66	1.65	-0.03	1.68
Oct 24 02	126	1.66	1.65	-0.02	1.68
Oct 31 02	133	1.66	1.65	-0.04	1.68
Nov 07 02	140	1.68	1.67	-0.02	1.70
Nov 14 02	147	1.67	1.66	-0.05	1.69
Nov 21 02	154	1.69	1.68	-0.04	1.72

1. Find the asked price for the U.S. Treasury Note maturing in February of 2005 and carrying a coupon rate of 7 ½ %.

2. By how much did this price change from the previous day?

Corporate Bonds

Corporate bonds are debt obligations of private and public corporations. Corporate bonds are also denominated in $1,000 increments and usually pay interest on a semiannual basis. The secondary market for corporate bonds is not as liquid as that of U.S. government bonds – there is less buying and selling activity. The degree of liquidity also varies across issuers, as some large corporations have many bonds outstanding that are actively traded while smaller corporations issue bonds less frequently. Most corporate bonds are traded in over-the-counter markets. However, many bonds from large issuers are traded on the organized exchanges (e.g., NYSE and AMEX). A key gauge of the corporate bond market is the Dow Jones Bond Average found in The Markets Lineup of the *WSJ* each day.

In addition to the prices, current yields, year of maturity, and coupon rates of these bonds, the tables in the U.S. Exchange Bonds column of the *WSJ* report the volume, and the number of bonds traded. Corporate bond prices are also quoted per hundred dollars of face value, but in percent of one hundred, not 32nds. For example, a bond selling for 102.20 is selling for 102.2% of 1,000, or $1,022.00.

Exercise 6-2

U.S. Exchange Bonds

4 p.m. ET Tuesday, June 18, 2002

Explanatory Notes

For New York and American Bonds

Yield is Current yield. **cv**-Convertible bond. **cf**-Certificates. **cld**-Called. **dc**-Deep discount. **ec**-European currency units. **f**-Dealt in flat. **ll**-Italian lire. **kd**-Danish kroner. **m**-Matured bonds, negotiability impaired by maturity. **na**-No accrual. **r**-Registered. **rp**-Reduced principal. **st, sd**-Stamped. **t**-Floating rate. **wd**-When distributed. **ww**-With warrants. **x**-Ex interest. **xw**-Without warrants. **zr**-Zero coupon.

vj-In bankruptcy or receivership or being reorganized under the Bankruptcy Act, or securities assumed by such companies.

NEW YORK BONDS
Corporation Bonds

BONDS	CUR YLD	VOL	CLOSE	NET CHG
AES Cp 4½05	cv	109	59	0.25
AES Cp 8s8	11.5	95	69.50	0.13
ATT 6½02	6.5	275	100.13	0.13
ATT 6½04	6.91021		97.38	-0.13
ATT 5½04	5.92678		95	-0.25
ATT 7s05	7.3	522	95.75	-1.38
ATT 7½06	8.0	830	93.88	-0.88
ATT 7½07	8.11500		95.88	0.88
ATT 6s09	7.3	720	82.38	-1.50
ATT 8½22	9.6	640	84.50	-0.38
ATT 8½24	9.7	505	84.13	0.13
ATT 8.35s25	9.6	42	87	0.50
ATT 6½29	9.0	710	72.63	-1.50
ATT 8½31	9.8	208	88.50	0.25
AForP 5s30	8.3	20	60.25	0.25
Aquila 6½11	cv	7	92	2.00
vjArmW 9½08f		16	49	-1.00
BkOne 7½04	6.8	10	107	4.13
Bauschl 6½04	6.6	30	102.50	0.50
Bauschl 7½28	8.5	22	83.50	
BayView 9s07	9.1	41	99.25	
Bellso 6½28	6.8	12	93.75	-1.13
BellsoT 5½09	5.8	5	101.63	-0.63
BellsoT 7s25	6.8	75	103.13	0.13
BellsoT 7½32	7.6	31	103	-0.38
BellsoT 7½33	7.4	80	101.63	
BellsoT 6½33	7.1	168	95.50	-0.13
Bluegrn 8½12	cv	40	87	-1.00
BordCh 8½16	10.4	70	80.88	0.88
BosCelts 6s38	9.6	3	62.38	0.88
BoydGm 9½03	9.0	15	103.25	
BoydGm 9½07	9.2	70	103.50	1.75
CallonP 11s05	12.2	6	90	0.13
CallonP 10½04	11.8	20	87	0.50
Case 7½16	9.5	10	76	-4.00
Chiq 10.56s09	10.0	20	106	0.25
Coeur 13½03	cv	1	136.38	1.38
CoeurDA 7½05	cv	20	77	-0.50
Coeur 6½04	cv	85	80.13	-0.88
Consec 8½03	9.3	25	87	0.47
ConPort 11½06	15.0	10	76.50	2.00
CrwnCk 7½26	11.2	10	66	1.00
CrwnCF 6½03	8.1	175	83.75	-6.25
CypSemi 4s05	cv	46	88	0.50
DR Hrtr 10s06	9.7	47	103	
DVI 9½04	9.8	98	101.13	

BONDS	CUR YLD	VOL	CLOSE	NET CHG
Hilton 5s06	cv	122	95	0.50
Hollngr 9½06	9.0	20	102.50	...
Honywll zr05		10	85.13	...
Honywll zr07		15	75	...
Honywll zr09		375	64.13	0.38
HuntPly 11½04f		326	55	35.00
IBM 7½13	6.6	84	113	1.00
JPMChse 6½08	6.3	20	107	2.00
JCPL 7½04	7.1	25	100.88	-0.25
JCPL 7½23	7.4	25	101.50	-0.75
KCS En 8½06	11.5	16	77.38	-1.63
K&B Hm 7½04	7.5	56	103.50	0.25
K&B Hm 9½06	9.3	25	104	...
Leucadia 7½13	7.7	65	100.88	...
Lucent 7½06	9.3	305	77.75	-0.63
Lucent 5½08	7.9	119	69.88	-1.75
Lucent 6½28	10.6	10	61.38	0.88
Lucent 6.45s29	10.5	40	61.38	-0.63
MBNA 8.28s26	8.5	82	98	0.50
MDC Hld 8½08	8.1	16	103.50	0.50
Malan 9½04	cv	216	93.75	2.75
McDnl 6½05	6.5	20	102	0.50
MPac 4½05	4.4	5	96.50	0.25
Moran 8½08f	cv	22	100	0.25
Motrla zr13	...	7	76	1.00
NatData 5s03	cv	15	100.50	-1.50
NETelTel 6½23	7.0	50	99	0.25
NYTel 7½24	7.3	60	99.50	-0.50
NYTel 6½10	6.2	20	99.50	-0.50
NYTel 7½23	7.6	535	100	-1.88
NYTel 7s25	7.2	50	96.88	-0.75
NYTel 7s33	7.2	75	97.50	1.00
Noram 6s12	cv	15	77	0.88
OffDep zr07	...	3	83	0.88
OreStl 11s03	10.8	75	101.50	0.50
ParkerD 5½04	cv	5	93	...
PhilPt 6.65s18	6.7	15	99	-1.00
PhilPt 7.92s23	7.6	5	104	...
PhillP 7½28	7.1	70	100.25	-0.50
PrmHsp 9½06	8.9	48	104.25	1.13
PSEG 6½03	6.8	50	101.66	...
PSvEG 7s24	7.0	11	100	-0.38
ReynTob 8½04	8.4	20	104.38	0.50
ReynTob 8½05	8.3	37	105.88	0.75
ReynTob 8½07	8.2	5	107	1.13
Safwy 9½07	8.4	8	117.88	4.63
Sequa 9s09	9.0	61	100.50	0.50
Solectrn zrN20		9	45	...
Sprint 6½28	9.3	10	74	-2.00
StdCmcl 07	cv	1	95	...
StdPac 8½07	8.3	10	102.75	0.25
TVA 5½11	5.5	25	103	2.38
TVA 6½17	6.0	25	105	0.25
TVA 6.35s18	6.5	5	98.50	...
TVA 6½43	6.7	18	103	0.63
Tenet 6s05	cv	20	100	0.50
TmeWar 7.98s04	7.6	10	104.25	-1.25
TmeWar 7½05	7.4	20	105	1.00
TmeWE 7½08	7.1	20	102	1.00
TmeWar 9½13	8.4	120	108.38	-0.63
TmeWar 9.15s23	8.4	45	109	-1.50
TolEd 8s03	7.9	10	101.75	...
TollCp 8½06	8.4	39	104.50	0.88
THilfig 6½03	6.5	10	100.50	0.22
THilfig 6.85s08	7.2	48	95	...
US Timb 9½07f	...	688	62	3.00
vjUSG 8½05f		50	80	-3.00
UtdAir 10.67s04	13.4	58	79.88	0.88
Webb 9s06cld		15	101.50	-0.50
WebbDel 9½09	8.9	54	105.50	-0.13
Weirton 10½05f		40	55	9.00
XeroxCr 7.2s12	9.0	5	79.88	1.25

1. Find the closing price for the bond issued by AT&T (ATT) with a coupon rate of 7%, maturing in 2005.

2. How many of these bonds traded on this day?

Municipal Bonds

Bonds are also issued by government bodies all around the country. These bonds are called *Municipal bonds* and are issued by states, counties, cities, schools, and many other government entities. Municipal bonds appeal to many investors because the interest is normally exempt from taxation by the Federal government and by the issuing government if the holder resides in that district. This tax exemption allows the issuer to offer a lower rate of interest than can be found on taxable issues such as Corporate Bonds.

Information on the most actively traded Municipal issuers can be found under the Tax-Exempt Bonds heading of the Bond Market Data Bank in the *WSJ*. Municipal bonds are also quoted in hundred dollars of face value. For each issue listed, the coupon rate, maturity date, current price, and current yield-to-maturity are reported. For comparison purposes you can review the Municipal Bond Index information that gives the average yield on various types of municipal issuers.

Exercise 6-3

Bond Market Data Bank

June 17, 2002

Bond Yields

Treasury Issues*

MATURITY	COUPON	PRICE	YIELD
05/31/04	3.250	100.20	2.918
05/15/05	6.750	109.01	3.456
05/15/07	4.375	101.04	4.113
02/15/12	4.875	100.05	4.854
02/15/31	5.375	98.21	5.467

*Most recent auctions.

Municipal Issues †(Comparable Maturities)

AAA YIELD	TAX EQUIV	MUNI/TREAS YIELD RATIO	52-WEEK RATIO HIGH	LOW
2.17	3.14	74.2	94.8	65.6
2.60	3.77	75.2	90.4	67.5
3.20	4.63	77.7	89.4	72.3
4.05	5.86	83.4	91.1	79.5
5.11	7.40	93.4	103.1	89.9

†From Delphis Hanover. Tax equiv. based on 31% bracket.

Tax-Exempt Bonds

Representative prices for several active tax-exempt revenue and refunding bonds, based on institutional trades. Yield is to maturity. n-new.
Source: The Bond Buyer.

ISSUE	COUPON	MAT	PRICE	CHG	BID YLD
BaltimoreMDprojectRv	5.125	07-01-42	97.893	+.071	5.25
CaliforniaStBd	5.000	04-01-27	98.048	-.231	5.14
CAStatewideComDevAuth	5.500	11-01-32	98.271	-.225	5.62
ChgILGenArpt3rdLnRv	5.375	01-01-32	98.941	-.382	5.45
ChgILGenPrj&Refnd	5.000	01-01-42	93.743	-.227	5.38
ConnHlth&EdFc	5.125	07-01-27	99.953	-.212	5.13
CookColLcapitalim	5.000	11-15-25	96.823	-.219	5.23
FairfaxCoWtrAuthVA	5.000	04-01-27	98.761	-.229	5.09
GreaterOrlandoAvFLA	5.125	10-01-21	99.190	-.184	5.19
HarrisCoTXRvRf	5.125	08-15-31	97.288	-.216	5.31
HillsbrghColDAFLA	5.500	10-01-23	99.888	-.195	5.51
ILLStGenObBdsIll 1s	5.250	04-01-27	99.839	-.161	5.26
IlSportsFcAthSr	5.000	06-15-32	96.524	-.159	5.23
IndianapolisPublmprvBd	5.250	07-01-33	99.080	-.160	5.31
Louisiana PbFcsAth bds	5.000	07-01-32	96.593	-.229	5.22
LuisvleJeffsnSwr KY	5.000	05-15-36	96.103	-.268	5.25
MassWtrResAuthbds	5.125	08-01-27	98.982	-.202	5.20
MD Hlth&Hghr EdFc	5.000	07-01-32	97.128	-.219	5.19
MetropolitanWasArptVA	5.250	10-01-32	98.805	-.256	5.33
MetroTransAuthNY	5.125	01-01-29	97.145	-.190	5.32
MetroTransAuthNY	5.000	07-01-30	96.826	-.312	5.21
MetroTransAuthNY	5.000	07-01-25	97.688	-.287	5.17
Miami-Dade Co FL Avtr	5.375	10-01-32	99.753	-.247	5.39
MinneapolisMNHlthcr	5.625	05-15-32	98.104	-.219	5.76
NCCapFcFnRvbd	5.125	10-01-41	96.927	-.197	5.31
NYC Gen Ob Bds	5.250	06-01-27	98.140	-.233	5.38
NYC Gen Ob Bds	5.375	06-01-32	99.212	-.184	5.43
OmahaConvHtlCpNE	5.125	04-01-32	98.937	-.274	5.19
OrangeCoHlthFcAuthFL	5.750	12-01-32	99.278	-.530	5.80
OrangeCoSchBdFLA	5.000	08-01-27	97.960	-.220	5.14
PalmBeachCoSchFL	5.000	08-01-27	98.140	-.168	5.13
PhoenixCivicImpCorpAZ	5.250	07-01-27	99.551	-.251	5.28
PhoenixCivicImpCorpAZ	5.250	07-01-32	99.145	-.354	5.31
PortAuth of NY&NJ125	5.000	04-15-32	97.953	-.187	5.13
PrtoRicoHwy&Trns	5.000	07-01-32	98.803	-.255	5.08
RichmondVAPubUtilty	5.000	01-15-33	97.580	-.135	5.16
SanDiegoCoWtrAuthCA	5.000	05-01-32	97.783	-.228	5.14
Univ of CA Regents	5.125	09-01-31	99.186	-.209	5.18
UnivMed&DentistryNJ	5.000	12-01-31	98.927	-.296	5.07
WestVAEcoDev	5.000	06-01-26	97.440	-.237	5.19

Mortgage-Backed Securities

Indicative, not guaranteed; from Bear Stearns Cos./Street Pricing Service

RATE		PRICE (JUL) (PTS-32DS)	PRICE CHANGE (32DS)	AVG LIFE (YEARS)	SPRD TO AVG LIFE (YEARS)	SPREAD CHANGE (BPS)	PSA (PREPAY SPEED)	YIELD TO MAT*
30-year								
FMAC GOLD	6.5%	101-27	-14	4.3	212	-4	398	5.98
FMAC GOLD	7.0%	103-12	-15	2.7	232	+23	630	5.53
FMAC GOLD	7.5%	104-18	-09	1.6	167	+30	833	4.31
FNMA	6.5%	101-26	-14	4.1	214	-1	428	5.91
FNMA	7.0%	103-10	-16	2.4	222	+28	709	5.32
FNMA	7.5%	104-18	-08	1.5	144	+33	883	4.02
GNMA	6.5%	101-30	-16	4.5	204	-1	379	5.97
GNMA	7.0%	103-21	-17	2.9	220	+22	516	5.49
GNMA	7.5%	105-07	-11	2.0	166	+27	673	4.62
15-year								
FMAC GOLD	6.5%	103-14	-02	4.2	170	-2	300	5.51
FNMA	6.5%	103-12	-02	4.2	165	-3	300	5.48
GNMA	6.5%	103-30	-02	4.2	155	-2	300	5.37

*Extrapolated from benchmarks based on projections from Bear Stearns prepayment model, assuming interest rates remain unchanged.

Collateralized Mortgage Obligations

Spread of CMO yields above U.S. Treasury securities of comparable maturity, in basis points (100 basis points = 1 percentage point of interest)

MAT	SPREAD	CHG FROM PREV DAY
Sequentials		
2-year	185	...
5-year	155	...
7-year	155	...
10-year	143	...
20-year	105	...
PACS		
2-year	110	...
5-year	115	...
7-year	120	...
10-year	123	...
20-year	95	...

International Government Bonds

COUPON	MATURITY MO/YR	PRICE	CHANGE	YIELD*
Japan (3 p.m. Tokyo)				
4.10%	06/04	108.08	-0.01	0.06%
3.30	06/06	111.92	-0.03	0.29
1.40	06/12	100.22	-0.09	1.38
2.00	03/22	99.72	-0.07	2.02
United Kingdom (5 p.m. London)				
8.00%	06/03	103.35	-0.04	4.460%
7.50	12/06	109.68	-0.09	5.060
5.00	03/12	99.68	-0.17	5.041
4.25	06/32	90.26	-0.24	4.871

COUPON	MATURITY MO/YR	PRICE	CHANGE	YIELD*
Germany (5 p.m. London)				
4.25%	02/05	100.11	-0.08	4.198%
5.00	02/06	101.85	-0.11	4.436
5.00	01/12	99.85	-0.22	5.016
5.50	01/31	101.62	-0.18	5.400
Canada (3 p.m. Eastern Time)				
5.00%	12/03	101.89	-0.02	3.654%
5.00	09/04	101.91	-0.06	4.079
6.00	06/08	104.75	-0.19	5.064
8.00	06/27	129.37	-0.47	5.765

*Equivalent to semi-annual compounded yields to maturity

Guaranteed Investment Contracts

GIC rates quoted prior to 10:30 am (Eastern) net of all expenses, no broker commissions. Rates represent best quote for a $2-$5 million immediate lump sum deposit with annual interest payments. Yield spreads based on U.S. Treasury yields, as of 10:30 am (Eastern), versus the index rate unadjusted for semi vs. annual interest payments. CHANGE reflects change in rate from previous day. Index is average of all rates quoted. Universe is investment grade. Source: T. Rowe Price GIC Index

| | 1 YEAR | | 2 YEARS | | 3 YEARS | | 4 YEARS | | 5 YEARS | |
	RATE %	CHANGE	RATE %	CHANGE	RATE %	CHANGE	RATE %	CHANGE	RATE %	CHANGE
High	2.65	+0.27	3.79	+0.07	4.55	+0.02	4.96	+0.02	5.38	+0.03
Low	2.02	+0.02	3.46	+0.02	3.99	+0.05	4.46	+0.05	4.92	+0.05
Index	2.28	+0.12	3.62	+0.03	4.30	+0.04	4.74	+0.03	5.10	+0.03

Top Quartile Range (in percent)

2.65	2.65	3.79	3.67	4.55	4.48	4.96	4.90	5.38	5.27

Spread vs. Treasuries

	+0.19		+0.77		+0.88		+0.90		+0.97	

Total Rates of Return on International Bonds

In percent, based on J.P. Morgan Government Bond Index, Dec. 31, 1987=100

| | LOCAL CURRENCY TERMS | | | | U.S. DOLLAR TERMS | | | |
	INDEX VALUE	1 DAY	1 MO	3 MOS	SINCE 12/31	INDEX VALUE	1 DAY	1 MO	3 MOS	SINCE 12/31
Japan	214.69	-0.02	+0.17	+0.98	+0.88	208.80	-0.28	+1.27	+4.70	+6.23
Britain	388.25	-0.08	+2.47	+2.58	+1.88	304.24	-0.03	+3.66	+6.38	+3.46
Germany	254.70	-0.16	+1.79	+2.44	+1.89	192.75	-0.67	+4.29	+9.38	+7.96
France	339.12	-0.16	+1.75	+2.40	+1.94	259.37	-0.67	+4.24	+9.33	+8.02
Canada	371.12	-0.17	+2.22	+3.09	+1.87	311.73	+0.05	+1.98	+5.77	+5.10
Netherlands	271.94	-0.17	+1.83	+2.53	+2.03	205.48	-0.68	+4.32	+9.47	+8.12
EMU-d	179.28	-0.16	+1.79	+2.44	+1.98	137.92	-0.68	+4.27	+9.37	+8.06
Global-a	306.00	-0.16	+1.60	+2.61	+2.13	256.27	-0.42	+2.92	+6.66	+6.22
EMBI+-b	208.41	+0.67	-2.89	-2.65	+4.03	208.41	+0.67	-2.89	-2.65	+4.03

a-18 int'l govt. markets. b-external-currency emerging mkt. debt, Dec 31, 1993=100. d-Jan. 2, 1995=100.

High-Yield Bonds

Monday, June 17, 2002

	TOTAL DAILY RETURN	INDEX VALUE	AVERAGE PRICE CHANGE	YEAR TO DATE	VOL
SSMB Index	+0.09	95.10	+0.05	-0.75	M

Volume Key: H = Heavy, M = Moderate, L = Light
Dec 31, 1998 = 100

Key Gainers

	TYPE/ RATING	COUP	MAT	3 PM BID	NET CHG	PRINC RET	YLD-y
Allied Waste	b/	10.000	8/09	100.00	+0.50	+0.50	10.00

Key Losers

	TYPE/ RATING	COUP	MAT	3 PM BID	NET CHG	PRINC RET	YLD-y
Worldcom	e/	7.500	5/11	48.50	-1.50	-2.96	20.17

SSMB Components

NAME	TYPE/ RATING	COUP	MAT	3 PM BID	NET CHG	YLD-y
Trump AC	e/CCC	11.250	5/06	76.00	...	20.52
Vintage Pet.	b/B	8.625	2/09	96.00	+0.50	9.45
AK Steel	a/BB	9.125	12/06	104.00	-0.75	6.87

American Std	a/BB+	7.375	2/08	102.50	...	6.83
Nextel Comm	c/B	0.000	9/07	63.00	...	22.17
Revlon	a/CCC	8.125	2/06	71.00	...	19.70
Chancellor	b/NR	8.125	12/07	103.00	...	7.14
HMH Prop.	a/BB-	7.875	8/08	96.50	...	8.63
Level 3	a/CCC-	9.125	5/08	43.00	...	30.58
Intermedia	a/B+	8.600	6/08	68.00	...	17.46
Global Xing	a/NR	9.625	5/08	2.00	...	z
Lyondell Che	a/BB	9.875	5/07	96.75	-0.25	10.74
Echostar	a/B+	9.375	2/09	96.50	...	10.11
Federal Mogu	e/D	7.500	1/09	20.00	...	z
Williams	a/D	10.875	10/09	10.00	...	z
Charter	a/B+	8.625	4/09	77.00	...	13.98
Packaging Co	b/BB+	9.625	4/09	108.50	...	7.03
Allied Waste	b/B+	10.000	8/09	100.00	+0.50	10.00
Chesapeake E	a/B+	8.125	4/11	99.50	+0.50	8.20

Volume indicators are based solely on the traders' subjective judgement given the relative level of inquiry and trading activity on any given day. Price quotes follow accrued interest conventions.
a-Senior. b-Senior Sub. c-Senior, Zero To Full. d-Senior, Split Cpn. e-Secured. y-yield is the lower of yield to maturity and yield to call. z-omitted for reset or bankrupt bonds, negative yields, or yields above 35%.
Source: Salomon Smith Barney

1. Find the closing price for the bond issued by the Indianapolis Public Improvement Board with a coupon rate of 5.25%. When does this bond mature?

2. Is this bond selling at, above, or below par value?

Pricing Bonds

As with any financial asset, the value of a bond is the sum of the present value of all its cash flows. We can find the *current yield* on a bond by dividing the stated coupon rate by the price of the bond. A better estimate of the return on a bond, however, is the *yield to maturity*, or YTM. This measure incorporates the present value of all cash flows from the bond. The YTM is the rate of return that sets the present value of the future cash flows equal to the bond's current price. We can use our time value of money skills to compare this total rate of return across different bonds. In the present value formula, YTM is the discount rate, r, that makes all future payments (the interest, or coupon, payments from the issuer of the bond) equal to the present value of the bond, its current price.

$$PV = \frac{coupon}{(1+r)^1} + \frac{coupon}{(1+r)^2} + \dots \frac{coupon}{(1+r)^t} + \frac{principal}{(1+r)^t}$$

For example, suppose a bond due in two years is selling at its $100 par value, or $1,000 per bond, and pays interest twice a year at the stated annual coupon rate of 6.25%. To find the YTM for this bond we first set the price of the bond, $1,000, equal to the present value of the four remaining interest payments and the final principal payment of $1,000. The semiannual interest payment of the bond is $31.25 (1,000 x 0.0625/2). We can then determine the YTM by solving for the semi-annual discount rate using a financial calculator or a spreadsheet program.

$$1000 = \frac{31.25}{(1+r)^1} + \frac{31.25}{(1+r)^2} + \frac{31.25}{(1+r)^3} + \frac{31.25}{(1+r)^4} + \frac{1000}{(1+r)^4}$$

In this case it turns out that the YTM equals the coupon rate of 6.25% since the bond is selling at par, the original issue amount.

On the same day, another bond due in two years is selling at 102, or $1,020.00 per bond. The bond also pays interest twice a year at a stated annual coupon rate of 7%. We follow the same steps to find the YTM on this bond. The price of the bond is set equal to the present value of its future payments.

$$1020 = \frac{35}{(1+r)^1} + \frac{35}{(1+r)^2} + \frac{35}{(1+r)^3} + \frac{35}{(1+r)^4} + \frac{1000}{(1+r)^4}$$

The rate r that solves this equation, or the yield-to-maturity for this bond, is 5.92%. This is the rate of return that makes all of the future cash payments received by the bond holder equal to the price of the bond today. The YTM gives us a better picture of our actual return on investment than the current yield ($70/$1,020, or 6.86%). As you can see, the price of the bond and its YTM or inversely related. The higher current price on this bond lowers its YTM to 5.92% from the coupon rate of 7%.

Exercise 6-4

Assuming you will receive semiannual payments for three years, calculate the annualized YTM for the U.S. Treasury Note and the AT&T Corporation bond from Exercises 6-1 and 6-2, respectively.

The Yield Curve

A particularly useful framework for describing the relationship between an issuer's bonds with short terms to maturity and those with long terms to maturity is a yield curve. More specifically, the *yield curve* is a graphical representation of the relationship between interest rates on a particular debt security with different terms to maturity. Here we are using the term 'yield' to mean the return received when a bond is held to maturity, or YTM. This is not the bond's current yield. Recall that the YTM includes both the interest return and the return of principal.

The shape of the yield curve, upward sloping (higher long-term rates) or downward sloping (lower long-term rates) is dependent on a number of factors. These factors can be classified into two general categories. First, the shape of the curve is influenced by investors' expectations of future interest rates. If the yield curve is flat – short-term rates and long-term rates are very similar – or downward sloping it is likely that investors' believe that rates will be lower in the future. In this case, investors are buying more and more long-term securities to capture the high current rates pushing their yield down (the yield on a bond and its price are inversely related). Conversely, if the yield curve is upward sloping investors expect future rates to rise. To capitalize on this expectation, investors sell current long-term securities and buy short-term securities, respectively raising and lowering the yields on each.

A second factor that can explain the shape of the yield curve is that investors perceive the risks of holding securities for longer periods of time to be greater than those of shorter periods. This preference for shorter term securities is called the *liquidity premium* and raises the yield on long-term securities. The liquidity premium is due to the fact that the longer the time until the principal is due to be returned, the higher the probability that the principal will not be returned. As the preference for short term debt becomes greater, investors sell current long-term securities and buy short-term securities, respectively raising and lowering the yields on each.

Exercise 6-5

Construct a yield curve for U.S. Government securities. Use the table "Treasury Bonds, Notes, and Bills" from Exercise 6-1. Interest rates for a representative Treasury with 2, 5, 10, and 30 years to maturity are in bold face. Use the indicated asked yield (found in the last column) for these four Treasurys to create a yield curve. Plot the values on the graph below and draw a yield curve for U.S. Treasurys.

Asked Yield

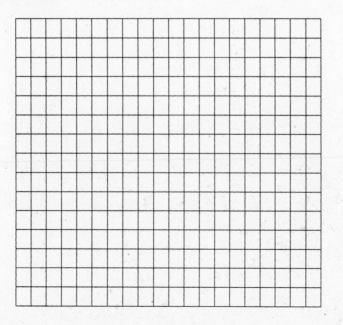

Maturity

1. Is this yield curve downward or upward sloping?

2. Given your answer to question 1, and assuming investors have no preference for shorter or longer term securities, what is the expectation for future interest rates on U.S. Treasurys?

Project 6-1

Repeat Exercise 6-1 using a recent edition of the *WSJ*.

Date _____

1. Find the asked price for a U.S. Treasury Note with 3 or 5 years to maturity.

2. By how much did this price change from the previous day?

Project 6-2

Repeat Exercise 6-5 using a recent edition of the *WSJ*. Using rates for the same terms to maturity, create a new yield curve for U.S. Treasurys below.

Asked Yield

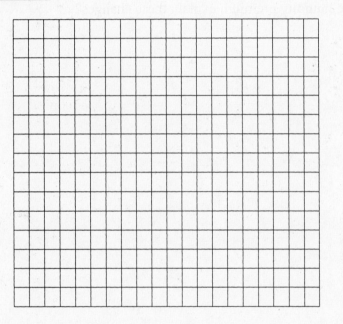

Maturity

Compare this yield curves to the one created in Exercise 6-5.

1. How has the shape of the yield curve changed?

2. How may investor's expectations explain these changes?

3. How may the liquidity premium explain these changes?

Project 6-3

Using a recent addition of the *WSJ*, review the Credit Markets column found in the Money and Investing Section.

Date of report:_____

1. What was the change, if any, in Treasury prices for the given trading day?

2. What reason was given in the article for the Treasury market activity?

3. What other bond issues (corporate, municipal, etc.) are discussed in the column? What was the change, if any, in these prices for the given trading day?

Discussion Questions

Treasurys Are Lifted by a Volatile Stock Market

By JOY C. SHAW
Dow Jones Newswires

NEW YORK—Treasurys ended higher, lifted by the same two factors that have been supporting government securities recently: volatility in stocks and geopolitical news.

Some repositioning by people in the market also lifted prices of longer maturities in particular.

At 4 p.m., the benchmark 10-year note was up 7/32 point, or $2.19 per $1,000 face value, at 98 25/32. Its yield fell to 5.035% from 5.062% Friday, as yields move inversely to prices.

The 30-year bond's price was up 22/32 point at 96 21/32 to yield 5.609%, down from 5.659% Friday.

Stocks attempted to rally. But gains were pared late in the session, with the Nasdaq Composite Index finishing down 4.79 points at 1530.69 and the Dow Jones Industrial Average up 55.73 points at 9645.40.

Investors often move money into government securities when stocks are weak, and anticipation of such shifts can boost bond prices. That happened yesterday, after people in the Treasurys market concluded that the stock rally wasn't strong enough to suggest that equities had stabilized.

The rise in stocks mostly was a correction of an oversold condition and doesn't likely mean a fundamental improvement, said Jeffery Meyerson, a trader at M.H. Meyerson & Co., Jersey City, N.J. "There's still a lot of general pessimism in the [equities] market," he said.

Yield Comparisons

Based on Merrill Lynch Bond Indexes, priced as of midafternoon Eastern time.

	6/10	6/7	52-WEEK HIGH	LOW
Corp. Govt. Master	4.99%	5.00%	5.72%	4.35%
Treasury				
1-10 yr	3.60	3.61	4.66	2.92
10+ yr	5.63	5.65	5.96	4.83
Agencies				
1-10 yr	4.01	4.01	5.26	3.25
10+ yr	6.08	6.12	6.50	5.38
Corporate				
1-10 yr High Quality	4.84	4.85	5.74	4.20
Medium Quality	6.04	6.04	6.67	5.52
10+ yr High Quality	6.76	6.80	7.16	6.27
Medium Quality	7.52	7.55	7.93	7.08
Yankee bonds (1)	5.78	5.80	6.36	5.10
Current-coupon mortgages (2)				
GNMA 6.50%	6.24	6.16	6.74	5.75
FNMA 6.50%	6.25	6.15	6.91	5.65
FHLMC 6.50%	6.28	6.20	6.92	5.65
High-yield corporates	11.48	11.43	13.70	10.92
Tax-Exempt Bonds				
7-12 yr G.O. (AA)	4.10	4.10	4.62	3.84
12-22 yr G.O. (AA)	5.08	5.08	5.32	4.67
22+ yr revenue (A)	5.27	5.27	5.46	4.91

Note: High quality rated AAA-AA; medium quality A-BBB/Baa; high yield, BB/Ba-C.
(1) Dollar-denominated, SEC-registered bonds of foreign issuers sold in the U.S. (2) Reflects the 52-week high and low of mortgage-backed securities indexes rather than the individual securities shown.

Late in the morning, investors were reminded of geopolitical risk when the government announced the arrest of a suspect who allegedly was planning an attack involving a radioactive bomb. The news helped push Treasurys higher.

However, some of that support dissipated after it was learned that the arrest had been made more than a month ago.

"It is certainly disturbing that someone is planning an attack in the country, but at the same time, it's not posting danger to security today, so the market sold back," said Vinnie Verterano, head of trading at Nomura Securities International in New York.

William Strazzullo, vice president of fixed-income trading at State Street Global Markets in Boston, said repositioning played a role in bond-market movements. Among other things, some people were reversing previous so-called steepening trades. The activity lifted 30-year issues.

In addition, traders cited a large purchase of 30-year bonds as a reason for strength in that area of the market.

Others also cited a belief that the Federal Reserve will continue to keep its interest-rate target at the current level until September as a factor in trading.

Speaking yesterday at a conference in California, Federal Reserve Bank of Dallas President Robert McTeer said second-quarter economic growth will be between the low rate of the fourth quarter and the high rate in the first three months of this year. Gross domestic product grew at a 1.7% rate in the fourth quarter, compared with a 5.6% rate in the first calendar quarter.

A Dow Jones-CNBC survey of dealers in Treasurys Friday of 20 banks found that most expect Fed policy makers to keep rates unchanged until the Sept. 24 Fed policy meeting.

Corporate and High-Yield Bonds

High-yield bonds fell slightly as credit concerns continued to weigh on the market despite a rise in stocks.

Adelphia Communications Corp. bonds fell, dragging the cable sector lower, after the company dismissed its auditor and revised 2000 and 2001 results.

Adelphia's $10\frac{7}{8}\%$ notes due 2010 were quoted down six points at 54 bid. The bonds have already priced in expectation of a bankruptcy filing, said traders.

Other cable bonds lost two to three points in price on concerns that accounting methods that had been used by Adelphia previously might be disclosed elsewhere in the industry, traders said.

Charter Communications Inc. $8\frac{5}{8}\%$ notes due 2009 were quoted at 78 bid, while **Cablevision Systems** Corp. $7\frac{5}{8}\%$ notes of 2011 were quoted at 89 bid.

In the new-issue market, **Intermet** Corp. sold $175 million of seven-year senior notes through Deutsche Bank Securities and Banc of America Securities. Rated single-B2 by Moody's Investors Service and single-B-plus by Standard & Poor's, the notes offer a 9.75% yield.

Investment-grade bond investors were expecting only about $2 billion in new securities this week, a relatively low level. The largest was expected to be from the General Electric Capital Corp. unit of **General Electric** Co.

GE Capital was expected to sell $500 million of 30-year public income notes, or PINEs, in $25 denominations via Salomon Smith Barney. The notes were expected to yield about 6.75% and are rated triple-A by both Moody's and S&P.

—Tom Barkley and Richard A. Bravo
contributed to this article.

1. According to the article, what effect, if any, did activity in the stock market have on the market for Treasury notes and bonds? How are the stock market and bond market related?

2. According to the article, what effect, if any, did political activity have on the market for Treasury notes and bonds? Explain how "geopolitical" news affects the bond market?

3. Why are bond traders interested in what the Federal Reserve will do at its next meeting? What effect can the Federal Reserve have on the price of existing bonds?

Chapter 7

Stock Valuations

Objectives

1. Distinguish between the primary and secondary markets for stocks.

2. Learn to read the price and other information given in the stock market tables of the *WSJ*.

3. Distinguish between the book value of a stock and its market value.

4. Describe two models of stock valuation using time value of money principles.

Key Terms

Primary market	Dividend Yield	Book value
Secondary market	Price-to-Earnings Ratio	Dividend Discount Model
Dividends	Market Value	Dividend Growth Model

Just as time-value-of-money concepts help us find the value of bonds, these principles can help us understand the value investors place on the stock of a corporation. In this chapter, some basic models of determining stock prices are introduced. Described first are the markets where firms issue stock and the markets where investors trade their shares of stock with other investors. Information from both of these markets is reported daily in the *WSJ*. A large amount of information is given for companies whose stock trades in the U.S. markets, as well as a fair amount of information for companies from around the world. We will learn what information is available and use it in our pricing models.

Stock Markets

The types of bonds issued by governments and corporations to fund their operations was discussed in the previous chapter. Corporations can also raise money by selling shares of ownership in the company. Shares in a company are called stock. Firms raise money through stock offerings in financial markets. The first, or initial, sale of stock to the public occurs in the ***primary market***. Corporations sell stock to the public with the help of investment banks, or underwriters. We can find information on the latest primary market activity in the *WSJ*. Articles on new stock issues are found in the Deals & Deal Makers column, and new offerings of both debt (bonds) and equity (stock) are listed each day under the "New Securities Issues" column (both columns are located in section C).

After these initial offerings, a company's stock will trade in the *secondary market*. Unlike the primary market, secondary financial markets do not provide funds to the issuer of the security (corporation). Funds are transferred amongst investors. Investors that wish to sell their shares can do so by offering them for sale through dealers operating in these secondary markets. There exists both organized and over-the-counter exchanges for trading in the secondary market. The New York Stock Exchange, or NYSE, is an example of an organized exchange - a visible marketplace where buyers and sellers meet to exchange shares. The National Association of Securities Dealers Automated Quotation system, or NASDAQ, is an example of an over-the-counter exchange. The NASDAQ is a telecommunication system of securities dealers. Buyers and sellers do not meet face-to-face.

Reading the Stock Market Listings

Trading activity for these, and many other, secondary markets is listed daily in the *WSJ*. Each day, the stock market tables of the *WSJ* report ten pieces of information about the trading activity on these markets for the previous day. They are the year-to-date percentage change in the price of the companies stock, the highest trading price over the past year (52 weeks), the lowest trading price over the past year, the name of the company (including a short, 3 or 4 letter, symbol for the company), the annual dividend paid, the dividend yield on the stock, the price-to-earnings (PE) ratio of the stock, the volume of shares traded on the previous day, the last price at which the stock traded, and the change in this price from the previous day's last price.

The year-to-date percentage change in the price of the stock reflects the return on an investment in this stock for the current calendar year. The 52-week high and low price are the highest and lowest price at which this stock traded over the past year, excluding the previous trading day. The dividend amount is the latest amount per share that the company has indicated (declared) it will pay shareholders over the course of one year. *Dividends* are cash distributions from the corporation to its owners and are normally paid every quarter. The *dividend yield* is calculated by dividing the annual dividend amount by the last price at which the stock traded.

The PE, or *price-to-earnings ratio*, is the ratio of the stock price to the earnings per share of the company for the past twelve months. Calculating earnings per share can be quite complicated but simply stated is net income of the company (excluding any extraordinary expenses or income) divided by the number of shares currently outstanding. The PE is a statistic that is often used to compare the values of two different corporations. The ratio indicates the number of years of current earnings per share that investors are willing to pay to own the stock. That is, the PE measures how many years of current earnings will return, or payback, the cost of an investment in the company today. For example, a PE ratio of 15 indicates that if an investor was to receive all the earnings each year, in 15 years the investor will have received the price of the investment. Low PE ratios indicate a quick payback on the investment and may indicate a good value relative to high PE ratio stocks.

The volume information indicates the number of shares traded, quoted in hundreds, during the previous day. Underlined information for stocks indicates there was a large change in the number of shares traded compared to the stock's average trading volume. A large volume of trading indicates strong interest, whether positive or negative, in this corporation.

Exercise 7-1

How to Read This Table

The following explanations apply to the New York and American exchange listed issues and the Nasdaq Stock Market. NYSE and Amex prices are composite quotations that include trades on the Chicago, Pacific, Philadelphia, Boston and Cincinnati exchanges and reported by the National Association of Securities Dealers.

Boldfaced quotations highlight those issues whose price changed by 5% or more if their previous closing price was $2 or higher.

Underlined quotations are those stocks with large changes in volume, pe exchange, compared with the issue's average trading volume. The calculation includes common stocks of $5 a share or more with an average volume over 65 trading days of at least 5,000 shares. The underlined quotations are for the 40 largest volume percentage leaders on the NYSE and the Nasdaq National Market. It includes the 20 largest volume percentage gainers on the Amex.

YTD percentage change reflects the stock price percentage change for the calendar year to date, adjusted for stock splits and dividends over 10%.

The 52-week high and low columns show the highest and lowest price of the issue during the preceding 52 weeks plus the current week, but not the latest trading day. These ranges are adjusted to reflect stock payouts of 1% or more, and cash dividends or other distributions of 10% or more.

Dividend/Distribution rates, unless noted, are annual disbursements based on the last monthly, quarterly, semiannual, or annual declaration. Special or extra dividends or distributions, including return of capital, special situations or payments not designated as regular are identified by footnotes.

Yield is defiend as the dividends or other distributions paid by a company on its securities, expressed as a percentage of price.

The P/E ratio is determined by dividing the closing market price by the company's diluted per-share earnings, as available, for the most recent four quarters. Charges and other adjustments usually are excluded when they qualify as extraordinary items under generally accepted accounting rules.

Sales figures are the unofficial daily total of shares traded, quoted in hundreds (two zeros omitted; f-four zeros omitted.)

Exchange ticker symbols are shown for all New York and American exchange common stocks, and Dow Jones News/Retrieval symbols are listed for Class A and Class B shares listed on both markets. Nasdaq symbols are listed for all Nasdaq NMS issues. A more detailed explanation of Nasdaq ticker symbols appears with the NMS listings.

Footnotes:

i-New 52-week high.

↑-New 52-week low.

a-Extra dividend or extras in addition to the regular dividend.

b-indicates annual rate of the cash dividend and that a stock dividend was paid.

c-Liquidating dividend.

cc-P/E ratio is 100 or more.

dd-Loss in the most recent four quarters.

e-indicates a dividend was declared in the preceding 12 months, but that there isn't a regular dividend rate. Amount shown may have been adjusted to reflect stock split, spinoff or other distribution.

FD-First day of trading.

f-Annual rate, increased on latest declaration.

g-indicates the dividend and earnings are expressed in Canadian money. The stock trades in U.S. dollars. No yield or P/E ratio is shown.

gg-Special sales condition; no regular way trading.

h-Temporary exemption from Nasdaq requirements.

I-indicates amount declared or paid after a stock dividend or split.

j-indicates dividend was paid this year, and that at the last dividend meeting a dividend was omitted or deferred.

k-indicates dividend declared this year on cumulative issues with dividends in arrears.

m-Annual rate, reduced on latest declaration.

n-Newly issued in the past 52 weeks. The high-low range begins with the start of trading and doesn't cover the entire period.

p-initial dividend; no yield calculated.

pf-Preferred.

pp-Holder owes installment(s) of purchase price.

pr-Preference.

r-indicates a cash dividend declared in the preceding 12 months, plus a stock dividend.

rt-Rights.

s-Stock split or stock dividend, or cash or cash equivalent distribution, amounting to 10% or more in the past 52 weeks. The high-low price is adjusted from the old stock. Dividend calculations begin with the date the split was paid or the stock dividend occured.

stk-Paid in stock in the last 12 months. Company doesn't pay cash dividend.

un-Units.

v-Trading halted on primary market.

vj-In bankruptcy or receivership or being reorganized under the Bankruptcy Code, or securties assumed by such companies.

wd-When distributed.

wi-When issued.

wt-Warrants.

ww-With warrants.

x-Ex-dividend, ex-distribution, ex-rights or without warrants.

z-Sales in full, not in 100s.

Wall Street Journal stock tables reflect composite regular trading as of 4 p.m. and changes in the closing prices from 4 p.m. the previous day.

Tuesday, June 18, 2002

NEW YORK STOCK EXCHANGE COMPOSITE TRANSACTIONS

YTD %CHG	52-WEEK HI	LO	STOCK (SYM)	DIV	YLD %	PE	VOL 100s	CLOSE	NET CHG
-2.1	12.24	6.21	CP Ships TEU n	.08e	.8	...	244	10.63	-0.02
35.2	17.50	5.50	CSK AutoCp CAO		...	dd	783	13.45	-0.15
12.5	38.70	20.63	CSS Ind CSS		...	15	128	34.77	-0.53
-1.6	41.40	25.44	CSX CSX	.40	1.2	24	6103	34.49	-0.10
-19.4	24	12.20	CTS Cp CTS	.12	.9	dd	691	12.81	-0.11
13.2	49.24	22.89	CVS Cp CVS	.23	.7	39	17150	33.50	-0.13
2.5	24.98	22.60	CabcoTr BFH	1.69	6.9	...	31	24.60	0.28
-44.9	18.66	7.90	CblWrels ADS CWP	.79e	9.7	...	1434	8.16	-0.07
-22.7	16.35	10.40	CableDsgn CDT		...	dd	2881	10.58	-0.17
-66.3	62	12.57	CablevsnNY A CVC		...	dd	38967	16	0.61
-35.1	29.06	14.55	CblvnRnbw A RMG		...		2188	16.03	0.18
-17.0	42.24	22.95	Cabot Cp CBT	.52	1.8	17	2533	29.63	0.05
-7.4	27.50	16.25	CabotO&G COG	.16	.7	83	965	22.28	0.28
10.9	31.91	23.55	CadburySch ADS CSG	.70e	2.5	...	999	28.53	0.13
-22.9	24.94	14.10	CadenceDsgn CDN		...	28	6282	16.91	-0.08
0.4	9.89	6.91	CalgonCarb CCC	.12	1.4	44	1688	8.38	-0.07
-5.4	27.75	23	CalWtrSvc CWT	1.12	4.6	23	148	24.35	-0.15
-13.8	20.68	11.83	CalwyGlf ELY	.28	1.7	22	2886	16.50	0.30
-32.1	12.40	3.96	CalnPete CPE		...	dd	127	4.65	-0.10
-46.4	46	6.15	Calpine CPN		...	7	67544	9	-0.07
-4.8	54.45	30.40	Cambrex CBM	.12	.3	41	737	41.49	0.14
3.7	41.66	33.97	CamdnProp CPT	2.54f	6.7	29	1574	38.05	-0.15
8.2	30.70	19.25	CamecoCp g CCJ	.50bg	...	...	105	26.78	0.27
-6.7	31.44	25.52	CampblSoup CPB	.63	2.3	22	4604	27.86	-0.18
-10.6	31.26	23.30	CanLifeFnl CLU	.60g	2.4	12	107	24.80	-0.26
-8.3	36.95	29.67	CIBC g BCM	1.64g	...	...	234	31.54	-0.13
3.2	53.75	33	CanNtlRlwy g CNI	.86g	...	...	1149	49.81	0.01
31.2	34.27	22.80	CndNatRes CED	.50g	1.6	7	110	32.01	0.05
17.2	23.80	13.20	CanPacRlwy CP n	.51g	2.2	...	460	22.85	-0.01
5.1	42.30	25	Canon ADS CAJ	.08e	.2	...	566	36.85	-0.11
35.9	19.70	11.47	CantelMed CMN s		...	24	424	17.29	-0.52
-23.9	10.20	5.57	CanwestGlbl g CWG	.30g	...	...	82	5.67	-0.22
10.8	67.25	36.40	CapOneFnl COF	.11	.2	19	26441	59.79	0.19
-7.3	51.37	42.65	CapOne un n	1.01p	...	...	3243	47.30	0.10
5.4	4.25	1.39	CapSrLvng CSU		...	14	15	3.13	0.03
-14.8	6.50	4.70	CapTr A CT		...	13	2	4.91	-0.04
-17.5	29.50	13.80	CapstdMtg CMO s	6.21e	32.0	3	306	19.38	-0.02
-11.1	42	25.50	CarboCermcs CRR	.36	1.0	19	155	34.81	-0.49
-1.1	77.32	59.45	CardnlHlth CAH	.10	.2	27	13418	63.94	-0.61
11.0	21.95	11.90	CaremarkRx CMX		...	22	13232	18.10	-0.25
17.4	44.85	25.50	Carlisle CSL	.84	1.9	28	2803	43.40	0.42
3.6	34.64	16.95	Carnival CCL	.42	1.4	18	21543	29.08	-0.11
4.4	34.05	27.70	Carolina CG n	.45p	...	...	3504	30.39	-0.61
6.9	30.55	19.80	CarpTch CRS	1.32	4.6	dd	894	28.46	-0.01
0.8	33.30	27.78	CarrAmRlty CRE	2.00	6.6	62	2475	30.35	-0.39
-18.4	8.74	3.85	CarriagScv A CSV		...	3	98	4.30	0.02
25.7	15.25	8.50	CascadeCp CAE	.40	2.6	66	321	15.10	-0.04
0.9	24.17	18.20	CascadeNG CGC	.96	4.3	16	158	22.25	-0.45
-0.5	10.50	6.92	CashAmInt PWN	.05	.6	dd	381	8.46	0.16
-10.2	39.70	25.05	CatalinaMkta POS		...	29	9299	31.16	1.94
1.9	24.90	19.25	CLECO CNL	.90f	4.0	15	1543	22.39	-0.01
42.0	32.25	13.65	ClvIndClfs CLF	.40	1.5	dd	173	25.99	0.21
-1.2	26.74	25.10	ClevelandElec CVEU n	2.25	8.9	...	346	25.20	-0.28
14.3	47.95	33.40	Clorox CLX	.84	1.9	41	5608	45.20	-0.27
-25.6	28.22	17.70	CMS Engy PEPS	1.81	9.3	...	656	19.54	0.19
41.7	60.23	20	Coach COH		...	32	5990	55.24	0.51
34.2	19.50	8.25	Coachmen COA	.20	1.2	cc	1438	16.10	-0.05
-57.1	8.40	2.10	Coastcast PAR	e	...	dd	18	2.20	-0.05
258.2	22.80	3.99	Cobalt CBZ	.05	.2	dd	1189	22.85	0.97
17.3	57.91	42.59	CocaCola KO	.80	1.4	35	35693	55.30	0.05
22.6	29.89	17.40	CC Femsa ADS KOF	.42e	1.7	...	479	24.60	-0.23
21.3	23.40	13.46	CocaColaEnt CCE x	.16	.7	85	9051	22.98	-0.34
113.8	2.20	0.63	Coeur dAMn CDE		...	dd	13095	1.71	0.05
12.7	19.65	10.70	ColeNtl A CNJ		...	41	82	18.65	-0.30
-12.4	37.40	24	ColesMyer ADS CM	1.05e	3.5	...	20	29.90	0.25
-8.3	61	51.30	ColgatePalm CL	.72	1.4	27	18572	52.94	-0.79
-36.4	22.70	7.52	CollnsAikman CKC s		...	dd	12455	9.80	-0.20
8.2	16.19	11.52	ColonlBcgp CNB	.52	3.4	14	2015	15.25	0.01
19.1	37.80	27.23	ColonlProp CLP	2.64	7.1	16	784	37.10	-0.39
1.3	25.85	24.76	ClmbsSo A CSJ	2.09	8.2	...	47	25.53	0.13
-60.2	59	20.05	Comcast DECS	1.43	6.9	...	141	20.82	0.52
10.5	66.09	44.02	Comerica CMA	1.92	3.0	14	7407	63.31	0.30
-3.4	4.99	2	CmfrtSysUSA FIX		...	dd	3938	4.90	0.02
15.9	50.49	30	ComrcBcpNJ CBH s	.60f	1.3	28	3175	45.60	-0.06
7.2	42.11	33.52	CommrcCGInc CGI	1.24f	3.1	15	432	40.42	-0.08
22.2	30.03	21.10	ComrclFed CFB	.36f	1.3	13	839	28.72	-0.28
27.8	47.99	24.50	CmrclMtls CMC	.52	1.2	15	869	44.70	0.10
20.6	16	11.25	CmrclNetRlty NNN	1.26	8.0	18	1392	15.68	-0.02
-40.9	24.45	11.59	Commscope CTV		...	70	2623	12.57	-0.03
18.1	34.21	24.75	CmntyBkSys CBU	1.08	3.5	18	58	30.95	0.25
14.5	35.35	20.29	CmntyHlth CYH		...	44	2635	29.20	-0.20
-16.1	11.94	9.05	CoSaoPlo ADS SBS n		...		141	9.65	-0.13
-12.9	16.39	8.02	EngGr-Cmg ADS CIG n	.88e	7.1	...	47	12.35	0.25
-37.1	8.47	4.65	Copel ADS ELP	.26e	5.3	...	1191	4.94	-0.12
3.6	21.10	9.10	CmpnhiaSidr SID	.82e	4.9	...	87	16.70	-0.38
1.6	25.15	24	CompassTr n	.51p	...	...	232	24.50	0.04
-49.1	38.74	14.30	CptrAssoc CA x	.08	.5	dd	17010	17.57	-0.14
-0.6	53.47	30.96	CptrSci CSC		...	24	8550	48.71	0.36
15.5	6.08	1.30	CptrTask CTG	.05	1.1	dd	93	4.55	-0.05
-4.2	14.65	8.50	CompxInt A CIX	.50	4.0	39	43	12.42	0.02
12.7	10.90	4.96	ComstkRes CRK		...	46	1344	7.89	0.66
4.8	25.71	18.80	ConAgraFoods CAG	.94	3.8	19	11126	24.91	-0.08
91.1	4.45	1.11	ConeMills COE		...	dd	105	3.44	-0.10
2.4	25.24	21.40	Conectiv CIV	.32	8.5	12	4307	25.09	0.24
5.9	21.83	17.51	Conectiv A CIVA	.50	2.3	...	420	21.59	0.22
-5.3	32	23.77	Conoco COC	.76	2.8	16	12401	26.81	0.01
-53.1	16.20	1.87	Conseco CNC		...	dd	13083	2.09	-0.12
-7.0	29.49	18.30	ConsolEngy CNX	1.12	4.8	11	2622	23.11	-0.15
3.4	45.40	36.50	ConEd ED	2.22	5.3	13	10507	41.75	0.14
0.4	25.70	24.45	ConEd QUICS	1.94	7.7	...	62	25.15	0.14

Source: *The Wall Street Journal*, June 19, 2002. Reprinted by permission of Dow Jones & Company, Inc. (c) 2002 Dow Jones & Company, Inc. All Rights Reserved Worldwide.

Use the above listing from the *WSJ* to locate the price and trading information for the

Coca Cola Corporation (symbol KO).

1. What is the YTD % change?

2. What was the last price?

3. What is the current dividend and yield?

4. What is the PE Ratio?

5. Compare these values to those of Colgate Palmolive Corporation (symbol CL).

Book v. Market Value

The current price of a stock is the rate at which buyers and sellers of the stock are willing to exchange shares of ownership in the company. Multiplying this market price by the number of shares currently outstanding determines a company's *market value*. The market value will likely be different than the value reported in a company's annual financial statements. Analyzing these accounting statements is an important aspect of determining firm value, but different analysts may view the statements differently. The accounting value of the company is called *book value*, and is equal to the net worth of the company - the total assets of the company less its total liabilities. Dividing this value by the number of shares currently outstanding gives the book value per share.

Comparing these two values is useful when analyzing a company as an investment. Market value will reflect the value that investors are currently placing on the future earnings of the company. The book value of a company represents the current value of the funds that the company has raised from shareholders plus all the earnings the company has retained from previous years of operation. Thus, market value is forward looking and book value is backward looking. The ratio of these two values reflects investors'(the market's) expectation of the earning power of these assets. When the market/book ratio exceeds one, the earning power of the assets exceeds their accounting value.

Exercise 7-2

According to the accounting statements at the end of 2001, the net worth of Coca Cola was $11,366,000,000 and the number of shares outstanding were 2,487,000,000. For the same period, the net worth of Colgate Palmolive was $505,100,000 and the number of shares outstanding were 557,800,000 . Use this information to answer the following questions.

1. Calculate the market value for these two companies using the last price information you found in Exercise 7-1.

2. Calculate the book value per share of Coca Cola and Colgate Palmolive based on the number of shares outstanding.

3. Calculate the market-to-book ratio for these two companies using the last price information you found in Exercise 7-1.

4. Compare these ratios with the PE ratios found in Exercise 7-1. Based on this example, do firms with high market-to-book ratios also have high PE ratios?

Present Value Models of Value

Market-to-book and PE ratios are two methods of analyzing the value that investors place on a stock. Time-value-of-money principles are also useful in analyzing stock value. As a financial asset, the value of a stock will equal the present value of all future cash flows generated by this asset. The return on an investment in the common stock of a corporation will come from cash dividends and any capital gains or losses. Recall, dividends are cash distributions from the corporation to its owners. The capital gain or loss on a stock depends on the future price of the stock at which the investors sells his or her share. Accordingly, the present value of a stock, its current market price, will equal the present value of all future cash dividends and the present value of the future price.

$$PV = \frac{dividend_1}{(1+r)^1} + \frac{dividend_2}{(1+r)^2} + ... \frac{dividend_t}{(1+r)^t} + \frac{price_t}{(1+r)^t}$$

In this relationship the discount rate, r, is the investor's expected rate of return for this stock. In a competitive market, investors compare expected returns, based on expected dividends and price changes, with comparable returns on similar securities. That is, the expected return, r, is an investor's opportunity cost of investing in this particular company.

This model can be simplified by assuming that the investor holds the stock forever. Just as a corporation is an ongoing concern, the stock of the company is on-going. In this case, the financial asset is a perpetuity, and the present value is equal to all future cash dividends.

$$PV = \frac{dividend_1}{(1+r)^1} + \frac{dividend_2}{(1+r)^2} + \frac{dividend_3}{(1+r)^3} + ...$$

or

$$PV = \frac{dividend}{r}$$

This valuation model of stocks is called the ***Dividend Discount Model***. Rearranging this equation we can estimate investors' expected rate of return for a given stock.

$$r = \frac{dividend}{PV}$$

For example, suppose a company currently pays an annual dividend of $1 per share and each share in the company is selling for $20. The expected rate of return that investors are placing on this stock is 5% ($1/$20 = 0.05).

Unfortunately this model assumes that there is no growth in the company- the dividend is constant. This may be true if all the earnings of the corporation are being paid out to the shareholder. Most corporations, however, reinvest earnings in order to pursue new business opportunities and to maintain existing operations (some corporations do not pay any dividends). To incorporate this reinvestment we can assume that dividends will grow at some constant rate *g*.

$$PV = \frac{dividend\ (1+g)}{(1+r)^1} + \frac{dividend\ (1+g)^2}{(1+r)^2} + ... \frac{dividend(1+g)}{(1+r)^\infty}$$

This equation can be simplified to:

$$PV = \frac{dividend}{r - g}$$

This is called the **Dividend Growth Model**, or the Gordon Growth Model for Myron Gordon who developed the model. As before, we can rearrange this equation to estimate investors' expected rate of return on the stock.

$$r = \frac{dividend}{PV} + g$$

Suppose that the company's stock is currently selling for $20 and the company is expected to increase its $1 annual dividend 5% each year. The expected rate of return in this case is 10% ($1/$20 + 5% = 10%).

Exercise 7-3

Use the dividend and price information from Exercise 7-1 to answer the following questions.

1. Estimate the expected rate of return for Coca Cola using the Dividend Discount Model.

2. From 1996 through 2001, the Coca Cola Corporation increased its dividend by an average of 8.5% each year. Assuming this growth will continue, estimate the expected rate of return for Coca Cola using the Dividend Growth Model.

Project 7-1

Find the stock listing for the Coca Cola company in a recent edition of the *WSJ*. Use this information to answer the following questions from Exercises 7-1 and 7-3.

Date _____

1. What is the YTD % change? What was the last price?

2. What is the current dividend and yield? What is the PE Ratio?

3. Estimate the expected rate of return for Coca Cola using the Dividend Discount Model.

4. From 1996 through 2001, the Coca Cola Corporation increased its dividend by an average of 8.5% each year. Assuming this growth will continue, estimate the expected rate of return for Coca Cola using the Dividend Growth Model.

Project 7-2

Using a current edition of the *WSJ*, find the last-trade prices, PE Ratios, and dividend yields for ten of the 30 stocks in the Dow Jones Industrial Average (DJIA). A listing of the thirty companies in the DJIA is located in the Markets Lineup section (page C2).

	Company	Price	PE	Dividend Yield
1				
2				
3				
4				
5				
6				
7				
8				
9				
10				
Average				

1. Calculate an average price, average PE ratio and average dividend yield for these 10 companies.

2. The PE ratio for the Dow Jones Industrial Average is reported each Monday in the Money and Investing Section of the *WSJ*. Compare your calculation of the average PE for your 10 companies to the recently reported PE for the DJIA.

3. Using these companies as a proxy for the market as a whole, estimate the current expected rate of return using the dividend discount model (assuming a constant dividend). Find the average dividend by multiplying the average price by the average dividend yield.

4.   Now assume that this average dividend is expected to grow at 5 percent per year. Find the expected rate of return.

5.   Compare these estimates of the market rate of return to the return on medium quality corporate bonds (10+ years to maturity). This rate can be found in the "Credit Markets" column of the Money and Investing Section. Is the expected rate of return on stocks greater or less than the current rate of return on these bonds?

Discussion Questions

Getting Going / *By Jonathan Clements*

FedEx Delivers: Its Small New Dividend Gives Hope That More Firms Will Follow

IT SEEMED ALMOST anachronistic: On Friday, FedEx Corp. announced it would deliver not only letters and packages, but also a dividend.

Big news? Maybe not. The quarterly payout, the first in the company's history, will be just five cents a share, amounting to a 0.4% yield on FedEx's $52.65 stock price. That won't make most shareholders rich, and it won't do much for the stock market's overall dividend yield, which remains mired at a paltry 1½%.

Still, I hope this is the beginning of a trend. When management regularly returns cash to shareholders, it's a plus not only for investors, but also for the companies themselves. Here's why you should cheer every time a company raises its payout or starts paying a dividend:

■Restoring Faith: Despite FedEx's announcement, the outlook for dividends isn't bright. Only yesterday, for instance, Qwest Communications International eliminated its dividend.

In fact, in the first five months of 2002, the dividends paid by companies in the Standard & Poor's 500-index slipped 2.8% compared with the same period last year. That follows declines in 2000 and 2001, says Arnold Kaufman, editor of Standard & Poor's Outlook, a weekly newsletter.

"If we have a full-year decline for 2002, it would be the first time we've had three consecutive declines since 1931-33," he says. "I'm expecting a pick up in dividends as the

year progresses. But to this point, there's been no evidence of improvement."

If management does start raising dividends, it could bolster the flagging stock market. This year, the firms in the S&P 500 will pay dividends equal to just 31% of operating earnings, as estimated by analysts at Standard & Poor's, a division of McGraw-Hill.

What if, instead, companies started paying out 50% of operating earnings, which is the historical average? The resulting yield of 2½% might make shares more appealing.

Higher payouts could also boost confidence in corporate profits. After all, if companies fork over more cash to shareholders, investors might be more inclined to believe earnings were the result of real corporate progress, rather than accounting shenanigans.

■Cushioning Investors: If companies increase payouts, it would represent a huge turnaround. As the accompanying chart makes clear, yields have been falling for 20 years.

Today's skimpy yield is due, in part, to the rapid rise in stock prices over the past two decades. But it also reflects the scorn heaped on dividends in the 1990s. As stock prices rocketed higher, the New Era crowd dismissed dividends as all but irrelevant.

Their argument: What really matters are share-price gains. If a company wants to return cash to investors, it can always buy back stock, thereby bolstering earnings growth when figured on a per-share basis. That, in turn, will lead to further gains in a company's stock price.

Dwindling Yields

Dividend yields on the Dow Jones Industrial Average have slumped as companies focus on lifting stock prices instead.

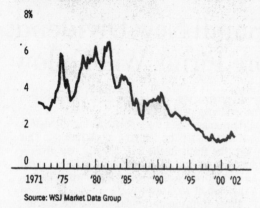

Source: WSJ Market Data Group

This relentless focus on capital gains was partly justified on grounds of tax efficiency. Dividends are immediately taxable as ordinary income, while share-price gains are taxed at the lower capital-gains rate and this tax isn't due until a stock is sold.

A convincing argument? Think about all the folks investing through tax-sheltered accounts. They don't care whether their stock-market earnings come from dividends or capital gains.

Meanwhile, among taxable investors, there are plenty of folks who wouldn't mind receiving quarterly checks. Dividends may have seemed like a trifling matter in the 1990s, as performance-hungry baby boomers struggled to amass enough for retirement. But now that the boomers are quitting the work force, collecting part of their return in cash may seem increasingly attractive.

If the stock-market slump drags on, other investors are also likely to look kindly on dividends. Even as share prices swoon, those dividend checks keep coming, helping to offset the market decline and providing cash for investors who don't want to sell shares at fire-sale prices.

■**Disciplining Companies:** In the 1990s, dividends weren't just scorned as tax inefficient. They also fell out of favor because of a single-minded focus on earnings growth. The hope: If management reinvested earnings, rather than paying them out as dividends, then faster profit growth would follow.

That notion is looking increasingly shaky. As one company after another is forced to restate earnings, it seems the rapid profit growth of the late 1990s wasn't quite as rapid as we thought.

But maybe we shouldn't be surprised by the recent earnings debacle. Money managers Robert Arnott and Clifford Asness analyzed the period since the Second World War.

They found that, when management retained the most earnings, profit growth over the next 10 years was flat or negative, once you figure in the impact of inflation. Meanwhile, when management retained the least earnings, real earnings per share over the next 10 years grew at an average 4% a year, faster than the 2% historical average.

"Dividends seem to be associated with good corporate behavior," says Mr. Asness, managing principal of New York's AQR Capital Management. "When companies in aggregate pay more dividends, subsequent earnings growth is faster. You'd expect the exact opposite."

What explains this bizarre result? Mr. Asness's theory: "Let's say you're paying a dividend and you want to embark on a new project. Then, you have to go to the capital markets and get the money. There's a lot of discipline imposed by that."

1. According to this article, what is the current dividend yield for the stock market (average dividend yield)? Is this rate high or low by historical standards?

2. What reasons are given in the article for why corporations may not want to pay dividends?

3. According to the article, what is typically the relationship between dividend payout ratios and earnings growth ('real earnings per share')? Given this relationship, are stocks currently under or over-valued?

Chapter 8

Foreign Exchange

Objectives

1. Describe the basic structure of the foreign exchange market.

2. Learn the difference between the spot exchange market and the forward exchange market.

3. Learn to read the foreign currency tables found in the *WSJ*.

4. Describe the basic parity conditions found in foreign exchange markets.

Key Terms

Exchange Rate	Forward Rate Discount	Law of One Price
Spot Rate	Forward Rate Premium	Purchasing Power Parity
Forward Rate	Cross Rate	Interest Rate Parity

One of the oldest and largest financial markets in the world is the market for foreign exchange. Each business day, billions of dollars and other currencies are traded amongst banks, international corporations, and brokers. In this chapter, the currency trading, and other information on world markets, reported in the *WSJ* is used to describe the operations of the market for foreign exchange and understand the economic effects of changes in value of one currency with respect to another.

Exchange Rate Quotations

The foreign exchange rate market is unlike many other markets for financial assets that trade in centralized marketplaces, such as the New York Stock Exchange. The foreign exchange market is an electronic network of commercial banks and foreign exchange (forex) dealers. These banks and dealers in the foreign exchange market serve as financial intermediaries for individuals, international businesses and governments wishing to exchange one currency for another. Participants in this market trade via a communications network, and normally in dollar volumes greater than $1 million. The rate at which a forex dealer will exchange one currency for another is called the ***exchange rate.*** Like other markets, dealers buy and sell currencies at different prices to earn a profit. The price, or exchange rate, at which banks or dealers will buy a currency (bid price) is lower than the price at which they will sell it (ask price).

Since the currency is exchanged one for another, the exchange rate is a ratio and can be quoted as one currency in terms of another and vice versa. The *WSJ* reports exchange rates every business day in each of these two ways. First, the exchange rates are reported in terms of the U.S. $ Equivalent. That is, the amount of U.S. Dollars needed to purchase one unit of the foreign currency. For example, on Thursday, March 14, 2002 the U.S. $ Equivalent rate for one British Pound was 1.4207. This means that one British pound can be exchanged for approximately $1 and 42 cents. If the U.S. $ Equivalent rate for the Pound rises (falls) the currency has appreciated (depreciated) relative to the U.S. Dollar.

Second, exchange rates are reported as the Currency per U.S. $. That is, the amount of foreign currency necessary to purchase one U.S. Dollar. For example, On Thursday, March 14, 2002 the exchange rate for the Japanese Yen, in currency per U.S. $, was 129.25, or 129.25 Yen for each U.S. Dollar. If the Currency per U.S. $ rises (falls) the U.S. Dollar has appreciated (depreciated) relative to that currency.

The Currency Trading Column of the *WSJ* reports foreign exchange market activity from New York on the previous business day. Quotes are given by commercial banks at 4 p.m. Eastern Time by various sources. These quotes apply to transactions of $1 million dollars or more. Rates on smaller transactions, such as currency exchange for tourists, will not be as favorable.

Exercise 8-1

CURRENCY TRADING

Key Currency Cross Rates

Late New York Trading Tuesday, May 21, 2002

	Dollar	Euro	Pound	SFranc	Peso	Yen	CdnDlr
Canada	1.5388	1.4162	2.2463	0.9757	.16192	.01240	...
Japan	124.11	114.22	181.18	78.695	13.059	...	80.654
Mexico	9.5035	8.7461	13.873	6.0259	...	.07657	6.1759
Switzerland	1.5771	1.4514	2.3023	...	.16595	.01271	1.0249
U.K.	.68500	.6304	...	.4344	.07208	.00552	.44517
Euro	1.08660	...	1.5862	.68899	.11434	.00876	.70614
U.S.	...	.9203	1.4598	.63408	.10522	.00806	.64986

Source: Reuters

Exchange Rates

The New York foreign exchange mid-range rates below apply to trading among banks in amounts of $1 million and more, as quoted at 4 p.m. Eastern time by Reuters and other sources. Retail transactions provide fewer units of foreign currency per dollar.

	U.S. $ EQUIVALENT		CURRENCY PER U.S. $	
Country	Tue.	Mon.	Tue.	Mon.
Argentina (Peso)-y	.2907	.2813	3.4400	3.5553
Australia (Dollar)	.5569	.5553	1.7955	1.8007
Bahrain (Dinar)	2.6525	2.6525	.3770	.3770
Brazil (Real)	.4020	.4033	2.4875	2.4795
Britain (Pound)	1.4598	1.4586	.6850	.6856
1-month forward	1.4571	1.4557	.6863	.6870
3-months forward	1.4517	1.4504	.6888	.6895
6-months forward	1.4433	1.4422	.6929	.6934
Canada (Dollar)	.6499	.6486	1.5388	1.5418
1-month forward	.6495	.6483	1.5397	1.5426
3-months forward	.6486	.6473	1.5419	1.5448
6-months forward	.6470	.6457	1.5456	1.5486
Chile (Peso)	.001534	.001534	651.95	651.95
China (Renminbi)	.1208	.1208	8.2769	8.2769
Colombia (Peso)	.0004233	.0004237	2362.50	2360.25
Czech. Rep. (Koruna)				
Commercial rate	.02998	.03007	33.353	33.255
Denmark (Krone)	.1237	.1241	8.0845	8.0605
Ecuador (US Dollar)	1.0000	1.0000	1.0000	1.0000
Hong Kong (Dollar)	.1282	.1282	7.7995	7.7987
Hungary (Forint)	.003776	.003746	264.83	266.93
India (Rupee)	.02042	.02040	48.960	49.010
Indonesia (Rupiah)	.0001107	.0001106	9035	9040
Israel (Shekel)	.2056	.2060	4.8640	4.8550
Japan (Yen)	.008057	.007974	124.11	125.40
1-month forward	.008070	.007988	123.91	125.19
3-months forward	.008095	.008012	123.53	124.81
6-months forward	.008141	.008057	122.84	124.11
Jordan (Dinar)	1.4124	1.4124	.7080	.7080

	U.S. $ EQUIVALENT		CURRENCY PER U.S. $	
Country	Tue.	Mon.	Tue.	Mon.
Kuwait (Dinar)	3.2862	3.2798	.3043	.3049
Lebanon (Pound)	.0006605	.0006604	1514.13	1514.25
Malaysia (Ringgit)-b	.2632	.2632	3.8001	3.8000
Malta (Lira)	2.2660	2.2671	.4413	.4411
Mexico (Peso)				
Floating rate	.1052	.1053	9.5035	9.4985
New Zealand (Dollar)	.4687	.4679	2.1336	2.1372
Norway (Krone)	.1221	.1223	8.1899	8.1769
Pakistan (Rupee)	.01665	.01665	60.075	60.075
Peru (new Sol)	.2885	.2889	3.4660	3.4619
Philippines (Peso)	.02022	.02027	49.455	49.325
Poland (Zloty)	.2441	.2453	4.0963	4.0760
Russia (Ruble)-a	.03198	.03198	31.273	31.273
Saudi Arabia (Riyal)	.2666	.2666	3.7505	3.7505
Singapore (Dollar)	.5587	.5587	1.7900	1.7900
Slovak Rep. (Koruna)	.02113	.02131	47.322	46.918
South Africa (Rand)	.0992	.0999	10.0790	10.0150
South Korea (Won)	.0008035	.0008009	1244.60	1248.60
Sweden (Krona)	.1002	.1001	9.9770	9.9941
Switzerland (Franc)	.6341	.6344	1.5771	1.5763
1-month forward	.6344	.6348	1.5762	1.5754
3-months forward	.6351	.6354	1.5746	1.5738
6-months forward	.6364	.6366	1.5714	1.5708
Taiwan (Dollar)	.02914	.02910	34.320	34.360
Thailand (Baht)	.02347	.02347	42.600	42.600
Turkey (Lira)	.00000071	.00000070	1407500	1434000
United Arab (Dirham)	.2723	.2722	3.6730	3.6731
Uruguay (Peso)				
Financial	.05790	.05792	17.270	17.265
Venezuela (Bolivar)	.001005	.001000	995.50	1000.50
SDR	1.2799	1.2799	.7813	.7813
Euro	.9203	.9214	1.0866	1.0853

Special Drawing Rights (SDR) are based on exchange rates for the U.S., British, and Japanese currencies. Source: International Monetary Fund.

a-Russian Central Bank rate. b-Government rate. y-Floating rate.

Source: *The Wall Street Journal*, May 22, 2002. Reprinted by permission of Dow Jones & Company, Inc. (c) 2002 Dow Jones & Company, Inc. All Rights Reserved Worldwide.

Use the above table from the *WSJ* to answer the following questions.

1. Find the U.S. $ Equivalent rate for the Australian Dollar. By how much has this rate changed from the previous day's trading?

2. Relative to the U.S. Dollar, did the Australian Dollar appreciate or depreciate?

3. find the amount of Philippine Pesos necessary to purchase one U.S. Dollar. By how much has this rate changed from the previous day's trading?

4. Relative to the Philippine Peso, did the U.S. Dollar appreciate or depreciate this day?

Spot Rates and Forward Rates

The exchange rates you found in Exercise 8-1 are *spot rates.* The spot exchange rate is a quote for an immediate transaction, the amount of one currency that may be exchanged for another currency today. The commercial banks and forex dealers also serve their clients by providing the contracts for the exchange of currencies in the future. The *forward rate* is the exchange rate, determined today, of foreign currency delivered at some future date. Forward exchange contracts help international businesses hedge against the risk that the currency they plan to receive from, or use in, their foreign operations will not be worth as much in the future as it is today. Speculators may also use forward contracts to speculate on the future price of foreign currency.

Forward exchange rates may be quoted at a premium or discount relative to the spot rate. When the forward U.S. $ Equivalent rate is lower than the spot rate the foreign currency is selling forward at a discount; or the exchange rate is at a *forward rate discount*. In this case, the foreign currency is expected to depreciate against the U.S. Dollar. When the forward U.S. $ Equivalent rate is higher than the spot rate the foreign currency is selling forward at a premium; or the exchange rate is at a *forward rate premium.* In this case, the foreign currency is expected to appreciate against the U.S. Dollar. Using the U.S. $ Equivalent rate, the expected annual rate of change in the value of the foreign currency relative to the U.S. Dollar is found by subtracting the spot rate from the forward rate, dividing by the spot rate and annualizing.

Expected rate of change = (Forward Rate – Spot Rate)/ Spot Rate x 360/n

In this formula, *n* is the number of days forward for the given forward rate. For example, on Thursday, March 14, 2002 the six-month forward rate (U.S. $ Equivalent) for one British Pound was 1.4064. The spot rate was 1.4207. The expected rate of change in the value of the British Pound over the next six months is

Expected rate of change $= (1.4064 - 1.4207)/ 1.4207 \times 360/180 = -0.02$ or -2%

On March 14, 2002, the British pound was expected to depreciate relative to the U.S. Dollar. at an annual rate of 2% over the next six months. The Currency Trading Column of the *WSJ* reports forward rates of 1, 3, and 6 months for most major currencies. It is important to remember, however, that these are only expected rates, not perfect forecasts. The future value of a currency will be determined by many factors.

Exercise 8-2

Using the Currency Trading Column from Exercise 8-1 to answer the following questions.

1. Find the U.S. $ Equivalent forward rates for the Canadian Dollar. Is the Canadian Dollar selling at a forward premium or a forward discount?

2. Find the U.S. $ Equivalent forward rates for the Swiss Franc. Is the Swiss Franc selling at a forward premium or a forward discount?

3. Based on the six-month forward rate, calculate the expected annual rate of appreciation or depreciation in each of these currencies.

Cross Rates

The quotation tables we have been using so far express the value of currencies relative to the U.S. Dollar. For many reasons, international firms and other traders in the foreign exchange market need the exchange rate for two currencies other than the U.S. Dollar. For example, a U.S. multinational corporation may need to exchange Japanese Yen received from its Asian operations for Mexican Pesos needed to fund its manufacturing operations in Mexico. This company wants to know the value of the Yen in terms of Pesos, or the Yen/MexPeso exchange rate. This *cross rate* can be found using the U.S. $ Equivalent rates used above. The Yen/MexPeso cross rate equals the exchange rate of the Yen in terms of U.S. Dollars divided by the exchange rate of the Mexican Peso in terms of U.S. Dollars.

For example, if the U.S. $ Equivalent value of the Japanese Yen is 0.007737 and the U.S. $ Equivalent value of the Mexican Peso is 0.1097, the value of the Yen in terms of Pesos is

Yen/MexPeso Cross Rates =

U.S. $ Equivalent for Yen / U.S. $ Equivalent for Mexican
Pesos

Yen/MexPeso Cross Rates = 0.007737 / 0.1097 = 0.07052.

Thus, a Yen is worth 0.07052 of a Peso. Of course, the exchange rate can also be expressed as the value of Mexican Peso in terms of Yen. This can be found by taking the reciprocal of the Yen/MexPeso cross rate. In this example, the value of the Mexican Peso in terms of Yen is 1/.07052, or 14.18.

Exercise 8-3

The *WSJ* reports cross rates for major currencies (in terms of trading volume) based on the quotes given by commercial banks in New York at 4 p.m. Eastern Time the previous day. For each currency listed in the first column, the exchange rate is given as the currency needed to purchase one unit of the currency listed in the subsequent column headings. Use the Key Currency Cross Rates chart included in the Currency Trading column from Exercise 8-1 to answer the following questions.

1. Find the value of the Euro in terms of Japanese Yen. That is, how many Japanese Yen are needed to purchase one unit of the Euro? Verify this rate using the U.S. $ Equivalent rate for the Euro and the Yen from the table given for Exercise 8-1.

2. To calculate the previous day's cross rate find the U.S. $ Equivalent rate for the Euro and the Yen for the previous trading day from the table given in Exercise 8-1. By how much has this cross rate changed from the previous day's trading?

3. In terms of Yen, has the Euro appreciated or depreciated?

Parity Conditions

A basic economic principle states that the prices of similar goods in different locations must be equal. If it were not so, supply and demand conditions in each location would change until it was true. For example, if Canadian wheat is currently selling for much less than U.S. wheat of similar quality, more firms will begin purchasing Canadian wheat and transporting it to where it is needed. If nothing else is changing, it shouldn't take long for the price differential to disappear. As demand for Canadian wheat increases, the price rises closer to the level of the U.S. wheat. The economic *law of one price* theory states the prices of similar goods in all countries should be equal when translated to a common currency.

Inflation is an increase in the overall price level of a country. When the overall price of goods in a country is rising, the purchasing power of that country's currency declines. For the law of one price to hold, exchange rates must vary with inflation to provide similar values for currencies across countries. This condition is known as *purchasing power parity* (PPP). For example, assume that the current spot rate for the British Pound is $1.42, and inflation in Britain and the United States is 3 percent annually. If inflation in the United States increases to 5% while inflation in Britain remains at 3%, PPP predicts that the British Pound will appreciate by 2% against the U.S. Dollar. As U.S. prices rise, demand for British goods rises. The increase demand for British goods leads to an increase in the supply of U.S. Dollars in exchange for the British Pound. This increase supply of Dollars and increased demand for Pounds increases the value of the Pound in terms of Dollars.

Of course PPP does not hold exactly –other factors also affect the value of one currency in terms of another. However, countries that experience high levels of inflation will see their currencies decline in value. In turn, countries that experience low levels of inflation or a decline in prices will see their currencies increase in value. PPP is more likely to be a long-run condition only. That is, exchange rates tend to reflect long-run differences in prices, but short-run differences may exist.

The following charts from the March 14, 2002 issue of the *WSJ* show recent exchange rate values and prices for the United States.

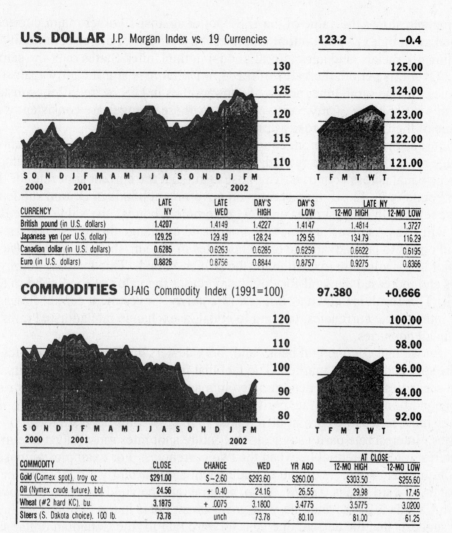

U.S. DOLLAR J.P. Morgan Index vs. 19 Currencies

123.2   −0.4

CURRENCY	LATE NY	LATE WED	DAY'S HIGH	DAY'S LOW	LATE NY	
					12-MO HIGH	12-MO LOW
British pound (in U.S. dollars)	1.4207	1.4149	1.4227	1.4147	1.4814	1.3727
Japanese yen (per U.S. dollar)	129.25	129.49	128.24	129.55	134.79	116.29
Canadian dollar (in U.S. dollars)	0.6285	0.6263	0.6285	0.6259	0.6622	0.6195
Euro (in U.S. dollars)	0.8826	0.8756	0.8844	0.8757	0.9275	0.8366

COMMODITIES DJ-AIG Commodity Index (1991=100)

97.380   +0.666

COMMODITY	CLOSE	CHANGE	WED	YR AGO	AT CLOSE	
					12-MO HIGH	12-MO LOW
Gold (Comex spot), troy oz	$291.00	$−2.60	$293.60	$260.00	$303.50	$255.60
Oil (Nymex crude future), bbl.	24.56	+ 0.40	24.16	26.55	29.98	17.45
Wheat (#2 hard KC), bu.	3.1875	+ .0075	3.1800	3.4775	3.5775	3.0200
Steers (S. Dakota choice), 100 lb.	73.78	unch	73.78	80.10	81.00	61.25

Source: *The Wall Street Journal*, March 14, 2002. Reprinted by permission of Dow Jones & Company, Inc. (c) 2002 Dow Jones & Company, Inc. All Rights Reserved Worldwide.

The top graph shows the value of the U.S. Dollar against 19 other major currencies (reported as an index). The bottom graph shows an index of major commodity prices (including oil, metals, and agricultural goods) in the United States over the same period. Over this period, the value of the U.S. Dollar rose significantly against other currencies. At the same time, prices of commodities in U.S. were falling substantially. While this is not proof of any parity conditions, these changes are consistent with PPP- the value of the U.S. Dollar rose as prices fell.

Just as prices in different countries will tend to be equal, by adjustments in the exchange rates, the exchange rate adjusted rate of return on similar investments will tend to be equal across countries. Suppose again that the current spot rate for the British Pound is $1.42. If interest rates on government bonds in Britain suddenly increase relative to interest rates on U.S. government bonds, the value of the British Pound will rise. As investors sell U.S. bonds and exchange their U.S. Dollars for British Pounds to take advantage of higher rates in Britain, there is an increase in the supply of U.S. Dollars in exchange for the British Pound. This increase supply of Dollars and increased demand for Pounds increases the value of the Pound in terms of Dollars. This result is known as ***interest rate parity*** - investment capital flows towards higher interest rate currencies, tending to equalize exchange rate adjusted rates of return in all countries.

Recall that commercial banks and forex dealers provide exchange rates for both the spot and forward market. The fact that investors can easily invest in money market securities and bonds denominated in many different currencies gives rise to a special condition of interest rate parity. The forward premium or discount for any currency must reflect the current differential in interest rates between the two countries. Interest rate parity suggests that future spot rates must adjust to eliminate any interest rate differential between the two currencies. For example, suppose the U.S. $ Equivalent spot rate on the Canadian Dollar is currently 0.6285, and the current six-month forward rate is 0.6274. Also, assume that the yield on one-year government notes in Canada is 3.5%, and one-year government notes in the U.S. is 3%. Interest Parity suggests that the current one year forward rate for the Canadian dollar should be 0.5% lower. That is, the Canadian Dollar should trade at a forward discount. The exchange rate will adjust to equate the real rate of return on these two investments.

The *WSJ* reports on the interest rate differentials between the U.S., Japan, the United Kingdom, Germany, and Canada. Included in the Bond Market Data Bank are interest rates on international government bonds. The rates reported are for maturities similar to the U.S. Treasury 2-year, 3-year, 5-year, and 10-year Notes.

Exercise 8-4

Bond Market Data Bank

May 21, 2002

Bond Yields

Treasury Issues*

MATURITY	COUPON	PRICE	YIELD
04/30/04	3.375	100.08	3.232
05/15/05	6.750	108.05	3.822
05/15/07	4.375	99.18	4.473
02/15/12	4.875	97.29	5.151
02/15/31	5.375	95.29	5.666

*Most recent auctions.

Municipal Issues †(Comparable Maturities)

AAA YIELD	TAX EQUIV	MUNI/TREAS YIELD RATIO	52-WEEK RATIO HIGH	52-WEEK RATIO LOW
2.49	3.60	76.9	94.8	65.6
2.93	4.25	76.7	90.4	67.5
3.51	5.08	78.4	89.4	72.3
4.28	6.21	83.1	91.1	79.1
5.28	7.65	93.2	103.1	89.9

†From Delphis Hanover. Tax equiv. based on 31% bracket.

International Government Bonds

COUPON	MATURITY MO/YR	PRICE	CHANGE	YIELD*	COUPON	MATURITY MO/YR	PRICE	CHANGE	YIELD*
Japan (3 p.m. Tokyo)					**Germany (5 p.m. London)**				
4.10%	06/04	108.38	−0.01	0.06%	4.25%	02/05	99.52	+0.12	4.433%
3.30	06/06	111.92	−0.05	0.34	5.00	02/06	101.04	+0.11	4.684
1.40	03/12	100.09	−0.08	1.39	5.00	01/12	98.69	+0.09	5.172
2.00	03/22	99.65	−0.14	2.03	5.50	01/31	99.77	+0.27	5.514
United Kingdom (5 p.m. London)					**Canada (3 p.m. Eastern Time)**				
8.00%	06/03	103.46	....	4.590%	5.00%	12/03	101.63	+0.05	3.889%
7.50	12/06	108.93	+0.03	5.264	5.00	09/04	101.43	+0.10	4.328
5.00	03/12	97.94	+0.03	5.271	6.00	06/08	103.38	+0.28	5.337
4.25	06/32	87.49	+0.05	5.062	8.00	06/27	125.88	+0.74	5.991

*Equivalent to semi-annual compounded yields to maturity

Source: *The Wall Street Journal*, May 22, 2002. Reprinted by permission of Dow Jones & Company, Inc. (c) 2002 Dow Jones & Company, Inc. All Rights Reserved Worldwide.

Use the above table from the *WSJ* to answer the following questions.

1. Compare the yields on U.S. government bonds to similar dated bonds in Japan. Are interest rates in Japan higher or lower than those in the United States?

2. According to interest rate parity, should the Japanese Yen be selling at a forward discount or premium? Check your answer using the U.S. $ equivalent spot and forward rates from the table in Exercise 8-1.

Project 8-1

Repeat Exercises 8-1 and 8-2 using a recent edition of the *WSJ*.

Date _____

1. Find the U.S. $ Equivalent rate for the Australian Dollar. By how much has this rate changed from the previous day's trading? Relative to the U.S. Dollar, did the Australian Dollar appreciate or depreciate?

2. Find the amount of Philippine Pesos necessary to purchase one U.S. Dollar. By how much has this rate changed from the previous day's trading? Relative to the Philippine Peso, did the U.S. Dollar appreciate or depreciate this day?

3. Find the U.S. $ Equivalent forward rates for the Canadian Dollar. Is the Canadian Dollar selling at a forward premium or a forward discount?

4. Find the U.S. $ Equivalent forward rates for the Swiss Franc. Is the Swiss Franc selling at a forward premium or a forward discount?

5. Based on the six-month forward rate, calculate the expected annual rate of appreciation or depreciation in the Canadian Dollar and the Swiss Franc.

Project 8-2

U.S. investors in foreign markets must be concerned with the effect of changes in exchange rates on their investments. The return potential of any foreign investment can be severely affected by changes in the local currency relative to the U.S. dollar. In the World Stock Markets section of the *WSJ*, trading activity and pricing information is reported for many stock markets around the world. The Dow Jones Country Indexes are recorded and reported for more than 30 countries. These indexes are reported in U.S. dollar terms, while major indexes for many of these countries are reported in terms of their local currency. Using a recent addition of the *WSJ*, complete the table below for the Dow Jones Country Index values and their percentage change from the previous day. Also find the percentage change in their currency's value relative to the U.S. dollar and answer the following questions.

COUNTRY	Dow Jones Country Index (In U.S. dollar terms)	% CHG.	Current currency value (U.S. $ EQUIVALENT)	Previous day's currency value (U.S. $ EQUIVALENT)	%CHG.
Canada					
Mexico					
Germany					
Switzerland					
Australia					
Japan					

1. Which stock market had the greatest gain in value (in terms of U.S. dollars)?

2. Which currencies rose in value, and which currencies fell in value against the U.S. dollar?

3. For which countries was the stock market gain or loss in U.S. dollar terms largely due to changes in the local currency value?

Discussion Questions

As Optimism Buoys Currencies, Many in Asia Grow Nervous

By Phillip Day

SINGAPORE—A surge in Asian currencies against the U.S. dollar is exposing a paradox for governments and central banks in the region: when their currencies rise on expectations of economic recovery, the rise hurts exporters and threatens to nip any recovery in the bud.

As a result, officials in Tokyo and Seoul have been trying to talk down the currency markets in recent days with threats to buy dollars.

"I don't believe the unusual moves of the last few days reflect (economic) fundamentals. We are ready to take the proper measures, if necessary," Japanese Vice Finance Minister for International Affairs Haruhiko Kuroda said yesterday.

But officials are reluctant to actually intervene when currencies are reflecting increasing optimism about their economies. Much of the renewed enthusiasm for Asian assets springs from the assumption that the U.S. recovery is just around the corner, and the demand for Asian exports will soon grow because of it.

In just the past week, the yen has gained more than 3.5% against the dollar, while the South Korean won is up almost 5%. Other Asian currencies have also risen: the Indonesian rupiah is up more than 4%, while the Philippines peso has gained more than 3%. The gains make exports

---

A weakening dollar raises concerns that U.S. investors will pull back funds.

---

from those countries to the U.S. relatively less competitive, threatening the economic expansion that is driving the currencies up.

The currency moves are particularly painful for countries that are the most dependent on exports for growth, such as Singapore and Taiwan, although South Korea, for one, has tried to diversify its economy after the implosion of the technology bubble showed the danger of overdependence. But even in economies where exports are a small percentage of gross domestic product, rising local currencies and a falling dollar could hurt.

In Japan, for example, exports make up only about 10% of GDP. But the export sector is the most dynamic of the economy, says Mark Matthews, Asia-Pacific strategist for Standard & Poor's Equity. Japanese car companies, for example, have been making gains overseas while domestic consumption continues to languish. "With local consumption so flat, any marginal increase in exports has a very big impact in Japan," he says.

A weakening dollar also raises concerns that foreigners will begin to pull back funds from the U.S., because it will make their investments worth less when translated back to their local currencies. Any pullback could knock the dollar down further, spawning a troubling cycle, analysts say.

Indeed, part of the reason for the currency gains is that stock market investors are returning to Asia. For example, foreigners were net buyers of Japanese and Korean stocks last week to the tune of about $582 million and $150 million respectively.

Currency traders are making the same

Good News, Bad News

Stronger Asian currencies...

Year-to-date change in the U.S.-dollar value

South Korean Won +5.2%

Japanese Yen +5

Singapore dollar +3.2

Taiwan dollar +1.8

Could throw the region's export rebound off course

Year-to-year change in merchandise exports

Singapore* South Korea Taiwan

bet as some global stock investors: given the lingering questions about the U.S. economic rebound and the still-high prices for shares of U.S. companies, Asia seems a safer place to be right now.

"Right now, given all the questions about the U.S., Asia is a much cheaper and much cleaner proxy for the U.S. recovery," says Mr. Matthews of Standard & Poor's Equity.

1. According to the article, what is the cause of the recent appreciation in the value of Asian currencies?

2. Why is the weakening dollar a concern for foreign investors?

3. How have the government's of Japan and Korea responded to the recent strengthening of their currencies?

PART IV

INVESTMENT ANALYSIS

Chapter 9

Financial Statements

Objectives

1. Understand the three basic financial statements of the corporation.

2. Learn some important ratios used to analyze company performance.

3. Learn how to use the Digest of Earnings Reports in the *WSJ* to review a firm's financial performance.

4. Use financial statement and pricing information in the *WSJ* to forecast stock prices.

Key Terms

Fundamental Analysis	Cash Flow Statement	Price to Sales
Income Statement	After-tax Profit Margin	Ratio
Balance Sheet	Payout Ratio	

In this chapter we explore one of two main areas of, or approaches to, investment analysis – fundamental analysis. *Fundamental analysis* is an examination of corporate accounting reports to assess the value of the company. The *WSJ* regularly reviews the accounting statement reports from many companies and contains a tremendous amount of information that investors can use to analyze a company's stock prices. In this chapter we will review the daily information available in the *WSJ* and discuss other sources of financial information. We will also use the *WSJ* information to calculate a few ratios that are useful in assessing the financial outlook of companies.

Financial Statements

In many ways, financial statements are the story of a company. Financial statements provide shareholders and other interested parties a view of the company's operation and current position. These statements tell anyone reading them how the company operated, bought and sold goods, over the indicated period and what remained after these operations. There are three primary, and interrelated, financial statements: the income statement, the balance sheet, and the cash flow statement. Following is a brief review of each statement. In the United States, all public companies are required to prepare and distribute these financial statements.

The *Income Statement* summarizes the revenue received from the sales of the firm's goods and the expenses associated with these sales for the given period. The statement begins with the firm's total sales and subtracts cost of goods sold (expenses directly related to production of the product) to determine gross profit. From gross profit all other operating expenses, such as administrative payrolls, insurance, and other office expenses, are deducted to find operating profit. From operating profit, all expenses associated with capitalizing the business, such as interest expense, plus any income the company received in its investments is subtracted to determine the net income of the company.

The subtraction of expenses from the revenues gives the company's net income, or profits. Thus, the income statement is a firm's measure of profit. The profits of the company are used to either pay dividends to its shareholders, providing a return on their investment, or retained for future growth. Therefore, the income statement is an important reporting source for determining the worth of a company's stock. Without profits, either now or in the future, a company will not be worth anything.

The *Balance Sheet* of the company reflects the firms assets and liabilities for a given date. The balance sheet is a picture of the company at any given point in time. This statement shows what the company owns and how these assets were financed (i.e., borrowed money or investor equity). The assets of a company, what it owns, can be attributed to either the company's lenders (its liabilities), or its owners. Subtracting the firm's total liabilities from its total assets determines stockholder's equity. In other words, by subtracting what is owed to lenders (suppliers, bankers, etc.) from what the firm owns (i.e., its assets) you can determine what is left for the owners.

Both assets and liabilities are generally grouped by their age. That is, assets and liabilities are usually separated by the length of time that they are used or due. For example, current assets are those assets that can be used or sold quickly by the firm. These include any cash the company currently holds and any inventory that can be sold immediately. Current liabilities are the bills and other commitments that the company must pay soon (within one year). The other categories on a balance sheet are long-term, or fixed, assets, and long-term liabilities. Fixed assets include the company's plant and equipment, or any assets that will be held more than one year. Long-term liabilities include debt and other obligations that are not due to be paid within the year.

The third financial statement serves in one manner to reconcile the previous two. The *Cash Flow Statement* is an analysis of the firm's sources of cash and its uses of cash. The cash flow statement begins with the net income reported on the income statement. Added to net income is any item on the income statement that did not involve cash, such as depreciation. Then, any changes in the balance sheets current assets and current liabilities are added to or subtracted from this value to determine the firm's cash from operations. Next, cash from investing activity is measured by subtracting cash used for investment purposes and adding cash received from the sale of investments. Next, any cash raised from borrowing or selling of stock is measured to determine the firm's cash from financing activity. The statement then summarizes these three areas, cash from operations, cash from investing activity, and cash from financing activity, to calculate the net change in cash from the beginning to end of the period.

As you can see, the cash flow statement reconciles the income statement and the balance sheet by showing how the firm raised cash over the period (through profits, borrowing, selling stock, etc.) with how it used it cash (building inventories, building plants, paying debt, etc.). It is important to note that net income, or profits, and cash flow are not the same thing. Even if a company has high profits, these profits may not be available to shareholders because the company has not received cash for all its sales or it used the cash for new investment or to pay off debt. This is why the cash flow statement is just as important as the income statement and balance sheet when analyzing a company.

The *WSJ* reports on the financial statement reports of all major companies in the U.S. and abroad. Public companies in the U.S. are required to prepare and release financial statements each quarter of their fiscal year. The *WSJ* reports on these quarterly reports and discusses the financial results included in each report. Often, the *WSJ* article will include a comparison of the reporting firm's financial results to the previous year's or quarter's results and to the expected results of professional security analysts.

Exercise 9-1

On May 21, 2002 the *WSJ* reported the latest financial statement results of Limited, Inc., a retailing company. Use the following information from the article to answer the questions below:

"Net income for the fiscal first quarter ended May 4 rose to $49.9 million from $30.7 million for the same period a year earlier"

"Sales for the period fell 4.7% to $2 billion from $2.1 billion in the same period last year"

1. On which of the three financial statements would the above financial information be reported.

2. According to the information, were expenses during the period higher or lower?

3. Since Limited, Inc.'s net income was higher for the period, is it true that the company also had more cash flow for the period?

Ratio Analysis

To make comparisons across different time periods and different companies, it is useful to convert much of the information contained in the financial statements to ratios. Financial ratio analysis involves transforming the accounting numbers found in financial statements to provide a better understanding of a firm's performance and position. Financial ratios tell the analyst how efficient the firm is at employing its resources. There are many different ratios that may be calculated using all three financial statements. In this section we will look at two – profit margin and payout ratio.

Profit margins identify how efficiently the management of a company is utilizing its resources. Firms with high profit margins are able to generate more profit for a given level of expenses. Profit margins can then be useful for comparison of efficiency by scaling a company's earnings. The ***After-tax profit margin*** of a firm is equal to net income divided by sales. For example, a firm with $20 billion in sales and net income of $2 billion has an after-tax profit margin of 10%. Although this firm has large profits, they are equally as efficient as a firm with only $2 million in sales and $200,000 in profits. Profit margins therefore make comparisons between the performance of two companies of much different size possible. It is also important to analyze profits margins over time. Companies that show increasing profit levels, but declining profit margins, may be losing their competitive position.

It is also important for investors to analyze the strategies the company has in place for future growth. If a company's current strategy is to pay out most of its earnings it will not have cash available when new opportunities come about. A company that pays out all or much of their earnings is essentially telling its shareholders that they do not foresee a great deal of growth potential in their industry. The ***payout ratio*** is calculated by dividing the dividends per share by the firm's earnings per share. Earnings per share is calculated by dividing net income by the number of shares outstanding. Low payout ratios are normally found in industries with high expectations for future growth, while high payout ratios are associated with more mature industries.

Exercise 9-2

DIGEST OF CORPORATE EARNINGS REPORTS

COMPANY	PERIOD	REV (mill)	% CHG	INC CT OP (mill)	NET (mill)	% CHG	PER SHARE CURR	PREV	% CHG
Aqua Care Systems... AQCR (Sc)	Q3/31	1.91	-44	(0.45)	(0.45)	...	(.14)	(.13)	...
Arrow-Magnolia... ARWM (Sc)	Yr12/31	13.6	-4.4	...	a0.36	-54	.10	.22	-55
a-Includes a settlement charge of $125,000.									
Balchem Corp... BCP (A) ▲	Q3/31	14.4	79	...	1.44	29	.29	.23	26
British Airways... BAB (N)	Q3/31	1,953	-7.9	...	a(43.0)	...	...	...	...
	Yr	8,340	-10	...	a(142.0)	...			
Amounts in British pounds. a-Includes charges of 70,000,000 in the quarter and gains of 65,000,000 in the year, related to restructuring and sale of assets and investments.									
Cambridge Antibody... CATG (Nq)	6mo3/31	4.85	43	...	(9.15)	...	...	...	...
Amounts in British pounds.									
Charming Shoppes... CHRS (Nq) ▲	Q5/4	630.6	60	...	16.3	95	.14	.08	75
DRS Technologies... DRS (N)	Q3/31	156.4	20	...	6.60	50	.38	.34	12
	Yr	517.2	21	...	20.3	69	1.41	1.01	40
2002 reflects a change in method of accounting and recent acquisitions.									
Environ Elements... EEC (A)	Q3/31	16.2	-6.4	...	0.13	-21	.02	.02	...
	Yr	71.9	18	...	1.48	...	.20	(.88)	...
GMX Resouces... GMXR (Nq) ▼	Q3/31	1.72	21	...	0.10	-73	.01	.10	-90
GameStop Corp... GME (N) P	13wk5/4	271.4	35	...	4.91	...	.08	(.20)	...
Gart Sports Co... GRTS (Nq) ▲	13wk5/4	245.0	51	...	2.59	328	.22	.08	175
Global e-Point... GEPT (Nq)	Yr12/31	0.44	472	a(1.91)	1.23	...	.27	(.78)	...
a-Includes a charge of $477,000 from restructuring.									
IXYS Corp... SYXI (Nq) L	Q3/31	20.4	-36	...	(0.58)	...	(.02)	.13	...
	Yr	82.8	-26	...	1.94	-86	.07	.49	-86
Revised by company.									
Imperial Cred Ind... ICII (Nq) L	Q3/31	...	...	(18.2)	(18.6)	...	(.44)	.01	...
Jos. A. Bank Cloth... JOSB (Nq) ▲	Q5/4	55.8	18	...	1.73	242	.25	.08	213
Limited Inc... LTD (N) ▲	13wk5/4	2,027	-4.7	...	a49.9	62	.10	.07	43
a-Includes a pretax nonrecurring charge of $33,808,000.									
Longs Drug Stores... LDG (N) L	13wk5/2	1,090	5.6	11.0	(13.7)	...	(.36)	.31	...
2002 reflects a change in method of accounting.									
Lowe's Companies... LOW (N) ▲	13wk5/3	6,471	23	...	345.8	54	.44	.29	52
Major Automotive... MAJR (Nq) ▼	Q3/31	91.3	3.7	...	0.55	-30	.06	.11	-45
Makita Corp... MKTAY (Nq)	Yr3/31	170,529	6.5	...	133.0	-94	...	...	...
Amounts in Japanese yen.									
Milestone Scient... MS (A)	Q3/31	1.02	-19	...	(0.52)	...	(.04)	(.12)	...
Overhill Corp... OVH (A) L	Q3/31	10.6	22	(0.22)	(0.18)	...	(.01)	.02	...
	6 mo	19.4	14	(0.35)	(0.32)	...	(.02)	.03	...

COMPANY	PERIOD	REV (mill)	% CHG	INC CT OP (mill)	NET (mill)	% CHG	PER SHARE CURR	PREV	% CHG
Pacific Magtron... PMK (Sc)	Q3/31	17.6	-12	...	(0.74)	...	.07	.05	...
Pro-Dex Inc... PDEX (Sc)	Q3/31	2.51	-24	(0.10)	(0.34)	...	(.04)	(.04)	...
	9 mo	7.84	-36	(0.38)	(0.85)	...	(.10)	.01	...
Radica Games Ltd... RADA (Nq)	Q3/31	17.5	49	...	(1.57)	...	(.09)	(.21)	...
Rurban Financial... RBNF (Nq) ▼	Q3/31	...	...	...	0.21	-87	.05	.35	-86
SED Int'l Hldgs... SECXD (Nq)	Q3/31	117.4	-18	...	a(1.15)	...	(.30)	(.15)	...
	9 mo	351.5	-14	a(4.41)	(10.7)	...	(2.76)	(.06)	...
2002 reflects a change in method of accounting. a-Includes a nonrecurring charge of $362,000.									
Smartserv Online... SSOL (Nq)	Q3/31	0.03	-98	...	(4.11)	...	(.66)	(.68)	...
Tat Technologies... TATTF (Sc)	Q3/31	5.86	-16	...	0.85	-1.6	.19	.19	...
Telekomunik Indo... TLK (N) ▲	Q3/31	4,431,019	30	...	1,498,764	46	...	...	...
Amounts in Indonesian rupiah.									
Toys "R" Us Inc... TOY (N)	13wk5/4	2,095	1.6	...	(4.00)	...	(.02)	(.09)	...
Tweeter Home Ent... TWTR (Nq) ▲	Q3/31	185.8	58	...	2.59	-31	.11	.20	-45
	6 mo	437.7	56	...	16.1	19	.66	.71	-7.0
Tyco Int'l... TYC (N) L	Q3/31	9,815	11	a(1,905)	(1,905)	...	(.96)	.62	...
	6 mo	19,883	15	a(450.9)	(454.4)	...	(.23)	.80	...
2002 reflects a change in method of accounting. a-Includes nonrecurring charges of $2,816,600,000 in the quarter and $2,836,500,000 in the six months.									
Unifab Int'l Inc... UFAB (Nq)	Q3/31	9.86	-55	...	(2.14)	...	(.26)	(.20)	...
Company has changed its fiscal year-end from March 31, to a calendar year.									
US Timberlands... TIMBZ (Nq)	Q3/31	2.15	-77	...	(9.07)	...	(.70)	(.68)	...
Union Acceptance... UACA (Nq) L	Q3/31	...	...	...	a(6.93)	...	(.22)	.49	...
Company has changed its fiscal year end from June 30 to a calendar year. a-Includes a nonrecurring net charge of $12,000,000 or 39 cents a share.									
United Online Inc... UNTD (Nq)	Q3/31	50.9	299	...	a(7.25)	...	(.19)	(3.95)	...
	9 mo	113.1	150	...	a(45.1)	...	(1.32)	(7.27)	...
a-Includes restructuring charges of $680,000 in the quarter and $3,115,000 in the nine months.									
USA Interactive... USAI (Nq)	Q3/31	1,373	4.6	25.9	(284.7)	...	(.73)	(.07)	...
2002 reflects a change in method of accounting.									
Wilshire Oil-Texas... WOC (A) ▲	Q3/31	5.02	-25	...	0.29	-72	.04	.13	-69

EXPLANATORY NOTES

Revenue, income and net figures are in millions, except * indicates full amount. INC CT OP figure is income from continuing operations, if applicable; otherwise it is income before extraordinary items or accounting adjustments. PREV under per share indicates year-earlier period. Figures in parentheses are losses.

▲ indicates net income increase of 25% or more. ▼ indicates net income decrease of 25% or more. P-Profit in latest period vs. year-earlier loss. L-Loss in latest period vs. year-earlier profit.

(N)-New York Stock Exchange (A)-American Stock Exchange (Pa)-Pacific
(Nq)-Nasdaq National Market (Sc)-Nasdaq Small Cap (C)-Chicago
(P)-Philadelphia (B)-Boston (T)-Toronto (F)-Foreign

WSJ.com

For more detailed earnings reports, go to WSJ.com. Five-day archive available

NEW YORK STOCK EXCHANGE COMPOSITE TRANSACTIONS

L

YTD %CHG	52-WEEK HI	LO	STOCK (SYM)	DIV	YLD %	PE	VOL 100s	CLOSE	NET CHG
3.7	4.44	2.01	LLE RoyalTr LRT	.32e	14.1	...	253	2.27	0.0?
15.6	38.44	25.90◆	LNR Prop LNR	.05	.1	9	878	36.05	-0.6?
-18.9	25.05	9.70	LSI Logic LSI	...		dd	21865	12.79	-0.1?
28.3	8.42	4	LTC Prop LTC	.20e	2.5	...	142	8.15	-0.1?
39.4	133.56	60.70	L3Comm LLL	...		39	7204	125.50	-1.8?
-2.3	67	63.60	L3Comm wi n	...			10	64.50	-0.3?
26.0	8.04	3.60	LaQuintaCorp LQI	...		dd	1664	7.23	-0.1?
30.6	30.94	14.70	LaZ Boy LZB	.40f	1.4	37	1904	28.50	-0.31
67.7	9.43	2.75	LaborRdy LRW	...		41	743	8.57	0.2?
20.0	52.38	32.64	LabCpAm LH s	...		33	5293	48.50	-0.3?
-17.2	45.17	19.11	LaBranche LAB	...		24	2631	28.53	-0.67
-1.5	25.48	21.75	LacledeGrp LG	1.34	5.7	23	150	23.55	0.21
12.0	25.50	17.35◆	Lafarge ADS LR n	.52e	2.0	...	12	25.60	0.10
16.6	45.15	28.60◆	LafargeNoAm LAF	.60	1.4	13	713	43.80	-0.30
-4.8	12.48	3.10	LamsonSes LMS	...		dd	172	5	...
-23.5	10.20	5.25	LanChil ADS LFL	.02e	.3	34	3	5.79	-0.06
13.0	37.10	23.20	LandAmFnl LFG	.20	.6	8	962	32.43	-0.39
19.5	41.91	27.25◆	Landauer LDR	1.40	3.5	24	126	40.46	-0.39
40.2	29.10	11.82	LandryRes LNY	.10	.4	20	2068	26.15	1.10
23.2	61.90	28.05	LandsEnd LE	...		24	3115	61.82	-0.05
21.3	18	6.89	LaSalleHtl LHO	.04	.3	95	178	14.24	-0.66
15.0	1.33	1.02	LaserMtg LMM s	3.00c		...	2	1.30	...
31.5	53.84	22.60	Lear LEA	...		50	2340	50.15	-0.48
6.3	40.09	29.40	LeeEnt LEE	.68	1.8	28	753	38.65	-0.64
11.8	57.15	34.25	LeggMason LM	.40	.7	25	2918	55.88	-1.09
15.4	27.40	16.85	LegPlatt LEG	.48	1.8	27	3839	26.55	-0.25
-0.3	10.30	9.44	Lehmn 2001-34 XKK n	.40p		...	80	9.97	-0.03
-0.8	25.50	24.20	LehCBTCS 2001-22 CXH n	1.91e	7.7	...	37	24.90	-0.15
0.0	26.50	24	Leh CBTCS 2001-25 CXO n	1.84e	7.4	...	4	25	0.30
-17.2	25.30	19.14	Lehmn 2001-33 XXU n	.91p		...	82	19.70	0.20
0.5	26.35	24.08	Leh CBTCS 2001-18 CLH n	1.35e	5.4	...	8	24.88	-0.01
-30.7	24.90	13.70	Lehmn 2001-35 XXOM n	.89p		...	127	15.30	0.10
-0.4	25.69	22.85	Leh CBTCS 2001-26 XXA n	1.40e	5.7	...	20	24.75	0.15
-6.0	25.20	22.50	*LehCBTCS 2001-32 n	.92e	4.1	...	66	22.55	-0.10
-22.8	10.20	7.15	LehCBTCS 2001-28 XXC n	.48e	6.7	...	35	7.20	-0.10
-8.3	26	19.30	LehCBTCS 2001-29 CYK n	1.62e	7.1	...	25	22.74	0.14
-1.7	26.75	24.20	LehCBTCS 2001-4 CYF	2.10e	8.3	...	1	25.35	-0.05
-1.6	26.30	23.81	Struc ABS n	1.27e	5.1	...	43	24.85	-0.05
-11.0	10.30	8.40	LehCBTCS 2001-31 XXE n	.45e	5.1	...	17	8.90	-0.10
10.8	10.15	6.02	LehCBTCS 2001-30 XXD n	.56e	6.4	...	27	8.75	-0.10
8.6	25	13.50	Leh CBTCS 2001-27 CWZ n	1.77e	7.8	...	39	22.80	-0.20
-0.4	27.10	24.90	LehCBTCS 2001-2	2.00e	7.7	...	12	26	0.15
-21.4	25.32	19.66	LehCBTCS 2001-21 CJO n	1.50e	7.6	...	3	19.73	0.07
8.2	26.30	19.36	LehCBTCS2001-19 CXC n	1.34e	6.0	...	18	22.15	-0.10
2.0	25.62	24.23	Leh CBTCS 2001-20 CXL n	1.94e	7.5	...	42	25.70	0.08
-1.9	82.90	43.50	LehmnHldg LEH	.36	.5	17	17938	65.55	-0.68
2.3	26.25	24.30	LehCBTCS 2001-5 CYG	2.13	8.4	...	62	25.30	-0.16
16.2	60.24	31.04	Lennar LEN	.05	.1	9	5364	54.42	-0.55
71.1	16.44	7.89	LennoxIntl LII	.38	2.3	dd	3982	16.60	0.23
21.1	38.16	26.31	LeucdaNat LUK	.25e	.7	78	291	34.95	-0.25
-1.5	16.40	13	LexgtnProp LXP	1.32	8.7	16	1399	15.26	-0.34
3.2	70.75	41.20	LexmarkInt LXK	...		31	14506	60.90	0.40
13.5	42.20	27	Libbey LBY	.30	.8	15	227	37.05	-0.05
-7.7	4.35	3	LibrteInvst LBI	.13e	3.6	dd	5	3.60	...
1.1	45	37.54	LbtyCp LC	.88	2.1	50	168	41.60	-0.30

YTD %CHG	52-WEEK HI	LO	STOCK (SYM)	DIV	YLD %	PE	VOL 100s	CLOSE	NET CHG
-16.9	18.04	9.75	LibertyM L	...		dd	58287	11.63	0.13
-18.4	18.82	10.85	LibertyM B LMCB	...		23	105	12.40	-0.04
9.3	34.70	25.60◆	LbtyProp LRY	2.36	7.2	15	930	32.62	-0.03
-18.5	88.47	62.79	EliLilly LLY	1.24	1.9	26	25215	64	-1.00
46.1	22.25	9	Limited LTD	.30	1.4	18	36480	21.50	-0.75
11.8	28.35	22.86	LinTVcorp TVL n	...			2512	27.95	0.34
-5.9	53.65	40	◆LncInNtl LNC	1.28	2.8	17	5717	45.71	-0.59
21.3	25.87	16.40	LindsayMfg LNN	.14	.6	29	102	23.48	...
37.3	37.35	17.37	LinenThings LIN	...		47	2002	35	-0.14
44.0	31.20	11.85	LithiaMtr A LAD	...		17	660	29.80	-0.17
28.8	32.45	18	LizClaib LIZ s	.23	.7	13	1433	32.03	-0.14
-0.3	48.85	39.10	LloydsGp ADS LYG n	1.50p		...	355	44.85	-0.49
30.6	63.48	35.36	LockhdMartin LMT	.44	.7	dd	15473	60.96	-0.74
4.3	72.50	41.05	LoewsCp LTR	.60	1.0	dd	4744	57.77	-0.62
-81.1	6.90	2.15	LndnPac ADS LDP	.13e	17.3	dd	10026	0.75	-1.45
41.8	50.74	10.10	LoneStarTch LSS	...		dd	1515	24.96	0.36
37.3	32	19.90	LongsDrg LDG	.56	1.7	25	2813	32.09	0.09
-14.6	13.98	8.30	LongvwFibr LFB	...		48	1614	10.09	0.10
-26.8	3.48	1.10	Loral Space LOR	...			21055	2.19	0.04
39.8	13.95	5.46	LA Pac LPX	...		dd	10063	11.80	-0.03
0.8	48.88	24.99	Lowes Cos LOW s	.08	.2	36	98541	46.80	2.04
-0.5	37.69	27.25	Lubrizol LZ	1.04	3.0	17	762	34.93	0.01
17.3	10.05	5.50	Lubys LUB	j	...	dd	101	6.70	-0.12
-86.6	3.81	3.50	LucentTch wi	...		dd	931	3.90	0.10
-21.7	10.50	3.78	LucentTch LU	...		dd	197940	4.93	0.02
18.2	20.90	11.60	LuxottGp LUX	.15e	.8	...	1023	19.48	-0.19
50.0	16.08	6.05◆	Lydall LDL	...		27	103	15	-0.75
19.7	17.65	9.45	Lyondell LYO	.90	5.2	dd	3825	17.16	-0.31

Source: *The Wall Street Journal*, May 21, 2002. Reprinted by permission of Dow Jones & Company, Inc. (c) 2002 Dow Jones & Company, Inc. All Rights Reserved Worldwide.

Use the above table and stock listings from the *WSJ* to answer the following questions.

1. What was Lowe's Companies after-tax profit margin for the quarter (13 weeks)?

2. Using the percentage change given for revenue and net income, calculate the revenue and net income for Lowe's Companies in the previous period.

3. What was Lowe's Companies after-tax profit margin for the same quarter a year earlier? What is the trend in the company's after-tax profit margin?

4. What is Lowe's Companies current annual dividend? What is Lowe's quarterly dividend?

5. What is Lowe's Companies payout ratio?

Price Analysis

Price ratios are widely used to assess a company's current value. A price ratio measures the cost of investing in a company, the price of its stock, relative to the company's financial performance. The price-to-earnings ratio, or PE is the ratio of the stock price to the earnings per share of the company for the past twelve months. The PE is a statistic that is often used to compare the values of two different corporations and is included in the stock listings of the *WSJ*. Low (high) PE ratios indicate a low (high) expectations of growth in earnings.

Another important price ratio, and one widely used for new companies with little or no current earnings, is the *Price to Sales (PS) ratio*. The PS ratio is calculated by dividing the company's current stock price by the sales per share. Sales per share is found by dividing the company's revenue (net sales) by the number of shares outstanding. To find the number of shares outstanding, divide net income by the earnings per share. The PS ratio identifies the firm's expected ability to generate growth in sales. Investors that expect high growth in sales will likely pay more for the company's stock. Thus, firms in industries with higher levels of growth will have higher PS ratios. Firms with low PS ratios are likely to grow their sales no more than the industry average, or no faster than the overall growth rate in the economy.

Exercise 9-3

Use the table and stock listings from Exercise 9-2 to answer the following questions.

1. What is the PS ratio for Lowe's Companies? What is the PS ratio for the Limited, Inc.?

2. What is the PE ratio for Lowe's Companies? What is the PE ratio for the Limited, Inc.?

3. What is the Payout ratio for Limited, Inc.? Compare this to the payout ratio for Lowe's Companies found in Exercise 9-2. Are both companies retaining earnings to support growth?

Using Ratios to Forecast

As mentioned, ratios are helpful for comparing one company's performance to another. Ratios can also be used to compare a given company to its industry or the market as a whole. Each day, the *WSJ* reports the PE ratio for the Dow Jones Industrial, Transportation, and Utility Averages, as well as broader market indexes like the S&P 500 and the Russell 2000. The PE ratio for each of these market indexes is found in the Markets Lineup column of the Money and Investing Section. To identify a high growth company an investor can compare the company's PE ratio found in the stock listing pages of the *WSJ* with the PE ratio for the market as whole. High growth companies will have PE ratios above the market average. The PE, PS, and other ratios for many Dow Jones indexes, including economic sectors and countries, are available on the Internet at http://indexes.dowjones.com.

Ratios are also used by many analysts to forecast stock prices . PE ratios are commonly used to calculate future stock prices based on current earnings per share and historical growth rates in earnings. PS ratios are also used to find future stock prices based on current sales per share and historical growth rates in sales. Assuming these ratios stay the same and that earnings or sales continue to grow at their current rates, the future stock price can be found by multiplying the ratio by the current per share data and 1 plus rate of growth. For example, on May 22, 2002 the *WSJ* reported that the office supply retailer, Staples, Inc., had 3% sales growth over the previous year in the current quarter. Staples, Inc.'s current sales per share was $5.85 and its PS ratio was 3.74. Assuming sales continue to grow at this rate, and the PS ratio remains the same, Staples Inc.'s expected stock price next year is $22.54 [3.74 x 5.85 x (1 + .03)].

Exercise 9-4

Use the table and stock listings and your answers from Exercises 9-2 & 9-3 to answer the following questions.

1. What is the growth rate in Lowe's Companies earnings per share? What is growth rate in Lowe's Companies revenue (sales)?

2. Using the PS ratios for Lowe's Companies and Limited, Inc. found in Exercise 9-3, calculate the expected price of the stocks in one year.

Project 9-1

Find the Digest of Earnings Report from a recent edition of the *WSJ*. Using a company of your choice, answer the following questions from Exercises 9-2 and 9-3.

Company_____   Date_____

1. What was the company's after-tax profit margin for the quarter?

2. Using the percentage change given for revenue and net income, calculate the revenue and net income for the company in the previous period.

3. What was the company's after-tax profit margin for the same quarter a year earlier? What is the trend in the company's after-tax profit margin?

4. What is the company's current annual dividend? What is the company's quarterly dividend? What is the company's payout ratio?

5. What is the PS ratio for the company? What is the PE ratio for the company?

Project 9-2

In this chapter it was mentioned that there are many different ratios that can be calculated using the income statement, balance sheet, and cash flow statement. Public Companies make their financial statements available to anyone who asks and the *WSJ* provides a valuable service through its Annual Reports Service. Through this service the *WSJ* distributes free of charge the annual financial statements of many companies. In the daily stock listings of the *WSJ* all entries marked by the shamrock symbol are included in this service. You can quickly order the annual report for a company with the symbol over the internet at http://wsj.ar.wilink.com.

In a recent issue of the WSJ, locate a company with the shamrock symbol and order the annual report. Use the income statement, balance sheet, and cash flow statement from this report to complete the following table of three additional ratios.

Name of Company: _____

Ratio	Calculation	Year	Year
Debt Ratio	Total Liabilities / Total Assets		
The total debt ratio measures the proportion of assets financed by debt.			
Current Ratio	Current Assets / Current Liabililities		
The current ratio measures the level of circulating assets available to cover current obligations.			
Return on Equity	Net Income / Average Equity		
Return on equity measures the return per dollar of invested equity capital. *Average equity is the calculated by taking the average of stockholder's equity for the current and previous year.*			

1. Have the changes in each ratio over the previous year been favorable or unfavorable?

2. Based on your assessment of these ratios, is this company a good a bad investment?

Discussion Questions

QUESTIONING THE BOOKS

Tweaking Results Is Hardly a Sometime Thing

Many Firms, Under Diverse Pressures, May Play With Numbers

HEARD
ON THE
STREET

BY KEN BROWN
Staff Reporter of THE WALL STREET JOURNAL

Many companies, at one time or another, massage their numbers using creative accounting techniques, and more

---

Crossing Over

Global Crossing insiders sold $1.3 billion of stock in the three years before the company flamed out, besting the tally of Enron executives. Inside Track, Page C22.

---

probably do it now than ever. But the extent to which companies do it varies widely, from a little to a lot.

In the wake of **Enron**'s debacle, in large part due to highly questionable accounting, many investors are worrying where the next big blowup might come. Instead, professional money managers, accounting gurus and financial analysts

agree, investors should focus on the big picture, how hundreds of companies have used the gray areas of accounting to paint prettier pictures of themselves than they deserved over the past decade.

And they should invest accordingly, taking into account that earnings juiced by aggressive accounting mean that some stocks may be overpriced.

The issue isn't so much whether many companies are committing fraud—that's likely confined to a small group of dishonest executives. It's more question of how many companies tweaked their earnings numbers here and there just to make the crucial number, earnings per share, look better.

"Because the accounting is not being a very good reflection of the economic activity it's meant to report, I think it allows the boundaries to be loosened," explains Sam Eddins, managing director of equity research at CSFB HOLT, a financial-research organization that focuses on businesses' cash flows rather than the net income numbers provided by accountants that most investors follow.

The analysts at HOLT, which had

been independent until it was bought by Credit Suisse First Boston last week, spend their time stripping the accounting gimmicks out of corporate earnings to provide institutional investors with a picture of a company's economic reality.

Over the past several years, Mr. Eddins says, they have had to work hard to keep up with the accountants. "From my perspective, we don't necessarily adjust for outright fraud. I can't identify that," Mr. Eddins adds. "But lacking that, there seem to me more adjustments that we make to the data; people have gotten more creative."

It's virtually impossible to quantify, even for sleuths like Mr. Eddins. But the reasons that executives became so obsessed with hitting their numbers are clear. A company that shows steady growth with few surprises often gets rewarded with a sweet premium from investors—a high stock price—which goes a long way toward keeping the executives' stock options in the money. And if competitors are doing everything they can to make their numbers look as good as possible, companies often have no

choice but to follow along.

"Penny differences in earnings per share matter a lot," notes Patricia Walters, a senior vice president at the Association for Investment Management and Research, the professional group for investment analysts. "So that in conjunction with their compensation schemes tied to what earnings might be, there's a lot of pressure on companies to manipulate earnings, or manage earnings, as they would probably describe it. Yes, I do think companies do push the envelope."

The current state of affairs is the result of a confluence of events. First, there was the bull market, which created a mass of quick-on-the-draw investors who would dump a stock at the slightest whiff of bad news, which gave an added incentive for company's to find ways to make the news look as good as possible.

The huge increase in executive stock options—which can dwarf even multimillion-dollar salaries when the stock goes up—created the incentive to manipulate. And the growing intricacy of accounting that came with the shift in the U.S. economy from manufacturing to service industries, as well as the rise of complex financial instruments such as derivatives, introduced a higher level of subjectivity in reporting everything from sales to earnings to debt.

"There's a lot more things to account for than there were before and they're different, and therefore we need to address in our financial reporting standards how best to act for those," explains said Ms. Walters, who has a doctorate in accounting.

Ultimately, the goal for most companies is to smooth out bumps to show steady growth or, even better, consistently high growth. That works while the economy is roaring. But for companies that made optimistic assumptions during good times, a recession can be disastrous. A credit-card issuer, for example, can report higher earnings by estimating a too-low level of defaults—and then, when more people than expected stop paying their bills, the losses can be far worse than investors anticipated.

"There is smoothing, and there is smoothing," says Julia Grant, associate dean and a professor of accounting at the Weatherhead School of Management at Case Western Reserve University in Cleveland. "If you're smoothing a little rough edge, it's probably not a big deal. But if you're smoothing a big trough, then the problem is inevitable."

How do you smooth earnings? There are lots of tricks. A company can push inventory out to its dealers and book the revenue, a not uncommon practice that was taken to the extreme at **Sunbeam**, which had to restate results in the late 1990s, with a seeming profit turning into a big loss. Or a company can pay its employees in stock options rather than cash.

Companies also can juggle the numbers to make the business seem more efficient. By signing a lease on a building rather than buying it, a company will have the same costs, but won't have an asset on its balance sheet. Taking it a step further the company can do what's called a "synthetic lease" and keep the asset off the balance sheet completely, forcing investors to dig into the footnotes of the financial statements to figure out liabilities.

While many of these sharp accounting practices have been around for a while, "all that stuff is far more significant now than it was 10 or 15 years ago," says Mr. Eddins of CSFB HOLT.

Some veteran investors turn the tables and in part blame the accounting gimmickry on investors who will flee a stock in droves if a company doesn't meet its numbers. These so-called momentum investors generally focus on the earnings-per-share numbers that companies report in their news releases and rarely delve more deeply to determine the underlying prospects.

So, many companies, in massaging their "headline" numbers, have reacted to how investors have treated companies that have missed their numbers by even a narrow margin. "What is the companies' motivation for doing it?" asks Ed Antoian, a money manager at Chartwell Investment Partners who also is an accountant. The answer: "You know, a lot of investors out there worry about this stuff."

1. According to the article, what are some of the ways firms can manipulate earnings per share?

2. Why do company executives focus on earnings per share?

3. What other portion of the financial statements must investors review in order to gauge a company's commitments?

4. Why do you think the analysts at CSFB HOLT look at the cash flow of companies rather than earnings?

Chapter 10

Technical Analysis

Objectives

1. Describe the difference between fundamental and technical analysis.

2. Describe the various charting methods of technical analysis.

3. Describe the various technical indicators used in investment analysis.

4. Use the money flow data in the *WSJ* to analyze trends.

Key Terms

Technical Analysis	Moving Average	Downtick
Dow Theory	Closing Arms	Closing Tick
High-Lo-Close	Uptick	Block trades

In the previous chapter we introduced the fundamental approach to analyzing stock prices. Fundamental analysis involves study of the firm's operations to determine a stock's value. A completely different approach, focusing only on market conditions for stocks (i.e., supply and demand), is technical analysis. Technical analysis is a method of forecasting stock prices using historical price data and other current market statistics. In this chapter we review the origins of technical analysis. We will also review the types of historical price charts, the many technical indicators, and money flow statistics found in the WSJ.

Dow Theory

Developed in the late 1800s and early 1900s by Charles Dow, part owner of the *WSJ*, the Dow theory is considered the first technical analysis method of forecasting stock prices. The theory was not presented as one complete model, but was pieced together from the editorial page writings of Charles Dow over several years.

The ***Dow Theory*** is based on three types of price movements for the Dow Jones Industrial (DJIA) and Transportation averages (DJTA) - primary movements, secondary movements and daily fluctuations. Primary movements can last for just a few months or for many years. These movements represent the underlying trend of the market. Secondary, or reactionary, movements last from just a few weeks to a few months. These movements are counter to the primary trend. The third set of price movements are daily fluctuations. These price movements may be with the primary trend, or against it.

The basic idea of the Dow Theory is to identify changes in the primary trend. An investor that knows that the primary trend has changed can profit from following the new trend until it changes again. To identify the trend change, the analyst watches the two indexes, DJIA and DJTA. When one of the averages departs from the primary trend, but the other average remains unchanged, the price movement is considered secondary. If a change in the trend of one index is followed by a change in the trend of the other, the price movement is considered a change in the primary trend. The Dow theory is not widely used today since its historical performance is mixed – the theory has mostly under-performed in rising (bull) markets, and outperformed in declining (bear) markets. However, the theory's principles are the foundation of many modern technical analysis programs.

The Markets Lineup includes historical price charts for all three Dow Jones Averages – Industrial (DJIA), Transportation (DJTA), and Utilities (DJUA). The DJIA chart is located at the top, the DJTA and the DJUA are directly below. In each chart, the index values are listed vertically on the right and the months are listed across the bottom.

Exercise 10-1

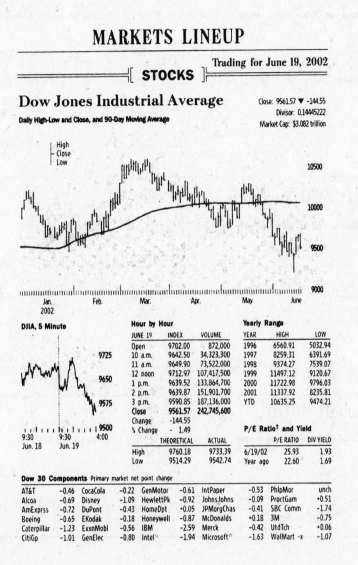

MARKETS LINEUP

Trading for June 19, 2002

=[STOCKS]=

Dow Jones Industrial Average

Daily High-Low and Close, and 90-Day Moving Average

Close: 9561.57 ▼ -144.55
Divisor: 0.14445222
Market Cap: $3.082 trillion

Hour by Hour

JUNE 19	INDEX	VOLUME
Open	9702.00	872,000
10 a.m.	9642.50	34,323,300
11 a.m.	9649.90	73,522,000
12 noon	9712.97	107,417,500
1 p.m.	9639.52	133,864,700
2 p.m.	9639.87	151,901,700
3 p.m.	9590.85	187,136,000
Close	9561.57	242,745,600
Change	-144.55	
% Change	- 1.49	

	THEORETICAL	ACTUAL
High	9760.18	9733.39
Low	9514.29	9542.74

Yearly Range

YEAR	HIGH	LOW
1996	6560.91	5032.94
1997	8259.31	6391.69
1998	9374.27	7539.07
1999	11497.12	9120.67
2000	11722.98	9796.03
2001	11337.92	8235.81
YTD	10635.25	9474.21

P/E Ratio[†] and Yield

	P/E RATIO	DIV YIELD
6/19/02	25.93	1.93
Year ago	22.60	1.69

DJIA, 5 Minute

9725
9650
9575
9500

9:30   9:30   4:00
Jun. 18   Jun. 19

Dow 30 Components Primary market net point change

AT&T	-0.46	CocaCola	-0.22	GenMotor	-0.61	IntPaper	-0.53	PhlpMor	unch
Alcoa	-0.69	Disney	-1.09	HewlettPk	-0.92	JohnsJohns	-0.09	ProctGam	+0.51
AmExprss	-0.72	DuPont	-0.43	HomeDpt	+0.05	JPMorgChas	-0.41	SBC Comm	-1.74
Boeing	-0.65	EKodak	-0.18	Honeywell	-0.87	McDonalds	+0.18	3M	-0.75
Caterpillar	-1.23	ExxnMobl	-0.56	IBM	-2.59	Merck	-0.42	UtdTch	+0.06
CitiGp	-1.01	GenElec	-0.80	Intel	-1.94	Microsoft	-1.63	WalMart -x	-1.07

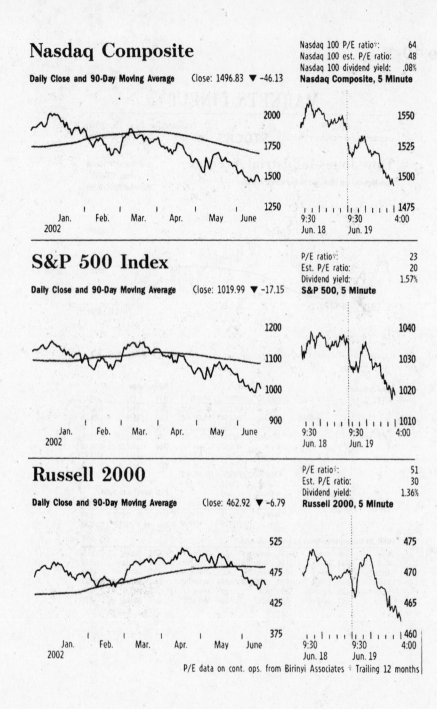

Nasdaq Composite

Nasdaq 100 P/E ratio*:	64
Nasdaq 100 est. P/E ratio:	48
Nasdaq 100 dividend yield:	.08%

Daily Close and 90-Day Moving Average   Close: 1496.83 ▼ -46.13

Nasdaq Composite, 5 Minute

2000
1750
1500
1250

Jan. Feb. Mar. Apr. May June
2002

1550
1525
1500
1475

9:30   9:30   4:00
Jun. 18   Jun. 19

S&P 500 Index

P/E ratio*:	23
Est. P/E ratio:	20
Dividend yield:	1.57%

Daily Close and 90-Day Moving Average   Close: 1019.99 ▼ -17.15

S&P 500, 5 Minute

1200
1100
1000
900

Jan. Feb. Mar. Apr. May June
2002

1040
1030
1020
1010

9:30   9:30   4:00
Jun. 18   Jun. 19

Russell 2000

P/E ratio*:	51
Est. P/E ratio:	30
Dividend yield:	1.36%

Daily Close and 90-Day Moving Average   Close: 462.92 ▼ -6.79

Russell 2000, 5 Minute

525
475
425
375

Jan. Feb. Mar. Apr. May June
2002

475
470
465
460

9:30   9:30   4:00
Jun. 18   Jun. 19

P/E data on cont. ops. from Birinyi Associates * Trailing 12 months

Dow Jones Transportation Average

Close: 2755.10 ▲ +21.42
Divisor: 0.20545179
Volume: 18,879,900

Daily Closes

3000	
2750	
2500	
2250	

D J F M A M J
2002

P/E Ratio[†] and Yield

	P/E RATIO	DIV YIELD
6/19/02	neg.	1.06
Year ago	24.51	1.49

Components

AMR	-0.89
AirbrnInc	-0.28
AlxBldwn*	-0.17
BurlNthSF	+0.56
CNF	+0.79
CSX	-0.11
DeltaAir	-0.95
FedExCp	-0.56
GATX	-0.30
JBHunt*	+2.49
NorflkSo	+0.06
NowestAir*	-0.82
Roadway*	+2.25
RyderSys	-0.03
SowestAir	-0.55
UAL Cp	-0.35
UnPacific	-0.11
US Airways	+0.06
USFrght*-x	+1.34
YellowCp*	+2.06

Dow Jones Utility Average

Close: 281.59 ▼ -1.74
Divisor: 1.72347290
Volume: 27,191,000

Daily Closes

325	
300	
275	
250	

D J F M A M J
2002

P/E Ratio[†] and Yield

	P/E RATIO	DIV YIELD
6/19/02	11.54	4.31
Year ago	68.03	3.57

Components

AEP	-0.35
AES Cp	+0.26
ConEd	-0.35
DominRes	-0.63
DukeEngy	-0.09
EdisonInt	unch
Exelon	+0.14
FstEngy	+0.60
NiSource	-0.47
PG&E	-0.44
PubSvcEnt	-0.79
ReliantEn	-0.56
SouthernCo	-0.14
TXU	-0.07
WillmsCos	-0.11

* Trades on Nasdaq † Trailing 12 months x- Ex-dividend

Source: *The Wall Street Journal*, June 20, 2002. Reprinted by permission of Dow Jones & Company, Inc. (c) 2002 Dow Jones & Company, Inc. All Rights Reserved Worldwide.

Use the charts from the Markets Lineup section above to answer the following questions.

1. Reading from the beginning of the chart on the left to the current price on the right, what is the primary trend in the DJIA? (Hint: Draw a trendline. A trendline is a straight line that connects two or more price points, high or low.)

2. Reading from the beginning of the chart on the left to the current price on the right, what is the primary trend in the DJTA?

3. Are there any secondary trends in the two charts?

Charting

As you can see from the Dow Theory the primary tool of the technical analyst is the price chart. This is why technical analysts are sometimes call "chartists". A price chart is a sequence of prices plotted over a specific timeframe. The most basic of charts is the line chart. It is formed by plotting one price point, usually the close price of a stock or index, over a period of time. By connecting the price points over a period of time, a line is created. The are many more types of price charts that provide additional information. In this section we will review two that are found in the *WSJ* each day – the hi-lo-close and the moving average chart.

In the *WSJ*, the chart of the DJIA includes small bars for each trading day. This a **hi-lo-close** chart. The high, low and closing prices for each day form the price plot of each bar on the chart. The high and low are represented by the top and bottom of the vertical bar and the close is the short horizontal line crossing the vertical bar. The hi-lo-close chart is ideal for analyzing the close relative to the high and low.

Most of the charts in the Markets Lineup section of the *WSJ* are line charts with moving averages. A **moving average** chart plots prices with the average prices for each period. A moving average is an average of prices for a given period of time, say 90 days, that is updated, or "moved", each day. For example, say we wish to find a 90-day moving average. First, the average closing price for the previous 90 days is calculated. This is then repeated each day by dropping the oldest and adding the newest day. To construct a 90-day moving average line, these values are plotted along the graph. Moving average charts quickly identify trends in price movements. When the closing price is above (below) the moving average, the index or stock is in an upward (downward) trend.

Exercise 10-2

Use the Markets Lineup charts from Exercise 10-1 to answer the following questions.

1. Is the current closing price of the DJIA currently at, above, or below its 90-day moving average?

2. Is the current closing price of the NASDAQ Composite Index currently at, above, or below its 90-day moving average?

3. Is the current closing price of the S&P 500 currently at, above, or below its 90-day moving average?

4. Is the current closing price of the Russell 2000 currently at, above, or below its 90-day moving average?

5. Given the trend in each of these indexes, how would you characterize the overall trend in the market?

Technical Indicators

Each day in the NYSE and NASDAQ Scorecard columns of the *WSJ* many indicators of market demand are listed. The Diaries section of this table reports on many aspects of the day's trading activity. Each listing includes a comparison of the day's activity to the previous trading day and the same trading day one week earlier. The first listing is the number of issues (# of companies) traded on the given day followed by the number and volume of issues that closed higher than the previous day (advances), those that closed lower than the previous day (declines), and those issues that remained unchanged. The volume of trading supporting a general movement in the stock market gives an idea of the strength of any trend.

If many issues advance on the day but the volume of trading was higher for the declining issues, any upward trend in the market prices lacks strength. Alternatively, if both volume and number of issues closed higher for the day, a market's upward price movement is strong. The **Closing Arms** is the ratio of the average trading volume in declining issues to the average trading volume in the advancing issues.

$$Arms = \frac{Declvol / Declines}{Advvol / Advances}$$

A Closing Arm greater than 1 indicates declining shares had greater volume for the day, implying a weak upward trend or a strong downward trend depending on the movement in prices. For example, suppose advancing volume on the NYSE is 650,000,000 shares and declining volume is 500,000,000 shares for the day. The number of advancing issues for the day was 1500 and the number of declining issues was 1750. The Closing Arms ratio for the day is

$$0.66 = \frac{500,000,000 / 1,750}{650,000,000 / 1500}$$

This value less than one indicates that advances shares where stronger.

Of more importance to many technical analysts is whether or not the issue closed higher or lower compared to the trade just prior to the final trade of the day, as opposed to its relationship to the previous day's closing price. An ***uptick*** trade is one at a higher price than the previous trade, while a ***downtick*** trade is one at a lower price than the previous trade. The ***Closing Tick*** is the net difference between the number of issues closing higher than their previous trade from those closing lower. The closing tick for the NYSE is reported each day in the NYSE Scorecard table of the *WSJ*.

Exercise 10-3

Nasdaq Scorecard

June 19, 2002 4 p.m. ET

Price Percentage Gainers... And Losers

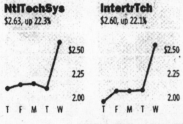

NtlTechSys $2.63, up 22.3%

IntertrTch $2.60, up 22.1%

CntnlComm $1.99, down 30.4%

SilicnImg $5.98, down 29.1%

	VOLUME	CLOSE	CHG	% CHG		VOLUME	CLOSE	CHG	% CHG
NtlTechSys	40,600	2.63	+0.48	+22.3	OakTch	16,520,300	4.52	-5.38	-54.3
IntertrTch	2,440,800	2.60	+0.47	+22.1	Rambus	8,345,000	4.12	-2.31	-35.9
LMI Aero	2,400	4.96	+0.66	+15.3	CntnlComm	54,600	1.99	-0.87	-30.4
CeladonGp	527,600	13.00	+1.69	+14.9	SilicnImg	3,808,900	5.98	-2.45	-29.1
XOMA	696,400	4.39	+0.53	+13.7	ATI Tch	8,609,300	7.01	-2.87	-29.0
MicroTherp	38,000	3.75	+0.45	+13.6	ReptronElec	12,500	2.01	-0.79	-28.2
Aksys	522,500	6.01	+0.70	+13.2	AmkorTch	2,902,400	7.00	-1.85	-20.9
VersaTelTele	13,000	2.60	+0.30	+13.0	FountnPwrbt	11,800	1.60	-0.42	-20.8
HycorBio	17,400	3.92	+0.42	+12.0	Presstek	50,200	5.02	-1.27	-20.2
HaggarCp	22,300	16.59	+1.73	+11.6	Conexant	6,753,100	3.78	-0.91	-19.4

Most Active Issues

	VOLUME	CLOSE	CHG
WorldCom	118,075,200	1.52	-0.04
OracleCp	107,103,900	8.80	-0.18
SunMicrsys	63,254,900	6.03	-0.32
Intel	61,619,200	20.09	-1.93
CiscoSys	56,063,100	14.49	-0.22
Microsoft	38,396,900	54.36	-1.63
AppleCptr	30,092,900	17.12	-3.03
DellCptr	27,320,500	24.73	-1.98
AppldMatl	26,412,400	19.69	-0.77
Ciena	22,742,600	3.96	-0.44

Diaries

	WED	TUE	WK AGO
Issues traded	3,724	3,685	3,756
Advances	1,065	1,535	1,531
Declines	2,372	1,840	1,884
Unchanged	287	310	341
New highs	65	58	46
New lows	126	66	229
Adv vol (000s)	165,442	684,989	1,115,796
Decl vol (000s)	1,504,083	858,429	865,641
Total vol (000s)	1,691,439	1,559,482	1,999,971
Block trades	n.a.	17,319	20,711

Volume Percentage Leaders

	VOLUME	% DIF*	CLOSE	CHG		VOLUME	% DIF*	CLOSE	CHG
Inergy	155,300	2213.8	30.50	-0.85	CeladonGp	527,600	565.7	13.00	+1.69
OakTch	16,520,300	1724.3	4.52	-5.38	StFranCap	130,400	557.9	22.16	-0.57
WorldAcpt	755,700	1445.4	7.45	...	YellowCp	1,942,500	525.4	31.05	+2.06
Rambus	8,345,000	1145.3	4.12	-2.31	ChamppsEntn	210,600	496.0	11.35	-0.10
UtdStatnrs	1,836,700	967.3	31.59	-2.39	ThrRvrsBcp	152,300	475.4	17.58	+0.11
GntvaHlth	2,036,800	695.5	8.67	+0.37	AppleCptr	30,092,900	471.4	17.12	-3.03
CorusBksh	195,100	679.3	45.15	-1.29	ATI Tch	8,609,300	462.1	7.01	-2.87
FstCtzBk A	50,600	586.6	106.64	-0.91	SteelTch	249,700	457.8	13.07	+0.07

*Common stocks of $5 a share or more with average volume over 65 trading days of at least 5,000 shares.

Highs & Lows

New 52-Week Highs — 65

BobEvFrm	33.30	Dynex pfC	28.05	HaggarCp	16.59	LSB Bk NC	19.50	PapaJohns	35.19	SunBcp	24.00
BonTonStr	5.06	EagleBcsh	26.00	HampshrGp	22.46	LancastrCol	41.16	PepBcp OH s	27.75	SwedMtch	83.33
BrightHrzn	33.60	Electrolux	.38.80	HlthTrncSrg	16.22	LandstarSys	110.30	QltyDining	5.00	TippingPt s	13.50
CFC Int	5.10	EonLabs n	17.76	JBHunt	32.37	LoneStarStk	22.40	R&G Fnl B	25.25	Trader.com A	7.90
CH Robinsn	35.40	ExpeditrInt	63.35	IntertrTch	2.75	Massbk s	34.45	RubioRestr	9.74	UrbanOutfit	37.23
CeladonGp	13.00	FstEsxBcp	34.90	Intuit	49.09	Middleby	8.45	SlvrStrm	8.95	USANA Hlth	7.80
CntlGarden	18.49	FstFedAR	26.45	JJillGp	36.83	MS VlyBcsh	52.05	SonicCp s	32.26	WSFS Fnl	25.80
CtznFstBcp	21.50	FstFnlOH	20.42	Jamesnlnn pfA	18.59	NtlTechSys	2.63	SpartnMtr	.14.98	WainwrtBk s	9.20
CmrcBcsh	46.85	FstSentinl	15.19	Jamesnlnn pfS	13.89	NewCentFnl	31.95	SteelTch	13.44	WellsFnl	23.19
CptrPrgms n	21.45	Fossil s	23.74	KSwiss A	48.87	PAM Transpt	27.50	Stericycle s	40.54	YellowCp	32.30
CorVel s	35.40	GlacierBcp	23.50	LNB Bcp	25.80	PacerIntl n	16.65	StrayerEd	64.50		

New 52-Week Lows — 126

ADC Tel	2.33	BroadVisn	0.52	EMCORE	4.80	Intrgroup	16.63	OpticalComm	1.26	SonusNetwks	1.50
ARM ADS	5.92	CNET Ntwrks	2.32	EdsnSchls A	0.97	InterNAP	0.23	PLX Tch	4.22	Spectrx	2.90
ATS Med	0.46	CmbrdgHrt	0.91	ElecFuel	0.82	LJ Int	1.00	Pantry	3.16	SuprcndTch	2.10
ACLARA	1.80	CarmikeCnms n	24.62	ElectroRent	11.50	L90	0.84	ParametTch	3.20	Surmodics	27.20
aEtrnaLab	3.85	CarrierAcc	1.20	Electroglas	11.41	LatticeSemi	8.22	PDF Sol n	7.80	Syntroleum	3.50
AkamaiTch	1.19	CatEngySys wi	2.90	ElronElec	8.18	LegatoSys	4.25	Plumtree n	6.18	TII NtwkTech	0.36
Alcide	18.45	Ceragon	1.75	Endocare	11.16	Level 8	0.40	PwrwaveTch	7.46	TTR Tch	0.34
Altiris n	6.42	Ciena	3.90	Endologix	0.77	LexiconGns	4.99	PrnctnVid	0.80	TargetGene	1.04
AmSuprcnd	4.59	CitrixSys	7.64	EvrgrnSolar	1.59	MacrovsnCp	12.90	Printcafe n	6.63	Tellabs	6.26
AmkorTch	6.90	CptrMotion	1.00	EXFO ElecEng	1.37	MetroOne	13.12	ProcomTch	0.64	Tellium	1.00
ANADIGICS	7.80	Conexant	3.75	FlowInt	6.85	MissionRes	1.70	Provant	0.20	TelularCp	3.90
AndrewCp	13.77	Corel	0.89	FocalComm s	1.90	Moldflow	7.53	QRS Cp	7.50	3DO Co	0.47
AnsoftCp	6.20	Cryptologic	7.28	GT Gp Tele.	0.10	MultilinkTch n	0.56	RF MicroDvc	6.90	TrnWldEntn	6.15
AppldFilm	10.80	D&E Comm	11.90	GenesisMcro	8.02	NeoRx	1.60	Rambus	4.00	TranSwitch	0.62
AppldMicro	4.90	DDiCp	1.18	GenomicSol	0.63	NtSrCommADS s	8.53	ReadRite	1.49	VINA Tch	0.22
AspenTch	7.51	Deltagen	3.01	GldnVintnr B	2.78	NetRtngs	8.74	ReptronElec	1.86	Vical	4.97
Avanex	1.92	Dendreon	2.19	HeskaCp	0.47	NextelPtnrs	2.70	ResCare	5.70	VionPharm	0.50
Avigen	7.30	Diacrin	1.47	hi/fn	6.29	NIC Inc	1.55	RuralCell A	1.25	VitesseSemi	3.38
BEI Tch	12.75	DiamondClstr A	5.09	HollywdMed	1.80	OYO Geospce	8.50	SEMX	0.90	Westaim	1.97
BoneCare	5.37	DigeneCp	15.11	IONA Tch ADS	5.85	OakTch	4.44	SecureCmptg	7.78	WrldHeart	2.43
BriteSmile	2.70	DbsnComm A	1.46	InfoVista ADS	1.61	ONI Sys	2.77	SmartServ	0.70	Zygo	8.47

Use the Diaries data for the Nasdaq market above to answer the following questions.

1. Is total volume on the Nasdaq market higher or lower than the previous week?

2. Calculate the Closing Arms ratio for the Nasdaq market?

Money Flows

The final listing in the Diaries section of the Scorecard columns is Block Trades. **Block Trades** are any trades in excess of 10,000 shares. This is an indicator of institutional investor activity. Institutional investors are often referred to as the "smart money" investors. Therefore, technical analysts sometimes follow large trades to indicate strong buying or selling pressure in the market. The listing includes Block

Trades for the previous day and the same day one week earlier. An increase in block trades week after week during upward price trends indicates higher demand from institutional investors.

Another important indicator of supply and demand activity in the market is money flow. The money flow indicator represents the relative buying and selling pressure each day on share prices. Money flow data are used by many technical analysts to assess whether price trends are sustainable. The money flow indicator compares the dollar value of uptick trades with the dollar value of downtick trades. It is calculated as the dollar value of composite uptick trades minus the dollar value of downtick trades. The up/down ratio reflects the value of uptick trades relative to the value of downtick trades. The money-flow dollar value is computed by multiplying the price by the number of shares traded.

A greater volume of stock changing hands on an uptick indicates the buyers are being relatively more aggressive at accumulating stock than the sellers are at selling it. For example, suppose a stock had five trades in a day in this order - $50, $50 (no change), $52 (uptick), $48 (downtick), and $50 (uptick). At the close of the day the trend in this stock's price would be flat (unchanged). However, if 10,000 shares traded on an uptick and only 1,000 shares on the downtick, the net inflow for those trades would be $10,000 minus $1,000, or a positive $9,000. This indicates there was much more activity for the day at the higher prices.

The daily *WSJ* Money Flows report includes composite money flow figures for the Dow Jones Industrial Average, the Dow Jones U.S. Total Market Index, the S&P 500 stock index and the Russell 2000 index. Also, individual issues with the largest net up or down money flow for the day are listed with their closing prices. The report also gives the ratio of positive to negative money flow. A greater volume of stock changing hands on an uptick indicates the buyers are being relatively more aggressive at accumulating stock than the sellers are at selling it.

Exercise 10-4

Money Flows

Total money flows (in millions of dollars)

June 19, 2002 4 p.m. ET

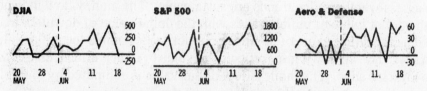

Uptick vs. Downtick Trading by Dollar Volume

MARKET	MONEY FLOW (IN MILLIONS)	MONEY FLOW PREV DAY	UP/DN RATIO	MARKET	MONEY FLOW (IN MILLIONS)	MONEY FLOW PREV DAY	UP/DN RATIO
DJIA	+16.2	+144.2	101/100	S&P 500	+432.2	+615.9	105/100
Blocks	−56.6	+149.8	95/100	Blocks	+399.0	+703.8	109/100
DJ US Total Mkt	+621.2	+756.2	106/100	Russell 2000	+50.2	+9.4	103/100
Blocks	+591.3	+936.8	112/100	Blocks	+39.3	+64.5	110/100

Issue Gainers

ISSUE (EXCH)	CLOSE	MONEY FLOW (IN MILLIONS)	UP/DN RATIO
Nasdaq 100 (A)	27.34	+103.4	113/100
NorthrpGrum (N)	132.50	+40.4	146/100
Lennar (N)	59.18	+37.8	202/100
KLA Tencor (Nq)	47.41	+37.5	120/100
NtwrkAssoc (N)	20.09	+35.6	554/100
TycoInt (N)	15.50	+34.4	128/100
eBay (Nq)	61.82	+33.6	134/100
CiscoSys (Nq)	14.49	+31.4	119/100
MedImmune (Nq)	29.11	+30.2	192/100
Amgen (Nq)	43.03	+28.2	116/100
AppldMatl (Nq)	19.69	+27.3	123/100
Qualcomm (Nq)	28.13	+26.0	126/100
Comcast spA (Nq)	26.12	+25.8	150/100
VeritasSftwr (Nq)	22.89	+25.0	134/100
GoldmanSachs (N)	74.45	+23.0	155/100

...And Losers

ISSUE (EXCH)	CLOSE	MONEY FLOW (IN MILLIONS)	UP/DN RATIO
JohnsJohns (N)	56.37	−72.4	66/100
Diamond (A)	95.81	−66.9	78/100
AnheuserB (N)	50.55	−46.0	48/100
AmIntGp (N)	68.38	−42.3	71/100
Kookmin ADS (N)	47.70	−34.5	32/100
CitiGp (N)	42.06	−29.3	84/100
WalMart (N)	57.41	−27.7	83/100
Semi HOLDRs (A)	32.25	−26.5	68/100
GenElec (N)	30.35	−25.8	87/100
LehmnHldg (N)	61.21	−24.3	66/100
CVS Cp (N)	33.00	−22.9	42/100
IBM (N)	73.35	−22.2	90/100
GileadSci (Nq)	34.89	−21.8	57/100
IShrRu2000V (A)	135.10	−16.8	48/100
Pfizer (N)	35.75	−16.2	86/100

Source: WSJ Market Data Group without block trades.
Money flow figures are the dollar value of composite uptick trades minus the dollar value of downtick trades. The up/down ratio reflects the value of uptick trades relative to the value of downtick trades.

Source: *The Wall Street Journal*, June 20, 2002. Reprinted by permission of Dow Jones & Company, Inc. (c) 2002 Dow Jones & Company, Inc. All Rights Reserved Worldwide.

Use the Money Flows data and charts above to answer the following questions.

1. According to the chart, is money flow in the DJIA currently declining or rising?

2. Which market index, DJIA, DJ US Total Mkt., S&P500, or Russell 2000, experienced the largest money flow for the trading day?

3. Which market index, DJIA, DJ US Total Mkt., S&P500, or Russell 2000, had the highest UP/DOWN ratio?

Project 10-1

Use the charts from a recent Markets Lineup section to answer the following questions from Exercises 10-1 and 10-2.

Date _____

1. Reading from the beginning of the chart on the left to the current price on the right, what is the primary trend in the DJIA?

2. Reading from the beginning of the chart on the left to the current price on the right, what is the primary trend in the DJTA?

3. Are there any secondary trends in the two charts?

4. Is the current closing price of the DJIA currently at, above, or below its 90-day moving average?

5. Is the current closing price of the NASDAQ Composite Index currently at, above, or below its 90-day moving average?

6. Given the trend in each of these indexes, how would you characterize the overall trend in the market?

Project 10-2

Use the Money Flows data and charts from a recent edition of the *WSJ* to answer the following questions from Exercise 10-4.

Date_____

1. According to the chart, is money flow in the DJIA currently declining or rising?

2. Which market index, DJIA, DJ US Total Mkt., S&P500, or Russell 2000, experienced the largest money flow for the trading day?

3. Which market index, DJIA, DJ US Total Mkt., S&P500, or Russell 2000, had the highest UP/DOWN ratio?

Project 10-3

A relative strength chart compares the performance of one stock to the market as a whole, or one market relative to another. The chart is constructed by plotting the price change for two stocks or indexes each day, setting the two equal at some beginning base date. The chart shows the relative performance of one investment to another. Each day, the *WSJ* includes a relative strength chart for small stocks. A relative strength chart of the Russell 2000 Index (an index of 2000 smallest stocks from the largest 3000 largest stocks in the U.S.) versus the Dow Jones Total Market Index is included in the Small Stock Focus column of the Money and Investing section.

Use a recent issue of the *WSJ* to answer the following questions.

1. Based on the chart, what has been the trend for small stocks, as measured by the Russell 2000 index, versus the overall market?

2. Estimate the return on an investment in each of the indexes over the period.

3. Can you identify any turning points in the two markets?

4. Compare this relative strength chart with the Russell 2000 chart in the Markets Lineup section. Does the relative strength chart give a different signal (trending up or trending down) than the moving average chart.

Discussion Questions

Market Timer Offers Chance To Spread Risk

Using Performance Data, Select Advisors Relies On a Variety of Managers

By KAJA WHITEHOUSE
Dow Jones Newswires

NEW YORK—Roger Schreiner knows about putting his money where his mouth is.

Mr. Schreiner was one of many a couple of years ago trying to determine whether market timing—the practice of trading to ride upswings and avoid drops—gave investors any edge over simply buying a stock and letting it ride.

So at the tail end of 1999, he forked over $250,000 of his own money to 250 professional market timers and asked them to manage it. The idea was to create an index of market timers.

Mr. Schreiner has since all but dumped the index idea, but the performance data he has collected from the firms have grown into a unique business in the world of market timing. His new firm, **Select Advisors**, allows investors to invest as little as $100,000 in a basket of market-timing managers, spreading out the money and the risk.

While whether market timing works remains debatable, Select Advisors at least points out to investors which shops have done well and which have fallen flat.

No Mean Feat

That is no mean feat, given the diversity of performances among the 300 firms he now follows. For example, the top performing manager in 2001, **Greenwich Capital Management**, posted gains of 57.25%, according to Select Advisors' database. That is extraordinary in a year when the Standard & Poor's 500-stock index dropped 11%. At the same time, the worst performing manager, **Progressive Ventures**, saw a 91.77% decline.

But, under the Select Advisors approach, performance isn't the only consideration in picking managers. By tracking management styles and other risk factors, Mr. Schreiner cobbles together a group of firms and spreads a client's money around, a diversification play in an often volatile area.

"The general rule of thumb is three to five managers," said Mr. Schreiner. "If one changes his style, you can fire him and it's not such a big deal."

It is an approach normally relegated to only the very rich because of high initial costs. With Select Advisors, the $100,000 threshold may be steep to some, but in some cases it is spread around to firms that carry a minimum initial investment many times higher.

There is a trick to the process. To determine the better managers, Select Advisors ranks managers based on both performance and risk. "If we wanted the biggest performers, we'd get more impressive numbers," Mr. Schreiner said. "The problem is the amount of ulcers, or risk, is not suitable for 90% of investors."

So Mr. Schreiner uses what he calls the "ulcer index," a rather complex equation that attempts to measure downside volatility. In essence, the ulcer index attempts to measure the percentage of days a fund falls below its highest value in a given time period, then compares that with performance.

The service doesn't come cheap. Investors who use Select Advisors' services can expect to be charged a 2.5% fee, based on the total invested assets, plus any costs attached to the underlying mutual funds (Mr. Schreiner tracks firms that use Rydex funds). Select Advisors takes 1%, it gives 1% to the adviser who referred the client, and the money managers split up 50 basis points based on the portion of assets they manage.

The business, which now serves about 85 investors with about $20 million in assets, plans to expand by grabbing the clients of investment advisers who can't otherwise offer market-timing options. Buy-and-hold advisers, for example, represent a much larger share of the money-management market, and, by their nature, have been hesitant to dip a toe into market timing.

Entering this new market could prove difficult, however. Most buy-and-hold money managers scoff at market timing as an expensive and risky strategy. "My personal feeling is that there is not a lot of evidence that market timers as a whole do well ... after you take into account their fees," said Charles Lee, professor at Cornell University's Johnson Graduate School of Management.

An Exception

Bob Bergstedt, financial adviser at **First Financial Planners** Inc. of Golden, Colo., might be an exception. The adviser has been using a buy-and-hold strategy since he opened for business in 1997, but finds himself looking at Select Advisors as an alternative.

"Some say, 'Let's just accept the S&P 500 average return,' " he said. "But I like to do the best I can to find the waves for the equity portion of accounts."

Still, Mr. Bergstedt wants to be sure that Select Advisors will benefit his clients. "The problem I've got is that performance numbers are so short-term," Mr. Bergstedt said, referring to the 2½ years Select Advisors has been tracking performance—roughly equivalent to the duration of the bear market.

Still, Mr. Bergstedt knows that market timing isn't for everyone. If he does use Select Advisors services, he plans to limit the service to his wealthier clients, or those with investable assets of at least $500,000. He also plans to allocate market timing to a small percentage of investors' portfolios.

"Right now, I'm just trying to make sure my clients surf out [of the bear market] safely," he said.

1. Based on the article, define the term "market timing".

2. Assume that you wanted to "time" the market as these advisors do. Which indicators mentioned in this chapter would you use? Why?

3. Market efficiency is the relationship between stock prices and the information available to investors. Market efficiency refers to the ability of anyone to "beat the market". If the market is efficient, it is only by luck that some investors outperform others. Based on the discussion and information in this article, do you think the market efficient?

PART V

DERIVATIVE SECURITIES

Chapter 11

Options

Objectives

1. Understand the basics of call and put options.

2. Use the *WSJ* to understand the determinants of option value.

3. Distinguish between speculative and hedging strategies with options.

4. Use the *WSJ* to understand the concept of expected volatility.

Key Terms

Call Option	Premium	At-the-money
Put Option	In-the-money	Intrinsic Value
Strike Price	Out-of-the-money	Volatility

     Many financial assets derive their value from other financial assets. Such assets are called derivatives. A derivative is any financial contract whose value is dependent upon the value of some underlying asset. In this chapter we will see how one such derivative, an option contract, can be used to both reduce risk (hedge) or take on risk (speculate). The *WSJ* reports prices and trading activity for option contracts each business day. Option prices vary with variations in the assets for which they are issued, such as stocks, and for a variety of other reasons we will discuss.

The Basics of Options

    An option is any contractual right to act in a specified manner within a specified period of time. Options are widespread in finance and investments. For example, most lending agreements give the borrower an option to pay off the debt prior to the specified due date of the loan. This option gives the borrower the right, but not the obligation, to refinance the asset for which they borrowed money whenever interest rates fall. Options like this can be written into any financial contract and tailored to the preferences of each party to the agreement. In this chapter we will look at more specific, standardized options – options that trade on exchanges for specified amounts and periods of time.

There are two classifications of options – calls or puts. ***Call options*** give their owners the right to buy (call from the seller, or writer of the option) the underlying asset for a specified price within a specified period of time. The seller of the call option is obligated to deliver (sell) the underlying asset at the specified price when called. For example, if you buy a call option on AT&T stock with an expiration date in April, you have the right to purchase AT&T stock from the writer of the option at the specified price sometime before the expiration date in April.

Put options give the owner the right to sell (put to the seller) the underlying asset at a specified price within a specified period of time. The seller of a put option is obligated to take delivery (buy) the underlying asset at the specified price. For example, if you buy a put option on AT&T stock with an expiration date in April, you have the right to sell AT&T stock to the writer of the option at the specified price sometime before the expiration date in April. The specified price of the option is called the exercise, or ***strike price***. Thus, when the owner of the option wishes, they can exercise their right under the option contract at the strike price.

To own these rights, either call or put, the purchaser of an option pays the seller a fee, or ***premium***, for the contract right. The seller, or writer, of the option receives the premium as compensation for taking the risk that they may have to deliver on their obligations when it may not be beneficial. Call writers risk that they may have to sell the underlying asset to the call option owner for a price below prevailing market prices. Put writers risk that they may to buy the underlying asset at prices above current market prices.

Standardized options have been trading on U.S. exchanges since the early 1970s. Exchanges, such as the Chicago Board Options Exchange, make it easier for the buyers and sellers of options to execute an option contract. There are standardized option contracts for common stocks, stock indexes, commodities, and currencies. The standards in these contracts are normally the quantity of the underlying asset and the date of expiration. For example, the underlying quantity of stocks is 100 shares and the expiration date is the third Friday in the specified month of expiration. The *WSJ* publishes the trading activity for the 700 most active stock options each day, as well as the 100 most active long-term stock options, under the column heading "Listed Options Quotations". Included for each option listing is the name of the Company (in bold), the strike price of the option, and the month of expiration. The next two columns list the volume (number of contracts traded) and premium of call options for the given strike price and expiration. The following columns list the volume and premium for put options. For stocks with significant activity under many different strike prices, the previous day's closing price for the stock is also listed below the name of the company.

Exercise 11-1

LISTED OPTIONS QUOTATIONS

Tuesday, May 7, 2002

Composite volume and close for actively traded equity and LEAPS, or long-term options, with results for the corresponding put or call contract. Volume figures are unofficial. Open interest is total outstanding for all exchanges and reflects previous trading day. Close when possible is shown for the underlying stock or primary market. **XC**-Composite. **p**-Put. **o**-Strike price adjusted for split.

OPTION/STRIKE	EXP	CALL VOL	CALL LAST	PUT VOL	PUT LAST
AOL TW 17.50	May	1349	0.65	594	0.80
17.26 20	May	1916	0.10	2864	2.80
AdobeS 35	May	1122	2.30	157	0.80
Altera 15	Jun	...	...	2660	0.70
17.49 17.50	Jun	5	1.95	6991	1.40
Amazon 12.50	Jul	...	...	2720	0.70
16.11 17.50	Oct	2461	2.45	2313	3.70
16.11 20	Jul	2705	0.70	20	4.50
A E P 40	May	950	6.40	...	...
46.36 45	May	1334	1.40	4	0.30
AmExpr 45	May	1020	0.10	...	...
AmIntGp 65	May	6	3.40	2565	0.65
67.65 65	Jun	3	4.50	899	1.90
67.65 70	May	48	0.80	1622	2.85
Amercrd 45	May	2888	0.25	...	...
Amgen 45	May	1131	2.75	380	0.95
46.54 45	Jun	139	4.10	1423	2.40
46.54 47.50	May	2064	1.35	153	2.20
46.54 47.50	Jun	797	2.70	67	3.20
46.54 50	May	4290	0.50	147	4
46.54 55	May	111	0.10	1446	8.10
46.54 55	Jul	795	0.85	611	8.80
AnnTay 45	May	150	1.70	3334	1.50
Apache 50	Oct	...	...	1820	2.50
AppldMat 17.50	Jul	...	...	9052	0.75
22.32 22.50	May	1262	1.30	298	1.40
22.32 23.75	May	871	0.70	39	2
22.32 25	Jun	3309	1.10	188	3.40
22.32 25	Jul	4206	1.45	198	3.80
22.32 27.50	May	439	0.10	3605	5.10
22.32 27.50	Oct	909	1.60	...	...
AMCC 5	May	140	1	1192	0.10
BJ Svc 37.50	May	1430	0.70	...	...
BancOne 40	May	707	1.05	1579	0.55
Bk of Am 65	Aug	932	9.40	...	...
72.96 75	Jun	1373	1.30	31	3.70
BarickG 20	May	1230	0.80	280	0.30
BestBuy 70	May	862	4.10	139	1.05
Biogen 35	Jun	...	...	2353	1.70
40.29 50	May	2352	0.75	...	...
BiotechT 90	Jun	3214	5.50	833	5.30
89.67 90	Jul	1040	6.60	...	...
89.67 130	Jul	...	...	1000	39.50
Biovail 35	May	2006	1.20	281	3.20
Broadcom 22.50	May	309	3.30	1487	1
24.72 25	May	4303	1.85	8995	2.10
24.72 25	Jun	2908	3.10	1120	3.10
24.72 25	Aug	257	4.70	833	4.20
24.72 30	May	3019	0.95	6406	5.50
24.72 30	Jun	1342	1.35	768	6.30
24.72 35	May	3029	0.10	6012	10.10
24.72 35	Jun	1053	0.50	398	10.40
24.72 40	May	295	0.05	2387	12.90
24.72 50	Aug	1084	0.15	15	24.50
Brocade 15	Jul	3	6.20	1460	1.20
19.90 20	May	882	1.60	1135	1.85
19.90 20	Jul	1	4.20	1329	3.40
19.90 22.50	May	1393	0.80	846	3.30
19.90 25	May	946	0.30	5034	5.10
19.90 30	Oct	1629	1.85	20	10.80
CVS Corp 35	May	936	0.40	3	1.70
Cablvision 25	Jun	30	1.50	800	3.30
CabotMc 40	May	1104	4.50	98	0.65
CallGolf 17.50	Jun	...	...	3100	1.70

OPTION/STRIKE	EXP	CALL VOL	CALL LAST	PUT VOL	PUT LAST
30.65 32.50	May	1706	0.20	873	2.10
30.65 40	Jun	1905	0.05	41	9.40
GenMotrs 60	May	61	5.10	1437	0.25
GaPacIf 27.50	May	...	...	7570	0.30
29.85 27.50	Jul	...	...	1755	1.05
29.85 35	Jul	1000	0.50	...	...
GlobalSFe 30	May	1030	3.90	...	...
33.75 35	May	2024	0.50	11	1.95
GoldmnS 80	May	1555	0.50	336	5.30
74.85 80	Oct	4645	5.30	...	...
74.85 85	May	4501	0.10	5	9.60
74.85 100	Jul	845	0.15	...	...
Goodyr 22.50	Jul	513	1.50	2050	2.15
Guidant 35	May	2502	2.60	46	0.45
HewlettPk 17.50	May	1178	1.20	188	0.15
ICN Phma 22.50	Dec	36	6	1186	1.85
IndevusPh 5	Jun	...	...	810	0.75
Intel 25	May	2758	1.85	19822	0.60
26.15 25	Jun	67	2.70	1461	1.20
26.15 25	Oct	26	4.10	1141	2.35
26.15 27.50	May	4222	0.50	3571	1.75
26.15 27.50	Jun	1632	1.20	418	2.40
26.15 30	May	1116	0.10	444	3.70
26.15 30	Jun	1160	0.45	107	4.20
26.15 30	Jul	19832	0.90	1098	4.50
26.15 35	Jul	156	0.20	5575	8.70
26.15 35	Oct	1077	0.65	...	...
I B M 60	Jun	1	17.60	2285	0.75
76.50 70	Jun	67	8.50	2923	1.85
76.50 75	May	3781	2.90	2571	1.80
76.50 75	Jun	812	4.50	485	3.50
76.50 75	Jul	79	5.80	931	4.30
76.50 80	May	1506	0.85	1188	4.70
76.50 80	Jun	6941	2.40	508	5.60
76.50 80	Jul	399	3.50	8528	6.90
76.50 80	Oct	1647	5.30	137	8.60
76.50 85	May	3239	0.15	2717	8.90
76.50 85	Jun	1113	1	60	9
76.50 85	Oct	827	3.40	130	11.90
76.50 90	May	1392	0.05	350	14.10
76.50 90	Jun	856	0.40	35	14.20
76.50 90	Oct	1364	2.15	86	15.20
In Pap 40	Jun	2632	3.30	75	0.70
42.99 42.50	Jun	1800	1.50	61	1.45
JPMorgCh 32.50	May	106	3.10	3125	0.50
34.63 35	May	944	1	627	1.35
34.63 37.50	Jun	1165	0.90	169	3.30
JohnJn 60	May	592	1.40	4284	1
60.42 65	Jul	179	2.90	2725	2.65
60.42 65	May	650	0.05	1664	4.80
60.42 65	Jun	932	0.45	109	5
60.42 70	Oct	1603	0.65	1	10
JnprNtw 10	May	1824	0.15	387	1.75
8.43 10	May	3065	0.50	47	1.85
KLA Tnc 60	May	1180	0.45	728	5.90
KingPh 30	May	109	0.30	887	2.20
LamRs 25	Jun	...	...	1703	3.60
23.29 30	Jun	...	...	1457	7.30
LehmBr 55	Oct	3600	2.55	3601	3.80
60.40 70	Oct	3620	2.40	...	...
Lucent 5	May	969	0.05	60	0.70
4.31 5	Jun	1634	0.10	178	0.85
Macrmd 17.50	Aug	...	...	1822	2.10
19.86 22.50	Aug	1779	1.60	...	...

OPTION/STRIKE	EXP	CALL VOL	CALL LAST	PUT VOL	PUT LAST
NextelCm 5	Jun	1070	0.50	...	...
NokiaA 20	Jul	79	0.20	1514	5
Novlus 50	May	1285	0.50	127	5
NvidiaCp 30	May	1406	3.40	1349	1.05
32.29 35	May	1036	0.90	469	3.60
OpenwvSys 5	May	46	0.30	1675	0.35
Oracle 7.50	May	1737	0.90	1189	0.20
8.25 7.50	Jun	869	1.25	567	0.60
8.25 10	May	1006	0.10	7060	1.75
8.25 10	Jun	1022	0.30	1766	2.05
8.25 12.50	May	102	0.05	4250	4.20
OxfordHlt 40	Jun	...	...	930	0.70
44.60 47.50	May	1005	0.25	...	...
PanAmSat 22.50	May	1650	1.05	650	0.10
Peoplesoft 25	Jun	2059	0.50	...	...
Pfizer 35	May	1339	1.90	2855	1.05
Pharmacia 40	Jun	1615	1.80	1910	2.45
Ph Mor 55	May	39	1.20	1911	0.60
55.62 55	Jun	1374	2.10	11036	1.15
ProcG 90	Jul	52	4.50	936	2.60
ProvidFn 7.50	May	1242	0.20	64	0.80
Qlogic 35	May	2252	5	3266	1.80
38.26 40	May	4334	2.10	3929	3.80
38.26 45	May	1591	0.65	3890	7.50
Qualcom 25	May	1702	1.30	954	1.60
24.80 30	May	1448	0.20	441	5.40
24.80 30	Jun	1163	0.75	103	6
24.80 55	Jul	2	0.10	1010	30
QwestCom 5	Oct	821	1.40	153	1.25
RF MicD 17.50	Jun	1407	0.90	5	3.20
RschMot 17.50	Jun	57	1.55	972	2.40
Schering 25	May	31	2.60	1110	0.65
27.01 27.50	May	96	0.45	1186	0.95
Schlmb 55	Jun	149	2.40	1765	3.40
SealdAir o 40	Jul	...	...	840	1.40
SemiHTr 12.50	Jun	1023	0.90	20	5.90
37.37 35	May	88	3.40	1388	0.65
37.37 37.50	May	3237	1.55	600	1.65
37.37 40	May	4438	0.60	1059	2.95
Semtech 25	Dec	...	...	1140	4
SiebelSys 20	May	1335	1.30	9907	1.45
19.89 20	Jun	401	2.25	905	2.40
19.89 22.50	May	1080	0.45	625	3
19.89 25	May	798	0.15	442	5.30
19.89 25	Aug	1149	1.40	88	6.30
SmithfldFd 20	Jun	...	...	1000	1.05
Starbcks 22.50	Jul	95	1.50	1327	1.15
StarwdHtl 35	Jun	20	2.35	3405	1.45
SunMicro 5	Oct	121	1.75	958	0.60
6.14 7.50	May	1582	0.05	315	1.40
6.14 7.50	Jun	1713	0.25	652	1.60
6.14 7.50	Jul	2429	0.40	1823	1.65
Synops 45	May	1131	3.40	361	0.75
TelMexL 50	Aug	2446	0.05	...	...
TenetHl 75	May	177	1	1149	2.35
Terdyn 30	May	144	1.25	1945	1.45
TexasInst 30	Oct	65	2.75	1060	5.10
3M Co 125	May	1345	2.10	733	2.90
TollBr 30	May	315	2	2029	0.50
Trnskry 35	May	10	0.95	1653	4
33.06 45	May	...	...	1250	12.50
TycoIntl 15	May	156	4.70	1245	0.25
19.10 17.50	May	625	2.35	2392	0.70
19.10 20	May	4834	0.80	1400	1.85

Use the above listings from the *WSJ* to answer the following questions.

1. What is the premium on the call option for Intel common stock with a strike price of $30.00 per share and an expiration date in June? How many of these contracts traded on the previous trading day?

2. What is the premium on the put option with the same strike price and expiration? How many of these contracts traded on the previous trading day?

3. According to the table, what was the closing price of Intel stock?

Option Values

The value of an option contract is first and foremost dependent on the price of the underlying asset. For example, if AT&T stock is currently selling for $20 a share, a call option on AT&T with a strike price of $15 is worth more than a call option that expires in the same month but has a strike price of $25. The option with the $15 strike price is *in-the-money*, while the option with the $25 strike price is *out-of-the-money*. When the strike price of a call option is equal to the market price, it is *at-the-money*. A put option with a strike price over the market price is in-the-money, while a put option with a strike price below the market price is out-of-the-money. Just as for a call option, when the strike price of a put option is equal to the market price, it is at-the-money.

The market price of the underlying asset, therefore, is the first determinant of the value of an option. The higher the market price relative to the strike price, the higher (lower) the call (put) option premium, all else being equal. The difference between the market price and the strike price of an option is called the option's *intrinsic value*. When the strike price exceeds the market price, a call option has zero intrinsic value. When the market price exceeds the strike price a put option has zero intrinsic value.

An option with an intrinsic value of zero may still be of interest to an investor and would therefore still have value. The second determinant of the value of an option is its length of time until expiration. For example, if AT&T stock is currently selling for $20 a share, a call option on AT&T with a strike price of $20, expiring three months from now, is worth more than a call option with a strike price of $20 that expires next month. There exists a greater probability the market price of AT&T stock will move farther above $20 in the next three months than in just one month. With more time, there is a higher probability that the market price will move farther from any strike price. More time until expiration allows the owner more time in which to exercise their option. Thus, the longer the option's time until expiration, the higher the option premium. This is true for both call and put options.

Exercise 11-2

Use the Listed Options Quotations and your answers from Exercise 11-1 to answer the following questions.

1. What is the premium on the Intel call options with a strike price of $25 per share and an expiration date in June? What is the premium on the put options with the same strike price and expiration?

2. Which option contract (call or put) is in-the-money? Which option contract (call or put) is out-of-the-money?

3. Are these premiums higher or lower than the ones you found in Exercise 11-1?

Volatility

Just as more time leads to a higher probability of a difference in market price and strike price, more volatility in the underlying assets also raises the likelihood that the market price will move farther from an option's strike price. The third determinant of an option's value is the level of *volatility* in the underlying asset of the option contract. The greater the volatility in the underlying asset, the greater the risk for the writer of the option contract. Recall that the premium in an option contract is compensation to the option writer for taking the risk that they may have to deliver on their obligations when it may not be beneficial. If the price of a stock significantly fluctuates in price, then the risk of having to buy or sell the stock at a loss compared to current market prices increases. Thus, options for stocks with greater volatility have greater value, or higher premiums.

Different types of stocks have different levels of volatility. The stock prices of smaller companies are generally more volatile than those of larger companies. The revenue and profits of smaller companies are often much harder to predict, leading to greater variations in the current market valuation of the company. Similarly, the revenue and profits of companies in some industries are difficult to predict. This can be seen in the greater volatility of the market valuations of technology companies versus the market valuation of industrial companies. For example, on March 14, 2002 the stock price of Intel and General Electric closed at $30.97 and $40.41, respectively. On the same day the Intel call option with a $35 strike price and expiration in April sold for a premium of $0.50. The General Electric call option with a $45 strike price and expiration in April sold for a premium of only $0.15. The intrinsic value (zero) and time till expiration in both options was identical, but the Intel option had a much higher value. This higher value can be attributed almost entirely the inherent volatility in the price of technology stocks versus manufacturing stocks. The share price of a technology company like Intel has a much higher probability of increasing more than the difference between the current share price and the option's strike price. To be higher than the strike price, Intel's market price would need to increase more than 13%, where as GE's price would only need to rise approximately 10%. In the case of these two companies, the higher premium on the Intel stock suggests that a 13% increase is more likely than a 10% increase for GE.

Exercise 11-3

Use the Listed Options Quotations from Exercise 11-1 to answer the following questions.

1. Compare the premium on the October 70 Calls for Johnson&Johnson, a pharmaceutical and consumer products company, to the premium on the

October 27.50 Calls for Applied Materials (ApdldMat), a high technology manufacturer. For the day listed, both of these options were out-of-the-money. Calculate the percentage change in the share price necessary for the option to have any intrinsic value (in-the-money).

2. Is the percentage change you calculated greater for the stock with the higher or lower premium?

Hedging and Speculating with Options

All financial assets, stocks or otherwise, carry some level of price volatility. With greater volatility comes greater risk. Options can be used to both take on this risk or transfer it to someone else. Individuals and institutions that want to reduce the risk associated with their financial assets use options to hedge. Individuals and institutions that wish to speculate on the future price movements of financial assets may also use options. A stock investor can use options to hedge the risk that the stock may fall in value. To hedge against the possible decline in the value of 100 shares of stock the investor can buy one put option.

For example, if an investor owns 100 shares of Intel, that is currently selling for $31 a share and wants to protect themselves against the possibility that the stock may fall below $30 in the next few months, they can buy 1 put option on Intel with an expiration in the months ahead. If the stock falls below this level, the investor can exercise their option to sell the stock above prevailing market prices and can avoid a loss on the initial stock investment. If the price remains at the current level or rises, the option expires worthless and the investor is out only the premium paid for the option. On March 14, 2002 the April this put option was selling at $1.55. The cost of this hedge would be $1,550.00.

The speculator that uses options may or may not own the underlying assets. Options provide an opportunity for investors to speculate on the future price movement of a stock without incurring the cost of investing in a large number of shares. The speculator can profit from the future stock price movement with only a small up-front investment. For example, suppose a speculator believes that the price of Intel stock will rise substantially above its current market price of $31 in the next two months. To profit from this expected move, the speculator can purchase a call option on Intel with a strike price of $30 and expiration in the next two months. The speculator incurs only the premium cost and is not required to invest $3100 in the actual stock.

There are many different strategies speculators can use to profit from future price movements or to profit from no change in the price of an investment. Speculators can sell options to profit from expected price moves. If the price of a stock is expected to fall, the value of call options will fall. To profit from this expectation, a speculator can sell (write) call options at or above the prevailing market prices. If the price of a stock is expected to rise, but the speculator is unsure as to what level the price will rise, put options with strike prices at, or close to, prevailing market prices can be sold (written). If the price rises as expected, the options expire worthless and the speculator gains the premium value. Combinations of both calls and puts can also be purchased or sold to profit on expected price movements. An options trader that expects a stock to be volatile, but is unsure of the direction of the stock price, can purchase both a call and a put option with identical strike prices. If the stock price rises, the call is profitable and the put expires worthless. If the stock price falls, the put is profitable and the call expires worthless. Of course for this type of investment to be profitable the stock price must change by an amount great enough to cover the premium cost of both options.

Exercise 11-4

Use the Listed Options Quotations from Exercise 11-1 to answer the following questions.

1. Suppose you own 200 shares of IBM. What would it cost to hedge against the risk that the price of IBM will fall below $75 per share between now and mid-July?

2. Suppose you think that Oracle Corporation will announce significantly higher profits for the period ending in May, leading to a strong rise in their stock price to $12 per share in early June. What would be the cost of one option contract that could profit from this expectation?

3. Now suppose you are unsure what Dell will announce, but you expect the announcement to cause a significant change in the price of the stock, either up or down (increased volatility). What combination of two different option positions could you take to profit from this expectation?

Project 11-1

Repeat Exercise 11-3 using a recent edition of the *WSJ*. In the Listed Option section find <u>out-of-the-money</u> calls with <u>identical expiration</u> months for two different companies.

Date_____

Company_____Strike_____Expiration_____

Company_____Strike_____Expiration_____

1. Calculate the percentage change in the share price necessary for each option to have any intrinsic value (in-the-money).

2. Is the percentage change you calculated greater for the stock with the higher or lower premium? Why?

Project 11-2

The options contracts we have looked at so far are generally short term in length. For some actively traded stocks, standardized long-term option contracts also exist. Each day the *WSJ* reports the 100 most active long-term option contracts called LEAPs. Just as with the option contracts described in this chapter, LEAPs can be used to hedge against risk or to speculate on future price movements. For speculators, LEAPs offer the opportunity to profit without a large investment.

To see the potential return on an LEAP option investment consider the following investment choices. Suppose you are deciding whether to invest in 100 shares of a company or purchase 1 LEAP option contract on the company's stock that expires in January of the next year. Using the information on LEAPs from a recent edition of the *WSJ*, complete the following table.

Stock Price on December 31	Profit on 100 Shares of Stock	Return on Investment	Profit on LEAP Option	Return on Investment
30				
35				
40				
45				
50				
55				
60				
65				
70				

Discussion Questions

Covered Calls Grow in Popularity As Stock Indexes Remain Sluggish

By KOPIN TAN
Dow Jones Newswires

NEW YORK—Stock indexes are up one day and down the next two. The result? Many stocks have hardly advanced in months.

With this range-bound market threatening to drag on, money managers under

OPTIONS REPORT

pressure to boost returns are looking to the options market. Michael Urias and Peter Fanelli, who co-head Morgan Stanley's quantitative strategies group, have noted more interest from money managers looking to devise "covered call writing" strategies, where an investor sells call options against stock he buys or already holds.

By doing so, the investor sets a price target at which he will be willing to sell a certain amount of stock; in return, he earns income even as stocks stall. "For many portfolio managers with longer-term views on stocks, it's also a way to enhance yields," said Matthew Carrara, Deutsche Bank's head of U.S. institutional equity derivatives sales.

Considered the second most popular option strategy (after the straight buying of calls or puts), covered call writing fell out of favor during the 1990s bull run, since a call seller surrenders any gain above the strike price of the calls sold—a bummer if stocks keep rising (which they did in the 1990s). But "a range-bound market is a call sellers' market," said Michael Schwartz, CIBC Oppenheimer's chief options strategist.

Some investors are hesitant because they believe volatility—a major part of option prices—is low. While volatility is at its lowest levels in recent years, the past four years have been more turbulent than usual. In fact, the average volatility of the S&P 500 index during the past five years was about 19.3%, higher than the average of 17.7% for 2002's first three months and 15.4% in March. But over the longer term, the recent levels still exceeded the average level of S&P 500 volatility since 1950, which is 12.4%, and since 1980, which is 14.6%.

Meanwhile, the Chicago Board Options Exchange launched a benchmark to help investors track potential returns from such covered call-writing (also called buy-writing or over-writing). The CBOE Buy-Write Monthly Index, or BXM, measures potential returns of a hypothetical portfolio made up of S&P 500 stocks, and where the investor also systematically sells S&P 500 Index call options.

Source: *The Wall Street Journal*, April 12, 2002. Reprinted by permission of Dow Jones & Company, Inc. (c) 2002 Dow Jones & Company, Inc. All Rights Reserved Worldwide.

1. According to the article, what is "covered call writing"?

2. Why has this strategy recently become more popular?

3. According to the article, what is the current level of volatility in the

    market?

4. At what level of volatility is selling calls a good strategy?

Chapter 12

Futures

Objectives

1. Explain the basics of commodity and financial futures markets.

2. Use the *WSJ* to understand the value of a futures position.

3. Distinguish between speculative and hedging strategies with future contracts.

4. Use the *WSJ* to explain the price movements of futures contracts.

Key Terms

Commodity futures	Settle price	Short position
Financial futures	Hedge	Long position
Spot price	Margin requirement	Basis Risk

Many types of assets - both tangible assets like gold and intangible assets like bonds - can be traded without ever making or taking actual delivery. This can be accomplished through the use of futures contracts. In this chapter we will discuss the basics of commodity and financial futures contracts. Futures can be used to both speculate on the future value of an asset as well hedge against any adverse change in the prices. Each day, the *WSJ* reports the previous day's trading activity in many different futures contracts. The price, volume, and other trading information found in the *WSJ* is useful in explaining how current market prices and future expectations affect the value of commodity and financial futures contracts.

The Basics of Futures Contracts

Futures contracts are derivative securities. That is, their value is derived from the value of some underlying asset. A futures contract is a standardized agreement to deliver or take delivery of an asset in the future. Since the contract is standardized, only the price is determined by traders in futures contracts. The actual contract specifies all other particulars, such as the exact quantity of the asset to be taken or delivered and the ending date of the contract. This trading of standardized contracts, that takes place on organized exchanges, provides liquidity and guaranteed settlement. The exchanges provide the guarantee to traders that the other party to the contract will meet their obligations. The organized exchanges include the Chicago Board of Trade and Chicago Mercantile Exchange. Most buyers and sellers of futures contracts do not actually make or take delivery of the underlying asset. The holder of a futures contract can close their position any time before the contract expiration date. To offset or close out their positions in the futures market by the settlement date, traders can buy or sell the same contract to close the position. All of the obligations are netted out when traders close positions in this manner.

  Commodities futures contracts are standardized agreements to exchange a specified amount of a given commodity on a specified date in the future. Futures contracts are traded for various grains (e.g., wheat and corn), livestock (e.g., cattle and hogs), foods (e.g., sugar and cocoa), metals (e.g., gold and silver), as well as oil and natural gas. ***Financial futures*** contracts are standardized agreements to exchange a specified amount of a given financial asset on a specified date in the future. Futures contracts are traded for many different financial assets including bonds, currencies, and stocks. The price of these contracts, the futures prices, may or may not equal the prices for the same quantities of the commodity or financial asset if bought or sold today. Today's price is known as the ***spot price***. The futures price reflects the market participants' expectation of the spot price in the future. The *WSJ* reports spot prices for commodities each day under the column heading "Cash Prices". Prices are listed for such commodities as grains, fibers, metals, and oils, and include the spot price of one year ago for comparison.

  Futures contract prices for the previous trading day are reported in the *WSJ* each day. In the Futures Prices column information on both commodity and financial futures contracts are listed. Each commodity or financial asset is listed in bold, followed by the name of the exchange where the contract is traded, the size of a single contract, and a description of how the prices are quoted. For example, corn is traded on the Chicago Board of Trade. 5,000 bushels make up one corn contract and corn prices are quoted as cents per bushel. As another example, Japanese Yen are traded on the Chicago Mercantile Exchange. Each Yen contract is for 12.5 million Yen and the price is quoted as $ per Yen.

  Under each of these commodity headings are price listings for each of the months for which delivery of the commodity or financial asset may be obtained. There are usually only 4 to 6 months for which futures contracts trade. The columns of information for each maturity month are the opening, the highest, the lowest and the settle (closing) price for the contract. The ***settle price***, is an estimate of the price at which the last trade for the contract occurred. Unlike stocks, trading in futures contracts closes over a period of a few minutes, not at some exact time. Many trades occur in this last period and the exchange maintains a system to average or estimate the prices of these final trades. For example, the settle price on the September corn futures contract on March 8, 2002 was 221.25 cents. Since corn futures contracts trade for 5000 bushels per contract, the estimated value of the September contract was $11,062.50 (2.2125 x 5000).

Also included for each listing is the change in the closing price from the previous day, the lifetime high and low, and the open interest, or how many contracts are outstanding for a particular maturity date. The change is the difference in the settlement price from the previous trading day. The lifetime high and low prices are the highest and lowest prices at which the contract traded since it began trading. This range of trading is one measure of the volatility in the prices for both the underlying asset and the futures contract. The open interest is the number of contracts outstanding, or open, at the beginning of the day's trading. Open interest is a measure of the level of activity from individuals and institutions in this asset and their interest in its future price.

Interest rate futures are priced like the bonds and notes that the futures contracts are based upon. The price quotations are given points per 100 percent of the contract value. The hundred price is followed by a line and then 32nds of 1 percent. That is, 101-01 means 101 and 1/32, or 101 and 0.33 % of contract value. As an example, the profit on a Treasury Bonds contract purchased at 92-10 (92 and 10/32% of $100,000) and sold for 101-01 (101 and 1/32 % of $100,000) is $8,718.75.

Exercise 12-1

FUTURES

Metal Futures

	OPEN	HIGH	LOW	SETTLE	CHG	LIFETIME HIGH	LIFETIME LOW	OPEN INT
Copper-High (CMX)-25,000 lbs.; cents per lb.								
June	74.90	74.90	73.90	74.20	-0.80	89.50	62.35	501
July	75.10	75.15	73.90	74.30	-0.85	88.90	62.30	42,307
Aug	75.10	75.10	74.65	74.65	-0.85	82.90	62.90	2,501
Sept	75.75	75.90	74.70	75.00	-0.85	88.00	62.95	11,279
Nov	75.40	75.50	75.40	75.45	-0.80	85.50	64.00	951
Dec	76.35	76.35	75.45	75.65	-0.80	83.00	63.50	9,418
Ja03	75.90	75.90	75.90	75.85	-0.80	80.10	64.90	596
Mar	76.35	76.35	76.35	76.25	-0.80	80.70	65.30	1,946
July	77.50	77.50	77.00	76.95	-0.80	80.80	66.80	723
Dec	78.00	78.00	78.00	77.75	-0.80	81.60	71.50	1,707
Est vol 21,000; vol Thu 15,190; open int 78,310, -4,381.								
Gold (CMX)-100 troy oz.; $ per troy oz.								
June	322.90	325.20	322.20	324.60	1.40	385.00	264.50	487
Aug	324.00	325.80	322.80	325.10	1.40	331.50	272.60	104,799
Oct	326.00	326.70	324.20	326.20	1.40	331.50	274.00	5,662
Dec	326.00	327.80	324.50	327.10	1.40	358.00	268.10	25,697
Fb03	326.70	328.50	326.70	328.10	1.50	333.70	286.50	7,661
June	329.00	329.50	329.00	330.10	1.50	338.00	280.00	4,771
Dec	332.00	333.50	332.00	334.00	1.50	359.30	280.00	7,225
Dc04	343.00	343.00	343.00	343.60	1.50	388.00	290.00	2,393
Dc05	353.00	353.00	353.00	354.80	1.50	353.00	298.40	164
Est vol 27,000; vol Thu 42,783; open int 172,068, +3,170.								
Platinum (NYM)-50 troy oz.; $ per troy oz.								
July	570.00	570.00	562.50	562.70	-6.40	572.00	405.00	4,755
Est vol 1,815; vol Thu 1,994; open int 7,380, -1.								
Silver (CMX)-5,000 troy oz.; cnts per troy oz.								
June	...	...	...	485.2	-1.5	515.0	440.0	4
July	488.0	490.5	482.5	485.5	-1.5	559.0	409.5	50,688
Sept	491.0	493.0	485.0	487.8	-1.5	517.0	412.5	24,355
Dec	492.5	494.5	487.0	490.4	-1.5	613.0	412.0	14,912
Mr03	494.0	494.0	494.0	492.3	-1.5	522.0	417.0	1,744
July	497.0	497.0	494.0	494.8	-1.5	551.0	421.0	3,942
Dec	498.5	502.5	498.5	498.7	-1.5	565.0	419.0	2,037
Est vol 13,000; vol Thu 16,533; open int 101,139, -769.								

Currency Futures

	OPEN	HIGH	LOW	SETTLE	CHG	LIFETIME HIGH	LIFETIME LOW	OPEN INT
Japanese Yen (CME)-12.5 million yen; $ per yen (.00)								
Sept	.8132	.8313	.8098	.8271	.0136	.8620	.7495	69,149
Dec	.8245	.8351	.8141	.8312	.0137	.8885	.7569	872
Est vol 9,480; vol Thu 8,406; open int 70,410, +755.								
Canadian Dollar (CME)-100,000 dlrs.; $ per Can $								
Sept	.6532	.6569	.6518	.6562	.0041	.6590	.6175	70,841
Dec	.6506	.6550	.6499	.6545	.0041	.6555	.6190	3,530
Mr03	.6525	.6530	.6525	.6529	.0041	.6530	.6198	662
June	.6472	.6510	.6472	.6513	.0041	.6524	.6197	384
Est vol 7,415; vol Thu 14,712; open int 75,520, +1,587.								
British Pound (CME)-62,500 pds.; $ per pound								
Sept	1.4908	1.4940	1.4874	1.4886	-.0022	1.4940	1.3990	44,600
Dec	1.4816	1.4848	1.4792	1.4794	-.0022	1.4848	1.4070	253
Est vol 1,762; vol Thu 6,164; open int 44,853, -618.								
Swiss Franc (CME)-125,000 francs; $ per franc								
Sept	.6571	.6638	.6560	.6622	.0062	.6638	.5860	44,026
Dec	.6621	.6645	.6592	.6632	.0062	.6645	.5875	148
Est vol 3,748; vol Thu 10,911; open int 44,215, +80.								
Australian Dollar (CME)-100,000 dlrs.; $ per A$								
Sept	.5674	.5708	.5671	.5692	.0025	.5728	.4790	33,624
Dec	.5653	.5660	.5644	.5647	.0025	.5660	.4980	542
Est vol 1,022; vol Thu 3,229; open int 34,834, +821.								
Mexican Peso (CME)-500,000 new Mex. peso, $ per MP								
Sept	.10020	.10020	.09810	.09900	-00082	.10830	.09810	17,840
Dec	.09790	.09790	.09680	.09710	-00104	.10673	.09680	1,781
Est vol 5,005; vol Thu 8,214; open int 19,840, +1,877.								
Euro FX (CME)-Euro 125,000; $ per Euro								
Sept	.9611	.9682	.9594	.9665	.0064	.9682	.8375	109,876
Dec	.9568	.9644	.9560	.9627	.0064	.9644	.8390	1,456
Est vol 11,938; vol Thu 31,752; open int 111,550, +400.								

Source: *The Wall Street Journal*, June 24, 2002. Reprinted by permission of Dow Jones & Company, Inc. (c) 2002 Dow Jones & Company, Inc. All Rights Reserved Worldwide.

Use the above listing from the *WSJ* to answer the following questions.

1. Calculate the value of one October Gold contract based on the settle price. What was the change in the value of this contract from the previous trading day?

2. Calculate the value of one September Canadian Dollar contract based on the settle price. What was the profit or loss on this contract from the previous trading day?

3. What is the profit or loss on one December British Pound contract if it was purchased at the contract's lifetime low and sold at the settle price listed?

Determinants of Futures value

As would be expected, the price of a futures contract is related to the price of the underlying asset. The futures contract price reflects the expected price of the underlying asset or index as of the settlement date. Overall, anything that affects the price of the underlying asset affects the futures price. If supply and demand conditions for the commodity or financial asset change, both the spot price and futures price are affected. If the spot price rises today, it is likely that the futures price will also rise. However, it is possible that traders expect the rise in the spot price to be temporary and that the futures value will be lower. Thus, futures prices reflect market participants' expectation of spot prices in the future. Lower futures prices reflect an expected decline in spot prices; higher futures prices reflect an expected increase.

Commodity futures prices are influenced by the many factors which determine supply and demand conditions in the food and energy markets. For example, wheat, corn, and soybean futures will move on current and expected weather conditions which influence the size of crops. Livestock and meat futures, such as cattle and hogs, move when changes in demand for meat, or meat products increases or decreases. Energy futures, such as oil and natural gas, will also be affected by changes in weather conditions. Colder weather increases the demand for heating oil and natural gas. The *WSJ* publishes weekly reports on supply conditions for many commodity markets. There are weekly reports on electrical production (Thursdays), oil supplies (Wednesdays), and lumber prices (Mondays).

Financial futures prices are influenced by many economic factors that affect interest rates, stock prices, and currency values. The inverse relationship between the price of a bond, or other debt instrument, and interest rates, or yields, also applies to futures prices. If interest rates are expected to rise, bond futures decline; if interest rates are expected to fall, bond futures rise. Just as with commodities, factors that affect the underlying financial assets, also affect financial futures. Anything that leads to higher interest rates, such as strong economic growth or an increase in expected inflation, leads to lower bond futures prices. Other factors may cause the effect of economic variables on the underlying assets to differ from the effect on financial futures. For example, an investor who buys a bond receives the regular interest payments. An investor in a bond futures contract does not receive any interest. This cost of holding bond futures over bonds themselves may lead to a differential affect of changing interest rates on bonds versus bond futures.

Exercise 12-2

Metal Futures

Copper-High (CMX)-25,000 lbs.; cents per lb.

	OPEN	HIGH	LOW	SETTLE	CHG	LIFETIME HIGH	LIFETIME LOW	OPEN INT
June	n.a.	76.00	75.85	75.85	-0.10	89.50	62.35	972
July	76.10	76.65	75.60	76.00	-0.10	88.90	62.30	46,486
Aug	76.10	76.75	76.10	76.35	-0.05	82.90	62.90	2,509
Sept	76.85	77.25	76.35	76.70	-0.05	88.00	62.95	10,129
Oct	76.90	77.20	76.85	76.90	-0.05	85.50	63.60	1,314
Nov	77.10	77.10	77.10	77.10	-0.05	85.50	64.00	969
Dec	77.00	77.70	77.00	77.30	-0.05	83.00	63.50	9,218
Ja03	77.60	77.60	77.60	77.50	-0.05	80.10	64.90	592
May	78.50	78.50	78.15	78.30	-0.05	81.05	65.80	2,005
July	78.90	78.90	78.90	78.60	-0.05	80.80	66.80	725
Ja04	79.90	79.90	79.90	79.55	-0.05	79.90	76.40	130

Est vol 8,000; vol Mon 7,825; open int 84,204, -1,278.

Gold (CMX)-100 troy oz.; $ per troy oz.

	OPEN	HIGH	LOW	SETTLE	CHG	LIFETIME HIGH	LIFETIME LOW	OPEN INT
June	317.00	319.10	317.00	319.20	1.80	385.00	264.50	824
Aug	317.80	320.20	317.20	319.70	1.60	331.50	272.60	101,150
Oct	318.70	321.00	318.70	320.70	1.60	331.50	274.00	5,514
Dec	320.00	321.80	319.50	321.60	1.60	358.00	268.10	26,451
Fb03	321.20	322.50	321.20	322.50	1.60	333.70	286.50	7,714
Dec	328.60	328.60	328.60	328.50	1.60	359.30	280.00	7,212
Dc04	336.00	337.50	336.00	338.20	1.60	388.00	290.00	2,394

Est vol 20,000; vol Mon 16,284; open int 169,227, +1,905.

Platinum (NYM)-50 troy oz.; $ per troy oz.

	OPEN	HIGH	LOW	SETTLE	CHG	LIFETIME HIGH	LIFETIME LOW	OPEN INT
July	563.00	567.50	561.50	565.80	3.50	569.80	405.00	6,133

Est vol 987; vol Mon 1,585; open int 7,172, +331.

Silver (CMX)-5,000 troy oz.; cnts per troy oz.

	OPEN	HIGH	LOW	SETTLE	CHG	LIFETIME HIGH	LIFETIME LOW	OPEN INT
June				484.2	2.2	515.0	440.0	4
July	482.3	486.5	481.5	484.5	2.2	559.0	409.5	60,194
Sept	484.0	488.5	483.5	486.6	2.3	517.0	412.5	19,456
Dec	487.0	491.5	487.0	489.1	2.4	613.0	412.0	13,113
Mr03	494.0	494.0	494.0	491.0	2.4	522.0	417.0	1,654
July	499.0	499.0	491.0	493.5	2.2	551.0	421.0	3,893
Dec	495.0	500.0	495.0	497.4	2.2	565.0	419.0	1,936

Est vol 12,000; vol Mon 6,855; open int 103,705, +768.

Weekly Oil Statistics

Oil statistics compiled by the American Petroleum Institute for the week ended June 14, 2002, with changes from the previous week and the total for a year ago (in barrels) follow:

	JUN 14 2002	JUN 7 2002	JUN 15 2001
Motor gasoline stocks	216,230,000	-451,000	r219,572,000
Motor gasoline prod	59,983,000	+1,953,000	59,185,000
Light fuel oil stocks	129,092,000	+898,000	108,755,000
Light fuel oil prod	26,089,000	+1,022,000	24,983,000
Heavy fuel oil stocks	34,666,000	-831,000	44,476,000
Heavy fuel oil prod	4,025,000	-119,000	5,824,000
Jet fuel stocks	40,648,000	+163,000	43,476,000
Jet fuel production	11,067,000	+777,000	11,249,000
Crude runs daily	15,417,000	+109,000	15,505,000
% Rated Capacity	94.2	+0.4	95.0
Domestic output daily	5,889,000	-5,000	r5,805,000
Domestic crd oil stocks	324,148,000	+2,532,000	312,912,000
Daily crude import U.S.	8,402,000	-91,000	8,392,000
Daily prod import U.S.	2,055,000	-221,000	2,728,000

Subject to revision.

Petroleum Futures

Crude Oil, Light Sweet (NYM)-1,000 bbls.; $ per bbl.

	OPEN	HIGH	LOW	SETTLE	CHG	LIFETIME HIGH	LIFETIME LOW	OPEN INT
July	26.00	26.15	25.37	25.43	-0.66	28.58	18.75	55,583
Aug	26.30	26.38	25.60	25.65	-0.69	28.18	18.70	125,745
Sept	26.04	26.18	25.50	25.56	-0.58	27.76	19.10	46,612
Oct	25.99	26.01	25.60	25.45	-0.54	27.42	19.50	28,012
Nov	25.87	25.87	25.50	25.34	-0.50	27.07	19.55	15,993
Dec	25.60	25.75	25.30	25.22	-0.47	26.95	15.50	53,301
Ja03	25.25	25.25	25.19	25.03	-0.45	26.50	19.90	19,517
Feb	25.08	25.10	25.08	24.84	-0.44	26.10	19.70	9,399
Mar	25.00	25.00	24.93	24.65	-0.43	28.85	20.05	8,501
June	24.60	24.60	24.40	24.20	-0.40	25.35	19.82	15,266
Dec	23.60	23.70	23.60	23.43	-0.34	24.44	15.92	19,864

Est vol 189,703; vol Mon 182,254; open int 464,716, -11,569.

Heating Oil No. 2 (NYM)-42,000 gal.; $ per gal.

	OPEN	HIGH	LOW	SETTLE	CHG	LIFETIME HIGH	LIFETIME LOW	OPEN INT
July	.6650	.6690	.6530	.6549	-.0100	.7300	.5210	27,145
Aug	.6710	.6750	.6610	.6620	-.0101	.7340	.5300	31,482
Sept	.6746	.6800	.6680	.6700	-.0096	.7300	.5390	13,783
Oct	.6900	.6900	.6795	.6785	-.0091	.7345	.5460	9,479
Nov	.6965	.6965	.6845	.6865	-.0091	.7500	.5570	7,905
Dec	.7000	.7000	.6940	.6930	-.0086	.7570	.5660	18,059
Ja03	.7060	.7060	.6990	.6960	-.0081	.7510	.5680	8,711
Feb	.7000	.7000	.6970	.6935	-.0076	.7441	.5710	7,961
Mar	.6910	.6910	.6860	.6810	-.0071	.7261	.5640	5,111
Apr	.6710	.6710	.6680	.6645	-.0066	.7041	.5500	2,448
May	.6575	.6575	.6500	.6475	-.0061	.6800	.5450	1,432
June	.6450	.6450	.6450	.6425	-.0056	.6751	.5600	3,346

Est vol 31,095; vol Mon 34,426; open int 139,239, -2,084.

Gasoline-NY Unleaded (NYM)-42,000 gal.; $ per gal.

	OPEN	HIGH	LOW	SETTLE	CHG	LIFETIME HIGH	LIFETIME LOW	OPEN INT
July	.7905	.7913	.7730	.7766	-.0144	.8510	.5925	40,193
Aug	.7910	.7948	.7765	.7786	-.0154	.8290	.5800	39,945
Sept	.7720	.7750	.7610	.7618	-.0137	.8000	.5788	16,924
Oct	.7370	.7370	.7300	.7258	-.0122	.7550	.5815	12,287
Dec	.7090	.7090	.7040	.6990	-.0115	.7285	.5700	3,256
Ja03	.7000	.7000	.7000	.6977	-.0118	.7260	.5775	1,917

Est vol 39,479; vol Mon 33,066; open int 119,505, +448.

Natural Gas (NYM)-10,000 MMBtu.; $ per MMBtu

	OPEN	HIGH	LOW	SETTLE	CHG	LIFETIME HIGH	LIFETIME LOW	OPEN INT
July	3.479	3.480	3.295	3.312	-.065	4.780	2.320	44,602
Aug	3.460	3.465	3.370	3.385	-.062	4.790	2.380	41,777
Sept	3.484	3.484	3.400	3.412	-.060	4.770	2.380	32,000
Oct	3.480	3.495	3.435	3.445	-.057	4.785	2.410	49,470
Nov	3.740	3.770	3.705	3.725	-.052	4.900	2.630	33,516
Dec	3.980	4.022	3.960	3.972	-.050	5.010	2.720	32,129
Ja03	4.130	4.130	4.060	4.062	-.044	5.049	2.730	29,610
Feb	3.990	4.040	3.990	3.998	-.042	4.874	2.700	23,461
Mar	3.980	3.980	3.905	3.908	-.032	4.710	2.710	20,440
Apr	3.820	3.820	3.770	3.778	-.022	4.520	2.610	17,931
May	3.770	3.770	3.770	3.753	-.017	4.490	2.630	12,838
June	3.810	3.816	3.780	3.783	-.013	4.400	2.610	16,764
July	3.820	3.840	3.815	3.822	-.013	4.530	2.550	13,127
Aug	3.880	3.880	3.855	3.850	-.010	4.535	2.890	13,333
Sept	3.880	3.880	3.850	3.850	-.010	4.445	2.880	11,163
Oct	3.920	3.920	3.885	3.885	-.015	4.455	2.910	15,632
Nov	4.110	4.110	4.060	4.080	-.010	4.673	3.050	8,186
Dec	4.290	4.290	4.270	4.265	-.005	4.820	3.250	12,203
Ja04	4.370	4.370	4.360	4.345	-.005	4.880	3.300	7,090
Feb	4.265	4.265	4.265	4.240	-.005	4.760	3.260	5,725
Mar	4.085	4.085	4.070	4.060	-.005	4.510	3.150	7,076
Apr	3.790	3.790	3.790	3.775	-.005	4.190	2.970	6,858
May	3.765	3.765	3.765	3.755	.010	4.155	3.030	9,982
June	3.760	3.760	3.760	3.780	.010	3.850	3.010	5,617

Est vol 98,131; vol Mon 91,686; open int 521,304, -6,880.

Brent Crude (IPE) 1,000 net bbls.; $ per bbl.

	OPEN	HIGH	LOW	SETTLE	CHG	LIFETIME HIGH	LIFETIME LOW	OPEN INT
Aug	25.05	25.10	24.75	24.79	-0.45	27.15	17.95	70,471
Sep	25.00	25.10	24.80	24.83	-0.47	26.80	18.19	42,893
Oct	24.99	24.99	24.78	24.76	-0.44	26.48	18.30	19,546
Nov	24.82	24.77	24.64	24.62	-0.42	26.08	19.10	8,310
Dec	24.70	24.70	24.50	24.50	-0.42	25.95	17.35	31,387
Ja03	24.48	24.48	24.30	24.31	-0.40	25.40	19.15	12,210
Jun	23.70	23.70	23.70	23.58	-0.27	24.22	19.45	7,330
Dec	22.90	22.90	22.83	22.85	-0.27	23.43	19.15	11,600

Est vol 45,000; vol Mon 64,295; open int 219,924, +6,692.

Use the listings on the previous page from the *WSJ* to answer the following questions.

1. According to the Metals Futures prices, what is market's expectation for the spot price of gold in December?

2. What is market's expectation for the spot price of NY Unleaded Gasoline in December?

3. According to the Weekly Oil Statistics listing, has the weekly supply of the motor gasoline increased or decreased over the past year? Assuming that all other factors are unchanging, does the market expect this trend in gasoline supply to continue or reverse course?

Hedging with futures

Anyone that may be adversely affected by a change in the future spot price of an asset, whether a commodity or a financial asset, can use futures contracts to *hedge* this risk. A hedge is a transaction designed to counterbalance another transaction so as to protect against risk. Farmers, dairy producers, and energy producers use futures contracts extensively to protect themselves against price risk. An alternative to using futures to hedge price risk is for these producers to simply agree to long-term price contracts that stipulate the exact price producers receive for their production. For example, a wheat farmer can agree on a price with the grain mill operators before planting his crop. The farmer would know for certain the profit per bushel to be received well in advance of harvest. Unfortunately, the mill operators may not be willing to agree to this contract. The operators may not want to take on the price risk themselves. Futures markets provide the ability for producers to transfer price risk to speculators or other market participants willing to take on the risk of future price changes.

To use futures for hedging, participants open trading accounts with futures brokers and make an initial deposit. The deposit is made to provide the necessary *margin requirement* for the commodity or financial future the hedger wishes to use. A benefit of standardized futures contracts is that it is not necessary for the contract buyer to pay for the entire value of the contract available upon purchase. Only a fraction of the contract's value is placed on deposit to insure compliance with the contract on the settlement date. This deposit is called the margin requirement and varies with different futures contracts and exchanges.

To offset the risk of lower prices in the future many farmers and other producers establish a *short position* in futures contracts. To establish a short position, hedgers sell futures contracts with characteristics similar to the product being hedged. If prices decrease, the hedger closes out the position at a profit in the futures market to offset the loss on their spot market production. If prices increase, hedger's spot market gains are offset by losses on their futures position. For example, a corn farmer with an expected crop of 100,000 bushels of corn in the late summer, can hedge the risk of falling prices by selling 20 corn futures contracts for September. Each corn futures contract is for 5,000 bushels. If prices fall, the producer buys the futures contract in September for less than they were sold and this profit at least partially offsets the lower price the farmer will receive for the 100,000 bushels of production.

An international firm has risks associated with its receivables and payables that are denominated in a currency other than their own. These risks can be hedged using currency futures. Firms with international sales can hedge receivables from other countries by selling currency futures. For example, a U.S. firm selling product in Japan may be interested in protecting itself against the risk that the Yen loses its value relative to the dollar. To hedge this risk, the firm would sell Yen futures contracts. If the value of the Yen falls, the firm's profit on the futures contract at least partially offsets the loss on the Japanese receivables. Conversely, a firm with payables due in other currencies can hedge the risk that these payables will be higher by buying currency futures. This firm is taking a *long position* – a purchase of a futures contract. For example, a U.S. based company with a significant amount of business in Europe may consider using Euro futures to hedge against changes in the Euro's value relative to the U.S. Dollar. A U.S. firm that is facing future expenses in Euros can hedge against the possibility that the Euro will rise against the U.S. Dollar (raising the expenses) by taking a long position in a Euro futures contract. If the Euro does rise the firm profits on the futures position at least partially offsetting the higher expenses payable in Euros.

Financial institutions also use futures contracts to hedge risks. Banks primarily use short-term funds, such as checking and savings deposits, to finance longer term assets, such as business loans and mortgages. This creates interest rate risk. The bank can be hurt by rising interest rates. The bank would be paying out higher rates on the short-term deposits while continuing to receive the lower interest payments from its loans. To protect against this risk, the bank can establish a short position in financial futures contracts. The bank sells futures contracts with characteristics similar to the long-term loans being hedged (i.e. Treasury Bonds, 10 year Agency Notes, etc.). If rates increase, hedger closes out the position at a profit in the futures market to offset losses in the spot market position. If rates increase, bond futures prices fall, and the hedger's spot market loses (higher deposit rates) are at least partially offset by gains on the short futures position.

A difficulty with using standardized futures contracts for hedging is that although price risk may be reduced, *basis risk* may remain. Basis risk is the risk that the amount of the asset that is covered in the futures contract is not exactly equal to the amount of the asset being hedged. For example, the corn farmer may be expecting only 100,000 bushels from the late summer harvest, but weather and other conditions lead a much higher yield of 110,000 bushels. There is also a risk that the price of the underlying asset of the futures contract is not exactly correlated with the assets being hedged. For example, the bank may want to hedge interest rate risk on business loans and mortgages using Treasury bond futures, but the interest rates on loans and treasury bonds, although related, may not move in the same way.

Exercise 12-3

Grain and Oilseed Futures

Corn (CBT)-5,000 bu.; cents per bu.

	OPEN	HIGH	LOW	SETTLE	CHG	LIFETIME HIGH	LIFETIME LOW	OPEN INT
July	208.00	209.00	205.75	206.75	-1.25	279.50	198.00	143,07
Sept	215.00	215.75	212.75	213.50	-1.75	262.00	205.25	88,64
Dec	224.50	225.75	222.00	222.75	-1.75	272.00	215.00	142,67
Mr03	233.00	233.00	230.25	231.25	-1.50	258.50	224.00	22,95
May	235.75	235.75	234.00	234.75	-1.25	252.00	229.25	7,47
July	238.50	238.50	236.75	237.50	-1.50	272.00	233.75	11,61
Sept	235.00	235.00	233.00	233.25	-1.25	242.00	233.00	74
Dec	237.50	237.75	236.00	237.00	-1.00	269.00	235.00	13,83

Est vol 67,203; vol Mon 55,461; open int 433,293, -1,690.

Oats (CBT)-5,000 bu.; cents per bu.

	OPEN	HIGH	LOW	SETTLE	CHG	LIFETIME HIGH	LIFETIME LOW	OPEN INT
July	181.00	187.00	178.25	183.75	1.75	204.25	129.00	4,34
Sept	147.00	149.75	146.25	148.25	-1.50	165.00	117.50	97
Dec	138.50	140.25	137.00	139.25	-1.25	153.00	123.00	5,031

Est vol 1,295; vol Mon 997; open int 10,566, +137.

Soybeans (CBT)-5,000 bu.; cents per bu.

	OPEN	HIGH	LOW	SETTLE	CHG	LIFETIME HIGH	LIFETIME LOW	OPEN INT
July	499.25	499.25	490.25	493.00	-5.75	533.00	425.00	73,386
Aug	492.50	492.75	486.00	488.00	-5.00	529.00	425.00	21,678
Sept	479.00	479.50	475.00	476.75	-4.00	496.50	425.00	12,125
Nov	473.50	474.00	468.50	470.75	-3.00	561.00	428.50	51,952
Ja03	474.00	475.50	472.00	473.50	-3.25	490.50	445.00	8,629
Mar	477.00	478.00	475.00	477.00	-2.50	491.00	449.00	6,876
May	477.00	478.50	476.00	478.50	-1.25	492.00	461.00	8,984
July	479.50	480.50	477.00	479.50	-1.50	525.00	450.00	2,757
Nov	476.50	477.00	473.00	473.00	-2.50	515.00	453.00	1,726

Est vol 52,463; vol Mon 39,546; open int 188,114, +778.

Soybean Meal (CBT)-100 tons; $ per ton.

	OPEN	HIGH	LOW	SETTLE	CHG	LIFETIME HIGH	LIFETIME LOW	OPEN INT
July	166.00	166.00	163.90	164.80	-1.10	171.50	141.00	43,448
Aug	162.50	162.60	161.30	162.00	-1.00	168.50	141.10	20,886
Sept	158.70	159.00	157.90	158.30	-.90	168.00	141.90	16,764
Oct	155.00	155.50	154.30	154.60	-.70	165.00	141.50	11,823
Dec	153.50	154.00	152.80	153.30	-.50	160.70	142.70	30,911
Ja03	153.10	153.30	152.30	152.80	-.50	160.00	143.50	4,696
Mar	151.30	151.40	150.70	151.00	-.50	156.50	145.50	4,237
May	149.10	149.70	149.10	149.70	.10	163.70	146.00	4,395
July	150.00	150.00	149.00	149.20	.20	156.00	147.00	2,037
Aug	149.20	149.50	149.20	149.20	.20	152.00	148.00	529
Sept	149.20	149.50	149.20	149.20	.20	152.00	148.00	487

Est vol 20,963; vol Mon 20,670; open int 140,894, -101.

Soybean Oil (CBT)-60,000 lbs.; cents per lb.

	OPEN	HIGH	LOW	SETTLE	CHG	LIFETIME HIGH	LIFETIME LOW	OPEN INT
July	18.15	18.15	17.85	17.86	-.27	20.55	15.48	49,722
Aug	18.09	18.09	17.94	17.96	-.27	20.33	15.62	20,079
Sept	18.17	18.17	18.05	18.07	-.26	19.11	15.73	11,890
Oct	18.18	18.22	18.14	18.16	-.24	19.17	15.15	7,377
Dec	18.42	18.45	18.33	18.39	-.21	20.50	16.10	24,633
My03	18.80	18.83	18.75	18.83	-.20	19.82	16.80	3,449
July	18.90	18.90	18.90	18.90	-.20	20.05	16.95	1,573

Est vol 17,304; vol Mon 17,112; open int 126,446, -3,002.

Wheat (CBT)-5,000 bu.; cents per bu.

	OPEN	HIGH	LOW	SETTLE	CHG	LIFETIME HIGH	LIFETIME LOW	OPEN INT
July	289.50	291.50	287.50	289.25	...	365.00	264.50	37,670
Sept	297.75	298.50	294.50	295.75	-.50	315.00	271.00	29,072
Dec	306.25	306.50	302.50	303.75	-1.00	365.00	283.50	25,206
Mr03	306.00	307.00	303.50	305.00	-1.50	320.00	288.50	3,395
May	300.00	301.00	299.00	299.50	-1.50	307.00	287.00	514
July	293.00	294.50	291.00	291.75	-2.25	336.00	280.50	2,942

Est vol 23,363; vol Mon 26,660; open int 98,899, -2,546.

Wheat (KC)-5,000 bu.; cents per bu.

	OPEN	HIGH	LOW	SETTLE	CHG	LIFETIME HIGH	LIFETIME LOW	OPEN INT
July	308.00	309.00	305.50	306.75	-1.25	384.50	279.00	29,400
Sept	311.50	312.25	309.00	310.00	-1.50	338.00	285.50	21,301
Dec	315.50	316.00	312.50	313.25	-2.00	348.00	293.00	16,378
Mr03	314.00	315.00	311.50	311.50	-3.00	326.00	297.50	4,258
May	311.00	312.00	311.00	311.00	-4.00	319.00	299.50	307

Est vol 11,277; vol Mon 10,100; open int 73,305, +2,650.

Wheat (MPLS)-5,000 bu.; cents per bu.

	OPEN	HIGH	LOW	SETTLE	CHG	LIFETIME HIGH	LIFETIME LOW	OPEN INT
July	300.00	301.00	298.50	299.25	-1.00	381.00	289.50	8,813
Sept	302.50	303.75	301.00	301.25	-.75	330.50	295.00	5,811
Dec	308.00	310.25	307.00	307.00	-1.00	390.00	305.00	3,976
Mr03	313.75	315.75	313.00	313.25	-.75	355.00	313.00	1,749
May	316.50	318.50	315.00	315.00	-1.50	345.00	315.00	663

Est vol na; vol Mon 2,437; open int 22,034, -250.

Interest Rate Futures

Treasury Bonds (CBT)-$100,000; pts 32nds of 100%

	OPEN	HIGH	LOW	SETTLE	CHG	LIFETIME HIGH	LIFETIME LOW	OPEN INT
June	104-15	105-00	104-06	104-13	3	110-00	96-30	30,760
Sept	103-09	103-30	103-00	103-07	3	109-00	96-07	396,857
Dec	102-15	102-20	101-30	102-03	2	103-00	96-06	31,113

Est vol 185,829; vol Mon 194,606; open int 458,732, -1,110.

Treasury Notes (CBT)-$100,000; pts 32nds of 100%

	OPEN	HIGH	LOW	SETTLE	CHG	LIFETIME HIGH	LIFETIME LOW	OPEN INT
June	08-215	08-215	108-05	08-095	2.5	08-255	101-10	77,734
Sept	106-31	07-115	06-245	06-295	2.5	08-165	100-25	705,598

Est vol 315,698; vol Mon 275,262; open int 784,416, -18,143.

10 Yr Agency Notes (CBT)-$100,000; pts 32nds of 100%

	OPEN	HIGH	LOW	SETTLE	CHG	LIFETIME HIGH	LIFETIME LOW	OPEN INT
June	104-02	104-04	104-02	104-04	3.0	104-13	97-04	7,360
Sept	103-10	103-11	102-27	02-295	2.5	03-135	97-19	26,094

Est vol 2,732; vol Mon 1,402; open int 33,454, -136.

5 Yr Treasury Notes (CBT)-$100,000; pts 32nds of 100%

	OPEN	HIGH	LOW	SETTLE	CHG	LIFETIME HIGH	LIFETIME LOW	OPEN INT
June	08-125	08-175	108-09	108-11	2.0	08-195	03-115	35,156
Sept	07-015	107-10	106-31	107-02	2.5	107-11	102-17	556,365

Est vol 123,978; vol Mon 116,844; open int 591,521, -8,257.

2 Yr Treasury Notes (CBT)-$200,000; pts 32nds of 100%

	OPEN	HIGH	LOW	SETTLE	CHG	LIFETIME HIGH	LIFETIME LOW	OPEN INT
June	105-18	105-20	05-147	105-17	1.5	105-20	03-005	11,205
Sept	04-257	04-287	104-24	04-257	2.0	05-155	103-11	94,754

Est vol 5,562; vol Mon 10,420; open int 105,959, -2,512.

30 Day Federal Funds (CBT)-$5,000,000; pts of 100%

	OPEN	HIGH	LOW	SETTLE	CHG	LIFETIME HIGH	LIFETIME LOW	OPEN INT
June	98.240	98.240	98.235	98.235	...	98.370	96.960	43,550
July	98.24	98.24	98.24	98.24	...	99.22	97.68	63,743
Aug	98.22	98.23	98.22	98.23	.01	98.24	97.47	32,809
Sept	98.19	98.20	98.19	98.20	.01	98.21	97.27	16,345
Oct	98.12	98.15	98.12	98.14	.02	98.16	97.75	14,464
Dec	97.91	97.91	97.90	97.91	.03	97.95	96.60	683

Est vol 10,760; vol Mon 14,862; open int 174,589, +2,490.

10 Yr Interest Rate Swaps (CBT)-$100,000; pts 32nds of 100%

	OPEN	HIGH	LOW	SETTLE	CHG	LIFETIME HIGH	LIFETIME LOW	OPEN INT
Sept	103-14	103-25	103-09	103-14	2	104-00	100-08	33,169

Est vol 705; vol Mon 2,937; open int 33,169, -9,777.

Muni Bond Index (CBT)-$1,000; times Bond Buyer MBI

	OPEN	HIGH	LOW	SETTLE	CHG	LIFETIME HIGH	LIFETIME LOW	OPEN INT
June	106-04	106-04	105-17	105-23	2	106-09	99-09	5,282
Sept	104-26	104-29	104-05	104-12	1	106-09	102-01	3,712

Est vol 1,286; vol Mon 1,296; open int 8,994, +282.
Index: Close 105-02; Yield 5.38.

Treasury Bills (CME)-$1,000,000; pts of 100%

	OPEN	HIGH	LOW	SETTLE	CHG	YIELD	CHG	OPEN INT
Sept	...	...	...	98.16	...	1.84	...	175

Est vol 0; vol Mon 43; open int 452, +11.

Libor-1 Mo. (CME)-$3,000,000; pts of 100%

	OPEN	HIGH	LOW	SETTLE	CHG	YIELD	CHG	OPEN INT
July	98.16	98.16	98.15	98.15	...	1.85	...	30,297
Aug	98.14	98.14	98.12	98.12	...	1.88	...	8,717
Sept	98.06	98.06	98.04	98.05	.02	1.95	-.02	4,353
Oct	97.97	97.99	97.97	97.99	.03	2.01	-.03	427
Nov	97.83	97.84	97.83	97.84	.05	2.16	-.05	300

Est vol 1,858; vol Mon 11,270; open int 57,980, +8,663.

Eurodollar (CME)-$1,000,000; pts of 100%

	OPEN	HIGH	LOW	SETTLE	CHG	YIELD	CHG	OPEN INT
July	98.09	98.09	98.07	98.07	...	1.93	...	53,245
Aug	98.02	98.02	98.01	98.01	.01	1.99	-.01	24,455
Sept	97.89	97.94	97.90	97.91	.02	2.09	-.02	669,292
Dec	97.50	97.58	97.49	97.54	.03	2.46	-.03	748,098
Mr03	96.95	97.03	96.94	96.99	.04	3.01	-.04	546,653
June	96.35	96.45	96.35	96.41	.05	3.59	-.05	317,073
Sept	95.92	95.97	95.89	95.93	.05	4.07	-.05	284,686
Dec	95.55	95.58	95.52	95.55	.04	4.45	-.04	210,347
Mr04	95.31	95.44	95.28	95.30	.02	4.70	-.02	176,236
June	95.14	95.15	95.07	95.09	.01	4.91	-.01	144,734
Sept	94.98	94.98	94.91	94.92	...	5.08	...	136,795
Dec	94.79	94.81	94.73	94.75	...	5.25	...	107,960
Mr05	94.70	94.74	94.66	94.67	...	5.33	...	110,659
June	94.63	94.63	94.54	94.56	...	5.44	...	67,919
Sept	94.47	94.51	94.43	94.45	...	5.55	...	65,089
Dec	94.36	94.37	94.29	94.32	...	5.68	...	54,613
Mr06	94.29	94.33	94.25	94.27	-.01	5.73	.01	46,986
June	94.19	94.24	94.16	94.18	-.01	5.82	.01	58,802
Sept	94.09	94.15	94.08	94.10	-.01	5.90	.01	49,984
Dec	93.96	94.02	93.95	93.97	-.01	6.03	.01	41,419
Mr07	93.91	93.98	93.91	93.92	-.01	6.08	.01	32,989
June	93.87	93.91	93.84	93.85	-.01	6.15	.01	17,535
Sept	93.77	93.82	93.77	93.77	-.01	6.23	.01	10,553
Dec	93.64	93.70	93.64	93.65	-.01	6.35	.01	10,293

Est vol 629,377; vol Mon 711,230; open int 4,526,315, -60,842.

	OPEN	HIGH	LOW	SETTLE	CHG	LIFETIME HIGH	LIFETIME LOW	OPEN INT
Euro-Yen (CME)-Yen 100,000,000; pts of 100%								
Sept	99.90	99.90	99.90	99.90	...	99.91	97.84	5,209
Dec	...	...	...	99.89	...	99.90	97.77	3,981
Mr03	99.85	99.85	99.85	99.85	...	99.85	97.72	2,875
June	99.85	99.85	99.85	99.85	...	99.85	98.32	3,495
Est vol 612; vol Mon 753; open int 48,104, +972.								
Short Sterling (LIFFE)-£500,000; pts of 100%								
June	95.80	95.82	95.79	95.81	.01	96.38	92.39	146,128
July	95.71	95.73	95.71	95.70	.02	95.73	95.64	451
Sept	95.42	95.54	95.42	95.49	.07	96.18	92.38	173,154
Dec	95.06	95.20	95.05	95.15	.10	95.93	92.45	171,926
Mr03	94.78	94.92	94.78	94.88	.10	95.51	92.49	120,096
June	94.58	94.69	94.57	94.65	.08	95.24	92.77	76,685
Sept	94.44	94.53	94.44	94.50	.07	95.08	92.90	98,966
Dec	94.38	94.46	94.38	94.42	.05	94.90	92.92	92,065
Mr04	94.36	94.43	94.36	94.38	.03	94.78	93.01	39,105
June	94.36	94.41	94.36	94.37	.03	94.75	93.04	15,299
Sept	94.39	94.41	94.36	94.37	.03	94.70	93.35	10,928
Dec	94.37	94.41	94.37	94.37	.02	94.62	93.25	7,910
Mr05	94.39	94.39	94.38	94.37	.02	94.60	93.29	3,791
Est vol 240,449; vol Mon 122,502; open int 959,810, +6,150.								
Long Gilt (LIFFE) (Decimal)-£50,000; pts of 100%								
June	113.48	113.80	113.47	113.55	.18	115.60	110.51	18,324
Sept	112.56	113.18	112.54	112.78	.18	113.18	110.26	96,286
Est vol 32,826; vol Mon 29,414; open int 114,610, +666.								
3 Month Euribor (LIFFE)-Euro 1,000,000; pts of 100%								
July	96.48	96.49	96.47	96.47	...	96.50	96.26	19,770
Sept	96.33	96.36	96.31	96.32	...	97.31	94.24	348,945
Dec	96.08	96.13	96.06	96.08	.01	97.08	94.06	278,455
Mr03	95.91	95.96	95.89	95.92	.02	96.91	94.05	234,616
June	95.74	95.78	95.71	95.73	.01	96.92	93.99	155,890
Sept	95.62	95.66	95.59	95.61	.01	96.54	93.91	120,501
Dec	95.48	95.52	95.46	95.47	.02	95.53	93.80	87,479
Mr04	95.42	95.46	95.39	95.42	.02	96.22	93.83	50,852
June	95.31	95.37	95.31	95.33	.02	96.07	93.79	32,052
Sept	95.23	95.29	95.23	95.25	.02	95.94	93.73	29,717
Dec	95.12	95.17	95.12	95.13	.02	95.74	93.64	15,972
Mr05	95.08	95.12	95.08	95.09	.02	95.66	94.07	14,264
June	95.03	95.06	95.03	95.03	.02	95.54	94.29	11,847
Sept	95.00	95.00	94.99	94.97	.02	95.43	94.29	1,860
Dec	94.90	94.90	94.90	94.86	.02	95.28	94.41	697
Est vol 379,395; vol Mon 260,360; open int 1,404,780, −269,756.								
3 Month Euroswiss (LIFFE)-SFr 1,000,000; pts of 100%								
Sept	98.49	98.52	98.46	98.49	−.01	98.55	94.24	90,410
Dec	98.00	98.04	97.98	98.00	...	98.06	94.06	45,096
Mr03	97.60	97.65	97.60	97.60	−.01	97.66	94.05	19,211
June	97.32	97.33	97.31	97.31	−.02	97.37	93.99	6,496
Sept	97.17	97.17	97.15	97.15	−.01	97.19	93.91	4,761
Est vol 12,599; vol Mon 20,425; open int 169,284, +37,785.								
Canadian Bankers Acceptance (ME)-C$1,000,000								
July	...	...	...	97.06	−0.02	97.05	97.05	139
Aug	...	...	...	96.95	−0.02	96.85	96.85	119
Sept	96.85	96.88	96.81	96.82	−0.02	97.80	93.11	69,371
Dec	96.49	96.51	96.41	96.42	−0.02	97.23	93.06	55,449
Mr03	96.09	96.10	96.01	96.03	...	96.80	93.98	18,910
June	95.77	95.77	95.68	95.71	0.03	96.40	93.96	6,121
Sept	95.38	95.38	95.38	95.38	0.02	95.86	93.82	3,486
Ju04	94.93	94.93	94.93	94.90	0.02	94.93	94.34	191
Est vol 16,784; vol Mon 17,320; open int 158,076, −49,868.								
10 Yr. Canadian Govt. Bonds (ME)-C$100,000								
June	...	...	...	104.32	0.01	104.05	99.55	13,509
Sept	103.79	103.82	103.30	103.47	0.02	103.90	101.45	61,712
Est vol 5,382; vol Mon 4,380; open int 75,221, +2,019.								
10 Yr. Euro Notional Bond (MATIF)-Euros 100,000								
Sept	...	...	...	88.54	0.25	...	...	n.a.
Est vol n.a.; vol Mon 70; open int n.a., .								
3 Yr. Commonwealth T-Bonds (SFE)-A$100,000								
Sept	94.33	94.34	94.25	94.30	−0.04	94.37	93.74	240,269
Est vol 56,108; vol Mon 171,900; open int 240,269, +12,320.								
Euro-Yen (SGX)-Yen 100,000,000 pts of 100%								
Sept	99.90	99.90	99.90	99.90	...	99.91	98.35	38,962
Dec	99.89	99.89	99.88	99.89	0.01	99.90	98.28	37,527
Mr03	99.85	99.85	99.85	99.85	0.01	99.85	98.45	34,977
June	99.85	99.85	99.85	99.85	...	99.85	98.40	50,036
Dec	99.76	99.76	99.76	99.76	0.01	99.76	98.09	13,482
Est vol 6,859; vol Mon 8,082; open int 233,034, −72,705.								
5 Yr. German Euro-BOBL (EUREX)-Euro 100,000; pts of 100%								
Sept	105.74	105.91	105.67	105.79	0.12	105.95	103.70	503,322
Dec	...	...	...	105.20	0.12	105.18	103.96	4,217
vol Tue 412,094; open int 507,539, +13,672.								

Source: *The Wall Street Journal*, June 19, 2002. Reprinted by permission of Dow Jones & Company, Inc. (c) 2002 Dow Jones & Company, Inc. All Rights Reserved Worldwide.

Use the listing on the previous pages from the *WSJ* to answer the following questions.

1. Suppose a soybean farmer wants to hedge 200,000 bushels of soybeans expected to be harvested and delivered in September. What contract and position should the farmer use to hedge this risk? Based on the settle price, what is the value of this contract?

2. A bank currently holds a $10,000,000 portfolio of business loans with long-term maturities. The bank managers are worried that interest rates will rise substantially through the end of this year. What futures contract position can be used to partially offset the risk that interest rates may rise? How many contracts should the bank use to match its loan portfolio? Based on the settle price, what is the value of this contract?

Speculating with futures

Speculators in futures markets are as equally likely to buy or sell futures contracts. A hedger uses the futures market to lay off risk on speculators. The hedger's sale of a futures contract, a short position, used to offset the risk of a decline in prices must be purchased by another futures market participant. A long position is a strategy used by speculators anticipating prices will rise. For example, a speculator that anticipates a decline in interest rates buys an interest rate futures contract; if rates drop, the contract's price rises above what it cost to purchase and the speculator sells it at a profit. If interest rates rise instead of fall, the futures contract price drops and it is sold for less than it cost to initially buy the contract and losses result. A speculator may also take short positions. The strategy to use if a speculator anticipates interest rates will rise and contract prices drop, is the sale of an interest rate futures contract. The speculator hopes to close the position by buying the contract back at a lower price. If rates rise, the price to buy the contract, and close the position, is less than the price received for the initial sale of the contract. The speculator loses money if rates drop.

Many individuals and institutions take positions in the futures market to profit from expected changes in exchange rates. These speculators use currency futures to profit from the changes in the relative values of different currencies. For example, a speculator that believes the Euro will gain in value relative to the Japanese Yen can purchase a Euro-Yen contract. If the Yen declines in value, the futures contract will rise.

Exercise 12-4

Use the listings in Exercise 12-1 to answer the following questions.

1.   What is the profit or loss on one December Gold contract if a speculator purchased the contract at its lifetime low and sold at the settle price listed? What is the profit or loss on one December Gold contract if a speculator sold the contract at its lifetime high and closed the position at the settle price listed?

2.   What is the profit or loss on one September Swiss Franc contract if a speculator purchased the contract at day's opening and sold at the settle price listed? What is the profit or loss on one September Swiss Franc contract if a speculator sold the contract at the day's low price and closed the position at the settle price listed?

Project 12-1

Use the Futures listing from a recent Wednesday edition of the *WSJ* to answer the following questions.

Date _____

1. What is market's expectation for the spot price of Crude Oil, Light Sweet in the next six months?

2. According to the Weekly Oil Statistics listing, has the weekly supply of the motor gasoline increased or decreased over the past year?

3. Assuming that all other factors are unchanging, does the market expect this trend in gasoline supply to continue or reverse course?

Project 12-2

Using a recent edition of the WSJ, assess the markets' expectation for future prices, interest rates, and the value of the U.S. Dollar by completing the following tables. Fill in the tables with as many contracts as possible for wheat, gold, oil, Treasury Bonds, Japan Yen, and Euro FX.

Wheat (CBT)		Gold (Cmx.Div.NYM)		Crude oil, Light Sweet	
Contract Month (Yr)	Settle	Contract Month (Yr)	Settle	Contract Month (Yr)	Settle

Treasury Bonds (CBT)		Japan Yen (CME)		Euro FX (CME)	
Contract Month (Yr)	Settle	Contract Month (Yr)	Settle	Contract Month (Yr)	Settle

1. Based on this information, Do you expect interest rates to rise, fall, or stay level for the next few months?

2. Do you expect the U.S. Dollar to rise in value, fall in value, or stay the same relative to the Euro and Yen?

3. Considering all the futures contracts reviewed here, do you expect overall prices to be rising (inflation), falling (deflation), or staying level for the next few months?

Discussion Questions

Using a recent addition of the *WSJ*, review the Commodities Report column found in the Money and Investing Section.

1. For the trading day discussed in this report, what futures contracts were most active?

2. What contracts rose in value? What contracts fell in value?

3. What are the reasons discussed for this activity?

Chapter 13

Index Options and Index Futures

Objectives

1. Understand the basics of index options and index futures.

2. Distinguish between speculative and hedging strategies with index futures and options.

3. Describe the use of index options and futures in investment portfolio management.

4. Understand the use of index options and futures in program trading.

Key Terms

Stock Index Options   Dollar Index Futures   Portfolio Insurance
Stock Index Futures   Options on Futures   Basis Risk
Commodity Index Futures   Index Arbitrage   Program Trading

Option and futures contracts are available for not only single underlying assets, such as gold or U.S. Treasury bonds, but also for portfolios of financial assets, or indexes. Options and futures on stock indexes provide numerous speculative and hedging opportunities for investors and financial institutions. Other options and futures are available for indexes of commodities, bonds, and currencies. This chapter explores the index option and index futures information reported in the *WSJ*. We will also see how these instruments are used by portfolio managers and how market expectations are reflected in the prices of these securities.

Index Options

Recall that an option is any contractual right to act in a specified manner within a specified period of time. An index option gives its holder the right to act on a specified bundle of assets, or index, in a specified manner within a specified period of time. For example, ***stock index options*** are trading rights on a portfolio of stocks. Stock index call options give the right to buy a specified stock index; stock index put options provide the right to sell a stock index. Just as with options on individual stocks, the buyer pays a premium for the right to buy or sell the underlying asset. The *WSJ* reports price quotations for many different stock index options each day. The most popular (widely traded) index options are on the S&P 500 index and the Dow Jones Industrial Average. Index options are also available for many different industrial sectors, such as oil service companies, and foreign markets, such as Japanese stocks.

If, and when, a stock index option is exercised, the option holder receives or pays the specified contract amount multiplied by the difference between the index value and the strike price. Thus, index options are settled in cash, not by the delivery of the actual stocks or other assets. For example, suppose an investor purchased a call option on the Dow Jones Industrial Index (symbol DJX) with a strike price of 99 and an expiration in April for a premium of $4. The DJX index option contract is based on one one-hundredth of the current value of the Dow Jones Industrial Average. So a strike price of 99 corresponds to a value of 9900 for the average. When the option expired the index was at 10200; giving the option a cash settlement value of $300. Since the option contract cost 4, or $400, the investor had a loss on this trade of $100.

The Index Options Trading section of the WSJ includes index options pricing and trading information from the Chicago Board Options Exchange, the American Stock Exchange, and the Philadelphia Stock Exchange. For each option, the listing includes the expiration month of the contract in the first column; the strike price (exercise price) followed by a "c" for call options and a "p" for put options. The third column lists the volume of trading, or the number of contracts traded on the previous trading day. The next two columns give the last price at which the option traded and the change in price from the previous trading day. The final column lists the open interest as of the previous trading day. This is the amount of contracts currently outstanding for the particular contract.

Exercise 13-1

INDEX OPTIONS TRADING

Tuesday, June 18, 2002
Volume, last, net change and open interest for all contracts. Volume figures are unofficial. Open Interest reflects previous trading day. p-Put c-Call. The totals for call and put volume are midday figures

Underlying Indexes

	HIGH	LOW	CLOSE	NET CHG	FROM 12/31	% CHG
DJ Indus (DJX)	97.22	96.37	97.06	0.19	-3.16	-3.2
DJ Trans (DTX)	274.39	272.04	273.37	0.38	9.37	3.5
DJ Util (DUX)	284.28	279.95	283.33	3.12	-10.61	-3.6
S&P 100 (OEX)	518.41	513.02	516.73	0.55	-67.55	-11.6
S&P 500 (SPX)	1040.78	1031.04	1037.14	0.97	-110.94	-9.7
CB-Tech (TXX)	425.22	415.79	416.08	-4.01	-125.41	-23.2
CB-Mexico (MEX)	86.48	85.36	85.36	-1.12	13.97	19.6
CB-Lps Mex (VEX)	8.65	8.54	8.54	-0.11	1.40	19.6
M5 Multinti (NFT)	594.63	587.69	591.87	0.31	-94.78	-13.8
GSTI Comp (GTC)	151.50	147.94	147.94	-1.50	-54.28	-26.8
Nasdaq 100 (NDX)	1163.46	1138.31	1138.47	-11.44	-438.58	-27.8
NYSE (NYA)	556.52	552.05	555.20	1.01	-34.60	-5.9
Russell 2000 (RUT)	474.64	469.49	469.71	-1.03	-18.79	-3.8
Lps S&P 100 (OEX)	103.68	102.60	103.35	0.11	-13.51	-2.3
Lps S&P 500 (SPX)	104.08	103.09	103.71	0.10	-11.09	-1.0
Volatility (VIX)	28.57	26.93	27.33	-0.27	4.11	17.7
S&P Midcap (MID)	514.06	508.59	509.31	0.21	1.00	0.2
Major Mkt (XMI)	1030.05	1023.42	1028.90	-0.27	2.53	0.2
Eurotop 100 (AEUR)	243.60	241.23	242.64	-1.65	-45.29	-15.7
HK Fltg (HKO)	211.49	211.49	211.49	0.19	-12.81	-5.7
IW Internet (IIX)	93.50	90.90	91.48	0.09	-54.45	-37.3
AM-Mexico (MXY)	102.74	101.21	101.21	-1.39	0.80	0.8
Institut'l-A.M. (XII)	548.04	542.61	546.40	0.45	-73.72	-11.9
Japan (JPN)			114.37	1.77	2.11	1.9
MS Cyclical (CYC)	566.08	559.85	564.74	3.37	32.87	6.2
MS Consumr (CMR)	566.64	563.09	565.42	0.04	0.55	0.1
Biotech (BTK)	380.60	367.77	370.77	-4.57	-209.81	-36.1
Gold/Silver (XAU)	76.41	73.41	76.39	2.74	21.96	40.3
Value Line (VAY)	1206.60	1194.74	1195.01	-2.14	-52.12	-4.2
Bank (BKX)	871.89	858.64	869.84	2.23	9.70	1.1
Semicond (SOXX)	462.83	441.97	441.97	-6.99	-80.19	-15.4
Street.com (DOT)	109.90	106.98	107.34	-0.39	-85.60	-44.4
Oil Service (OSX)	101.52	99.14	99.80	-1.31	12.66	14.5
PSE Tech (PSE)	563.34	552.52	552.65	-4.05	-134.80	-19.6

CHICAGO

DJ INDUS AVG (DJX)

STRIKE	VOL	LAST	NET CHG	OPEN INT
Dec 68p	30	0.45	-0.05	...
Dec 70p	4,500	0.55	-0.25	...
Dec 72p	15	0.70	-0.05	...
Sep 76p	30	0.30	-0.05	...
Dec 76p	10	1.10	0.10	...
Sep 80p	45	0.55	...	...
Dec 80p	6	1.40	...	...
Jul 84p	60	0.30	0.05	...
Jul 84p	41	0.85	-0.25	...
Dec 84p	9	2	-0.30	...
Jun 88c	1,000	8.90	-5.60	1,127
Jul 88c	400	9.30	2.90	39
Jul 88p	405	0.40	-0.25	...
Sep 88c	3	10	-0.30	132
Sep 88p	31	1.55	-0.15	...
Dec 88p	4	2.90	...	...
Jul 90p	118	0.60	0.10	...
Sep 90p	54	1.85	-0.15	...
Dec 90p	54	3.30	-0.10	...
Jun 92c	13	5	0.20	740
Jun 92p	494	0.05	-0.05	...
Jul 92c	10	6	0.20	741
Jul 92p	74	0.90	-0.15	...
Sep 92c	2	7.70	0.80	1,270
Sep 92p	19	2.25	-0.30	...
Dec 92p	5	3.80	-0.20	...
Jun 94c	367	3.40	0.60	1,110
Jun 94p	1,167	0.10	-0.25	...
Jul 94c	243	4.70	0.80	216
Jul 94p	296	1.30	-0.25	...
Sep 94c	16	6.10	0.30	1,922
Sep 94p	3	2.80	-0.40	...
Dec 94p	10	4.60	0.10	...
Jun 95c	28	2.50	0.45	1,604
Jun 95p	763	0.25	-0.15	...
Jun 96c	2,728	1.70	0.20	9,210
Jun 96p	2,369	0.50	-0.20	...
Jul 96c	169	3.80	0.95	2,328
Jul 96p	325	2	-0.15	...
Sep 96c	139	4.70	0.30	6,899
Sep 96p	239	3.60	-0.40	...
Jun 97c	1,074	0.95	0.05	6,740
Jun 97p	723	0.75	-0.25	...
Jul 97c	140	2.70	0.25	953
Jul 97p	129	2.40	-0.10	...
Jun 98c	2,640	0.55	0.05	23,133
Jun 98p	667	1.30	-0.20	...
Jul 98c	187	2.05	0.10	4,112
Jul 98p	140	3.10	...	...
Sep 98c	70	3.60	0.10	6,816
Sep 98p	52	4.90	-0.10	...
Dec 98p	7	6	-0.50	...
Jun 99c	259	0.25	0.05	3,862
Jun 99p	23	2.20	-0.10	...
Jun 100c	40	0.05	...	11,789
Jun 100p	344	2.45	-0.75	...
Jul 100c	930	1.30	0.15	3,944
Jul 100p	84	4.10	-0.30	...
Sep 100c	7	2.60	0.55	1,695
Sep 100p	9	5.50	-0.60	...
Dec 100p	25	7.30	-0.10	...
Jun 102c	40	0.05	...	28,350
Jun 102p	5	4.70	-0.30	...
Jul 102c	140	0.55	-0.05	4,968
Jul 102p	8	5.50	-0.60	...
Sep 102c	103	1.90	0.05	2,742
Dec 102p	83	8.10	-0.50	...

STRIKE	VOL	LAST	NET CHG	OPEN INT
Jun 500c	3,696	0.90	-0.75	7,500
Jul 500c	136	28	3.20	...
Jul 500p	244	7.50	-1.50	4,452
Aug 500p	14	12.50	-2.50	1,125
Sep 500p	12	17	-0.80	2,186
Jun 505c	502	16	...	...
Jun 505p	2,025	1	-1.50	3,977
Jul 505c	23	21.90	0.40	...
Jul 505p	15	9.80	-0.40	467
Jun 510c	1,427	12.30	2.30	...
Jun 510p	4,489	1.80	-2.00	7,543
Jul 510c	54	19.90	1.50	...
Jul 510p	158	10.50	-1.50	1,522
Jun 515c	4,562	8.30	1.40	...
Jun 515p	4,064	3	-2.70	3,518
Jul 515c	88	17.50	2.40	...
Jul 515p	178	13.10	-1.50	1,240
Jun 520c	6,104	4.50	0.50	...
Jun 520p	1,598	4.80	-3.80	3,659
Jul 520c	298	14.50	0.80	...
Jul 520p	78	14.70	-2.90	2,598
Aug 520p	4	21	-2.00	249
Sep 520c	77	22	-1.00	...
Sep 520p	81	24.50	-2.50	1,619
Jun 525c	1,797	2.20	...	...
Jun 525p	92	8.50	-2.80	2,069
Jul 525c	25	11.30	1.30	...
Jul 525p	3	18.20	-4.00	255
Jun 530c	1,830	1.30	0.05	...
Jun 530p	456	14.10	-1.80	3,623
Jul 530c	783	9.20	0.70	...
Jul 530p	14	22	-8.00	1,225
Jun 535c	525	0.40	-0.20	...
Jul 535p	10	17	-4.00	1,462
Jul 535c	32	5.80	...	...
Jun 540c	3,154	0.15	-0.15	...
Jun 540p	92	24.20	-0.80	2,602

STRIKE	VOL	LAST	NET CHG	OPEN INT
Jun 1100c	793	59.10	-4.90	40,310
Jul 1100c	2,272	5.30	0.30	...
Jul 1100p	1,237	66.50	-2.50	12,131
Aug 1100c	35	12.50	1.50	...
Aug 1100p	20	71.50	-3.50	4,292
Sep 1100c	1,898	18.50	0.80	...
Sep 1100p	1,206	77.50	-8.00	12,990
Jun 1110c	2	0.05	...	...
Jun 1110p	13	74	-20.00	5,639
Jun 1120c	1	0.05	...	...
Jun 1125c	2	0.05	-0.05	...
Jun 1125p	18	88.50	-1.50	30,380
Jul 1125c	841	2.25	0.15	...
Aug 1125c	44	7	1.00	...
Sep 1125c	7	12	1.70	...
Sep 1125p	5	102.50	-31.50	4,702
Jun 1130c	14	0.05	-0.45	...
Sep 1135c	72	104	24.00	553
Jun 1150c	65	0.05	...	...
Jun 1150p	2	112	-4.00	22,524
Jul 1150c	217	0.70	-0.30	...
Jul 1150p	202	113	-14.00	423
Aug 1150p	16	3.50	-0.20	...
Aug 1150p	1	115	38.50	100
Sep 1150c	877	7.50	0.50	...
Sep 1150p	2	122.50	1.50	6,031
Jun 1170p	13	134.50	-25.50	3,868
Jun 1175c	5	0.05	...	...
Jun 1175p	3,220	135.10	-9.90	6,763
Jul 1175p	15	141	50.00	90
Jun 1200p	9	159	-10.00	8,158
Jul 1200c	10	0.30	-0.05	...
Jul 1200p	4	168	-9.00	112
Jun 1225p	1	186	-8.00	638
Sep 1225c	1	1.70	0.85	...
Jun 1250p	848	209.60	-6.40	3,736
Jul 1250p	4	213	60.00	197

STRIKE	VOL	LAST	NET CHG	OPEN INT
Call Vol.	926		Open Int.	43,546
Put Vol.	1,439		Open Int.	35,879

OIL SERVICE (OSX)

STRIKE	VOL	LAST	NET CHG	OPEN INT
Sep 85p	50	2.40	-0.50	1,137
Jul 90p	425	1.45	-0.15	1,519
Jun 95c	5	5.20	-1.30	...
Jun 95p	250	0.35	-0.05	4,055
Jun 100c	55	2.25	...	...
Jun 100p	295	1.60	0.10	10,263
Jul 100c	80	4.60	-0.10	...
Jul 100p	30	4	-1.80	1,039
Aug 100c	5	7.10	1.10	...
Aug 100p	91	7.30	0.90	1,118
Jun 105p	250	4.40	-5.90	16,482
Jul 105c	50	2.90	-0.60	...
Jul 105p	6,325	8	1.00	1,729
Jul 110c	100	1.45	-0.30	...
Jul 115c	1,000	0.90	-3.30	...
Call Vol.	1,540		Open Int.	48,370
Put Vol.	13,745		Open Int.	58,516

PHLX KBW (BKX)

STRIKE	VOL	LAST	NET CHG	OPEN INT
Jun 400c	11	0.50	-0.10	39
Jul 400p	12	40.50	-11.50	...
Aug 400c	5	17.80	-0.80	200
Jun 460c	7	0.40	0.35	1,036
Jun 460p	7	82.40	33.60	...
Aug 700p	1	3.70	...	...
Jun 800p	5	0.40	-0.10	...
Jun 820p	2	0.30	-0.40	...
Jun 830c	6	40	2.00	20
Jul 835p	1	14.20	...	...
Jun 840p	100	1.75	-1.75	...
Jun 845p	10	3	-6.60	...
Jun 850p	5	3.10	-2.00	...
Jun 860c	10	12.40	10.30	35
Jun 865c	20	12.10	...	...

```
Sep 1150 p   58 100   -10.00   299
Jun 1175 c   53   9.10 -3.90
Jun 1175 c    5  30  -11.00     343
Jul 1175 c    8  53    9.00
Jun 1200 c  373   7.20  0.20
Jun 1200 p   13  46   -8.00   1,219
Jul 1200 c    1 37.10 10.10
Sep 1200 c   10  77   21.00
Jun 1225 c  145  1.75 -0.25
Jul 1225 c    3 36.50 16.90
Jun 1250 c   87  0.65 -0.35
Jul 1250 c   90  23   -4.40
Jul 1250 p   75 125    1.00    1,254
Sep 1250 p   50 152  -18.00     320
Jun 1275 c  150  0.40  0.05
Jul 1275 c   29 19.60  8.60
Jun 1300 c     4 155  -15.00   3,161
Jul 1300 c    9  13   -1.00
Sep 1300 c   15  50    5.00
Jul 1350 c    4  8.40  4.80
Aug 1350 c   20 18.40 -11.50
Sep 1350 p    9 226    4.00     150
Jun 1375 c  100  0.10 -0.20
Jul 1375 c    4  4.90  1.70
Jun 1400 c  164  0.10
Jun 1400 p   78 245  -40.00   2,760
Sep 1400 c    1  25    3.50
Jun 1500 p    3 355  -59.00     891
Jul 1500 c   10  1.20  0.10
Jul 1500 p   10 355
Jun 1600 p   10 455  165.00      76
Jun 2500 p    2 1350 368.00       3
Call Vol. ____ 1,537  Open Int. _ 49,148
Put Vol. ____ 2,078  Open Int. _ 44,820
```

RUSSELL 2000(RUT)

```
Sep  410 c   20  66
Jun  450 c   20  20   14.50
Jun  460 c    2 13.10  8.30
Jun  460 p  118  2.15 -0.25     214
Jun  470 c    2  4.80  2.10
Jun  470 p    5  2.45 -6.45     222
Sep  470 c   19  23  -36.30
Sep  470 p   19  21   -7.00     197
Jun  480 c   19  1.05 -0.05
Sep  480 c  100  18    4.60
Sep  480 p  250 24.50 -9.10     815
Jun  490 p   12 20.50 -1.50     568
Aug  490 c   40  9.50  1.20
Sep  490 p  300 31.80 19.30     350
Jun  500 c   19  0.25 -0.10
Jun  500 p   22  29   -5.60   2,195
Jul  500 p    2 31.50 10.20       3
Call Vol. ____ 85  Open Int. _ 13,426
Put Vol. ____ 2,154  Open Int. _ 12,428
```

S & P 100(OEX)

```
Jun  440 p 1,246  0.05        10,814
Jul  440 p  146  1.10 -0.30   3,033
Jun  460 p 1,214  0.05 -0.05  6,653
Jul  460 p   13  2.20 -0.70   2,566
Aug  460 p    1   5   -0.40     376
Sep  460 p    9  7.80 -0.20     341
Jun  470 p   41  0.15 -0.05   8,386
Jul  470 p  184  2.95 -0.55   3,686
Jun  480 p  269  0.25 -0.10   6,105
Jul  480 p   95   4   -0.70   1,535
Jul  485 p  209  0.25 -0.25   2,561
Jul  485 p   94  5.30 -0.20     302
Jun  490 c   97  28    1.40
Jun  490 p 1,528  0.35 -0.40   6,214
Jul  490 p   84  6.30 -0.60   1,004
Jun  495 c    3 22.50  0.50
Jun  495 p 2,229  0.55 -0.55   6,037
Jul  495 c    2 28.20  0.70
Jul  495 p   15  6.60 -0.80   1,672
Jun  500 p  586 20.10  2.10
```

```
Aug  900 c   20 140.50
Sep  900 p  507  9.70 -0.50  19,548
Jul  925 c    1 115
Jul  925 p  200  3.60 -1.40   8,815
Aug  925 c    1 121.40 25.80
Aug  925 p  652   8   -1.50   1,168
Sep  925 p   10 13.50 -6.00   5,119
Jun  930 p   20  0.20 -0.15   1,621
Jul  935 p    1  4.80
Jun  950 p  949  0.25 -0.05  23,647
Jul  950 c   20 91.60  5.60
Jul  950 p 1,330  5.20 -1.80  16,142
Aug  950 p 5,026  11   -1.00   4,464
Sep  950 p   10  17   -0.50  13,503
Jun  960 p  237  0.20 -0.30   2,816
Jul  960 p  900   7   -1.20     256
Jun  965 p  250  0.40 -2.80   1,261
Jun  975 c   51 60.50 -1.00
Jun  975 p 4,096  0.25 -0.55  21,515
Jul  975 c  675 72.50  1.40
Jul  975 p  762   8   -2.00  11,533
Aug  975 c  250 78.70 14.70
Aug  975 p    2 16.70 -4.10   3,113
Sep  975 p 1,008  22   -1.50  10,213
Jun  990 p  107  52    6.00
Jun  990 p  847  0.70 -0.60   5,844
Jul  990 p   17  11   -1.70   1,965
Sep  990 p    4  27
Jun  995 c   61  42   -2.00
Jun  995 p 5,471   1   -0.70  27,652
Jun  995 c  275 55.50  0.90
Jun  995 p 2,145 11.60 -2.20  12,579
Jul  995 c  401  73   12.00
Jul  995 p 1,435 28.50 -0.50   9,521
Jun 1005 p   70  34    2.50
Jun 1005 p  240   1   -1.90   3,631
Jul 1005 c   17  50    2.50
Jun 1005 p  204  15   -0.80   2,084
Jun 1010 c  155 32.90  4.90
Jun 1010 p  567  1.75 -1.55   6,308
Jul 1010 c   50  44    2.70
Jul 1010 p   14 15.50 -1.90     332
Sep 1010 p 1,000 32.50 -15.50  1,154
Jun 1020 c   31 24.10  3.10
Jun 1020 p  256  2.60 -2.40   1,008
Jul 1020 c    2  35    9.00
Jul 1020 p  158 20.40 -1.10     253
Jun 1025 c 1,332 21.50  3.50
Jun 1025 p 7,786  3.80 -2.20  25,471
Jul 1025 c  523 37.50  3.00
Jul 1025 p 1,239 20.60 -1.60  16,787
Aug 1025 c 1,562  44   18.00
Aug 1025 p   10  28   -5.00   3,957
Sep 1025 c  887 51.50  0.50
Sep 1025 p 1,776  39   -1.00  12,864
Jun 1030 c  184 11.50 -3.50
Jun 1030 p  721  5.50 -2.90     271
Jul 1030 c    7 31.50 -0.30
Jul 1030 p  718  24   -1.00      24
Jun 1050 c 3,513  5.20  0.60
Jul 1050 p 1,270 10.70 -7.30  29,973
Jul 1050 p 1,995 22.60  2.30
Jul 1050 p  264 34.80 -1.20  13,149
Aug 1050 p 1,776  31    2.00
Aug 1050 p    2  41  -19.00   3,315
Sep 1050 p 3,110  38    0.30
Sep 1050 p  920  50   -2.00  19,636
Jul 1075 c  224  0.60 -0.20
Jul 1075 p  398 39.10  0.30  19,418
Jul 1075 c  653 11.80  0.80
Aug 1075 c   49  48   -2.00   5,788
Aug 1075 c   61  19    0.80
Sep 1075 c   12  28    8.90
Sep 1075 p    2  63   -3.50   7,689
Jun 1080 c   32  0.35 -0.25
Jun 1090 p   14  0.05 -0.20
Jun 1100 p  201  0.05 -0.05
```

```
Call Vol. ____ 0  Open Int. ___ 455
Put Vol. ____ 1  Open Int. ___ 54
```

MS CYCLICAL(CYC)

```
Jul  560 c  250 19.70  4.00     810
Jul  560 p  250  14   -2.30
Jul  560 c  250 19.70  4.00     810
Jul  560 p  250  14   -2.30
Jun  570 c   26  3.80  2.80      26
Jun  570 c   26  3.80  2.80      26
Jun  580 c    5  0.50 -1.80     655
Jul  580 p    5  18   -3.80
Jul  580 p    5   7    1.00
Jul  580 c    5  25   -7.40
Jun  580 c    5  0.50 -1.80     655
Jul  580 p    5  18   -3.80
Jul  580 p    5   7    1.00
Jul  580 c    5  25   -7.40
Jun  600 c   10  3.30
Jun  600 c   10  3.30
Call Vol. ____ 296  Open Int. __ 3,109
Put Vol. ____ 260  Open Int. __ 2,372
```

MS HITECH 35(MSH)

```
Jul  360 p    4  3.50 -4.00     100
Jul  360 c   10 20.50          40
Call Vol. ____ 0  Open Int. __ 1,502
Put Vol. ____ 0  Open Int. ___ 515
```

PHARMACEUTICAL(DRG)

```
Jun  320 p  105   3   -4.00
Jun  340 p    5  20    0.10
Call Vol. ____ 0  Open Int. __ 2,777
Put Vol. ____ 110  Open Int. __ 1,962
```

S & P MIDCAP(MID)

```
Jun  500 c    2  13    7.00     131
Sep  500 p  100 17.70  6.70     140
Dec  500 p   10 25.50 -1.90      94
Jun  510 p    8  4.10 -10.80      8
Jul  510 c    5  14    0.50       5
Jul  520 p  100 17.70 -8.80     425
Jun  530 c    2  0.50 -13.70      2
Jun  530 p   45 18.40 -10.70     75
Call Vol. ____ 9  Open Int. __ 2,201
Put Vol. ____ 263  Open Int. __ 2,490
```

PHILADELPHIA

GOLD/SILVER(XAU)

```
Jul   60 c   55 17.20  1.80
Jul   60 p  800  0.55  0.25     232
Jun   65 c    1  10    0.60
Jun   65 p    5  0.10  0.05   1,655
Jul   65 p   35  0.85 -0.15     887
Jun   70 c   85  0.20 -0.20   3,581
Jul   70 c   16  8.50  1.70
Jul   70 p   52  2.20 -0.70   1,305
Sep   70 c   21  10    0.70
Sep   70 c    4  5.40  0.40     230
Jun   75 c  290   2    0.70
Jun   75 p  416  0.95 -1.35   2,844
Jul   75 c   52  5.10  1.10
Jul   75 p   23  3.90 -1.10   7,341
Aug   75 c    3  6.50  0.70
Jun   80 c   35  0.30 -0.05
Jun   80 p   14   4   -2.20   2,310
Jul   80 c   44  3.10  0.80
Aug   80 c   85   4   -0.50
Sep   80 c    1   5   -0.40
Jun   80 c   10  0.05 -0.05
Jun   85 c   18  1.40 -0.60
Aug   85 c   12  2.35 -0.75
Sep   85 c    5  4.30  0.60
Jun   90 c    2  0.10  0.05
Jul   90 c  180  0.90
Jul   95 c   10  0.50
```

```
Jun  490 c  167  0.40 -1.20
Jun  490 p   34  40  -38.70     458
Jun  500 c   20  0.20 -0.55
Jun  500 p  220 51.10 -0.50     283
Jul  500 c  139   9   -2.50
Jul  500 p   57  66    2.90     516
Jul  510 c    4  0.50 -0.40
Jul  510 p    2 51.40 -13.70     51
Jul  510 c   49  11    2.80
Jun  520 c   23  59  -15.60     588
Jun  530 c   10  0.05 -0.40
Jun  540 c    5  0.05 -0.15
Jul  540 c    8  3.90 -0.10
Jun  550 p   10 99.50 -16.80    612
Jul  550 c   65  2.90  1.75
Sep  550 p   10 115.70 16.40     12
Jun  560 p   14 115.60 -22.70     22
Jul  560 c    1  3.90  1.00
Jun  570 c   10  0.20 -0.05
Aug  600 c  100  4.50  3.50
Jun  630 c    3  0.40 -0.10
Sep  640 p 5,196 64.50      30
Jul  680 p    1 219.50 -17.00     1
Jun  690 c    3  0.10  0.05
Call Vol. ____ 2,016  Open Int. _ 19,490
Put Vol. ____ 2,179  Open Int. _ 15,250
```

UTILITY INDEX(UTY)

```
Sep  270 c   50  2.70 -0.30     200
Jun  300 p   10  0.25 -0.35      64
Sep  300 p   50   6   -2.00     200
Jun  310 c  200  11    4.00
Jul  310 p  200  0.50 -4.00     200
Jul  320 c  100  10
Jul  320 p  100  7.60
Call Vol. ____ 300  Open Int. ___ 992
Put Vol. ____ 410  Open Int. __ 1,377
```

LEAPS-LONG TERM

DJ INDUS AVG - CB

```
Dec03  64 p   20  1.35 -0.15   5,339
Dec03  68 p   10   2   -0.20   4,813
Dec03  80 p  272  3.80 -0.30  46,524
Dec03  84 c    3 18.70 -0.90
Dec03  88 c    4  16    0.70
Dec03  88 p  419   6   -0.30   8,955
Dec02  92 p   27  7.70 -0.20   1,670
Dec02  96 p    6  9.10 -1.20     853
Dec03 100 c    5  9.20 -0.50
Dec02 108 p  240 14.20 -1.70     606
Call Vol. ____ 12  Open Int. ____ 1
Put Vol. ____ 994  Open Int. _ 84,416
```

S & P 500 - CB

```
Dec02  80 p    4  0.85 -0.15   4,185
Dec02  90 p   85  1.90 -0.20   7,704
Dec03  90 p  226  4.90 -0.50  45,161
Dec04  90 p 1,000  6.40  0.10  14,963
Dec03  95 p    6  6.50 -0.10   1,760
Dec02 100 c    8  8.70  1.90     147
Dec02 100 p   10  4.60 -0.10   3,839
Dec03 100 p  218   8   -0.30  35,817
Dec04 100 c   15 18.80  1.80  16,104
Dec02 105 p    1  6.10 -2.00     160
Dec02 110 p   20   9   -0.40  32,984
Dec03 110 c    2  8.40  1.10  27,596
Dec03 110 p   60 12.30       22,482
Dec03 115 c    1  6.30 -3.10   9,510
Dec02 120 c    4  1.10  0.15   2,436
Dec04 120 p 2,000 18.30 -1.10   7,264
Dec02 125 c    5  0.60  0.10     555
Dec02 130 p    1  26   -1.80   7,010
Dec03 130 p   65 25.20 -1.90  27,268
Dec03 160 p    2  51   -0.80   7,904
Call Vol. ____ 32  Open Int. _ 666,653
Put Vol. ____ 3,698  Open Int. _ 514,374
```

Source: *The Wall Street Journal*, June 19, 2002. Reprinted by permission of Dow Jones & Company, Inc. (c) 2002 Dow Jones & Company, Inc. All Rights Reserved Worldwide.

Use the table on previous page from the *WSJ* to answer the following questions.

1. What is the premium on the call options for Dow Jones Industrial Average index with a strike price of 100 and an expiration date in July? How many of these contracts traded during the trading day? What is the open interest?

2. What is the premium on the put option with the same strike price and expiration? How many of these contracts traded? What is the open interest?

Index Futures

Recall that financial futures contracts are standardized agreements to exchange a specified amount of a given financial asset on a specified date in the future. Unlike option contracts, futures buyers are obligated to act on the underlying instrument. That is, futures are an obligation whereas options give the buyer the right to act, but not the obligation. Futures contracts are traded for many different financial indexes. *Stock index futures* provide the buyer the opportunity to lock in the purchase price for an index of stocks at some future date. An investor in a index future can gain or lose from the price movement of the stock market as a whole, rather than just an individual stock. The *WSJ* reports on the wide range of stock indexes that are available both in the U.S. and abroad, such as the Dow Jones Industrial Average, the Standard and Poor's 500 Stock Index, and FT-SE 100 Index (London).

Commodity index futures provide investors the opportunity to speculate on, or hedge against, the price movement of a group of commodities as opposed to a single product. For example, The Goldman Sachs Commodity Index (GSCI®), is a commodity index comprised of 26 exchange-traded futures contracts. The index is designed as a benchmark for world commodity prices and is weighted by the level of world production in each product. The most heavily weighted commodities in the index are energy related (e.g., crude oil and natural gas), but the index also includes agricultural goods like wheat and cattle. The GSCI futures contract trades on the Chicago Mercantile Exchange.

Dollar index futures are contracts based on the value of the U.S. Dollar relative to a group of other currencies. For example, The U.S. Dollar Index® is computed using a trade-weighted geometric average of six currencies. Currently, the six currencies and their trade weights are the Euro (57.6%), the Yen (13.6 %), The British pound (11.9%), the Canadian dollar (9.1%), the Swedish Krona (4.2%), and the Swiss Franc (3.6%). The U.S. Dollar Index futures contract trades on the Financial Exchange, a division of the New York Board of Trade. This index provides investors the opportunity to speculate on, or hedge against, changes in the overall value of the U.S. Dollar.

The *WSJ* reports price and trading activity for index futures each trading day. The information is listed in the same manner as regular futures contracts. Information on stock, commodity, and Dollar index futures contracts are listed in the Futures Prices column. Each contract is listed in bold, followed by the name of the exchange where the contract is traded, the size of a single contract, and a description of how the prices are quoted. For each maturity month of the contract, the opening, the highest, the lowest and the settle price are quoted. Also included for each listing is the change in the closing price from the previous day, the lifetime high and low, and the open interest, or how many contracts are outstanding for the contract. The listing may also include the price information on the current value of the underlying index, including the high, low, and closing value for the trading day.

As an example, the GSCI index is traded on the CME and the value of the contract is equal to $250 multiplied by the value of the index. On April 18, 2002, the GSCI index futures contract for May settled at 199.50, an increase of 0.30 from the previous day. At this price, the value of one May contract is $49,875.00 (199.5 * $250). The current, or spot price, of the GSCI index closed at 199.73 on that day. Thus, the futures contract was trading at a small discount to spot. Of course, just as with futures contracts on single underlying assets, investors in the GSCI index are only required to place a small margin deposit for each contract. As with index options, index futures are settled in cash, actual delivery of the assets within the index does not occur. Continuing with the previous example, an investor that bought the May GSCI contract above at a value of 190.5, and sold at the April 18 settle price of 199.5, would have a net gain of $2,250.00 ((199.5-190.5)*$250).

Exercise 13-2

Index Futures

	OPEN	HIGH	LOW	SETTLE	CHG	LIFETIME HIGH	LIFETIME LOW	OPEN INT

Russell 1000 (NYFE)-$500 times index

| June | ... | ... | ... | 553.45 | 4.70 | 622.00 | 526.25 | 19,256 |

Est vol n.a.; vol Mon 952; open int 68,241, +272.
Idx prl: Hi 551.87; Lo 546.47; Close 549.57, +.41.

NYSE Composite Index (NYFE)-500 times index

| June | ... | ... | ... | 557.45 | 2.80 | 611.50 | 383.50 | 1,173 |
| Sept | ... | ... | ... | 557.75 | 2.80 | 607.00 | 528.00 | 1,218 |

Est vol 820; vol Mon 1,884; open int 2,991, −273.
Idx prl: Hi 556.52; Lo 552.05; Close 555.20, +1.01.

U.S. Dollar Index (FINEX)-$1,000 times index

June	...	...	...	111.00	.20	121.23	110.30	1,356
Sept	111.19	111.28	110.60	110.66	−.74	121.00	110.60	11,391
Dec	111.75	111.60	111.30	111.22	−.74	122.15	111.30	2,009

Est vol 850; vol Mon 1,207; open int 14,698, −134.
Idx prl: Hi 110.87; Lo 110.10; Close 110.20, −.65.

Share Price Index (SFE)-A$25 times index

June	3297.0	3320.0	3291.0	3310.0	14.0	3516.0	2945.0	138,219
Sept	3310.0	3332.0	3309.0	3323.0	15.0	3511.0	3271.0	23,587
Dec	3336.0	3336.0	3336.0	3334.0	12.0	3497.0	3319.0	1,482
Mr03	3358.0	3358.0	3358.0	3354.0	15.0	3457.0	3335.0	1,037

Est vol 13,009; vol Mon 16,306; open int 164,720, +2,921.
Index: Hi 3322.6; Lo 3299.7; Close 3311.9, +12.2.

CAC-40 Stock Index (MATIF)-Euro 10.00 x index

June	4033.5	4056.0	3981.0	4004.5	−12.0	4980.0	3785.0	n.a.
July	4038.0	4042.0	3997.0	4011.5	−12.0	4205.0	3800.0	n.a.
Sept	4070.0	4070.0	4032.0	4034.0	−11.5	4645.5	3875.0	n.a.

Est vol n.a.; vol Mon 72,354; open int n.a., .

Xetra DAX (EUREX)-Euro 25 per DAX index point

June	4501.0	4501.0	4400.0	4420.5	−65.5	5520.0	4036.5	187,280
Sept	4538.0	4538.0	4439.0	4459.5	−65.0	5565.0	4295.5	86,729
Dec	4553.0	4553.0	4497.0	4501.0	−66.0	5552.5	4345.0	4,062

Vol Tue 118,070; open int 278,071, −698.
Index: Hi 4503.80; Lo 4398.73; Close 4433.85, −41.25.

FT-SE 100 Index (LIFFE)-£10 per index point

June	4765.0	4774.5	4695.5	4705.5	−58.5	5295.0	4563.5	249,338
Sept	4785.0	4785.0	4703.5	4714.0	−58.5	5310.0	4574.5	151,212
Dec	4776.0	4776.0	4761.0	4749.5	−59.5	5332.0	4621.0	11,768

Est vol 209,309; vol Mon 195,502; open int 416,629, +11,904.

DJ Euro STOXX 50 Index (EUREX)-Euro 10.00 x index

June	3219.0	3223.0	3166.0	3181.0	−34.0	3880.0	2997.0	808,142
Sept	3229.0	3232.0	3177.0	3190.0	−33.0	3871.0	3004.0	407,672
Dec	3260.0	3260.0	3206.0	3218.0	−35.0	3832.0	3045.0	34,821

Vol Tue 788,135; open int 1,250,635, +24,428.
Index: Hi 3216.88; Lo 3166.45; Close 3188.26, −4.74.

DJ STOXX 50 Index (EUREX)-Euro 10.00 x index

| June | 3146.0 | 3146.0 | 3090.0 | 3100.0 | −44.0 | 3728.0 | 2940.0 | 24,118 |
| Sept | 3137.0 | 3141.0 | 3099.0 | 3108.0 | −43.0 | 3665.0 | 2986.0 | 7,699 |

Vol Tue 9,102; open int 31,817, −1,276.
Index: Hi 3144.42; Lo 3089.04; Close 3106.54, −23.37.

Other Futures

Settlement prices of selected contracts. Actual volume (from previous session) and open interest of all contract months.

	VOLUME	HIGH	LOW	SETTLE	CHG	LIFETIME HIGH	LIFETIME LOW	OPEN INT

Euro-Sterling (FINEX)-100,000 Euros; Euro per Pound

| Sep | 1,646 | ... | ... | .6376 | −.0010 | .6493 | .6386 | 12,076 |

Euro-U.S. Dollar (FINEX)-200,000 Euros; $ per Euro

| Sep | 255 | ... | ... | .9457 | −.0010 | .9446 | .9340 | 2,826 |

Euro-Yen (FINEX)-100,000 Euros; Yen per Euro

| Sep | 1,677 | 117.07 | 117.07 | 117.15 | −.10 | 118.07 | 116.13 | 16,801 |

Lumber (CME)-110,000 bd. ft., $ per 1,000 bd. ft.

| Jly | 369 | 276.90 | 272.00 | 272.50 | 4.70 | 326.80 | 240.00 | 2,354 |

Palladium (NYM)-100 troy oz.; $ per troy oz.

| Jun | 83 | ... | ... | 334.50 | 0.50 | 436.00 | 333.00 | 1,849 |

Mini DJ Industrial Average (CBOT) $5 times average

| Jun | 7,514 | 9720 | 9641 | 9688 | 175 | 10399 | 9250 | 11,135 |

	OPEN	HIGH	LOW	SETTLE	CHG	LIFETIME HIGH	LOW	OPEN INT
10 Yr. German Euro-BUND (EUREX)-Euro 100,000; pts of 100%								
Sept	106.93	107.36	106.88	107.14	0.27	107.36	104.38	678,118
Dec	106.59	106.59	106.59	106.57	0.28	106.67	104.92	3,246
vol Tue 778,880; open int 681,364, +319.								
2 Yr. German Euro-SCHATZ (EUREX)-Euro 100,000; pts of 100%								
Sept	103.12	103.19	103.08	103.11	0.01	103.22	102.26	483,054
vol Tue 353,178; open int 483,055, +6,734.								

Currency Futures

	OPEN	HIGH	LOW	SETTLE	CHG	LIFETIME HIGH	LOW	OPEN INT
Japanese Yen (CME)-12.5 million yen; $ per yen (.00)								
Sept	.8082	.8085	.8048	.8080	.0006	.8620	.7495	66,489
Dec	.8104	.8125	.8090	.8120	.0006	.8885	.7569	871
Est vol 3,451; vol Mon 6,497; open int 67,738, -24,971.								
Canadian Dollar (CME)-100,000 dlrs.; $ per Can $								
June	.6464	.6484	.6464	.6480	.0019	.6700	.6180	21,521
Sept	.6450	.6469	.6447	.6457	.0011	.6590	.6175	70,257
Dec	.6446	.6452	.6435	.6441	.0011	.6555	.6190	3,484
Est vol 4,194; vol Mon 10,775; open int 96,370, -483.								
British Pound (CME)-62,500 pds.; $ per pound								
Sept	1.4708	1.4854	1.4702	1.4832	.0122	1.4854	1.3990	43,713
Dec	1.4642	1.4770	1.4616	1.4740	.0122	1.4720	1.4070	190
Est vol 3,197; vol Mon 4,929; open int 43,903, -13,706.								
Swiss Franc (CME)-125,000 francs; $ per franc								
Sept	.6410	.6469	.6403	.6456	.0049	.6469	.5860	38,925
Dec	.6442	.6472	.6413	.6466.	.0049	.6472	.5875	139
Est vol 3,216; vol Mon 10,519; open int 39,065, -32,030.								
Australian Dollar (CME)-100,000 dlrs.; $ per A$								
Sept	.5545	.5615	.5522	.5610	.0080	.5728	.4790	32,906
Dec	...	...	...	.5565	.0080	.5655	.4980	542
Est vol 1,277; vol Mon 3,397; open int 34,112, -13,117.								
Mexican Peso (CME)-500,000 new Mex. peso, $ per MP								
Sept	.10260	.10318	.10150	.10175	-0070	.10830	.09930	15,795
Dec	...	...	...	.10015	-0070	.10673	.09850	1,744
Mr03	.09880	.09880	.09875	.09875	-0070	.10495	.09780	134
Est vol 4,698; vol Mon 5,405; open int 17,746, -17,355.								
Euro FX (CME)-Euro 125,000; $ per Euro								
Sept	.9406	.9433	.9398	.9474	.0070	.9489	.8375	106,924
Dec	.9387	.9483	.9364	.9437	.0070	.9483	.8390	1,373
Ju03	.9400	.9400	.9400	.9382	.0068	.9400	.8615	176
Est vol 10,673; vol Mon 18,891; open int 108,504, -47,605.								

Index Futures

	OPEN	HIGH	LOW	SETTLE	CHG	LIFETIME HIGH	LOW	OPEN INT
DJ Industrial Average (CBOT)-$10 times average								
June	9690	9756	9630	9756	75	10951	9080	24,400
Sept	9700	9760	9625	9755	75	10705	9230	14,489
Dec	9635	9756	9635	9756	75	10740	9120	364
Est vol 22,798; vol Mon 28,729; open int 39,279, +586.								
Idx prl: Hi 9721.75; Lo 9636.96; Close 9706.12, +18.70.								
S&P 500 Index (CME)-$250 times index								
June	103100	104400	103100	104420	860	170550	95030	217,960
Sept	103640	104550	103080	104520	860	165670	95530	400,135
Dec	104200	104590	103440	104690	850	150070	96130	17,140
Est vol 183,518; vol Mon 192,465; open int 635,547, +13,518.								
Idx prl: Hi 1040.83; Lo 1030.92; Close 1037.14, +.97.								
Mini S&P 500 (CME)-$50 times index								
June	103575	104475	102950	104425	875	118000	97875	214,974
Vol Mon 421,807; open int 311,294, +10,483.								
S&P Midcap 400 (CME)-$500 times index								
June	507.00	513.50	507.00	513.10	3.25	555.90	417.85	8,963
Sept	509.00	515.80	509.00	514.25	3.25	554.00	422.85	10,848
Idx prl: Hi 514.06; Lo 508.57; Close 509.03, -.07.								
Nikkei 225 Stock Average (CME)-$5 times index								
Sept	10800.	10875.	10710.	10785.	-75	12100.	9245.	20,660
Est vol 1,244; vol Mon 2,445; open int 20,729, -16,810.								
Idx prl: Hi 10884.26; Lo 10747.68; Close 10839.93, +175.82.								
Nasdaq 100 (CME)-$100 times index								
June	113900	117100	113700	117000	2100	173650	105300	50,035
Sept	115250	117600	113700	117500	2100	169350	105800	35,051
Est vol 35,738; vol Mon 37,627; open int 85,141, +1,606.								
Idx prl: Hi 1163.46; Lo 1138.31; Close 1138.47, -11.44.								
Mini Nasdaq 100 (CME)-$20 times index								
June	1148.5	1171.0	1134.0	1170.0	21.0	1714.0	1054.5	168,763
Vol Mon 200,415; open int 220,977, -8,095.								
GSCI (CME)-$250 times nearby index								
July	199.80	200.70	197.30	197.40	-3.70	210.00	189.90	19,723
Est vol 280; vol Mon 599; open int 20,179, +81.								
Idx prl: Hi 203.67; Lo 197.66; Close 197.91, -.95.								
Russell 2000 (CME)-$500 times index								
June	468.00	476.00	468.00	474.90	4.00	528.95	394.95	11,834
Sept	469.50	476.10	469.00	475.50	4.00	525.50	402.55	20,004
Est vol 7,006; vol Mon 11,761; open int 31,838, +1,554.								
Idx prl: Hi 474.64; Lo 469.49; Close 469.71, -1.03.								

Source: *The Wall Street Journal*, June 19, 2002. Reprinted by permission of Dow Jones & Company, Inc. (c) 2002 Dow Jones & Company, Inc. All Rights Reserved Worldwide.

Use the above table from the *WSJ* to answer the following questions.

1. From the listing, what is the settle price for the Dow Jones Industrial Average index futures contract for September delivery? What has been the high and low price for this contract over its lifetime? What is the open interest?

2. Compare the settle price of the index futures contract to the closing price of the actual index for the trading day. Is the September contract selling at a premium or discount to the spot price?

Options on Index Futures

Recall that a futures contract obligates the buyer to deliver the underlying asset, whereas an option provides the buyer a right, but not an obligation. Options are also available on futures contracts. Call options on futures provide the buyer the right to purchase the underlying futures contract; put options on futures provide the buyer the right to sell the underlying futures contract. In comparison, consider the options on stock indexes described earlier. The buyer of a call option on the S&P 500 index has the right to purchase the S&P 500 index at the option's strike price within the specified contract period. Alternatively, this investor could have purchased an option on the S&P 500 Index futures contract, giving him or her the right to buy the futures contract at the strike price of the option within the specified contract period. The price of options on index futures will depend not only on the outlook for the underlying index, just as in the case of index options, but also on the relationship between the underlying index and the index futures contract.

For example, on April 18, 2002, a call option on the June DJIA Index Futures, with a strike price of 102 (index value of 10200) had a closing premium price of $28 ($2,800 value). This option contract gives its holder the right to buy the June DJIA index futures contract at a price of 10200 (contract value of $102,000.00). On that day, the June futures contract settled at 10175 and the DJIA index closed at 10205.28. Thus, the strike price of the option was above the underlying futures contract (out-of-the money), but the futures contract was below the spot price of the index. This shows that premiums for options on futures can vary for many additional reasons over those of index options. Like all options, options on index futures will carry a time premium (a greater value the longer until expiration), but the option may also vary in price based on the relationship between the underlying futures contract and the current value of the index.

The Futures column of the WSJ includes pricing and trading activity for many options on futures contracts. Quotes on options to purchase stock index futures, such as the DJIA and the S&P 500, are reported each trading day. Included for each index is a listing of the most active option contracts. For each strike, price call and put option premiums are listed for the next three months. Notice, however, that futures contracts do not trade for each of these three months. The option is for the right to buy or sell the futures contract for the next closest month of expiration. For example, a call option on the DJIA index with an April expiration is an option to purchase the June futures contract.

Exercise 13-3

FUTURES OPTIONS PRICES

Index

DJ Industrial Avg (CBOT)

$100 times premium

Price	Jun	Jly	Aug	Jun	Jly	Aug
96	18.50	33.75	...	3.50	18.75	22.50
97	11.50	27.25	...	5.00	24.05	...
98	4.95	21.50	...	9.00	26.50	35.50
99	2.25	17.00	...	16.00	32.00	...
100	0.75	11.95	...	24.00	38.00	...
101	0.25	9.75	...	34.00	44.75	...

Est vol 700 Mn 230 calls 667 puts
Op int Mon 8,743 calls 22,535 puts

S&P 500 Stock Index (CME)

$250 times premium

Price	Jun	Jly	Aug	Jun	Jly	Aug
1035	14.40	32.00	...	5.20	21.80	...
1040	11.20	29.10	38.60	7.00	23.90	33.40
1045	8.30	26.30	...	9.10	26.10	...
1050	5.70	23.60	32.90	11.50	28.40	37.70
1055	4.20	21.10	30.40	15.00	30.90	...
1060	2.80	18.80	27.90	18.60	33.60	42.60

Est vol 15,038 Mn 8,243 calls 14,996 puts
Op int Mon 103,726 calls 181,556 puts

Source: *The Wall Street Journal*, June 19, 2002. Reprinted by permission of Dow Jones & Company, Inc. (c) 2002 Dow Jones & Company, Inc. All Rights Reserved Worldwide.

Use the above table from the *WSJ* to answer the following questions.

1. What is the premium for a July call option on the Dow Jones Industrial Average index futures contract with a 100 strike price?

2. What is the premium for a July put option on the Dow Jones Industrial Average futures contract with a 99 strike price?

Trading Index Options and Index Futures

Index options and index futures provide numerous opportunities for speculation and hedging. These instruments are used by investors and financial institutions to enhance or protect their investment performance. Some speculators use these securities, as opposed to the underlying financial assets, to lower transaction costs or to increase the potential payoff from a given market position. For example, suppose an investor believes that the S&P 500 index will make a significant advance in the next few months. An investment in the all the stocks of the index will incur substantial commission fees whereas a single purchase of the S&P 500 Index option or futures contract incurs a much smaller commission charge and requires only a small deposit.

One trading strategy uses stock index futures to lock-in guaranteed profits. This is know as *index arbitrage*. Index arbitrage involves the simultaneous purchase (sale) of all stocks in an index and the sale (purchase) of an index futures contract. Suppose, for example, the NASDAQ 100 index is currently valued at 1240, while the NASDAQ 100 index futures contract, expiring in one month, is selling for 1246. An investor can arbitrage based on this 6 point positive differential. By simultaneously selling the futures contract and buying the 100 stocks in the index the investor locks-in a profit at expiration of the futures contract since the two must then have the same value. Suppose at expiration the index has a value 1230. The investors portfolio would lose 10 points, but the futures contract can be closed out at a profit of 16, for a net profit of 6 points. By trading many contracts at a time when these arbitrage situations arise, the potential profits are large. However, these situations require quick actions and do not arise frequently, making this trading strategy difficult.

Index options and index futures are also used to hedge a portfolio of assets against unfavorable changes in the price of the overall market. Investors and portfolio managers can use these instruments to insure against the loss of value when market prices fall. For example, if a mutual fund manager believes that there is a strong chance that the stock market will decline over the next few months, but rebound shortly thereafter, she can avoid the time and expense of selling numerous shares in the fund by utilizing index options or index futures. A put option on the S&P 500 will rise in value as the overall stock market experiences a decline. The mutual fund manager can purchase these put options, paying only the premium value, to protect against the potential market decline.

The fund manager could also sell S&P 500 index futures. If the stock market declines as expected, the index futures contract will be closed out at a profit, at least partially offsetting any losses in the fund's portfolio. Using index options and index futures to hedge against market risk is often called *portfolio insurance*.

Hedge positions such as these will be more effective the more closely the stocks held in the portfolio match the actual stocks in the S&P 500 Index. **Basis risk** represents the risk that the portfolio's value does not move in tandem with the index used to hedge the portfolio. If a portfolio is less diversified than the S&P 500 index, the correlation in the returns on these two groups of stocks will be small. In the case of a market downturn, any gains from index options and index futures positions may not completely offset the loss in portfolio value. Fortunately, many options and futures are available for a variety of market indexes. The opportunity to reduce basis risk exists given the indexes available on both broad and narrow market indexes. For example, index options are available for both the S&P 500 Index and the more narrow S&P 100 Index. The later index would more closely match a portfolio of only large U.S. corporations.

Exercise 13-4

Use the listing of Underlying Indexes in Exercise 1 and the listing of Index Futures in Exercise 2 to answer the following questions.

1. What index option could the manager of gold stock mutual fund use to hedge against a loss of value?

2. What index futures contracts could the manager of Japanese stock fund use to hedge against the loss value?

3. What index futures contract can U.S. fund managers use to protect against the risk of currency value changes that affect the portfolio's value?

Program Trading

Derivative products like index options and index futures are popular for their ability to control large amounts of financial assets with relatively small premium payments or deposits. These instruments are often used as part of a computer based trading strategy called program trading. **Program trading** generally involves the simultaneous purchase or sale of at least fifteen different stocks with a total value of $1 million dollars or more. When certain preset trigger points for the market are reached, a computer program automatically places an order to trade stocks. For example, an institutional investor could set a computer program to initiate a large scale sale of securities when the Dow Jones Industrial Average, or some other index, reaches a certain level. When many institutional investors are using index options and index futures for program trading purposes the level of market volatility can rise quickly. If, for example, thousands of S&P 500 index options or futures contracts are being sold through program trading, a chain reaction of stock selling and further derivatives selling can occur. In response to this concern the NYSE instituted a rule that automatically limits trading in the S&P 500 stocks when market prices move strongly up or down.

The NYSE tracks program trading by institutional investors and this information is reported in the *WSJ* (normally appearing every Friday). The Program Trading reports the percentage of all trades for the week that were executed through program trades. This listing reports the types of program trades executed by brokerage firms for their own accounts as well as trades made on behalf of their clients. The volume of trades (in million of shares) is reported for the 15 brokerage firms with the highest level of program trading activity.

Exercise 13-5

Program Trading

NEW YORK—Program trading in the week ended June 14 accounted for 30.1%, or an average of 447.6 million shares daily, of New York Stock Exchange volume.

Brokerage firms executed an additional 388 million daily shares of program trading away from the NYSE, with 14.9% of the overall total on foreign markets. Program trading is the simultaneous purchase or sale of at least 15 different stocks with a total value of $1 million or more.

Of the program total on the NYSE, 10.6% involved stock-index arbitrage. In this strategy, traders dart between stocks and stock-index options and futures to capture fleeting price differences. Less than 0.5% involved derivative product-related strategies. Index arbitrage can be executed only in a stabilizing manner when the Dow Jones Industrial Average moves 190 points or more from its previous day's close.

About 60.1% of program trading was executed by firms for their clients, while 33.4% was done for their own accounts, or principal trading. An additional 6.5% was designated as customer facilitation, in which firms use principal positions to facilitate customer trades.

Of the five most-active firms overall for the week, UBS AG's UBS Warburg and Morgan Stanley executed most of their program trading as principal for their own accounts. Goldman Sachs, RBC Dominion and Deutsche Bank Securities executed most of their program trading activity for customers as agents.

NYSE PROGRAM TRADING
Volume in millions of shares in the week ended June 14, 2002

TOP 15 FIRMS	INDEX ARBITRAGE	DERIVATIVE-RELATED*	OTHER STRATEGIES	TOTAL
Goldman Sachs	.....	.....	278.5	278.5
UBS Warburg	.....	.....	271.8	271.8
Morgan Stanley	46.8	.....	200.5	247.3
RBC Dominion	61.3	.....	144.9	206.2
Deutsche Bank Securities	11.9	.....	146.2	158.1
Credit Suisse First Boston	6.9	.....	126.8	133.7
Bear Stearns	23.0	.....	97.4	120.4
Interactive Brokers	.....	.....	114.3	114.3
BNP Paribas Brkg. Srvs.	.....	.....	99.4	99.4
Helfant Group	.....	.....	97.5	97.5
Salomon Smith Barney	.....	.....	88.0	88.0
Lehman Brothers	10.4	0.3	73.6	84.3
Merrill Lynch	6.4	.....	49.2	55.6
Susquehanna Bkrg. Srvs.	10.6	.....	42.1	52.7
TLW Securities LLC	0.5	.....	48.4	48.9
OVERALL TOTAL	236.1	0.5	2001.2	2237.8

*Other derivative-related strategies besides index arbitrage

Source: New York Stock Exchange

Source: *The Wall Street Journal*, June 21, 2002. Reprinted by permission of Dow Jones & Company, Inc. (c) 2002 Dow Jones & Company, Inc. All Rights Reserved Worldwide.

Use the above report and table from the *WSJ* to answer the following questions.

1. For the week, what was the percentage of all NYSE trades that were executed by program trading?

2. What were the top five firms executing program trades for the period reported? What was the total number of shares traded by these firms?

3. What firm had the highest level of index arbitrage trading? How many shares were traded?

Project 13-1

Use the Index Futures listings from a recent edition of the *WSJ* to answer the following questions.

Date_____

1. What is the settle price for the Dow Jones Industrial Average index futures contract for delivery in the next few months?

   What has been the high and low price for this contract over its lifetime?

   Compare the settle price of the index futures contract to the closing price of the actual index for the trading day. Is the contract selling at a premium or discount to the spot price?

2. What is the settle price for the S&P 500 index futures contract for delivery in the next few months?

   What has been the high and low price for this contract over its lifetime?

   Compare the settle price of the index futures contract to the closing price of the actual index for the trading day. Is the contract selling at a premium or discount to the spot price?

Discussion Questions

Using a recent addition of the *WSJ*, review the Options Report column found in the Money and Investing Section.

Date of Report: _____

1. For the trading day discussed in this report, what index option contracts were active?

2. What are the reasons discussed for this activity?

3. What does the level of activity imply about expectations of future volatility?

4. What program trading activity, if any, occurred?

5. What hedging activity, if any, occurred?

PART VI

PORTFOLIO MANAGEMENT

Chapter 14

Risk Management

Objectives

1. Learn the basics of measuring risk and return.

2. Understand the effect of diversification.

3. Introduce the Capital Asset Pricing Model.

4. Use the *WSJ* to measure risk and return for individual securities and portfolios.

Key Terms

Rate of return	Diversification	Unsystematic risk
Expected return	Correlation Coefficient	CAPM
Standard Deviation	Systematic risk	Beta

In this section we begin a discussion of the fundamental issues surrounding portfolio management. The key issue is risk and return. All investors require greater return for greater risk. Thus, all portfolio managers must be aware of not only the return they provide investors, but how the return measures up to the level of risk taken to achieve it. In this chapter we review a few basic statistical measures of risk and return using the pricing data found in the *WSJ*. However, this is not a textbook on statistics and the reader is encouraged to consult such a textbook for a more thorough discussion of these concepts. This chapter also introduces modern portfolio theory and the resulting model of investing behavior that is useful in measuring the performance of portfolio managers.

Measuring Risk and Return

The *rate of return* on any investment (e.g. stocks, bonds, gold) is a combination of dividend or interest payments plus any gain or loss on the originally invested capital. Rates of return are stated as a percentage of the investment. For example, the percentage return on an investment in stock is calculated by adding the capital gain or loss to any dividends received and dividing by the initial share price of the stock. To estimate the future return on any investment it is useful to look at historical returns. If all the possible future outcomes and their associated probabilities are known, they can be used to determine the likely future return. However, these values are unlikely to be known. Therefore, historical returns are used as a benchmark for estimating future rates of return. The statistics associated with these historical returns provide a description of possible outcomes for the investment.

Expected return refers to the expected, or average, rate of return on an investment. Say an investment has three possible outcomes. In statistical terms this means that the investment has a probability distribution with three different points. The investment's expected return is simply the most likely outcome from that distribution - the mean of that distribution. If K_i is the return on an investment in period i, then the expected return is

$$\overline{K} = \sum_{i=1}^{n} \frac{K_i}{n}$$

where n is the number of periods used to estimate the expected return. For example, an investment with returns of 5%, 10%, -5%, and 3% over the past four periods has an expected return of 13% divided by 4, or 3.25%.

The most common measure of risk is based on the dispersion of the distribution. If each of the outcomes (points in the distribution) are far from each other, the distribution is more disperse; this means more variation. The statistic that measures this dispersion is the standard deviation. The *standard deviation* measures the risk associated with a particular distribution of outcomes. Using the symbol σ, the standard deviation is calculated by taking the square root of the average value of all the squared deviations from the mean.

$$\sigma = \sqrt{\frac{\sum (K_i - \overline{K})^2}{n}}$$

The deviation from the mean, $(K_i - \overline{K})$ is the difference between the given return and the average of all returns. For example, an investment with returns of 5%, 10%, -5%, and 3% over the past four periods has a standard deviation of 5.40% as shown below.

Period	Return	$(K_i - \overline{K})$	$(K_i - \overline{K})^2$
1	5.00%	1.75%	0.03%
2	10.00%	6.75%	0.46%
3	-5.00%	-8.25%	0.68%
4	3.00%	-0.25%	0.00%
Total	13.00%		1.17%
Average	3.25%		0.29%
Standard Deviation			5.40%

The greater the standard deviation, the greater the volatility, or variability of returns, and therefore, the greater the risk. Recall that historical returns provide a benchmark for estimating future rates of return and the associated risk. The more historical observations available, the better the estimate.

Exercise 14-1

For the week ended May 24, 2002, the *WSJ* reported the following prices and price changes for the Coca-Cola Co.:

Day	Price	Change	Daily Return
Friday	56.20	-0.49	
Thursday	56.69	0.49	
Wednesday	56.20	0.74	
Tuesday	55.46	-0.74	
Monday	56.20	-0.80	

1. Calculate the daily return for each day (No dividends were paid during this period).

2. Find the expected daily return for the Coca-Cola Co.

3. Find the standard deviation of the daily return for the Coca-Cola Co.

Diversification

It is easy to assume that investors do not like risk (they are risk averse). Most people prefer to take less risk, all else being equal. One way to reduce risk is to hold a portfolio, or a collection of investments. *Diversification* is the reduction of risk from investing in a portfolio of assets whose returns do not move in synch. The risk reduction benefit of diversification is based on correlations - if assets' returns do not have perfectly positive correlations (that is, they don't move exactly by the same degree at the same time), then combining these assets in the same portfolio will reduce risk.

The measure of risk for a portfolio, its standard deviation, is not just the weighted average of each asset's standard deviation. The standard deviation of a portfolio is also determined by the correlation of all assets in the portfolio. The variability of each asset affects the variability of the portfolio, but the correlations between the assets also affect the variability of the portfolio. In a portfolio with equal amounts of just two assets, the standard deviation is given by

$$\sigma_p = \sqrt{(\tfrac{1}{2})^2 \sigma_i^2 + (\tfrac{1}{2})^2 \sigma_j^2 + 2r_{ij}(\tfrac{1}{2})\sigma_i(\tfrac{1}{2})\sigma_j}$$

where r_{ij} is the *correlation coefficient*, which measures the joint movement of the two assets. The correlation coefficient is found by dividing the covariance of the assets by the product of their standard deviations.

$$r_{ij} = \frac{\text{cov}_{ij}}{\sigma_i \sigma_j}$$

The covariance is found by averaging the product of the two assets' deviations.

$$\text{cov}_{ij} = \frac{1}{n}\Sigma(K_i - \overline{K}_i)(K_j - \overline{K}_j)$$

As an example, consider a two asset portfolio with equal weights of each asset and four periods of data. The following chart shows the calculation of the standard deviation for each asset, the covariance, and their correlation:

Period	K_i	$(K_i - \overline{K})$	$(K_i - \overline{K})^2$	K_j	$(K_j - \overline{K}_j)$	$(K_j - \overline{K}_j)^2$	$(K_i - \overline{K}_i)(K_j - \overline{K}_j)$
1	5.00%	1.75%	0.03%	3.00%	-0.25%	0.00%	0.00%
2	10.00%	6.75%	0.46%	5.00%	1.75%	0.03%	0.12%
3	-5.00%	-8.25%	0.68%	-1.00%	-4.25%	0.18%	0.35%
4	3.00%	-0.25%	0.00%	1.00%	-2.25%	0.05%	0.01%
Total	13.00%		1.17%	8.00%		0.26%	0.47%
Average	3.25%		0.29%	2.00%		0.07%	**0.12%**
Standard Deviation			5.40%			2.56%	
Correlation Coefficient							**0.849**

The two assets have a covariance of 0.12%. Dividing this covariance by the product of the two standard deviations gives the correlation coefficient of 0.849. The correlation coefficient is used to find the standard deviation of this portfolio.

$$3.85\% = \sqrt{\begin{array}{c} (\tfrac{1}{2})^2 5.4\%^2 + (\tfrac{1}{2})^2 2.56\%^2 \\ + 2(0.849)(\tfrac{1}{2})(5.4\%)(\tfrac{1}{2})(2.56\%) \end{array}}$$

The standard deviation of the portfolio (3.85%) is lower than the standard deviation of the most risky asset in the portfolio (5.4%). Anytime the correlation is less than perfect (+1), combining assets in a portfolio will reduce risk. Thus, diversification lowers the risk of portfolio investments.

Exercise 14-2

Use the information in Exercise 1 and the following prices and price changes for the Colgate Palmolive Corporation, as reported in the *WSJ* for the week ended May 24, 2002, to answer the questions below.

Day	Price	Change	Daily Return
Friday	53.46	-0.48	
Thursday	53.94	-0.14	
Wednesday	54.08	0.02	
Tuesday	54.06	-0.79	
Monday	54.85	-0.19	

1. Find the expected daily return for the Colgate Palmolive Corporation (No dividends were paid during this period).

2. Find the standard deviation of the daily return for the Colgate Palmolive Corporation.

3. Find the correlation coefficient for Coca Cola and Colgate Palmolive.

4. Find the standard deviation of a portfolio with ½ Coca-Cola Co. shares and ½ Colgate Palmolive shares.

Portfolio Theory

The idea of diversification is behind modern portfolio theory. Since investors are risk adverse, modern portfolio theory states that the standard deviation of an investment's return is not of particular interest to investors holding diversified portfolios. The historical return on a security is likely to be a good estimate of future returns, but the historical standard deviation of returns is not a good estimate for the risk of a stock that is held in a portfolio. Since stocks and other securities are usually held in diversified portfolios the most relevant risk is the impact of adding the stock to a portfolio. Does the stock reduce or increase variability (i.e., risk)? The incremental risk of a stock added to a portfolio depends on how the stock varies compared to the portfolio variation. If the historical correlation between the stock and the portfolio are highly positive, there is no diversification effect of the added stock. If the correlation is low, zero, or negative, the addition of the stock lowers the portfolio's standard deviation or risk.

In modern portfolio theory there are two types of risk – systematic and unsystematic. *Systematic risk* is the risk that as the market moves up or down, the price of the stock moves up and down as well. This risk is the risk associated with being invested in market securities in the first place and is therefore often called market risk. Systematic risk cannot be diversified away. No matter how many stocks the investor holds, market prices move up and down and therefore risk exists. *Unsystematic risk* is the risk that an investment's value will fluctuate regardless of market changes. These changes in the price of stock are not associated with changes in the market. That is, these changes are specific to a given stock and are not correlated with the market. The specific nature of these price movements implies they can be diversified away. Thus, in a diversified portfolio, unsystematic risk is very small, or even zero.

A key finding based on systematic risk is the capital asset pricing model (CAPM). The *CAPM* states that the expected return on an asset is the sum of the return on a risk-free asset and the return commensurate with the asset's market risk. There are many assumptions underlying the CAPM which are beyond our discussion here, but the basic premise is that investors hold diversified portfolios of all market securities and the return on a given investment is determined by the risk free rate and the asset's covariance with the market portfolio. This relationship can be described by what is called the security market line (SML) drawn in the diagram below.

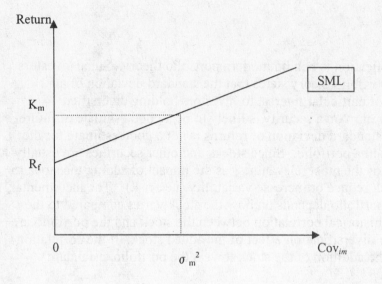

The vertical axis shows return on the market, K_m, and the risk-free-asset, R_f. The horizontal axis shows the risk on this asset as it compares to the market, Cov_{im} and the risk for the market itself, $\sigma_m{}^2$. The risk-free asset has no risk ($Cov_{im} = 0$ since the standard deviation of R_f is 0). When using the CAPM, a U.S. Treasury Bill or Note is most often used as the risk-free asset. The slope of the SML is called the asset's beta. **Beta**, *b*, is a measure of systematic risk. We can find the beta by calculating the slope of the SML and rearranging terms as follows:

$$K_i = R_f + \frac{(K_m - R_f)}{(\sigma_m^2 - 0)} Cov_{im}$$

which is equal to

$$K_i = R_f + \frac{Cov_{im}}{\sigma_m^2}(K_m - R_f)$$

The ratio of covariance between the asset and the market, Cov_{im}, to the market variance, $\sigma_m{}^2$ is the asset's beta.

$$K_i = R_f + b_i(K_m - R_f)$$

The greater the beta, the more sensitive are the returns on the stock to changes in the returns on the market as a whole.

As an example, consider the returns for an asset and the market over the past four periods shown in the table below.

Period	K_i	K_m
1	5.00%	4.00%
2	10.00%	9.00%
3	-5.00%	-3.00%
4	3.00%	2.00%
Total	13.00%	12.00%
Average	3.25%	3.00%

The covariance for this asset and the market is found just as in our previous discussion of the two asset portfolio.

Period	K_i	$(K_i - \overline{K})$	$(K_i - \overline{K})^2$	K_m	$(K_m - \overline{K}_m)$	$(K_m - \overline{K}_m)^2$	$(K_i - \overline{K}_i)(K_m - \overline{K}_m)$
1	5.00%	1.75%	0.03%	4.00%	0.75%	0.01%	0.01%
2	10.00%	6.75%	0.46%	9.00%	5.75%	0.33%	0.39%
3	-5.00%	-8.25%	0.68%	-3.00%	-6.25%	0.39%	0.52%
4	3.00%	-0.25%	0.00%	2.00%	-1.25%	0.02%	0.00%
Total	13.00%		1.17%	12.00%		0.74%	0.92%
Average	3.25%		0.2919%	3.00%		**0.1856%**	**0.23%**
Standard Deviation			5.40%			4.31%	
Beta							**1.24**

Taking the ratio of the covariance between the asset and the market, Cov_{im}, to the market variance, σ_m^2, gives the asset's beta,

$$Beta = \frac{Cov_{im}}{\sigma_m^2} = \frac{0.23\%}{0.1856\%} = 1.24$$

The beta value being greater than one indicates that the asset has more risk than the market as a whole. Or more specifically, the asset's incremental risk is high; adding risk to the portfolio. Given these historical returns for the asset and the market, the CAPM says that the expected return on this asset is calculated by

$$K_i = R_f + 1.24(K_m - R_f)$$

Therefore, the return on the asset can be estimated for a given risk-free rate and an expected return on the market. For example, if the market is expected to return 10% and the risk-free rate is 5%, the asset is expected to return 11.2%.

In practice, a beta is found by plotting the points for K_i and K_m on a graph and drawing a line of best fit, or through the process of regression analysis. Many years of daily price changes and dividends are used to find the asset returns, and the S&P 500 Index is most often used as the market portfolio. As mentioned earlier, a U.S. Treasury Bill or Note is used for the risk-free rate. The beta of a portfolio is the weighted average of the betas of the securities in the portfolio, where the weights are the proportion of the portfolio invested in the each asset.

Exercise 14-3

Following is information for S&P 500 Index for the week ended May 24,2002, as reported in the *WSJ*. Use this information and the information given in Exercises 1 and 2 to answer the questions below.

Day	Price	Change	Daily Return
Friday	1083.82	-13.26	
Thursday	1097.08	11.06	
Wednesday	1086.02	6.14	
Tuesday	1079.88	-12.00	
Monday	1091.88	-14.71	

1. Calculate the daily return on the market for each day (Assume no dividends were paid during this period).

2. Estimate the beta for Coca-Cola Company by taking the ratio of the covariance between the Coca-Cola's stock and the market, as measured by the S&P 500 Index, to the market variance.

3. Estimate the beta for Colgate Palmolive Corporation.

4. Assume the daily risk-free rate is .02% and the expected daily rate of return on the market is .05%. Given your answer for question 1, what is the expected daily rate of return for the Coca Cola Corporation? Colgate Palmolive?

Project 14-1

For one week, track the price changes in two stocks from the stock listing section of the *WSJ*. Enter your data in the tables below and Find the standard deviation of a portfolio with equal weights on the two shares (½ Company 1 shares and ½ Company 2).

Company 1_____ Ending Date_____

Day	Price	Change	Daily Return
Friday			
Thursday			
Wednesday			
Tuesday			
Monday			

Company 2_____ Ending Date_____

Day	Price	Change	Daily Return
Friday			
Thursday			
Wednesday			
Tuesday			
Monday			

Period	K_i	$(K_i - \overline{K})$	$(K_i - \overline{K})^2$	K_j	$(K_j - \overline{K}_j)$	$(K_j - \overline{K}_j)^2$	$(K_i - \overline{K}_i)(K_j - \overline{K}_j)$
1							
2							
3							
4							
5							
Total							
Average							
Standard Deviation							
Correlation Coefficient							

Project 14-2

As mentioned earlier, betas are normally calculated using many years of daily returns. The table below lists ten of the 30 stocks in the Dow Jones Industrial Average and their betas as of the end of May, 2002. You can find betas calculated for most companies using the internet. For example, go to http://moneycentral.msn.com and enter the company symbol, click go. On the next page, click on Company Report and scroll down to find the Beta.

Company	Symbol	Beta (May 2002)	Current Beta
Alcoa	AA	1.25	
General Electric	GE	1.18	
Johnson & Johnson	JNJ	0.42	
Microsoft	MSFT	1.77	
American Express	AXP	1.19	
General Motors	GM	1.12	
Procter & Gamble	PG	0.18	
Boeing	BA	0.81	
Home Depot	HD	1.24	
Coca Cola	KO	0.52	
Average			

1. Using the May 2002 information, find the beta for a equally weighted portfolio of these ten stocks.

2. Using the internet or a publication in your library like *The Value Line Investment Survey*, find the current beta for these ten stocks. Calculate a new beta for the portfolio.

3. How has the risk of this portfolio changed?

Discussion Questions

In a December 17, 2001 article entitled "Nasdaq Plans Fund To Track Entire Index", the *WSJ* reported on how investors would soon be able to invest in a fund that replicates the Nasdaq Composite Index. The following is an excerpt from that article.

> *Investors may be interested in jumping over to the Nasdaq Composite ETF[1] from the QQQ[2] because it holds more stocks and invests in a broader array of companies, including small-cap stocks, IPOs and financial-services companies.*

> *A Nasdaq Composite ETF would "have much more diversity" than the QQQ, says Thomas Mench, an investment adviser in Cincinnati who manages about $90 million in ETFs. Mr. Mench says he would consider using the Composite ETF for aggressive-stock accounts instead of the QQQ.*

> *This year, the Composite Index's relative diversification has helped cushion the sharp decline in the Nasdaq's largest tech stocks. Even though the Nasdaq 100 -- dominated by large stocks such as Microsoft Corp., Oracle Corp., and Intel Corp. -- accounts for about 70% of the market cap on the entire Nasdaq Stock Market, the Composite is only down 22% through November, while the Nasdaq 100 has plummeted 32%. (Of course, during a bull market, the 100 tends to rise faster. During the market's best year, 1999, it rose 102%, while the Composite Index trailed with an 86% gain.)*

1. An ETF is an exchange traded fund. ETFs are shares of a portfolio designed to track the performance of a market index.
2. The QQQ is an ETF for the Nasdaq 100 index.

Answer the following questions based on this information from the *WSJ*.

1. Why do investors seek diversification? What are the benefits?

2. How can an investment in an exchange traded fund (ETF) help investors achieve diversification?

3. Based on the theory behind the CAPM discussed in this chapter, is the new Nasdaq Composite ETF a "market portfolio? Why or why not?

Chapter 15

Asset Allocation

Objectives

1. Review the historical rates of return and volatility across different asset classes.

2. Review various classes of financial assets.

3. Understand the concept of the efficient frontier.

4. Use the *WSJ* to evaluate different asset allocation strategies.

Key Terms

Asset Allocation	Small-cap stocks	Bond Funds
Risk Premium	Value stocks	Real Estate Investment Trusts (REIT)
Large-cap stocks	Growth stocks	Gold Stocks

In this chapter the idea of diversification is expanded to include not just the effect of investing in more than one stock but the effect of investing in different classes of assets. The concept of asset allocation is introduced here and the *WSJ* is used to look at recent returns in each asset class. This chapter also reviews the various classifications of both stocks and bonds. Asset allocation across non-financial assets is also important and investments in real assets are therefore discussed here.

Asset Allocation

We have all heard the old saying, "Don't put all your eggs in one basket." This is the basic idea behind diversification. However, all your eggs in stocks can also be a bad idea. Furthermore, things may go wrong in one sector of stocks. For example, many people were heavily invested in technology stocks in the late 1990s. When the overall market corrected in 2000, many investors experienced even deeper losses in the technology sector. Therefore, investors can limit risk when they hold stocks in many sectors of the economy. Additionally, investors can hold other financial and real assets.

    Asset allocation is the process of designating investment funds into various categories of assets. To protect against the market risk of stocks, investors may put money into bonds. However, the bond market is not free of risk; returns on bonds will vary daily, monthly, and yearly. Another class of financial assets is short-term debt. To protect against the risk of both stocks and bonds many investors may hold money market accounts that investment in the virtually risk-free short-term debt of the U.S. government. Recall, however, less risk means lower rewards.

    To consider the effect of investing in different asset classes, consider the historical annual rate of return on the different investments listed in the table below.

Investment	Average Return	Standard Deviation	Minimum	Maximum
Dow 30 *	9.00%	15.95%	-27.57%	43.96%
Foreign Stocks *	9.54%	19.42%	-25.60%	66.80%
Long-term Government Bonds	6.58%	9.75%	-8.81%	43.11%
U.S. Treasury Bills	5.34%	2.93%	0.93%	14.91%
Gold	6.12%	24.62%	-32.81%	91.81%

* excluding dividends

Source: Author's calculations based on data from www.globalfindata.com

    The table lists the average annual return for five asset classes from 1950 through 2001. The 30 stocks in the Dow Jones Industrial Average are widely considered a good gauge for the performance of large company stocks. The return on Foreign Stocks is represented by the Morgan Stanley Capital International Europe Australia Far East Index (MSCI EAFE). This index has long been used as a proxy for stock market investment opportunities outside the United States. The information for investment in bonds is the average annual total return on 10-year U.S. Government bonds. The total return includes interest and changes in price. The U.S. Treasury Bills rate is also a total return figure. Finally, the table lists the average annual return on gold based on the London quoted prices for gold bullion.

    As you can see from the data in this table, the rates of return vary significantly across different types of investments. The level of volatility, or risk, in each investment class also varies significantly across investment types. The measure of risk used here is standard deviation. The greater the standard deviation, the greater the volatility, or variability of returns, and therefore, the greater the risk. For example, although Foreign Stocks outperformed U.S. stocks during this period (9.54% v. 9.00%) they have done so with greater risk (standard deviation of 19.42% v. 15.95%). U.S. Treasury Bills are considered risk-free since it is unlikely that investor will ever lose money in these securities. This is evident in the table since U.S. Treasury Bills have never had a negative annual return. Using standard deviations, the five classes in order of risk are Gold, Foreign Stocks, U.S. Stocks, Long-term Bonds, and U.S. Treasury Bills. The order is very similar when measured by the largest loss. This does not mean, however, that investors should not consider the most risky asset, gold, as an investment. Depending on the correlation in these returns going forward, the overall return could improve, and the overall risk decline, for an investment portfolio including all five asset classes.

Notice that the return on stocks has been higher than both U.S. Bonds and Bills. This extra return from stocks long has been called the risk premium. The *risk premium* is the premium received in exchange for owning a riskier, more volatile instrument, such as stocks. Since stocks don't offer the guaranteed returns of government bonds, investors need to receive extra returns to make investments in stocks worth their while. The risk premium is calculated by subtracting the rate on risk-free bonds or bills from the expected return on a stock, or other risky, investment.

Exercise 15-1

Markets Diary/ *Trading for Monday, June 10, 2002*

Stocks

Dow Jones Industrial Average   9645.40   ▲ +55.73

INDEX	CLOSE	NET CHG	% CHG	12-MONTH % CHG	YTD % CHG
DJIA	9645.40	+55.73	+0.58	-11.69	- 3.75
Nasdaq Comp.	1530.69	- 4.79	-0.31	-29.49	-21.52
S&P 500	1030.74	+ 3.21	+0.31	-17.83	-10.22
Russell 2000	469.29	- 1.22	-0.26	- 7.43	- 3.93

Global Stocks

DJ World Stock Index (excluding U.S.)   124.41   ▼ -0.07

INDEX	CLOSE	NET CHG	% CHG	12-MONTH % CHG	YTD % CHG
DJ World (ex. U.S.)	124.41	- 0.07	-0.05	-11.00	+ 0.41
Nikkei 225	11370.21	-68.32	-0.60	-14.03	+ 7.85
DJ Euro STOXX 50	3205.36	- 5.14	-0.16	-27.56	-15.78
MSCI EAFE	1133.00	- 0.82	-0.07	-12.64	- 1.91

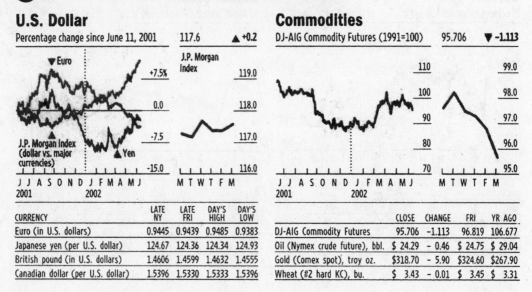

Bonds & Interest
10-Year Treasury Note Yield (4 p.m. ET)

Price Chg. ▲ + 7/32   Yield 5.035%

	MON	MON YIELD	FRI	FRI YIELD	TTL RTN YTD % CHG
10-year Treasury note	98.78	5.04%	98.56	5.06%	-1.03%
3-month Treasury bill	1.71	1.73	1.71	1.73	+1.18
DJ Corporate Bond Index	141.51	6.32	141.22	6.35	-1.10
Lehman Brothers MBS	993.41	5.98	992.95	5.98	+4.01

*For 24-hour updated news, stock quotes, and background information, see The Wall Street Journal Online at **WallStreetJournal.com**.*

U.S. Dollar
Percentage change since June 11, 2001

117.6   ▲ +0.2

J.P. Morgan Index

CURRENCY	LATE NY	LATE FRI	DAY'S HIGH	DAY'S LOW
Euro (in U.S. dollars)	0.9445	0.9439	0.9485	0.9383
Japanese yen (per U.S. dollar)	124.67	124.36	124.34	124.93
British pound (in U.S. dollars)	1.4606	1.4599	1.4632	1.4555
Canadian dollar (per U.S. dollar)	1.5396	1.5330	1.5333	1.5396

Commodities
DJ-AIG Commodity Futures (1991=100)

95.706   ▼ -1.113

	CLOSE	CHANGE	FRI	YR AGO
DJ-AIG Commodity Futures	95.706	-1.113	96.819	106.677
Oil (Nymex crude future), bbl.	$ 24.29	- 0.46	$ 24.75	$ 29.04
Gold (Comex spot), troy oz.	$318.70	- 5.90	$324.60	$267.90
Wheat (#2 hard KC), bu.	$ 3.43	- 0.01	$ 3.45	$ 3.31

Source: *The Wall Street Journal*, June 11, 2002. Reprinted by permission of Dow Jones & Company, Inc. (c) 2002 Dow Jones & Company, Inc. All Rights Reserved Worldwide.

Use the information from the *WSJ* above to complete the table below and answer the following questions.

Investment	Calculation	Return
U.S. Stocks (DJIA)	12-MONTH % CHG	
Foreign Stocks (MSCI EAFE)	12-MONTH % CHG	
Government Bonds (10 -year Treasury Note	Yield	
U.S. Treasury Bills (3 month)	Yield	
Gold (Comex Spot)	% change in price v. one year ago.	

1. Find a one year (12 month) return for each of the five assets classes discussed.

2. Which returns are higher than their historical average as given in the table above?

3. Which returns are lower than their historical average as given in the table above?

4. Using the U.S. Treasury Bill (3-month) rate, find the current risk premium for U.S. and Foreign stocks.

Stock Classifications

For purposes of asset allocation, there are two major ways to distinguish between stocks – size and relative value. Let's first distinguish companies by their size. Company size is most commonly measured by total market value. The total market value of a company is found by multiplying the price of the firm's stock by the number of shares outstanding. *Large-Cap stocks* have a high market value. As their name implies, large cap stocks make up a big portion of all the market value that is traded each day. For example, the Standard & Poor's 500 Stock Index is equivalent to approximately 75% of the total market value of the 3,000 firms listed on the New York Stock Exchange. Large caps stocks are usually in mature industries and have high-levels of fixed investment. Examples include General Electric, IBM, and Ford Motor. *Small-Cap stocks* have small market value. These firms constitute a small portion of the total value traded in the stock market each day. The Russell 2000 index is a widely value composite of these companies. A small firm may be in a mature industry, but it is more likely that small firms are competing in new industries with opportunity for growth. There are also many Mid-Cap stocks. As their name implies, their market capitalization is around the median of the market's total value. An example of mid-cap firms is the S&P 400 Mid-cap Index.

Assets may also be allocated across stocks based on the current market price. That is, stocks may be currently priced based on the growth opportunities, or stocks may be currently priced as value investments. To determine whether a stock is a growth stock or a value stock , investment analysts look at earnings and assets relative to the stock's current price. *Value stocks* are considered bargains. These stocks are currently out-of-favor stocks and are inexpensive relative to the company's earnings or assets. A stock priced low relative to assets or earnings is regarded as a value stock. *Growth stocks* represent companies with rapidly expanding earnings growth. High earnings growth typically indicates a growth stock.

Value companies have low or no sales growth; growth companies have sales growth greater than their competitors. Value companies have low earnings per share; growth companies have high earnings per share. Value companies have below-average earnings increases; growth companies have above-average earnings increases. Value companies have low price to earnings and price to book ratios; growth companies have high price to earnings and price to book ratios.

Exercise 15-2

Major Stock Indexes

	DAILY					52-WEEK			YTD
Dow Jones Averages	HIGH	LOW	CLOSE	NET CHG	% CHG	HIGH	LOW	% CHG	% CHG
30 Industrials	9718.09	9562.54	9645.40	+55.73	+0.58	10948.38	8235.81	-11.69	- 3.75
20 Transportations	2735.67	2685.21	2721.12	+34.46	+1.28	3049.96	2033.86	- 3.81	+ 3.07
15 Utilities	275.66	271.05	274.76	+ 1.96	+0.72	378.74	272.57	-27.38	- 6.53
65 Composite	2826.83	2783.15	2810.31	+21.45	+0.77	3249.64	2489.27	-13.52	- 2.83
Dow Jones Indexes									
US Total Market	241.77	239.06	240.01	+ 0.58	+0.24	291.31	222.35	-17.57	-10.01
US Large-Cap	228.79	225.70	226.99	+ 0.69	+0.30	287.21	218.90	-20.91	-12.22
US Mid-Cap	269.74	267.42	268.22	+ 0.55	+0.21	295.49	226.88	- 9.19	- 4.21
US Small-Cap	291.52	288.66	289.01	- 0.67	-0.23	320.03	233.12	- 5.87	- 4.12
US Growth	933.81	920.47	923.44	- 0.20	-0.02	1341.16	889.71	-31.02	-19.85
US Value	1247.15	1229.93	1239.51	+ 5.85	+0.47	1354.32	1134.22	- 8.48	- 4.39
Global Titans 50	172.57	170.53	171.45	+ 0.30	+0.18	217.24	168.34	-21.08	-14.15
Asian Titans 50	103.69	102.57	102.73	- 0.80	-0.77	123.23	86.94	-16.64	+ 7.03
STOXX 50	3193.02	3145.56	3170.07	+ 7.37	+0.23	4220.39	2915.64	-24.89	-14.48
Nasdaq Stock Market									
Composite	1551.80	1526.96	1530.69	- 4.79	-0.31	2170.78	1423.19	-29.49	-21.52
Nasdaq 100	1155.76	1132.12	1135.62	- 4.62	-0.41	1852.03	1126.95	-38.50	-27.99
Biotech	527.91	514.73	520.02	+ 3.76	+0.73	1014.84	516.26	-48.67	-42.78
Computer	731.44	715.50	717.99	- 3.65	-0.51	1091.98	653.13	-33.94	-26.77
Telecommunications	122.67	119.00	119.64	- 2.74	-2.24	333.15	119.64	-64.09	-49.44
Standard & Poor's Indexes									
500 Index	1038.08	1025.57	1030.74	+ 3.21	+0.31	1255.85	965.80	-17.83	-10.22
400 Mid-Cap	513.24	509.28	509.74	+ 0.46	+0.09	550.38	404.34	- 2.82	+ 0.28
600 Small-Cap	237.02	234.08	234.33	- 1.04	-0.44	257.81	181.09	+ 2.29	+ 0.93
1500 Index	229.49	226.90	227.84	+ 0.61	+0.27	272.14	209.52	-16.20	- 9.10
New York Stock Exchange									
Composite	556.55	550.68	553.39	+ 1.82	+0.33	637.37	504.21	-13.18	- 6.17
Industrials	693.83	686.92	689.86	+ 1.90	+0.28	792.23	620.11	-12.79	- 6.23
Finance	586.85	579.73	584.14	+ 3.38	+0.58	636.14	494.41	- 5.74	- 1.61
Others									
Russell 2000	473.50	468.60	469.29	- 1.22	-0.26	522.95	378.90	- 7.43	- 3.93
Wilshire 5000	9838.45	9738.52	9771.69	+19.00	+0.19	11631.79	8900.45	-15.95	- 8.74
Value Line	341.53	338.47	338.80	- 0.30	-0.09	405.56	294.60	-16.46	- 8.32
Amex Composite	927.06	914.63	915.03	-11.73	-1.27	962.69	780.46	- 1.43	+ 7.95

Use the above tables of stock indexes from the *WSJ* to answer the following questions.

1. According to the Dow Jones Indexes, which stock classification, Large, Mid, or Small, had the best performance over the past year (52 weeks)?

2. According to the Dow Jones Indexes, which stock classification, growth or value, had the best performance over the past year (52 weeks)?

Bonds and Bond Funds

Let's now consider allocating investment funds over different financial assets. Bonds are the most commonly purchased financial assets other than stocks. Investors can buy individual bonds or bond funds. There are many different individual bonds from which to choose. Individual bonds are bought and sold in the over-the-counter (OTC) market. Many brokers keep an inventory of bonds to buy and sell for their own account or their clients' accounts. Some corporate bonds are also listed on the New York Stock Exchange. In addition to the prices, current yields, year of maturity, and coupon rates of these bonds, the U.S. Exchange Bonds column found in the Money and Investing Section reports the volume and number of issues traded. U.S. Exchange Bonds can be purchased from most major brokerage firms.

Bond funds, like stock funds, offer professional selection and management of a portfolio of securities. The advantage of bond funds is diversification across a broad range of issues. Many bond funds invest in various types of bonds. However, there are also bond funds with specific objectives. These differing objectives include government or corporate bonds, taxable or non-taxable bonds, and short or long-term bonds. For example, a Long-term Government bond fund purchases U.S. Treasury and U.S. government agency securities. Short-term U.S. Government bond funds purchase U.S. Treasury bills and other short-term instruments from government agencies. A General Municipal bond fund invests in a variety of municipal securities. Municipals are bonds issued by state and local governments. Interest income from municipal bond funds is normally free from federal taxation. Municipal debt, or other non-taxable funds, will also vary by duration - long-term, intermediate-term, or short-term.

Another, more risky, category of bonds is the high-yield sector. A high-yield taxable bond fund purchases high-risk corporate bonds, issued by companies with little or no credit history operating in risky markets. Mortgage funds purchase the debt of the Government National Mortgage Association, Ginnie-Mae, and other U.S. agencies, as well as general mortgage and adjustable-rate mortgage securities.

A number of indexes exist to track the performance of bonds as an asset class. In the Markets Lineup section of the *WSJ* there are broad market indexes and the specific bond categories. These indexes track the total return, both interest payments and price changes, on these bond categories. The Yield Comparison table in the Credit Markets section of the *WSJ* shows the difference between the current yield to maturity for different bond classifications.

Exercise 15-3

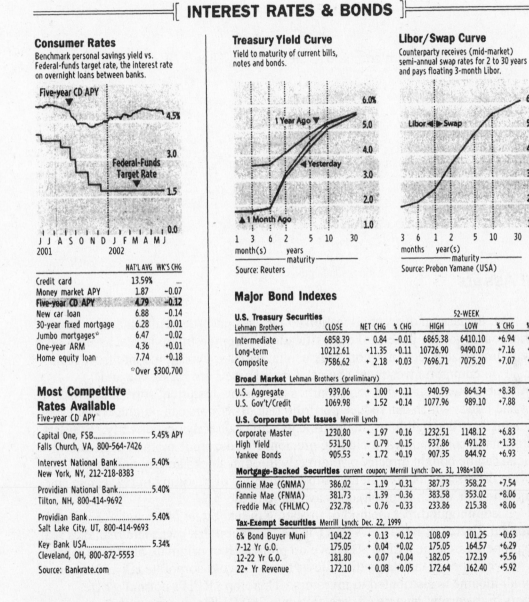

⟦ INTEREST RATES & BONDS ⟧

Consumer Rates
Benchmark personal savings yield vs. Federal-funds target rate, the interest rate on overnight loans between banks.

Five-year CD APY

Federal-Funds Target Rate

J J A S O N D J F M A M J
2001　　　　　2002

	NAT'L AVG	WK'S CHG
Credit card	13.59%	...
Money market APY	1.87	−0.07
Five-year CD APY	4.79	−0.12
New car loan	6.88	−0.14
30-year fixed mortgage	6.28	−0.01
Jumbo mortgages*	6.47	−0.02
One-year ARM	4.36	+0.01
Home equity loan	7.74	+0.18

*Over $300,700

Most Competitive Rates Available
Five-year CD APY

Capital One, FSB............................ 5.45% APY
Falls Church, VA, 800-564-7426

Intervest National Bank................ 5.40%
New York, NY, 212-218-8383

Providian National Bank................5.40%
Tilton, NH, 800-414-9692

Providian Bank 5.40%
Salt Lake City, UT, 800-414-9693

Key Bank USA................................. 5.34%
Cleveland, OH, 800-872-5553

Source: Bankrate.com

Treasury Yield Curve
Yield to maturity of current bills, notes and bonds.

1 Year Ago
Yesterday
1 Month Ago

1　3　6　2　5　10　30
month(s)　years
└──── maturity ────┘

Source: Reuters

Libor/Swap Curve
Counterparty receives (mid-market) semi-annual swap rates for 2 to 30 years and pays floating 3-month Libor.

Libor ◄ ► Swap

3　6　1　2　5　10　30
months　year(s)
└──── maturity ────┘

Source: Prebon Yamane (USA)

Major Bond Indexes

U.S. Treasury Securities				52-WEEK			YTD
Lehman Brothers	CLOSE	NET CHG	% CHG	HIGH	LOW	% CHG	% CHG
Intermediate	6858.39	− 0.84	−0.01	6865.38	6410.10	+6.94	+2.23
Long-term	10212.61	+11.35	+0.11	10726.90	9490.07	+7.16	+2.66
Composite	7586.62	+ 2.18	+0.03	7696.71	7075.20	+7.07	+2.39

Broad Market Lehman Brothers (preliminary)							
U.S. Aggregate	939.06	+ 1.00	+0.11	940.59	864.34	+8.38	+3.28
U.S. Gov't/Credit	1069.98	+ 1.52	+0.14	1077.96	989.10	+7.88	+2.72

U.S. Corporate Debt Issues Merrill Lynch							
Corporate Master	1230.80	+ 1.97	+0.16	1232.51	1148.12	+6.83	+2.08
High Yield	531.50	− 0.79	−0.15	537.86	491.28	+1.33	+2.37
Yankee Bonds	905.53	+ 1.72	+0.19	907.35	844.92	+6.93	+1.97

Mortgage-Backed Securities current coupon; Merrill Lynch; Dec. 31, 1986=100							
Ginnie Mae (GNMA)	386.02	− 1.19	−0.31	387.73	358.22	+7.54	+2.96
Fannie Mae (FNMA)	381.73	− 1.39	−0.36	383.58	353.02	+8.06	+3.30
Freddie Mac (FHLMC)	232.78	− 0.76	−0.33	233.86	215.38	+8.06	+3.24

Tax-Exempt Securities Merrill Lynch; Dec. 22, 1999							
6% Bond Buyer Muni	104.22	+ 0.13	+0.12	108.09	101.25	+0.63	+1.58
7-12 Yr G.O.	175.05	+ 0.04	+0.02	175.05	164.57	+6.29	+4.68
12-22 Yr G.O.	181.80	+ 0.07	+0.04	182.05	172.19	+5.56	+3.79
22+ Yr Revenue	172.10	+ 0.08	+0.05	172.64	162.40	+5.92	+3.38

Use the tables on the previous page from the *WSJ* to answer the following questions.

1. What has been the total return over the past year (52 weeks) according to the Lehman Brothers U.S. Treasury Securities Index for Intermediate term bonds?

2. How does this return compare to the return on Ginnie Mae Mortgage-Backed Securities?

3. How does this return compare to the return on 7-12 year Tax-exempt Securities?

Real Assets

Our discussion of asset allocation so far has concerned only financial assets. Another source for the benefit of diversification is an investment in real assets. Just like with financial assets, investors seek capital gains or current income from real assets. Two common investment choices for real assets are real estate and commodities. Real estate and commodities have a low historical correlation with stocks and bonds which can reduce portfolio risk. Investors can purchase real estate (land, houses, office buildings, or apartments) either directly or indirectly. Similarly, investments in commodities, including precious metals, crude oil, and agricultural products, can be bought directly or indirectly through stocks and mutual funds. The following discussion focuses on the indirect methods of investing in real estate and commodities for which information is available in the *WSJ*.

A common indirect method of investing in real estate is through **Real Estate Investment Trusts**, or REITs. A REIT is a corporation that owns and manages real estate properties. Some REITs also develop properties or originate mortgage loans. REITs have a special tax status that allows them to avoid corporate tax as long as nearly all income is distributed to investors. Therefore, REITs normally offer investors high current income. There are some 300 REITs, approximately one-third of which are private. The remainder trade on the stock exchanges, and pricing and trading information can be found each day in the *WSJ*.

There are three types of REITs - equity, mortgage and hybrid. An Equity REIT is a corporation that purchases, owns, and manages real estate properties but does not own or originate real estate loans. A Mortgage REIT purchases, owns and manages real estate loans; it does not own real estate properties. A Hybrid REIT does both; purchasing and manages both real estate loans and real estate properties.

A commodity mutual fund is an indirect method of investing in commodities. By investing in a mutual fund rather than a specific commodity, investors spread the risk over a broad range of commodities. Historically, one specific commodity has been a popular investment used to offset positions in stocks and bonds. That commodity is gold. Gold has been a good alternative to stocks and bonds during periods of high inflation. For example, in the late 1970s and early 1980s gold outperformed the stock market by wide margins. When inflation subsided, beginning in the mid-1980s and continuing through the 1990s, the return on gold has been very low.

There are many ways to invest in gold, including gold bullion, gold coins (such as the American Eagle coins) and gold futures contracts. Two indirect methods that are much more convenient than trading and storing gold are gold mining stocks and gold mutual funds. **Gold Stocks** are ownership interests in a gold mining company. The price of the stock, however, will depend not only upon the price of gold, but also upon the corporation's management. Therefore, the return on the stock may be more or less than the return on gold itself. Gold mutual funds are perhaps the safest method of buying and owning gold stocks since they allow the investor to diversify among many companies.

The *WSJ* tracks the market for real assets, including both real estate and commodities, each day. For example, to track the real estate market, investors can follow the Dow Jones Specialty Indexes for REITs. The Dow Jones Specialty Indexes are found each day in the Money and Investing section of the *WSJ*. Dow Jones has an index for equity REITs and a composite index that includes all three REIT types. Price information for gold and commodities can also be found in the *WSJ*. Gold futures prices and the Dow Jones - AIG Commodity Index (DJ-AIG), a benchmark for commodities, can be found in the Market Dairy charts and tables on page C1 of each day. The DJ-AIG tracks futures contracts on 20 physical commodities traded on U.S. and London exchanges. The major sectors within the index are energy (including petroleum and natural gas), precious metals, industrial metals, grains, livestock and softs (including fibers and textiles).

Exercise 15-4

Dow Jones Specialty Indexes

Monday, June 10, 2002

	CLOSE	NET CHG	% CHG	YTD % CHG	YLD		CLOSE	NET CHG	% CHG	YTD % CHG	YLD
Composite Internet	39.38	−0.68	−1.70	−36.77	...	Australia 30 -c	Closed	...	...	−2.43	...
Internet Commerce	43.35	−0.89	−2.01	−18.76	...	Canada 40 -c	1076.43	−2.78	−0.26	−6.46	...
Internet Services	28.51	−0.53	−1.83	−51.41	...	France 30 -c	264.90	+0.70	+0.26	−13.96	...
Equity REIT	159.74	+0.57	+0.36	+7.95	6.58	Germany 30 -c	280.12	−1.27	−0.45	−11.48	...
Equity REIT -tot ret	392.06	+1.46	+0.37	+10.60	...	Hong Kong 30 -c	3628.39	+21.68	+0.60	+0.46	...
Composite REIT	141.41	+0.53	+0.38	+8.19	6.44	Japan 100 -c	2377.14	−20.42	−0.85	+4.55	...
Composite REIT -tot ret	360.51	+1.42	+0.40	+10.87	...	Switzerland 30 -c	342.18	+1.23	+0.36	−4.33	...
Islamic Market	1379.91	+1.78	+0.13	−10.65	...	U.K. 50 -c	206.27	+0.46	+0.22	−6.94	...
Islamic Tech	1792.19	−8.70	−0.48	−26.28	...	Sustainability	791.07	+2.08	+0.26	−8.69	...
Islamic U.S.	1574.01	+2.33	+0.15	−13.49	...						

c-index in local currency

Use the above tables from the *WSJ* to answer the following questions.

1. What has been the total return year-to-date for Real Estate according to the Dow Jones Composite REIT?

2. What has been the total return year-to-date for Real Estate according to the Dow Jones Equity REIT?

Project 15-1

Repeat Exercise 1 using information from a recent edition of the *WSJ*.

Date_____

Find a one year (12 month) return for each of the five assets classes.

Investment	Calculation	Return
U.S. Stocks (DJIA)	12-MONTH % CHG	
Foreign Stocks (MSCI EAFE)	12-MONTH % CHG	
Government Bonds (10 -year Treasury Note	Yield	
U.S. Treasury Bills (3 month)	Yield	
Gold (Comex Spot)	% change in price v. one year ago.	

1. Which returns are higher than their historical average as given in the table below?
   Which returns are lower than their historical average as given in the table below?

Investment	Average Return	Standard Deviation	Minimum	Maximum
Dow 30 *	9.00%	15.95%	-27.57%	43.96%
Foreign Stocks *	9.54%	19.42%	-25.60%	66.80%
Long-term Government Bonds	6.58%	9.75%	-8.81%	43.11%
U.S. Treasury Bills	5.34%	2.93%	0.93%	14.91%
Gold	6.12%	24.62%	-32.81%	91.81%

* excluding dividends

Source: Author's calculations based on data from www.globalfindata.com

2. Using the U.S. Treasury Bill (3-month) rate, find the current risk premium for U.S. and Foreign stocks.

Project 15-2

The following table lists the risk of different portfolios for two asset classes – stocks and bonds. The historical standard deviation on the Dow 30 stocks and Long-term government bonds were used to calculate the standard deviation of the five different portfolios in the table. In a recent edition of the *WSJ*, find the current rate for the 10-year Treasury Note (See the Markets Diary on page C1). Using this rate for bonds and the historical average return on the Dow 30 of 9%, calculate the expected return for each portfolio over the next year. The expected return on the portfolio is equal to the sum of the two returns multiplied by their respective weights in the portfolio. Next, calculate the ratio of return to risk. This is a measure of the portfolio's efficiency; that is, how much the portfolio is expected to return relative to the amount of risk taken. A value of one indicates the portfolio has an equal amount of return relative to its risk. The first portfolio, 100% stocks, has been completed for you.

Date_____

Current rate on a 10-year Treasury Note: _____

| Portfolio Weights: | | | | |
Stocks	Bonds	Standard Deviation	Expected Return	Return/Risk
1.00	0.00	15.95%	9.00%	0.56
0.75	0.25	12.02%		
0.50	0.50	9.01%		
0.25	0.75	8.05%		
0.00	1.00	9.75%		

1. Which portfolio(s) has the highest expected return?

2. Which portfolio(s) has the highest risk?

3. Which portfolio(s) has the highest return relative to its risk?

Discussion Questions

MUTUAL FUNDS

Midas Touch: Gold Portfolios Surge

*Returns Vary Widely,
And Sector's Stock Prices
Are Notoriously Mercurial*

———

By Aaron Lucchetti

———

It's enough for investors to want to turn into prospectors.

Gold-stock mutual funds continued their hot streak in May, extending a run that has

left just about all other funds in the dust this year. Funds that focus on precious-metals shares returned an average of 19.06% last month through Thursday, the highest one-month gain for any fund category since technology funds soared more than 25% in February 2000, according to preliminary May data from Lipper Inc. In the first five months of the year, gold-oriented funds have gained almost 72%.

"I have the feeling that the high-tech guys had in 1999," says Jean-Marie Eveillard, co-manager of the **First Eagle SoGen Gold Fund.** After a long and steady decline during the 1990s, the assets of Mr. Eveillard's fund have spiked, doubling since the end of March to $61 million.

Diversified U.S.-stock funds lost ground in May, slipping an average 2.13%, while the Dow Jones Industrial Average, including dividends, was about flat for the month, according to the preliminary Lipper figures. (Full performance figures and rankings for May appear today in the Mutual Fund Monthly Review, starting on page R1.)

Investors tempted to jump on the gold bandwagon should realize that the performance of such funds is notoriously fickle and can vary widely even among gold portfolios themselves. Returns of the three dozen gold funds ranges between about 50% so far this year to about 125%.

Indeed, gold stocks are even more volatile than the price of the actual metal. And while gold-stock funds are having a good run now, they haven't had a great year since 1993. They have also lost more than 10% in six different years since 1990. Over the 15 years ended in April, the average gold fund gained only about 3% a year, far below the return of most other investments, according to Morningstar Inc.

Still, the metal is giving a silver lining to some portfolios. In May, gold rose while just about all types of stock funds fell, according Lipper's data. Even funds focusing on small, undervalued companies—which have been attracting gobs of new money recently—slipped about 3% in May through Thursday.

Investors are starting to believe again that "gold is legitimate as insurance against something bad happening," Mr. Eveillard says. Cash and inflation-protected bonds also play a defensive role, he says, but aren't likely to soar as much during tough periods for stocks. "The last two years have been the opposite of the previous 20," the portfolio manager says. "You've had the bursting of the Internet bubble, Sept. 11 and Enron. The cult of equities might be dead for a few years."

Some alternatives to U.S. stocks did well in May, as Japanese-stock funds rose 6.43%, bringing that long-suffering category to a gain of more than a 12% for the year. Bond funds remained in the black for the year, as funds focused on corporate and mortgage issues performed well in May, according to Andrew Clark, a senior research analyst with Lipper in Denver.

The price of gold, which has shot up above $320 an ounce from about $265 a year ago, has driven much of the rally in the stocks of gold-mining companies. Bill Martin, manager of American Century Global Gold Fund, says that a further increase in the price of gold-mining stocks depends in large part on a sharper rally in the price of the metal. That's more likely if the U.S. dollar continues to weaken and gold mining companies unwind more of their hedges, which in the past have held gold prices lower.

* * *

MANAGER MOVES: Ernst von Metzsch, stock portfolio manager of the $25 billion **Vanguard Wellington Fund** and the $1.6 billion **Vanguard Energy Fund,** will retire at year end.

Mr. von Metzsch, 62 years old, has run the stock portion of the Wellington fund, which is a balanced stock-and-bond portfolio, since 1995 and the energy fund since 1984. Technically, he isn't an employee of Vanguard. Rather, he is a senior vice president and partner with **Wellington Management** Co. of Boston, which manages $321 billion for Vanguard and other clients.

Taking up Mr. von Metzsch's mantle on the Wellington fund will be Edward P. Bousa, 43, currently a vice president at Wellington. Karl Bandtel, 35, a Wellington senior vice president and portfolio manager who runs several portfolios in the energy and natural resources sectors, will take over Mr. von Metzsch's duties on the Vanguard Energy Fund.

–Bridget O'Brian

1. According to the article, what has been the range of returns on gold funds for the year?

2. How does the return on these funds compare to the return on gold over the past year as indicated in the article?

3. Gold is considered a defensive investment. What other defensive investments are mentioned in the article?

Chapter 16

Benchmarking

Objectives

1. Understand the basics of mutual funds.

2. Review various mutual fund benchmarks.

3. Introduce measures of risk-adjusted performance.

4. Use the *WSJ* to evaluate mutual funds' relative and risk-adjusted performance.

Key Terms

Mutual funds	Lipper Indexes	Sharpe ratio
Variable annuities	Benchmark index	Treynor ratio
Index funds	Excess return	Jensen's alpha

In this chapter the tools of risk and return measurement are used to discuss performance evaluation of mutual funds and other portfolios. To start, the basic structure and operations of mutual funds are described and the extensive price and performance data for mutual funds in the *WSJ* is reviewed. Next, the various classifications of mutual funds and their respective benchmarks are described. Finally, three widely used measurements of risk adjusted performance for evaluating portfolio managers are introduced.

Mutual Funds

Mutual funds are investment vehicles that pool the money of many small investors and invest it in shares of companies, bonds, or other assets. A mutual fund is a company in itself with a board of directors that hires the fund's managers. The main advantage of mutual funds is that you can invest small amounts, and your money automatically buys a share in many different companies – instant diversification. Another advantage is the professional management of your money which you hire with your mutual fund investment. However, this management comes at a cost. Costs will vary depending on the type of fund, its investment style, and the method through which you buy it - direct or through a broker. The typical cost of a mutual fund is up to five percent to buy, and 1 to 2 percent a year in management and other fees. Many funds are sold directly to investors with no up-front fee.

There are thousands of individual funds to choose from, many with differing investment characteristics. Pricing and performance information for funds with at least $50 million in assets is found daily in the *WSJ*. Funds are listed by 'family', the company that administers the operation of the fund. For example, all the funds offered by Fidelity Investments are listed under their name in the Mutual Funds tables of the Money and Investing Section.

For each listing, the table includes the Fund's net asset value (NAV), the change in the NAV from the previous day, the year-to-date percent change, and the 3-year total return for the fund. The NAV is the current value of the investment fund. It is calculated as the ratio of total assets minus total liabilities to total shares outstanding. For example, a fund with $100 million in investments, $1 million in liabilities, and 9 million shares outstanding has a NAV of $11.00.

In addition to this daily listing of mutual funds, the *WSJ* also reports price and return information for variable annuities each Monday. ***Variable annuities*** operate just like mutual funds but are actually insurance products. The insurance company offering the annuity pays its owner returns that depend on the mutual fund performance of the investment option selected by the owner. The advantage of a variable annuity is deferred taxes on any dividends, interest, and capital gains that are credited to the owner's account until withdrawn at retirement (age 59 ½).

The *WSJ* listings for variable annuities are organized by the insurance company (sponsor) and include much of the same information as the mutual fund listings. For each annuity, the listing includes the unit value (similar to NAV), the total return for the past week, the year-to-date return, and the expense ratio. The expense ratio is calculated as the total expenses incurred by the investment fund divided by the fund's total assets.

Exercise 16-1

MUTUAL FUNDS

Price Funds

Balanced	17.26	-0.04	-0.5	1.7
Bd Index r	10.37	0.02	2.5	NS
BlChip	26.34	-0.12	-9.1	-4.2
CA Bond	10.80	0.01	2.5	5.0
CapApp	15.76	-0.06	7.7	13.4
CapOpp	11.16	-0.07	-6.3	-2.4
CorpInc	9.23	0.03	1.7	6.3
DivGro	20.23	-0.06	-2.6	-0.4
DvsfSmGr	10.48	-0.13	-7.3	0.6
EmgMktB	10.67	0.02	7.0	17.2
EmMktS	12.07	-0.08	12.1	7.1
EqInc	24.09	-0.07	2.6	3.8
EqIndex	28.75	-0.18	-6.6	-5.5
Europe	15.80	...	-1.3	-3.2
ExtIndex r	9.62	-0.08	-1.5	-2.0
FinSvcs	19.48	0.02	3.4	9.8
FL Inter	10.87	0.01	3.1	5.1
ForEq	13.28	-0.02	1.1	-4.0
GNMA	9.62	0.02	3.5	7.4
GA Bond	10.88	0.01	2.7	5.0
GlbStk	13.22	-0.04	-4.1	-2.1
GlbTech	4.01	-0.07	-15.6	NS
Growth	22.12	-0.10	-8.5	-0.6
Gr&In	21.14	-0.12	-6.7	-1.5
HelSci	17.06	-0.13	-15.0	11.6
HiYield	6.63	...	3.2	2.3
N Inc	8.69	0.03	2.3	6.9
IntlBond	8.19	0.02	5.6	-0.5
IntDis	19.15	-0.03	-0.2	10.1
IntlStk	11.10	-0.02	1.0	-4.3
InstSmCap	11.37	-0.10	2.1	NS
Japan	6.69	-0.02	10.6	-6.8
Lat Am	9.56	-0.14	4.3	7.1
MCapGro	38.29	-0.19	-2.8	6.4
MCapVal	18.13	-0.06	10.5	16.0
MCEqGr	18.90	-0.10	-2.8	6.8
MD Short	5.24	...	1.5	4.3
MD Bond	10.55	0.01	3.0	5.3
MediaTel	16.29	-0.20	-19.2	-3.2
N Amer	26.73	-0.23	-13.4	-10.0
N Asia	6.94	-0.03	11.8	5.6
New Era	24.49	-0.11	10.1	9.9
N Horiz	20.81	-0.22	-8.0	4.9
NJ Bond	11.43	0.01	3.5	5.0
NY Bond	11.01	0.01	3.3	5.0
PSBal	15.11	-0.01	0.7	2.9
PSGrow	17.55	-0.04	0.1	1.8
PSInc	12.87	...	1.2	4.1
RealEst	11.62	0.11	10.8	12.8
SciTec	16.10	-0.35	-23.0	-19.6
Sht-Bd	4.75	0.01	1.6	6.7
SmCapStk	25.76	-0.22	1.7	13.8
SmCapVal	25.51	-0.17	12.6	18.7
SpecGr	13.70	-0.07	-2.6	1.5
SpecInc	10.73	0.02	3.4	5.1
SpecIntl	7.90	-0.02	1.8	-1.5
SuGNMA	9.90	0.02	3.4	7.4
SuMuInc	10.55	0.01	3.1	5.2
SuMuInt	10.72	0.01	3.1	5.2
TaxEfGro t	8.87	-0.05	-6.2	NS
TFHY	11.42	0.01	2.6	3.1
TF Incom	9.72	0.01	3.1	5.1
TF Inter	11.13	0.01	3.0	5.2
TFSI	5.44	...	2.1	4.9
TotIndex	10.84	-0.07	-5.2	-4.4
USTInter	5.41	0.02	2.2	7.1
USTLg	11.30	0.05	2.2	6.7
Value	19.20	-0.11	1.7	3.9
VABond	11.32	0.01	2.9	5.2

The T. Rowe Price Company is a direct seller of mutual funds. Their many funds are listed in the Mutual Funds section of the *WSJ* under the heading Price Funds. Answer the following questions using the table on previous page from the *WSJ*.

1. What is the current NAV for the Price Growth Fund (Growth)?

2. What is the 3-year total return on the Price Growth Fund (Growth)?

3. What is the current NAV for the Price Small-Cap Stock Fund (SmCapStk)?

4. What is the 3-year total return on the Price Small-Cap Stock Fund (SmCapStk)?

Fund Categories

Mutual funds and other portfolios come in many shapes and sizes. The main distinction is based on the type of management involved – passive or active. Some funds simply try to track the movements of a particular index – passive management. In other funds the investments are chosen by the managers – active management. *Index funds* are passively managed funds that seek to match the performance of a particular stock market index or sector index. This is done by holding shares in all the companies of the index, or in a representative sample of those companies. Conversely, actively managed funds seek to better the indexes. That is, the fund manager chooses a portfolio of stocks that he or she believes will outperform 'the market'. Most funds are actively managed, but index funds have grown in popularity. This may be due to the fact that most active managers have failed to consistently outperform the indexes.

The second distinction amongst mutual funds is investment objective. The *WSJ* follows the Lipper classification system of investment objectives. Lipper is a research company that has followed the mutual fund industry for many years. For stocks, Lipper's system divides U.S. stock mutual funds into four broad categories based on the size of the companies in the fund, then subdivides them based on the investing style of the fund manager. These classifications are the basis for the ***Lipper Indexes***. These indexes are formed to track the investment performance of all funds in a given class, providing a measure by which the performance of a fund can be gauged against other funds with similar investment objectives. The *WSJ* reports the Lipper Indexes each day.

The Lipper Indexes differ from benchmark indexes. A ***Benchmark index*** is a market or sector index funds seek to match or outperform. The most common benchmark index for general U.S. stock market funds is the S&P 500. Other benchmarks for U.S. funds include the DJIA and the Dow Jones Total Market Index. For international funds, the key benchmark is the Morgan Stanley Capital International Europe Australia and the Far East index (MSCI EAFE).

Another category for funds is based on the size of the companies in which the fund invests. The size of a company is determined by its total market value (the company's stock price multiplied by the number of shares outstanding). The four broad categories are Large-cap, Mid-cap, Small-Cap, and Multi-cap. Large-cap funds invest in stocks of companies that have a market capitalization greater than 300 times the median of the Standard & Poor's Mid-Cap 400 index. Mid-cap funds invest in companies that have a market capitalization less than 300% of the market capitalization of the S&P Mid-Cap 400. Small-cap funds invest in stocks of firms that have a market capitalization less than 250% of the S&P 600 Small-Cap stock index. Multi-cap funds are those that like to buy small-company stocks and hold them as they get larger. Or they buy stocks of large and small companies, depending on the market.

The fund's investment philosophy is the next distinction. There are two main types of investment philosophies – value and growth. A third classification is called core – a combination of growth and value. Value funds look for stocks that are currently priced low relative to the rest of the market. These funds will typically have below-average price-to-earnings (PE) ratios. Growth funds look for stocks with strong potential for growth in earnings. The idea is that the stock price will rise because prices usually follow earnings. Growth funds will typically have above-average PE ratios and three-year earnings growth. Core funds invest in both growth and value stocks, and their PE ratios typically fall in the middle of their size group.

There are other Lipper classifications for mutual funds that focus on specific investment sectors. These classifications include science and technology funds, telecommunications, and financial service. Finally, there are Lipper classifications for the location of a fund's investments. These classification include international funds (outside U.S.), European region, Pacific region, and Latin America.

Exercise 16-2

=H[**MUTUAL FUNDS**]H=

How the Largest Mutual Funds Did

Stock Funds	DAY'S % CHANGE	YTD RETURN	52-WK RETURN
Fidelity Magellan	−0.58	−8.1	−16.4
Vanguard 500	−0.62	−6.5	−14.7
American ICAA	−0.35	−0.6	− 6.4
American WshA	−0.42	+1.4	− 2.2
American GrwthA	−0.59	−7.7	−15.9
Fidelity Contrafd	−0.09	+3.1	− 2.6
Fidelity GwthInc	−0.20	−4.6	− 9.5
American EupacA	−0.29	+2.6	− 8.3
American PerA	−0.50	+0.3	− 9.0
American CentUltr	−0.38	−5.5	−12.2
Bond Funds			
PIMCO TotRt	+0.19	+3.7	+11.7
Vanguard GNMA	+0.19	+3.7	+ 8.8
Vanguard TotBroad	+0.30	+2.4	+ 7.9
FrankTemp CA	+0.14	+1.6	+ 5.5
American America	+0.16	+2.3	+ 5.4

Lipper Indexes

		PERCENT CHANGE FROM		
Stock-Fund Indexes	PRELIM CLOSE	PREVIOUS CLOSE	WEEK AGO	DEC 31
Large-Cap Growth	2913.29	−0.66	−1.52	−10.70
Large-Cap Core	2089.35	−0.50	−1.09	− 5.88
Large-Cap Value	8929.52	−0.51	−0.66	− 2.29
Multi-Cap Growth	2367.54	−0.91	−1.44	−11.88
Multi-Cap Core	6239.73	−0.58	−0.90	− 5.17
Multi-Cap Value	3640.11	−0.52	−0.70	− 0.75
Mid-Cap Growth	581.33	−0.80	−1.21	− 9.29
Mid-Cap Core	551.28	−0.61	−0.66	− 0.18
Mid-Cap Value	818.28	−0.53	−0.50	+ 4.33
Small-Cap Growth	456.19	−0.98	−1.53	− 8.04
Small-Cap Core	328.44	−0.90	−1.43	+ 0.12
Small-Cap Value	490.25	−0.61	−0.95	+ 7.68
Equity Income Fd	3835.24	−0.40	−0.52	− 0.53
Science and Tech Fd	557.45	−1.88	−3.50	−22.20
International Fund	680.26	−0.15	−0.30	+ 5.06
Balanced Fund	4496.68	−0.24	−0.38	− 1.87
Bond-Fund Indexes				
Short Inv Grade	239.73	+0.11	+0.24	+ 1.43
Intmdt Inv Grade	269.33	+0.27	+0.57	+ 2.42
US Government	363.74	+0.29	+0.44	+ 2.56
GNMA	403.67	+0.19	+0.28	+ 3.54
Corp A-Rated Debt	957.67	+0.29	+0.53	+ 2.23

Indexes are based on the largest funds within the same invest ment objective and do not include multiple share classes o similar funds.

Source: Lipper Inc.

Each day in the MARKETS LINEUP column of the *WSJ*, the major Lipper Indexes for both stock and bond funds are reported. Answer the following questions using the table on previous page.

1. Based on the indexes, for all size classifications (Large, Multi, Mid, and Small) which investment philosophy has performed best since the beginning of the year (Dec 31) - value, growth, or core?

2. Based on the indexes, for all investment philosophies (value, growth, and or core) which size category has performed best since the beginning of the year (Dec 31) - Large, Multi, Mid, or Small?

Risk-Adjusted Performance

Mutual fund and other portfolio managers are evaluated not only on the performance relative to some index or benchmark, but also on their performance relative to the amount of risk undertaken. There are three popular measures of risk-adjusted performance – the Sharpe ratio, the Treynor ratio, and Jensen's alpha. Each of these measures is named for the researcher who originally suggested the measurement. These measures use the statistics describe in the previous chapter on Risk Measurement. Before describing each measure in turn, consider the return that matters most to investors – excess return. *Excess return* is the return on a portfolio or security that compensates the investor for the extra risk taken. This is also called the risk premium and is calculated by subtracting the risk-free rate from the expected return. For example, a portfolio earning 10% when the risk-free rate is 5% has an excess return of 5%.

The *Sharpe ratio* is a measure of reward relative to risk. It is calculated by subtracting the risk-free rate from the rate of return on a portfolio of individual security and dividing by the standard deviation of the portfolio or security. For example, when the risk-free rate is 5%, a portfolio with an expected return of 15% and a standard deviation of 20% has a Sharpe ratio of 0.5 [(15%-5%) /20%]. Since it uses the standard deviation of the portfolio or security, the Sharpe ratio measures return relative to total risk only. This measure does not account for any diversification benefits. Since standard deviation does not measure risk relative to the market as a whole, the Sharpe ratio is more appropriate for measuring portfolios that are already well diversified.

The ***Treynor ratio*** incorporates market risk into the evaluation of performance. The Treynor ratio is calculated by dividing excess return by the beta of the portfolio or security. Beta is a measure of systematic risk, or market risk, and is found by measuring the slope of the Security Market Line (SML). The SML shows the relationship between return on investment and market risk (the covariance of the asset and the market). Thus, the Treynor ratio measures risk-adjusted performance by looking at the risk of the portfolio relative to the market. For example, when the risk-free rate is 5%, a portfolio with an expected return of 15% and a beta of 1.25 has a Treynor ratio of 0.08 [(15%-5%) /1.25]. The higher the ratio the higher the excess return relative to the risk of adding the portfolio or security to a total market portfolio.

The Sharpe and Treynor ratios are useful for comparing portfolios or comparing a portfolio to the market. Ignoring dividends, the U.S. stock market has returned roughly 9% annually with a standard deviation near 16%. Assume that the market's expected return is 9% and the risk-free rate is 5%. The market has a beta of 1 by definition. Thus, the market's Sharpe ratio would be 0.25 [(9%-5%) /16%], and the market's Treynor ratio would be 0.04 [(9%-5%) /1].

Jensen's Alpha is the difference between a portfolio's actual return and the expected return on the portfolio based on the Capital Asset Pricing Model (CAPM). The CAPM says that the expected return is equal to the risk-free rate plus the Beta portfolio multiplied by the market risk premium (Return on the market – risk-free rate). Once the CAPM return is calculated, the portfolio's alpha is found by subtracting the portfolio return from this expected return. For example, a portfolio with an expected return of 9% based on the CAPM and an actual return of 12% has an alpha of 3% [12% - 9% = 3%]. Most estimates of a portfolio's alpha use the S&P 500 Index to find the return on the market and the U.S. Treasury Bill or Note for the risk-free rate. Portfolio managers that consistently achieve positive alphas are rewarded for essentially "beating the market", since the CAPM is a market based expected return.

Exercise 16-3

The Mutual Funds table in Exercise 2 includes performance information on the 10 largest mutual funds. The Fidelity Magellan Fund is the largest U.S. stock mutual fund with over $72 Billion in assets. As of May 2002, the fund's average annual return for the previous 10 years was 12.46% and the standard deviation was 17.08%.

1. Assuming the risk free rate was near its historical average of 5%, find the Magellan Fund Sharpe Ratio.

2. The historical beta for the Magellan Fund has been 1.01. Assuming the risk free rate is near its historical average of 5%, use the 12.46% average annual return to calculate the Magellan Fund Treynor Ratio.

3. Based on these two ratios, has the Magellan Fund had good or bad performance on a risk adjusted basis? Explain.

Project 16-1

Repeat Exercises 1 and 2 using a recent edition of the *WSJ*.

Date_____

1. What is the current NAV for the Price Growth Fund (Growth)?

2. What is the 3-year total return on the Price Growth Fund (Growth)?

3. What is the current NAV for the Price Small-Cap Stock Fund (SmCapStk)?

4. What is the 3-year total return on the Price Small-Cap Stock Fund (SmCapStk)?

5. Based on the indexes, for all size classifications (Large, Multi, Mid, and Small) which investment philosophy has performed best since the beginning of the year (Dec 31), value, growth, or core?

6. Based on the indexes, for all investment philosophies (value, growth, and or core) which size category has performed best since the beginning of the year (Dec 31), Large, Multi, Mid, or Small?

Project 16-2

Each day, the Mutual Funds section of the *WSJ* includes a detailed look at a specific fund classification. This look is titled the Mutual-Fund Scorecard. The Scorecard details the performance of the largest funds in the category and the best and worst performers over the past year. Use a recent Mutual-Fund Scorecard to complete the following Projects and questions.

Name of Scorecard (e.g. Large-Cap Core)

_____

Date _____

Describe the Investment Objective:

_____

_____

Of the Ten Biggest funds in the group, which fund has the best performance over the long-term (usually 5 years or more)? What was the return?

_____

_____

What was the average return for all funds in this category over the long-term (usually 5 years or more)? How many funds did this include?

_____

_____

Of the past year's bottom performers, what was the worst long-term performance? Was this performance less than or greater than the average performance over the same period?

_____

_____

Discussion Questions

Getting Going / *By Jonathan Clements*

Smart or Lucky? Despite 11 Great Years, Jury Is Still Out on Famed Mutual Fund

LEGG MASON VALUE TRUST'S William Miller has beaten the market for 11 consecutive years, making him the mutual-fund industry's most-celebrated stock picker. But to statisticians, he's just a coin flipper on a winning streak.

My goal here isn't to bash Bill Miller. In fact, I have a soft spot for the guy. I profiled him for another publication in 1989, when he was the Legg Mason fund's junior co-manager. Make no mistake: Mr. Miller is extraordinarily bright.

Still, for anybody who spends time hunting for superstar fund managers, it is sobering to think that even Mr. Miller's success could be attributed to luck. Indeed, whenever you see a record like Mr. Miller's, you should ask yourself three questions.

First, could you have foreseen Mr. Miller's success and thus taken advantage of his stellar results? Second, even though he has outpaced Standard & Poor's 500-stock index for 11 consecutive years, can you really be sure it wasn't luck? And finally, if you do decide that Mr. Miller is truly a talented stock picker, can you be confident his success will continue?

■ **Taking Charge:** Mr. Miller took sole control of Legg Mason Value Trust in late 1990, when co-manager Ernie Kiehne stepped down. Together, they had built a decent enough record, clocking 16.6% a year from the fund's April 1982 launch through year-end 1990, versus 17.3% for the S&P 500, according to Chicago's Morningstar Inc.

If that record was a buy signal, not many folks noticed. At year-end 1990, the fund had $636 million in assets, a healthy but hardly massive sum. In fact, the fund's assets were still just $2 billion at year-end 1996.

Instead, the big influx of money came in 1998 and 1999, and today the fund boasts assets of $11 billion. These investors may have been late to the party, but they have fared moderately well.

Legg Mason Value Trust lost money in 2000 and 2001, but it lost less than the S&P 500, thus further extending Mr. Miller's market-beating record.

■ **Checking the Tape:** But is all the hoopla over this winning streak justified? I asked William Bernstein, an investment adviser in North Bend, Ore., and author of "The Four Pillars of Investing," to analyze the Legg Mason fund's performance since year-end 1990. Over the past 11 calendar years, the fund has soared 19.6% a year, versus 14.4% for the S&P 500.

Mr. Bernstein's conclusion: Even after adjusting for the fund's relatively high risk, Mr. Miller's record is excellent, especially given the fund's hefty annual expenses. But the record isn't so exceptional that the performance couldn't be explained by luck alone.

The raw results, however, aren't Mr. Miller's real claim to fame. After all, Morningstar calculates that there are 30 other funds that boast even higher annualized returns over the past 11 years. Instead, what is remarkable is Mr. Miller's record for beating the market 11 years in a row.

Skeptics dismiss successful money managers as highly paid coin flippers who get lucky and flip

Market Beaters

Only 16 diversified funds have beaten the
S&P 500 in at least eight of the past 11 years.
Here are seven with low investment minimums
that still are open to new investors.

FUND	YEARS BEAT S&P 500	11-YEAR RETURN
Legg Mason Value Trust	11	19.58%
FPA Capital	8	21.87
Merrill Small Value A	8	20.48
Mairs & Power Growth	8	19.35
Davis NY Venture A	8	16.97
Heritage Capital Appreciation A	8	16.83
Frank Russell Quantitative Equity S	8	14.78
S&P 500	N.A.	14.42

Source: Morningstar Inc.

heads a few times in a row. But what are the chances of flipping heads 11 consecutive times? That would be one in 2,048.

To be fair, the odds are somewhat steeper than that, because half of all money managers don't beat the market in any given year. The reason: investment costs.

■ **Beating the Benchmark:** Let's say the chances of beating the S&P 500 in a single year are 45%. In that case, the odds of outperforming for 11 consecutive years would be one in 6,526.

If those sound like long odds, consider this: SEI Investments, in Oaks, Pa., tracks 7,000 mutual funds, separate accounts and other investment products that focus on U.S. stocks.

"Somebody has to come in No. 1," Mr. Bernstein argues. "It just happened to be Mr. Miller."

Mealymouthed quibbles? Let's presume Mr. Miller did indeed earn his success. Next question: Can this success continue?

■ **Sizing Up the Future:** Mr. Miller runs a fairly concentrated portfolio, holding just 36 stocks as of year-end 2001. That strategy has paid off handsomely in the past.

But as the Legg Mason Value Trust's assets grow larger, Mr. Miller will be increasingly limited to bigger-capitalization stocks. Will these big-capitalization stocks yield the sort of blowout winners that Mr. Miller has found in the past?

"If you believe there are skillful managers, then an obvious thing to do is look for managers with good records," says Steven Thorley, a finance professor at Brigham Young University's Marriott School of Management. "But even with this kind of record, there's no guarantee that he'll outperform the market again next year."

Mr. Miller, for his part, is both gracious and analytical about the question. He readily concedes that his record could be explained by luck and allows that his investment style may have been particularly attuned to the market of the past 11 years.

But he also points out that his performance relative to the S&P 500 has gotten better as his fund has grown larger.

In addition, he notes that he is focused primarily on figuring out what companies are really worth and then buying them at a big discount to those values—a strategy that has paid off handsomely for Warren Buffett and other successful value investors.

So is Mr. Miller truly skillful or just very lucky? "I don't think you'll know until all the numbers are in," says the 52-year-old Mr. Miller. "I have a few more trials to go, and we'll see what the results are. Of course, they may be inconclusive. So far, I'm happy to be lucky."

1. According to the article, what is the benchmark index for the Legg Mason Value Trust fund?

2. According to the chart, how many diversified funds have beaten the S&P500 for more than eight of the past eleven years.

3. What are the odds of beating the S&P 500 benchmark for each of the past eleven years?

4. What characteristic of fund mentioned in the article is likely the cause of the fund's "relatively high risk"?

PART VII

CORPORATE FINANCING

Chapter 17

Cost of Capital

Objectives

1. Describe the capital structure of a firm.

2. Determine the components of a firm's cost of equity capital.

3. Estimate a firm's Weighted Average Cost of Capital.

4. Use the *WSJ* to analyze the different cost of capital across firms.

Key Terms

Capital Structure	Preferred Stock	Equity
Market Value	Dividend Discount Model	CAPM
Cost of Debt	Cost of Common	Weighted Average Cost of Capital (WACC)

In this chapter specific information on firms' debt and equity found in the *WSJ* is used to illustrate the process of estimating a firm's cost of capital. First, how a firm is structured in terms of its different sources of capital is defined and described. Next, the process of estimating the cost of those different sources of capital is reviewed. And finally, the reasons and why firms use a weighted average of these costs to evaluate future investments is discussed. Again, this chapter simply illustrates the concept of cost of capital and we will therefore be making a number of assumptions since much of the information needed to accurately measure a firm's cost of capital is not available to the public. Regardless, the process is the same as that followed by corporate financial managers.

Capital Structure

Most companies finance their operations with both debt and equity. For some projects, firms issue bonds or borrow from the bank. For other, usually more risky, projects, firms issue new stock and use the proceeds to invest in the new venture. Debt and equity have different risks, which therefore implies that debt and equity have different costs. Investors require higher returns when they take higher risks. Furthermore, the debt issued by corporations faces a different tax consequence than equity issues. The interest paid on debt is tax-deductible for the corporation, whereas the dividends paid to equity shareholders is not.

If a corporation does not issue debt its value is solely determined by the value of its stock. As soon as a corporation takes out a loan or issues debt securities it has changed the value of the corporation since the debt holders have a claim to some part of the company. Therefore, the value of the company, and the cost of raising money for new investment, is determined by the company's financial structure. A firm's *capital structure* is the mix of debt and equity financing in use by the firm.

An important point to remember when looking at the capital structure of a company and estimating its cost of raising capital is that book value is inconsequential. *Market value* reflects the value that investors, both long-term debt holders and equity shareholders, are currently placing on the future earnings of the company. Therefore, market value will determine what the company needs to pay when it raises new capital for future projects.

The accounting value of the company, its book value, is equal to the net worth of the company divided by the number of shares currently outstanding. The net worth of a company is equal to the total assets of the company less its total liabilities. These values are historical. Book value is backward looking, while market value is forward looking. Adding the current value of the firm's outstanding long-term debt to the market price of the firm's stock multiplied by the number of shares currently outstanding determines a company's market value. That is, total market value is the sum of the market value of the firm's long-term debt (current price of total long-term debt outstanding) and the market value of the firm's stock. Note that only long-term debt is used as opposed to total debt. Many firms have short-term debt, but short-term debt is used more for cash needs, and is normally not used to finance investment projects for the firm. In summary, the market value of the firm, V, is the sum of the market value of its debt, D, and its equity, E ($V = D + E$).

Exercise 17-1

NASDAQ NATIONAL MARKET ISSUES

L

YTD %CHG	52-WEEK HI	LO	STOCK (SYM)	DIV	YLD %	PE	VOL 100s	CLOSE	NET CHG
63.6	2.71	0.58	LCA Vision LCAV	...		dd	301	1.44	0.05
-71.0	8.40	2.20	LCC Int LCCI	...		5	675	2.12	-0.17
0.8	2.50	1.10	LJ Int JADE	...		dd	30	1.30	0.05
15.7	6.59	2.03	LMI Aero LMIA	...		16	20	5	...
13.6	24.75	18.50	LNB Bcp LNBB	1.00b	4.1	12	1	24.15	0.05
-35.5	2.84	0.92	L90 LNTYE	...		dd	946	1	-0.10
38.9	19.10	11.28	LSB Bk NC LXBK	.60f	3.4	16	58	17.85	-0.35
8.7	14.02	9.81	LSB Cp LSBX	.44	3.2	19	120	13.80	-0.19
15.4	19.65	12.80	LSB Fnl LSBI	.44	2.3	11	2	18.75	...
-6.9	22.39	12.97	LSI Ind LYTS s	.24	1.5	19	422	16.20	-0.93
-23.5	32.15	10.36	LTX LTXX	...		dd	5055	16.02	-0.24
25.5	11.48	5.23	LVMH Moet LVMHY	.14e	1.4	...	1023	10.34	0.17
-39.7	10.75	3.40	LaJolla LJPC	...		dd	324	5.39	-0.22
50.0	25.92	5.82	LabOne LABS	j		dd	99	23.10	0.30
-11.6	4.81	2.04	LaCrosFtwr BOOT	...		dd	16	2.83	...
-6.0	16.20	7.10	Ladish LDSH	...		10	19	10.27	-0.03
10.7	19.43	11.10	LakelandBcp LBAI	.36b	2.0	21	296	18.04	0.09
57.3	28.40	13.90	LakelandFnl LKFN	.68f	2.5	15	54	27.72	0.47
6.4	13.74	5.40	LakelandInd LAKE	p		14	2	10.11	-0.19
25.5	10.10	4.95	LksGaming LACO	...			61	7.78	0.21
-4.2	32.20	14.73	LamRsch LRCX	...		dd	20838	22.24	-0.04
1.7	46.78	24.65	LamarAdvts A LAMR	...		dd	6987	43.65	0.24
9.0	40	24.96	LancastrCol LANC	.72	1.9	17	1391	38.70	0.37
5.7	16.50	10.25	Lance LNCE	.64	4.2	18	423	15.10	0.11
-6.4	2.15	0.39	Lndcrp LCOR	...		dd	18	1.17	-0.03
7.9	17.40	5.25	Landair LAND	...		15	18	15.86	-0.14
17.3	5.70	2.81	LandecCp LNDC	...		dd	5	4.40	0.11
11.4	23.25	17.14	LndmrkBcp LARK	.60b	2.6	9	10	22.72	0.12
44.8	107.25	60	LandstarSys LSTR	...		21	365	104.98	0.20

M

YTD %CHG	52-WEEK HI	LO	STOCK (SYM)	DIV	YLD %	PE	VOL 100s	CLOSE	NET CHG
-47.8	24.95	6.54	Micrvisn MVIS	...		dd	1098	7.44	0.54
16.2	21.05	13.90	MidStBcsh MDST	.40	2.1	16	252	18.92	1.02
53.8	8	4	Middleby MIDD	e			124	8	...
0.1	26.72	20.53	MidsexWtr MSEX s	.34	3.7	34	86	22.64	-0.95
4.8	8.05	4.05	MiddltnDoll DOLL	.65b	10.0	17	378	6.50	0.14
7.3	49.57	25	Midland MLAN	.35	.7	16	209	46.98	-0.04
31.1	29.95	18.51	MdwstBanc MBHI	.60	2.2	15	63	27.86	0.40
22.8	14.88	8.35	MdwstGrn MWGP	.15e	1.1	16	7	14.20	0.09
-40.6	10.06	3.14	MikohnGamg MIKN	...		dd	70	4.75	-0.20
10.4	53.05	31.71	Millea ADS	.33e		4	286	40.41	-1.02
-36.0	12.05	2.73	MinnumCell MCEL	...		dd	1506	3.34	0.10
-44.4	42.90	12.55	MillnmPhrm MLNM	...		dd	128485	13.62	0.64
0.1	27.11	18	MillerHrm MLHR	.14	.6	dd	3134	23.68	0.12
-75.5	30.50	3.20	MillicmInt MICC	p		dd	1919	2.98	-0.23
-24.0	5	1.03	Mind CTI MNDO	...		dd	8	1.27	...
-22.7	5.75	1.37	Mirae ADS MRAE	.02e	.8	...	3	2.55	0.05
-89.4	12.70	0.68	MiravantMed MRVT	...		dd	1204	1.02	0.07
-25.5	10.25	4.86	MISONIX MSON	...		dd	125	7.08	0.40
-38.6	8.42	1.95	MissionRes MSSN	...		dd	1095	2.15	...
12.2	47.11	35.35	MS VlyBcsh MVBI	.56	1.3	15	21	43.99	-0.73
-13.2	8.15	3	MitchamInd MIND	...		dd	45	3.95	0.20
42.1	14.99	7	MITY Ent MITY	...		69	50	11.72	0.41
-51.5	39.99	15.76	MobileMini MINI	...		14	771	18.99	0.33
57.6	3.50	0.66	MbltyElec MOBE	...		dd	374	1.97	0.02
-6.7	4.04	1.78	MobiusMgt MOBI	...		dd	241	2.80	-0.05
11.8	12.45	6.40	MOCON MOCO	.24	2.2	19	19	10.80	-0.15
36.2	23.50	6.21	McroGnrl MGEN	p		44	1906	18.67	0.16
22.9	5	2.05	MicroLinear MLIN	...		dd	146	3.44	-0.01
-30.0	8.24	3.88	MicroTherp MTIX	...		dd	127	4.40	0.05
-94.4	10.26	0.13	McroTele B MICT	...		dd	1767	0.14	-0.04
15.1	33.99	15.52	MicrochpTch MCHP s	...		65	25433	29.73	0.17
-55.0	47.04	5.30	Micromuse MUSE	...		dd	52 5513	6.75	0.18
8.1	30.78	16.10	MicrosSys MCRS	...		59	308	27.13	0.08
8.4	2.05	0.89	MicroToMain MTMC	...		dd	1731	1.55	0.03
-49.2	40.10	12.06	Microsemi MSCC s	...		43	7212	15.08	0.06
-22.0	76.15	47.50	Microsoft MSFT	...		45	327461	51.66	1.68
-66.5	4.98	1.10	MicroStrat MSTR	...		dd	2022	1.29	0.04
-57.2	29.45	8.01	Microtune TUNE	...		dd	6623	10.03	-0.34

M

YTD %CHG	52-WEEK HI	LO	STOCK (SYM)	DIV	YLD %	PE	VOL 100s	CLOSE	NET CHG
24.8	40.11	24.30	MAF Bcp MAFB	.60	1.6	14	937	36.81	-0.73
8.1	8.25	5	MAPICS MAPX	...		dd	395	6.66	0.01
16.1	32.48	21.20	MB Fnl MBFI	.30e	1.0	34	548	31.57	-0.17
8.1	19.84	14.74	MCG Cap MCGC n	1.13e	5.9	...	1071	19.24	0.04
-15.5	2.22	1	MCK Comm MCKC	...		dd	205	1.25	-0.01
-50.9	24.93	9.89	MCSi MCSI	...		dd	1664	11.51	-0.47
67.7	9.75	1	MDC A MDCA	...		dd	208	5.70	0.07
-6.3	5.31	2.23	MDSI Mobl MDSI	...			3	3.29	-0.03
0.5	3.26	1.20	META Gp METG	...		dd	49	2.20	-0.15
-14.8	11.60	7.40	MFC Bcp g MXBIF	...			24	9.80	0.20
-15.1	3.60	1.25	MFRI Inc MFRI	...		dd	25	2.65	0.25
-52.2	17.05	6.70	MGI Pharma MOGN	...		dd	693	7.30	0.01
-42.4	2	0.31	MH Meyersn MHMY	...		dd	5	0.38	0.03
-49.3	14.50	2.70	MIH Ltd A MIHL	...		dd	27	3.70	0.06
-38.1	22.95	4.38	MIM Cp MIMS	...		16	7289	11.02	0.39
-17.0	20.50	5.55	MIPS Tch A MIPS	...		dd	945	7.17	0.31
-17.4	19	4.85	MIPS Tch B MIPSB	...			348	6.59	0.31
-3.5	39.46	15.17	MKS Instr MKSI	...		dd	6398	26.08	-1.16
-8.3	2.45	0.75	MPW IndSvc MPWG	...		10	10	2.11	-0.02
-44.4	29.85	8.43	MRO Sftwr MROI	...		dd	960	13	-0.23
-67.7	11.20	1.20	MRV Comm MRVC	...		dd	2439	1.37	0.08
-29.4	12.85	3.65	M SysFlsh FLSH	...		dd	646	8.25	-0.16
-66.7	2.67	0.50	MTI Tch MTIC	...		dd	288	0.60	...
-3.9	17.82	7.19	MTR Gamg MNTG	...		26	1156	15.38	0.48
3.9	15.60	8.90	MTS Sys MTSC	.24	2.3	21	224	10.50	...
-16.8	8.16	3.60	M Wave MWAV	...		9	56	4.15	0.09
10.8	21.40	14.77	Macatawa MCBC sx	.32b	1.6	18	198	20.50	-0.17
-1.2	5.63	2.90	MackieDsgn MKIE	...		dd	21	4	...
-22.9	10.10	1.59	Macrochem MCHM	...			656	2.35	0.01
21.9	27.20	11.30	Macromedia MACR	...		dd	5821	21.69	-0.14
-11.9	11.50	4.25	Macronix ADS MXICY	b		...	3	6.78	-0.07
-57.6	72.25	13.85	MacrovsnCp MVSN	...		42	12362	14.94	-0.21
9.6	7.15	2.45	Made2Mnge MTMS	...		dd	6	4	-0.50
-33.3	1.45	0.24	MadgeNtwk MADGF	...			797	0.30	-0.02
3.8	29.35	23.09	MadsnGas MDSN	1.33	4.8	16	83	27.45	-0.35
-16.0	15.20	4.81	MagalSec MAGS	b		25	122	10.60	0.01
-30.0	2.33	0.80	MagicSftwr MGIC	...		dd	233	1.40	0.09
-43.9	30.90	13.97	MagmaDsgn LAVA n	...			968	17	0.01
9.3	10.25	5.02	MagnaEnt A MIEC	...		64	1339	7.65	0.20
18.8	14.52	10	Mahaskalnv OSKY x	.64	4.6	12	14	13.90	0.31
22.5	6.51	3.17	MainStMain MAIN	...		cc	796	6.05	-0.20
24.8	21	14.12	MainStBks MSBK	.42	2.1	20	44	20.46	0.21
30.5	25.45	15.11	MainsourceFncl MSFG	.68b	3.0	12	38	22.90	-0.30
87.4	3.33	0.45	MajrAutoCo MAJR	...		6	9	1.50	0.06
28.3	6.95	4.88	Makita ADS MKTAY	.14e	2.1	...	1	6.66	-0.09
-72.0	6.20	0.83	MallonRes MLRC	...		dd	76	0.85	-0.04
-66.7	7.66	2.33	MgtNtwk TMNG	...		38	456	2.34	0.14
11.7	2.98	2.07	MnchstrTch MANC	...		14	58	2.57	0.14
-9.1	42.16	12.75	ManhAssoc MANH	...		46	4058	26.50	-0.64
-10.6	4.61	0.85	Mannatech MTEX	...		dd	32	2.52	0.02
17.8	24.27	17.10	ManTch A MANT n	...			277	21.45	0.76
-72.0	42.37	4.94	Manugistics MANU	...		dd	201761	5.90	-2.04
-38.8	33.55	6.05	MapInfo MAPS	...		39	5325	9.60	-0.20
-82.1	11.21	0.17	Marconi ADS MONI	.11e	52.4	...	20198	0.21	...
-45.9	3.67	1.15	Marimba MRBA	...		dd	80	1.83	-0.01
212.2	2.65	0.51	MarisaChrist MRSA	...		26	6	2.31	0.05
40.1	5.49	1.06	MktWatch MKTW	...		dd	105	4.61	-0.27
4.7	16.75	12.40	MrshSupr A MARSA	.44	2.8	10	56	15.49	-0.11
3.7	15	10.75	MrshSupr B MARSB	.44	3.1	9	12	14.31	-0.24
-0.7	34.25	14	MartekBiosci MATK	...		dd	4301	21.60	-0.08
3.1	18.50	10	MartnTrnpt MRTN	...		14	86	18.25	-0.25
-29.1	46.24	12.51	MarvellTch MRVL	...		dd	76993	25.39	-2.70
32.0	33.31	21.77	Massbk MASB s	.88	2.8	14	77	31.50	...
-31.7	21.55	8.84	MatavCbl ADS MATV	e		28	3	11.20	0.05
-45.9	40	14.75	MatriaHlthcr MATR	...		28	939	18.74	-0.43
2.9	3.74	0.90	Matritech NMPS	...		dd	423	2.93	0.09
18.1	13.50	9.81	MatrixBcp MTXC	...		9	10	12.40	...
37.3	10.25	5.15	MatrixSvc MTRX	...		12	109	9.20	-0.24
-54.3	24	3.75	MatrixOne MONE	...		dd	1680	5.93	0.28
3.5	29	16.12	Matthwint A MATW s	.11	.4	...	245	25.43	0.06

Use the above stock listings from the *WSJ* to answer the following questions.

1. What is the current price of Microsoft Corporation stock (Symbol: MSFT)? Microsoft currently has 5.4 billion shares of stock outstanding. What is the market value of Microsoft stock?

2. Microsoft currently has no long-term debt. What is the market value of Microsoft Corporation?

3. What is the current price of LSI Industries Inc. stock (Symbol LYTS)? LSI Industries Inc. currently has 15.7 million shares of stock outstanding. What is the market value of LSI stock?

4. LSI Industries Inc. currently has approximately $17 million in long-term debt. What is the total market value LSI Industries Inc.?

Cost of Debt

Issuing debt carries a cost, but may also create a benefit to the firm. The ***cost of debt*** for a firm is the market's expected rate of return on their bonds minus any tax savings by incurring debt.

$$CostofDebt = r_{debt} \times (1 - T_c)$$

Where T_c is the tax rate for the firm, and r is the market's expected rate of return on the company's bonds. To find the rate a firm will need to pay when it issues new debt we must find the current expected return on the firm's existing bonds, or the expected return on bonds of similar risk and other characteristics. The expected return on bonds is the yield to maturity (YTM), or the rate of return that equates future cash flows with the price of the bond.

For example, suppose a bond due in two years is selling at $102, or $1,020.00 per bond. This is $2 above its par value of $100, or $1,000 per bond. This corporate bond pays interest twice a year at the stated annual coupon rate of 7%. To find the YTM we first set the price of the bond, $1,020, equal to the present value of the four remaining interest payments and the final principal payment of $1,000. We can then determine the YTM by solving for the semi-annual discount rate using a financial calculator or a spreadsheet program.

$$1020 = \frac{35}{(1+r)^1} + \frac{35}{(1+r)^2} + \frac{35}{(1+r)^3} + \frac{35}{(1+r)^4} + \frac{1000}{(1+r)^4}$$

The annual rate r that solves this equation, or the YTM for this bond, is 5.92%. This is the rate of return that makes all of the future cash payments received by the bond holder equal to the price of the bond today. Thus, the coupon rate that the firm would pay today for new bonds would be 5.92%. The cost of debt to the firm will equal this coupon rate less any tax savings from issuing debt. Most corporations face the standard corporate tax rate of 35%. We will assume that this is the firm's tax rate and use it in all calculations. The cost is debt is then found by

$$CostofDebt = 5.92\% + (1 - 0.35) = 3.85\%$$

The actually cost of debt is lower than the rate of interest on the bond because of the tax savings provided to the firm.

Exercise 17-2

U.S. Exchange Bonds

4 p.m. ET Wednesday, June 5, 2002

Explanatory Notes

For New York and American Bonds

Yield is Current yield.

cv-Convertible bond. cf-Certificates. cld-Called. dc-Deep discount. ec-European currency units. f-Dealt in flat. ll-Italian lire. kd-Danish kroner. m-Matured bonds, negotiability impaired by maturity. na-No accrual. r-Registered. rp-Reduced principal. st, ad-Stamped. t-Floating rate. wd-When distributed. ww-With warrants. x-Ex interest. xw-Without warrants. zr-Zero coupon.

vj-In bankruptcy or receivership or being reorganized under the Bankruptcy Act, or securities assumed by such companies.

NEW YORK BONDS
Corporation Bonds

BONDS	CUR YLD	VOL	CLOSE	NET CHG
AES Cp 4½05	cv	269	64.13	-1.38
AES Cp 8s8	11.4	82	70	-5.00
AMR 9s16	10.0	97	89.75	-0.38
ANR 9⅜21	8.8	2	109.25	-8.75
ATT 6½02	6.5	450	100.50	0.31
ATT 6¾04	6.8	2008	98.75	0.63
ATT 5⅞04	5.8	1453	97.38	1.38
ATT 7s05	7.2	485	97.38	...
ATT 7½06	7.5	460	99.75	2.50
ATT 7¾07	7.9	301	98.50	0.38
ATT 6s09	6.9	874	87.25	1.25
ATT 8½22	9.1	586	89.25	-0.25
ATT 8¼24	9.1	575	89	0.38
ATT 8.35s25	9.2	150	90.88	...
ATT 6½29	8.4	661	77.63	2.13
ATT 8⅛31	9.3	1230	92.88	...
ARetire 5½02	cv	103	90.50	-1.50
Baroid 8s03	8.0	25	100.50	2.47
BauschL 6¾04	6.7	32	101	-0.13
BauschL 7½28	8.4	10	84.50	0.50
BayView 9s07	9.1	30	99	1.00
Bellso 6½28	6.8	10	94.38	...
BellsoT 6⅛04	6.2	8	103.38	-1.25
BellsoT 7s05	6.6	52	106.13	-0.50
BellsoT 5⅞09	5.8	50	101.75	-0.25
BellsoT 7s25	6.9	34	102	-0.38
BellsoT 7⅛32	7.7	20	102.50	-0.25
BellsoT 7½33	7.4	5	102	0.63
BellsoT 6⅛33	7.1	117	95	-1.13
BellsoT 7⅞35	7.4	30	103.25	...
Bevrly 9s06	8.8	25	102	1.25
Bluegrn 8½12	cv	7	90	3.75
BordCh 8½16	10.4	5	80.50	-0.50
BosCelts 6s38	9.2	20	65	...
CallonP 11s05	12.4	26	89	6.00
CallonP 10¼04	11.6	109	88	2.00
Case 7⅛16	9.8	25	74	2.00
CaterpInc 9s06	8.0	40	112.13	0.13
Coeur 13⅜08	cv	149	142	-23.00
Coeur 6⅜04	cv	149	78.13	-3.38
Consec 8½03	8.8	112	92	2.50
Conseco 10½04	11.9	145	88.25	4.50
CSFB 6½11	6.2	30	99	-0.25
CrwnCk 7¼26	11.1	10	66.50	1.50
DR Hrtn 10s06	9.7	68	103	...
DelcoR 8¼07	8.8	95	98	-2.50
Dow 6.85s13	6.7	60	102	...
DukeEn 6¾23	7.0	81	98.38	0.25
DukeEn 6¼25	7.0	50	97.13	-1.63
DukeEn 7½25	7.3	70	102.38	0.25
DukeEn 7s33	7.0	35	100.75	1.75
FUnRE 8½03	9.4	52	95	...
FordCr 6⅜08	6.4	66	100.13	0.38
FrptMRP 8¼04	9.8	20	89	10.88
GMA 6⅝02	6.6	100	100.78	0.41
GMA 6⅜08	6.0	110	101.25	0.63
GMA dc6s11	6.2	31	96.13	0.75
GMA zr12	...	64	472.75	-2.13
GMA zr15	...	68	377.75	2.63
GoldmS 7½05	7.2	5	104.25	0.13
Hertz 7s03	6.8	15	103.50	1.50
Hexcel 7s03	cv	15	81	-2.00
Hilton 5s06	cv	53	94.63	0.13
Hollgnr 9¼07	8.9	5	104	...
Honywll zr03	...	70	95.38	-0.38
HuntPly 11½04f	...	27	20	...
IllPwr 7½25	7.5	20	100	3.00
IBM 7½02	7.2	39	101.06	0.03
IBM 5⅜09	5.5	17	98.50	-1.50
IBM 7⅛13	6.7	15	111.25	-0.50
IBM 7s25	6.6	30	105.50	1.63
KCS En 8⅜06	11.3	15	78.50	2.38
K&B Hm 9½06	9.2	59	104.50	0.13
Leucadia 7⅛13	7.7	10	101	-0.50
Lucent 7¼06	8.7	289	83.63	-0.13
Lucent 5⅛08	7.6	100	72	0.75
Lucent 6½28	10.0	75	65	...
Lucent 6.45s29	9.9	215	65	0.50
MBNA 8.28s26	8.5	103	97.75	...
Malan 9½04	cv	20	88.75	-0.25
McDnl 6⅜05	6.5	15	101.50	-0.50
ML PubSt 7s07	7.6	15	92	2.00
MPac 5s45f	...	50	59	0.50
NRurU 6.2s08	6.0	5	103.50	1.63
NatwFS 8s27	7.8	6	102.75	...
NYTel 5⅞03	5.5	29	101.75	...
NYTel 7¼24	7.2	20	101	1.00
NYTel 6⅛05	6.3	10	103.25	-1.38
NYTel 4⅞06	4.9	10	99	...
NYTel 6⅛10	6.2	85	99.25	...
NYTel 6.70s23	7.1	10	94.13	0.63
NYTel 7s25	7.2	130	97	-0.63
OffDep zr07	...	5	82	-2.00
ParkerD 5⅛04	cv	18	95	1.88
PhilPt 8.49s23	8.1	2	104.13	-3.38
PhilPt 7.92s23	7.6	58	104	...
PhilPt 7.2s23	7.1	20	101.13	2.13
PhilIP 7⅛28	7.1	43	100.25	-0.75
PrmHsp 9½06	9.0	10	103	0.50
PSvEG 7¾14	7.2	5	102	0.13
PSvEG 7s24	7.0	32	99.63	0.13
ReynTob 8¼02	8.0	14	100.50	-0.03
ReynTob 8¼04	8.4	11	104.75	-0.25
ReynTob 9⅛13	8.4	20	110	0.75
Safwy 9.65s04	8.9	55	108.25	-0.75
Sequa 9s09	9.0	74	100.50	-0.50
SilicnGr 5¼04	cv	152	69	1.00
Sizeler 9s09	cv	99	102	1.00
Solectrn zrM20	...	70	58	1.00
SoCG 5⅜03	5.6	25	103.13	1.13
Sprint 6⅞28	8.5	30	81	...
StdCmcl 07	cv	40	94	1.00
StdPac 8⅛07	8.3	7	103	1.00
TVA 5⅞11	5.6	1	100.13	-1.38
TVA 7¼43	6.9	125	104.75	0.25
TVA 6¾43	6.8	100	102	0.13
Tenet 6s05	cv	95	98	-0.38
TmeWar 8.11s06	7.5	10	108.50	1.50
TmeWar 8.18s07	7.9	65	104	1.00
TmeWar 7.48s08	7.3	5	102.13	0.13
TmeWar 9.15s23	8.4	55	109.38	-1.63
TolEd 8s03	7.8	30	102	...
TollCp 8s03	8.4	40	104.75	0.75
THilfig 6⅛03	6.5	265	100.50	-0.38
UtdAir 10.67s04	13.4	1136	79.38	-0.63
UtdAir 11.21s14	14.4	30	77.88	-0.13
WashMut 6⅞11	6.7	8	102.50	5.00
Webb 9s06	8.8	5	102	-0.50
WebbDel 9⅜09	8.9	115	105.38	-0.88
Weirton 11½04f	...	85	50	2.50
Weirton 10⅛05f	...	110	47	1.50
XeroxCr 7.2s12	8.9	31	80.75	2.25

Foreign Bonds

BONDS	CUR YLD	VOL	CLOSE	NET CHG
Inco 7¼16	cv	122	100.63	-0.25
SeaCnt 12½04A	12.9	166	97.25	-0.13
SeaCnt 12½04B	13.0	50	96.50	-1.50
SeaCnt 10½03	10.5	88	99.50	...
SeaCnt 9½03	9.5	42	99.50	0.50
TelMex 4¼04	cv	2	116	-7.75
TelArg 11¾04	25.8	84	46.13	2.13
TrnMarMx 03	...	45	90.88	-0.38

AMEX BONDS

BONDS	CUR YLD	VOL	CLOSE	NET CHG
ABN GE 11s03	cv	20	84	0.50
ABN INTC 12s03	cv	10	91	1.00
ABN SCH04	cv	31	95	0.88
Leh Prudents04	...	52	90	...
Leh Prudents06	...	18	94	-1.50
TrnsLux 7½06	cv	13	88	1.50
Trump 11½03f	...	66	92	1.00

NASDAQ BONDS

BONDS	CUR YLD	VOL	CLOSE	NET CHG
Avatar05	cv	10	99.50	...

Source: *The Wall Street Journal*, June 6 ,2002. Reprinted by permission of Dow Jones & Company, Inc. (c) 2002 Dow Jones & Company, Inc. All Rights Reserved Worldwide.

Most corporate bonds are traded in the over-the-counter (OTC) markets. However, many bonds from large issuers are traded on the organized exchanges (NYSE, NASDAQ, and AMEX). Use the tables on previous page from the U.S. Exchange Bonds column of the *WSJ* to answer the following questions.

1. Find the closing price for the bond issued by AT&T (ATT) with a coupon rate of 7%, maturing in 2005.

2. Calculate the YTM for this AT&T Bond that matures in 3 years (six semi-annual payments).

3. Assuming AT&T will finance any new investments for 3 years and their tax rate is 35%, what is AT&T's cost of debt?

Cost of Preferred Equity

All public corporations issue stock, but many firms also issue both common and preferred stock. *Preferred stock* is equity that takes priority over common stock with regard to dividends. Preferred stock is somewhat of a hybrid security between debt and equity. Holders of preferred stock receive dividends, just like common equity shareholders, but usually at a fixed level like bonds. Preferred stock holders do not normally have voting rights like common equity holders, and unlike interest on debt, preferred stock dividends are not tax-deductible.

Preferred stock with fixed dividends are valued using the *dividend discount model*. The present value of preferred stock (its current market price) will equal the present value of all future cash dividends and the present value of the future price.

$$PV = \frac{dividend_1}{(1+r)^1} + \frac{dividend_2}{(1+r)^2} + ... \frac{dividend_t}{(1+r)^t} + \frac{price_t}{(1+r)^t}$$

In this relationship the discount rate, r, is the investor's expected rate of return for the company's preferred stock. If the dividend is perpetual (or at least very long-term, say 30+ years), the present value is equal to all future cash dividends.

$$PV = \frac{dividend_1}{(1+r)^1} + \frac{dividend_2}{(1+r)^2} + \frac{dividend_3}{(1+r)^3} + ...$$

or

$$PV = \frac{dividend}{r_{preferred}}$$

Rearranging this equation we can estimate investors' expected rate of return for the preferred stock.

$$r_{preferred} = \frac{dividend}{PV}$$

The expected return, $r_{preferred}$, is the firm's cost of preferred stock.. For example, suppose a company currently pays an annual dividend of $1 per share and each share of preferred stock is selling for $20. The expected rate of return that investors are placing on the company's preferred stock is 5% ($1/$20 = 0.05).

Exercise 17-3

PREFERRED STOCK LISTINGS

STOCK	DIV	YLD	CLOSE	NET CHG
ANZ pf	2.00	7.9	25.36	0.01
ANZ II pf	2.02	7.9	25.41	0.02
AT&T 8 1/4 PNS	2.06	8.9	23.04	0.34
AT&T 8.125 PNS	2.03	8.9	22.75	0.31
AbbeyNtl pfA ADS	2.19	8.4	26.06	0.03
Aetna nts	2.13	8.3	25.59	0.09
Agrium COPrS	2.00	9.1	21.94	0.44
AL PwrCap pfQ	1.84	7.4	24.90	-0.35
AL Pwr pfO	1.46	6.4	22.95	0.20
AL PwrCap pfR	1.90	7.6	25.02	-0.05
AL Pwr pfN	1.30	6.2	20.90	0.15
AL Pwr ntsA	1.78	7.1	25.02	-0.23
AL Pwr ntsB	1.75	7.0	24.85	0.05
AL Pwr ntsC	1.75	7.1	24.78	-0.03
AL Pwr ntsJ	1.69	6.6	25.48	-0.17
AlbEngy pfA g	2.38	...	26.59	-0.38
AlexREEq pfA	2.38	9.1	26.20	0.05
AlexREEq pfB	.52e	2.0	25.86	0.05
AllenTele pfD	.60e	1.5	40.43	0.43
Allstate QUIBS	1.78	7.1	25.12	0.22
AllstFng CorTS	2.00e	7.6	26.25	0.40
Alltel pf	2.06	.7	300	4.51
Amerco pfA	2.13	9.3	23	-0.30
AmAnnuity TOPrS	2.32	9.3	25.05	-0.03
AmExpress pfA	1.75	6.9	25.21	0.06
AmFnlCap TOPrS	2.32	9.2	24.85	-0.05
AmGenl TOPRS A	1.97	7.4	26.45	-0.19
AmGenCap TruPs	2.01	7.4	27.25	-0.10
Apartmtlnv pfC	2.25	9.0	25.12	0.02
Apartmtlnv pfD	2.19	8.8	24.84	0.09
Apartmtlnv pfG	2.34	9.0	26	0.08
Apartmtlnv pfH	2.38	9.3	25.51	0.03
Aptlnv CIP Pfd.	2.25	8.9	25.25	0.19
Aptlnv CIQ Pfd	2.53	9.7	26	-0.25
Apartmtlnv prf	2.50	9.5	26.25	...
AppalchPwr ntsA	1.80	7.3	24.64	0.14
AppalchPwr pfA	2.06	8.1	25.40	0.14
AppalchPwr ntsB	1.83	7.4	24.70	-0.09
AppalchPwr pfB	2.00	7.9	25.24	-0.03
Aquila QUIBS	.50p	...	20.81	-0.26
ArchstoneSmith pfA	2.29	6.2	37	0.25
ArchstoneSmith pfD	2.19	8.4	26.02	0.17
ArmWdind QUIBS	1.86	13.3	13.99	-0.01
AssocEstate pf	2.44	9.8	25	0.18
AtlCap QUIPS	2.06	8.1	25.31	...
Aus&NZ Bk pf	2.28	8.6	26.60	0.05
AvalnBay pfA	2.00	8.0	24.88	-0.02
AvalnBay pfH	2.17	8.2	26.40	-0.10
Avista pfA	1.97	8.9	22.15	-2.20
BBVA pfA	1.96	7.7	25.50	0.10
BCH Cap pfB	2.36	8.5	27.62	0.02
BGE Cap pfA	1.79	7.2	24.92	0.08
BNY CapII pfC	1.95	7.8	25.07	-0.11
BNY CapIII pfD	1.76	7.0	25.10	0.10
BNYCapTr pfE	1.72	6.9	24.80	-0.09
BRE Prop pfA	2.13	8.2	25.93	-0.16
BSCH Fin pfF	2.03	7.9	25.60	...
BSCH Fin pfG	2.03	7.9	25.62	...
BSCH Fin pfH	1.95	7.8	24.85	0.03
BSCH Fin pfJ	1.84	7.4	25	...
BSCH Fin pfQ	2.16	8.2	26.36	...
Goodrich QUIPS	2.08	8.2	25.30	...
BAC Cp Tr	1.75f	6.9	25.21	-0.04
BAC Cap Tr II		...	25	-0.01
Bancoltau ADS	.57e	1.7	32.95	-0.69
BancwestCap pf	2.38	8.8	27.15	0.01
BkAm CorTS	.58e	2.3	25.20	0.35
BankAm TOPrS	1.75	7.0	25.12	0.17
BkOneCap	2.00	7.8	25.80	...
BankOneCap pf	1.50e	5.7	26.18	0.15
BnkOne pf II	2.13	7.9	26.96	...
BnkOne pf VI	1.80	7.2	24.93	0.08
◆ColonlProp pfC	2.31	8.7	26.48	-0.02
◆ColonlProp pfA	2.19	8.6	25.32	0.07
ClmbsSo pfB	1.98	7.9	25.15	-0.07
ComEd TOPrS	2.12	8.3	25.40	0.05
ComericaCap pfZ	1.27e	5.0	25.27	0.02
CommCap pfT	2.19	8.8	24.80	-0.15
ComrclRlty pf	2.25	9.0	24.95	...
ConAgraCap pfB	1.30e	5.6	23.35	0.45
Conseco pfG	2.25	27.3	8.25	0.42
Conseco pfH	2.36	26.7	8.85	0.57
Conseco pfT	2.29	27.4	8.37	0.47
Conseco pfV	2.17	27.0	8.05	0.40
ConEdPINES	.42e	1.6	25.95	0.23
ConEd PINES	1.84	7.1	25.80	...
ConEd pf	5.00	6.6	75.25	0.25
ConEdsn PINES	1.88	7.3	25.85	0.09
CnsmrsEngy TOPrS	2.31	9.5	24.40	-0.10
CnsmrEngyII TOPrS	2.05	8.9	23	0.25
CnsmrEngy pfA	4.16	7.4	56	-0.96
CnsmrEngy pfB	4.50	7.6	59.50	-0.50
CnsmrEngy TOPrS	2.09	9.0	23.22	-0.33
Corng nts	1.71e	8.3	20.70	-0.10
CpOfficProp pfB	2.50	9.5	26.30	0.09
◆CpOfficProp pfE	2.56	9.5	27	...
◆CpOfficProp pfF	2.47	9.3	26.45	0.10
CorrCorp pfA	2.00a	9.7	20.55	0.20
CorrCorp pfB	stk	...	24.10	0.10
CntrywdCap CorTS	2.00e	7.8	25.50	0.05
Cntrywd CorTS	2.00	7.9	25.40	0.05
CoxComm DECS	6.86	19.3	35.47	1.22
CoxComm pf	3.50	7.8	45	-0.31
◆Crescent pfB		...	.25	0.15
◆CrescentRE pfA	1.69	8.4	20	0.05
Criimi pfG	j	...	8.01	0.26
◆CrownAmRlty pf	5.50	10.0	55.15	0.25
DQE PINES	2.09	8.5	24.60	...
DamlrBnz nts	3.73e	6.1	61.45	-1.55
DelmarPL pfA	2.03	8.0	25.35	-0.10
DeltaAir nts	2.03	8.8	22.95	0.07
DetEd 7 3/8	1.84	7.4	24.82	0.02
DetEd 7 5/8	1.91	7.7	24.88	...
DetEd QUIDS Jr	1.89	7.6	24.83	0.13
DevDivRlty pfC	2.09	8.5	24.50	-0.05
DevDivRltyN pf	.47e	1.9	24.70	-0.05
Disney Quibb	.91e	3.6	25	-0.25
DominRes pfA	2.10	8.0	26.19	-0.01
DuPont pfA	3.50	5.8	60	0.50
DuPont pfB	4.50	5.9	76	-0.50
DukeCap QUIPS	1.84	7.3	25.15	-0.08
DukeCap TOPrS	1.84	7.3	25.24	0.05
DukeCap TruPs	2.09	7.8	26.70	0.05
DukeCap pfQ	1.80	7.2	25.05	...
DukeCap pfV	1.80	7.0	25.71	-0.04
DukeEngy pfA	1.59	6.2	25.60	-0.15
DukeEngy ntsC	1.65	6.4	25.70	-0.06
DukeRlty pfD	1.84	7.1	25.91	0.01
DukeRlty pfE	2.06	8.0	25.90	-0.25
DukeRlty pfF	2.00	8.0	25.10	-0.13
DukeRlty pfI	2.11	8.0	26.25	-0.15
DuqsnCap pfA	2.09	8.4	25.01	0.06
DuqsnLt QUIBS	1.84	7.5	24.55	0.10
DuqsnLt pf		...	25.25	...
DuqsnLt pfG	2.10	7.5	28	1.00
DuqsnLt pfC	2.00	7.8	25.75	-0.50
EDF London pfA	2.16	8.5	25.47	0.01
EIX QUIPS A		...	22.13	-0.12
EIX QUIPS B		...	23.40	...
Eksprtfinans pf	2.17	8.3	26.20	0.05
ElPasoGrwth	.06	.4	15.90	0.15
ElPasoCGPlnc	1.66	10.2	16.25	0.03
ElPasoEngy pfA	2.38	6.3	37.80	0.40
ElPasoTN pfA	4.13	8.3	49.95	0.45
FrptMcCG pfC	.92e	3.5	25.95	-0.95
FremontGen TOPrS	2.25	11.5	19.60	0.60
FresensMed pf	.27e	2.1	12.90	-0.30
G&L Rlty pfA wd	2.56	11.4	22.50	0.04
G&L Rlty pfB	2.45	11.2	21.84	0.34
Gabelli PRD	.48e	1.9	25.05	-0.35
GabelliConv pf	2.00	7.7	26.05	0.05
GabelliEqTr pf	1.80	6.8	26.40	0.15
GabelliTr pf	1.81	7.0	25.95	0.15
GabelliMlti pf	1.98	7.6	26.15	0.05
GblsRsdntl pfA	2.08	8.5	24.59	0.02
◆GenAmInv pf	1.80	7.0	25.88	-0.02
◆GenGrthProp pf	1.81	5.9	30.45	-0.15
GenMoPINES2031	1.83	7.3	25	-0.13
GenMotor QUIBS	1.81	7.2	25.06	0.01
GenMot nts	1.81	7.2	25.09	0.01
GenMtr nts	.46p	...	24.88	-0.07
GenMotor nts	1.84	7.3	25.11	-0.13
GA PwrCapTr pfA	1.71	6.8	24.98	...
GA PwrCapTr pfT	1.94	7.6	25.48	0.18
GA PwrCapTr pfU	1.90	7.5	25.20	0.05
GA PwrCapTr pfV	1.94	7.7	25.35	-0.05
GA Pwr PINES	1.72	6.9	24.84	0.02
GA Pwr ntsB	1.65	6.5	25.50	0.12
GA Pwr ntsD	1.66	6.5	25.60	...
Glenborough pfA	1.94	8.4	23	...
GlimchRlty pfB	2.31	9.3	24.91	-0.09
GrandMetro pfA	2.36	8.6	27.35	...
GtAtlPac QUIBS	2.34	9.9	23.75	-0.65
◆GtLakes REIT pfA	2.44	9.3	26.30	-0.20
GtWstFnl TOPRS	2.06	8.1	25.39	0.10
GulfPwrCap QUIPS B	1.75	7.0	25.15	0.15
GulfPwrCap	.69p	...	25.22	0.20
HL&P Cap pfA	2.03	8.9	22.70	0.62
HRPT Prcp pfA	2.47	9.4	26.18	0.17
HnckJ PtPfd	.86	7.0	12.33	-0.02
HarrisPfCap pfA	1.84	7.3	25.04	0.09
HrtfrdCap pfA	1.93	7.7	25.02	...
HrtfrdLf pfA	1.80	7.2	24.93	0.12
Hrtfrd TruPs B	1.91	7.5	25.60	0.03
Hl ElecInd TOPrS	2.09	8.2	25.48	-0.17
HlthCrProp pfA	1.97	7.9	24.95	...
HlthCrProp pfB	2.17	8.5	25.60	0.07
HlthCrProp pfC	2.15	8.4	25.50	0.10
◆HlthCrRE pfB	2.22	8.8	25.32	0.09
HlthcrRlty pfA	2.22	8.9	25.01	-0.29
HeclaMin pfB	j	...	24.58	-1.78
HecoCapTr QUIPS	2.01	8.2	25	...
Heco QUIPS	1.83	7.5	24.35	-0.05
Hercules TOPrS	2.36	9.9	25.95	-0.15
◆HighwdProp pfB	2.00	8.3	24.10	...
◆HighwdProp pfD	2.00	8.3	24.02	-0.34
HiltnHtls QUIBS	2.00	8.0	24.90	0.08
◆HomeProp pfF	.04e	.1	26.95	0.03
HsptlyProp pfA	2.38	8.9	26.65	-0.05
HostMar pfA	2.50	9.3	26.90	0.06
HostMar pfB	2.50	9.4	26.47	0.02
HostMar pfC	2.50	9.5	26.30	-0.10
HshldCapVI pfF	2.06	8.0	25.85	0.05
HshldCapIV pfP	1.81	7.5	24.21	-0.01
HshldCapI pf	2.06	8.2	25.16	-0.09
HshldCapVII pfV	1.88	7.6	24.65	...
HshldCapV pfX	2.50	9.0	27.90	-0.28
HshldInt pfG	.51e	2.1	24.85	-0.04
HshldInt pfM	2.50	7.6	32.94	...
HshldInt pfN	4.50	7.9	56.80	0.05
HshldInt pfO	4.30	7.7	55.50	-1.00
HshldInt pfS	1.88	7.7	24.54	-0.21
HshldInt pfZ	2.06	8.2	25.25	-0.15
IAC Cap pfA	2.06	8.2	25	...
IBM DebCorTSII	1.78e	7.1	25	
IBM CorTS	1.80e	7.2	25.05	...

Source: *The Wall Street Journal*, June 6 ,2002. Reprinted by permission of Dow Jones & Company, Inc. (c) 2002 Dow Jones & Company, Inc. All Rights Reserved Worldwide.

Preferred Stock Listings are found in the Money and Investing Section of the *WSJ* each day. Most preferred stocks are issued for very long periods (25 or more years). Therefore, when answering the following questions assume that each dividend is perpetual.

1. What is the closing price for AT&T's 8.125 preferred stock?

2. What is the annual dividend for these preferred shares?

3. Use the dividend discount model to calculate the cost of preferred stock for AT&T?

Cost of Common Equity

The next cost of financing to measure for a firm is the cost of common equity. A firm's *cost of common equity* is the market's expected return on the firm's stock. Just as we were concerned with market value, not book value, when measuring the total value of the firm, we are concerned with the market's expected return when estimating the cost of common equity. Determining a firm's cost of equity is somewhat subjective. However, the models of stock valuation, both the CAPM and the dividend discount model, provide reasonable estimates. When measuring the cost of equity capital using the *CAPM*, the expected return is equal to the sum of the risk-free rate and the firm's beta multiplied by the market risk premium. For example, for a firm with a beta of 1.24, if the market is expected to return 10% and the risk-free rate is 5%, the asset is expected to return 11.2% (5% + 1.24(10% -5%) = 11.2%).

One problem with using the dividend discount model to measure a firm's cost of capital is that the model assumes that there is no growth in the company. This is likely to be true only if all the earnings of the corporation are being paid out to shareholders. Most corporations, however, reinvest earnings in order to pursue new business opportunities and to maintain existing operations. To incorporate this reinvestment we can assume that dividends will grow at some constant rate *g*.

$$PV = \frac{dividend\ (1+g)}{(1+r)^1} + \frac{dividend\ (1+g)^2}{(1+r)^2} + \dots \frac{dividend(1+g)^\infty}{(1+r)^\infty}$$

This equation can be simplified to:

$$PV = \frac{dividend}{r-g}$$

(This is called the Dividend Growth Model, or the Gordon Growth Model for Myron Gordon who developed the model) The terms can be rearranged to estimate the expected rate of return on common stock.

$$r_{equity} = \frac{dividend}{PV} + g$$

For example, suppose that the company's stock is currently selling for $20 and the company is expected to increase its $1 annual dividend 5% each year. The expected rate of return in this case is 10% ($1/$20 + 5% = 10%).

Exercise 17-4

NEW YORK STOCK EXCHANGE COMPOSITE TRANSACTIONS

A

YTD %CHG	52-WEEK HI	LO	STOCK (SYM)	DIV	YLD %	PE	VOL 100s	CLOSE	NET CHG
22.6	17.45	6.96	AAR AIR	.10	.9	dd	751	11.05	-0.10
9.4	19.75	12.48	ABM Ind ABM s	.36	2.1	27	750	17.15	-0.41
14.6	20.44	14.20	ABN Am ADS ABN	.80e	4.3	...	1444	18.65	-0.02
-15.8	44.98	18.10 ◆ ACE Ltd ACE	.68f	2.0	dd	22653	33.79	0.84
-68.0	44.50	3.40 ◆ AES Cp AES	...	...	9	43757	5.24	-0.41
-46.5	70.50	11.20	AES Tr	3.38	18.3	...	2426	18.50	-0.35
31.2	35.24	23	AFLAC AFL	.24f	.7	25	17102	32.23	1.01
39.7	23.70	8	AGCO Cp AG	.04	.2	58	8148	22.04	1.26
-2.7	24.50	18.95	AGL Res ATG	1.08	4.8	...	2649	22.40	-0.12
12.8	51.91	35.02	AIPC PLB	...	...	24	433	47.40	0.52
20.2	15	7.50 ◆ AK Steel AKS	j	...	dd	3226	13.68	0.40
11.8	29.50	23.08 ◆ AMB Prop AMB	1.64	5.6	22	3662	29.08	-0.06
-20.1	7.50	5.15	AMCOL ACO	.08f	1.4	16	174	5.75	...
-3.6	26.98	22.30	AMLI Rsdntl AML	1.92	7.9	12	468	24.30	-0.10
-10.3	38.40	15.10	AMR AMR	stk	...	dd	7999	20	0.35
⬆ -46.7	55	16.87	AOL Time AOL	...	...	dd	218335	17.10	-0.10
-10.3	4.18	2.15	APT Satelt ATS	.05e	1.7	...	27	2.97	0.02
-44.5	19.92	7.31	AT&T Wrls AWE	...	...	...	67223	7.98	0.25
⬇ -35.8	21.46	11.76	AT&T T s	.15	1.3	4	299847	11.65	-0.60
-12.8	25.40	14.51	AVX Cp AVX	.15	.7	dd	2467	20.58	-0.37
-9.5	30.75	15.40 ◆ AXA ADS AXA	.50e	2.6	...	2221	19.03	0.11
-14.8	25.79	14.20	AZZ AZZ	.16	.9	12	67	17.95	-0.56
39.6	28.49	14.45	AaronRent RNT	.04	.2	42	1424	22.75	0.61
75.2	27.50	10.50	AaronRent A RNTA	.04	.2	44	8	23.65	-0.60
-3.9	18	6.10	ABB ADS ABB	...	...	...	102	9.04	0.12
-0.5	25.12	23.70	AbbeyNtl SUA	1.75	7.1	...	92	24.66	0.05
0.2	25.90	24.30	AbeyNtl ADS ANBB n	1.02e	4.0	...	179	25.25	0.05
-0.4	25.75	24.12	AbeyNtl nts SXA n	1.97	7.9	...	388	25	-0.05
-0.2	25.80	24.10	AbeyNtl 7 1/4% SUD	1.81	7.3	...	57	24.84	-0.01
⬇ -19.2	58	44.05	AbbottLab ABT	.94f	2.1	27	37548	45.05	0.38
5.8	46.20	16.21	Abercrombie A ANF	...	...	17	8097	28.08	0.67
18.2	9.50	6.06	Abitibi g ABY	.40g	...	...	602	8.65	0.07
11.7	7.59	5.80 ◆ AcadiaRlty AKR	.52	7.3	13	459	7.09	0.19
-26.9	30.50	11.61	Accenture ACN n	...	...	...	40120	19.69	0.06
-7.7	6.05	4.54 ◆ Acceptins AIF	...	...	dd	141	4.70	0.11
5.0	19.10	8.50	AcrlyGp AK	.02	.1	12	469	18.30	0.18
12.5	51.99	14.75	ActionPerf ATN	...	...	16	2605	34.44	-0.01
19.9	46.15	16	Actuant A ATU	...	...	19	1120	40.27	0.84
33.1	19.40	10.70	Acuity Br AYI n	.30e	1.9	...	563	16.10	-0.58
14.4	16.95	7.30	Adecco ADO	.15e	1.0	...	285	15.45	0.05
-56.3	36.48	11.45	Administaff ASF	...	...	39	9782	11.99	-0.09
-13.3	27.50	22.25	AFP Prov ADS PVD	1.53e	6.4	...	67	23.85	0.15
16.5	62.19	39.70	AdvanceAuto AAP n	...	...	...	2197	57.95	-0.92
-6.2	27	12.75 ◆ AdvMktg MKT	.04f	.2	15	2035	17.12	0.22
-30.8	31.79	7.69	AdvMicro AMD	...	...	dd	42297	10.97	-0.02
-6.6	5.68	1.75	AdSemEg ADS ASX s	stk	...	...	1082	4.10	-0.01
17.1	23	9.95	Advntst ADS ATE n	.08e	.5	...	23	17.07	0.17
-5.9	46.58	32.25	Advo AD	...	...	17	335	40.45	-0.04
-22.1	31.99	19.69 ◆ AEGON AEG	.73e	3.5	...	1243	20.85	0.14
5.3	26.50	23.47	Strurd AonCapA KOE n	.90e	3.6	...	5	24.75	-0.10
⬆ 2.6	27.85	24.25	Aeropostale ARO n	...	...	...	2498	28.46	1.01
43.6	51	24.05	Aetna AET	.04p	...	dd	9386	47.39	0.91
3.7	57.05	35.10	AffilCmptr A ACS s	...	...	35	4705	55.02	1.39
-3.5	74.50	53.21	AffilMangr AMG	...	...	30	1345	68	...
-3.0	25.85	22	AffMagrInm AMGI n	1.50	6.2	...	17	24.25	-0.06
-27.5	4.33	2.90	AgereSys B wi n	...	...	...	279991	3.08	-0.02
-46.4	7.91	2.50	AgereSys A AGRA	...	...	dd	77032	3.05	0.04
-12.0	38	18	AgilentTch A	...	...	dd	20765	25.10	-0.39
64.6	17.98	7.91 ◆ AgnicoEgl AEM	.02g	.1	dd	9537	16.25	-0.94
2.9	20.60	14.40	AgreeRlty ADC	1.84	9.7	10	138	19.02	0.12
-6.3	11.75	8.72	Agrium AGU	.11g	1.1	dd	4278	9.93	0.07
-28.5	31.95	20.68	Ahold AHO	.65e	3.1	...	3874	21.02	0.17
0.1	15.03	15	AimSelREIF RRE n	...	...	...	1828	15.02	0.02
5.2	11.05	5	AirNetSys ANS	...	...	18	133	8.67	0.06
5.0	53.52	32.25	AirProduct APD	.84f	1.7	21	6206	49.25	0.72
49.8	23.34	7	AirborneInc ABF	.16	.7	cc	4119	22.21	0.20
9.3	20.74	9.40	Airgas ARG	...	...	25	3286	16.52	0.50
⬇ -48.0	11.20	3.65	Airlease FLY	.44a	12.9	57	324	3.40	-0.30
-13.0	12.25	2.60	AirTranHldg AAI	...	...	dd	2226	5.74	0.09
13.7	17.15	12.60	AlamoGp ALG	.24	1.5	15	168	16.20	-0.05
-69.4	20	3	Alamosa APS	...	...	dd	1992	3.65	0.15
-9.8	33.90	17.40	AlaskaAir ALK	...	...	dd	2532	26.25	0.04
13.9	30.65	14.18 ◆ AlbanyInt AIN x	.15e	.6	26	718	24.72	0.29
34.4	32.60	16.50	Albemarle ALB	.52	1.6	24	1917	32.25	0.89
17.7	57.91	37.35	AlbertoCl ACV	.36	.7	25	2185	52.66	0.66
24.9	51.95	31.70	AlbertoCl A ACVA	.36	.7	23	616	48.83	0.28
7.5	36.99	26.88	Albertsons ABS	.76	2.2	28	14264	33.86	-0.43
5.2	46.89	28	Alcan AL	.60g	1.6	dd	15715	37.81	0.22
-31.8	26.39	10.53	Alcatel ADS ALA	.14e	1.2	...	11997	11.28	-0.28
-6.0	44.98	27.36	Alcoa AA	.60	1.8	42	36028	33.40	-0.02
11.3	39.30	29.90	Alcon ACL n	...	...	...	5264	37.85	0.85

YTD %CHG	52-WEEK HI	LO	STOCK (SYM)	DIV	YLD %	PE	VOL 100s	CLOSE	NET CHG
⬇ 28.3	72.90	55.75	Alexanders ALX	...	...	59	55	73.01	1.50
14.0	47.27	35.86	AlexREEq ARE	2.00f	4.3	27	590	46.84	0.02
-1.8	219.84	176.47	Allghny Y s	stk	...	dd	103	185.25	-0.15
-4.3	52.44	31.89	AllghnyEngy AYE	1.72	5.0	9	4907	34.66	-0.46
2.0	21.07	12.50	AllghnyTch ATI	.80	4.7	dd	2224	17.08	0.10
-37.1	15	4.64	AllenTele ALN	...	...	dd	1415	5.35	0.10
-17.2	93.30	56.06 ◆ Allergan AGN	...	...	38	9953	62.13	-0.44
15.8	31.10	21.14	Allete ALE	1.10	3.8	16	1398	29.19	0.30
-7.0	15.06	13.33	AllianceCal. AKP nx	.91	6.5	...	181	13.95	-0.11
-21.6	54.32	35.36	AllncCapMgt AC	2.64e	7.0	...	5195	37.90	1.81
9.3	26.20	11.05	AllianceData ADS n	...	...	dd	263	20.93	-0.43
⬇ 18.6	14.40	9.85	Alliance AIQ n	...	...	35	1597	14.47	0.37
-6.5	15.05	12.90	AllianceNa AFB nx	.95	6.8	...	401	14.03	0.16
-7.3	15.11	13.24	AllianceNY AYN nx	.92	6.6	...	66	13.90	0.17
⬇ -12.4	32.29	26.60	AlliantEngy LNT	2.00	7.5	14	1890	26.60	-0.20
32.0	115.40	56.07	AlliantTech ATK s	...	...	30	4868	101.90	2.64
-9.3	30.20	18	Allianz ADS AZ	.13e	.6	...	230	21.40	-0.02
-3.1	29	20	◆ AlldCap ALD	2.20f	8.7	11	12179	25.20	0.61
21.0	28.75	16.80	AldIrhBk ADS AIB	.77e	2.8	...	928	27.96	0.36
-21.8	19.90	8.90	AlldWaste AW	...	...	...	4074	11	0.04
6.6	57.50	36.70	AllmericaFnl AFC	.25	.5	99	1052	47.50	0.43
11.5	44.98	30	Allstate ALL	.84	2.2	25	17262	37.59	-0.26
-16.9	65.15	46.74	Alltel AT x	1.36	2.7	18	10380	51.29	0.05
3.5	51.98	47.95	Alltel un n	...	...	...	1903	51.45	0.10
-35.9	32.47	13.75	Alpharma A ALO	.18	1.1	dd	5991	16.95	-0.50
-32.4	2.15	1.10	AlpineGp AGI	...	...	dd	11	1.15	-0.01
3.1	30.25	10.35	Alstom ADS ALS	.47e	4.0	...	2061	11.70	0.02
-6.2	55.10	50.30	AltanaAG AAA n	...	...	...	29	51.50	1.00
7.8	24.70	16.67	AluCpChina ACH n	.21p	...	...	19	18.85	0.40

Using the listing on previous page from the *WSJ*, find the price and trading information for AT&T (symbol: T).

1. What was last price? What is the current dividend?

2. Assuming AT&T can grow its dividend at a 5% annual rate, calculate the cost of common equity?.

Weighted-Average Cost of Capital

The final step is to put each of these component costs of financing together. For most, if not all, investment projects a firm is likely to use a combination of financing sources. By putting these component costs together we can find the cost of financing an average project for the firm. Recall that if the company does not issue any debt its total market value is equal to the market value of its equity. Similarly, the cost of capital for a company without any debt is equal to its cost of common equity. Most corporations, however, have both debt and equity outstanding. The cost of capital is the weighted average of each component. The **Weighted Average Cost of Capital** (WACC) is the expected return on the total value of the firm. The WACC is equal to the expected returns on the debt portion of total value, (D/V x r_{debt}), plus the expected return on the preferred stock portion of total firm, (P/V x r_{equity}), plus the expected return on the equity portion of total firm, (E/V x r_{equity}).

$$WACC = r_{debt} \times (1 - T_c) \times D/V + r_{preferred} \times P/V + r_{equity} \times E/V$$

When finding a WACC for the firm, the weights for each component are determined by their portion of the firm's current market value. For example, suppose a firm has a current market value of $100 million, and its capital structure of 40% debt, 10% preferred stock equity, and 50% common equity. The cost of capital for this firm is 6% on debt, 5% on preferred stock, and 10% on common equity. Assuming once again that the firm's tax rate is 35%, the WACC for this firm is found by calculating the weighted average of these three components.

$$\left(\ 6\% \times (1 - 0.35) \times 0.4 \ \right) +$$
$$\left(\ 5\% \times 0.1 \ \right) + \left(\ 10\% \times 0.5 \ \right) = 7.06\%$$

It is important to note that this cost of capital should only be used to consider investment projects with risks similar to the average business risk of the company. Any project with higher or lower risk than average business risk should be discounted with rates above or below the WACC. Also, since debt is tax deductible and its after-tax cost is lower than the cost of common equity, many people will think that financing projects with more and more debt will lower the firm's WACC. This is not true. A higher debt ratio increases the cost of debt and equity by increasing the risk of the firm. Debt is riskier for the firm as it requires the firm to make regular interest payments even if the firm's cash flow is low. For this reason, shareholders will expect a higher return when the firm faces more payments on debt (both interest and principal).

Exercise 17-5

As of June 2002, the market value of AT&T's equity was approximately $37.8 billion, the value of AT&T's debt outstanding was approximately $32.5 billion, and the value of its outstanding preferred stock was approximately $5 billion. Use this information and your answers from Exercises 2, 3, and 4 to estimate the WACC for AT&T.

Project 17-1

Using a recent edition of the *WSJ*, estimate the WACC for a company of your choice. Start by examining the U.S. Exchange Bonds listing in the Money and Investing Section. First find a company with outstanding bonds listed here and estimate the cost of debt. For this Project, ignore preferred stock as it is usually a very small portion of a firm's capital. Next, check the stock listings to estimate the cost of equity for your firm. Use the dividend growth model (be sure to choose a company that pays dividends) and assume a 5% growth rate. To find the weights for the calculation check the debt to equity ratio of your firm by going on the Internet to wsj.com. Enter your company's name or symbol in the Quotes and Research box, then click on Valuations and Ratios.

Company:	Date:
Cost of Debt:	
Cost of Equity:	
Debt to Equity ratio:	
WACC:	

Discussion Questions

The following quote by Sung Won Sohn, chief economic officer at Wells Fargo, regarding corporate investment policies appeared in a June 6, 2002 *Dow Jones Newswires* article.

> "Econometric studies show that the three most important factors influencing capital spending (in order of importance) are the outlook for sales revenues, cash flow, and the cost of capital. If stocks don't do well, that increases the cost of capital. However, some capital is raised in the debt market, which has the added attraction that interest costs are tax deductible."[*]

1. Why do you think revenues and cash flow are more important than the cost of capital when firms are deciding what projects to undertake?

2. How does capital raised in the debt market reduce the cost of capital?

3. Why does the cost of capital rise when stock prices are not performing well?

---

[*] http://online.wsj.com/article/0,,BT_CO_20020606_005507.djm,00.html; **retrieved June 13, 2002.**

Chapter 18

Public Offerings

Objectives

1. Describe how corporations issue securities to the public.

2. Describe the role of investment banks in public offerings.

3. Review the history of initial public offerings and some of the costs.

4. Use the *WSJ* reports on new securities issues to analyze the market for public offerings.

Key Terms

Initial Public Offering (IPO)	Prospectus Underwriter	Underpricing
Secondary Offering	Spread	Winner's Curse
Securities Exchange Commission (SEC)	Syndicate	

In order to begin operations, corporations must raise capital. This chapter looks at how corporations raise capital from public, as opposed to private, investors. How corporations issue new equity securities to the public with the help of investment banks is described. Also, some of the costs associated with public offerings and their historical performances are discussed. Throughout this chapter, the regular and extensive reporting on new securities issues in the *WSJ* is used to analyze the market for public offerings.

The IPO Market

To raise cash, corporations sell both debt and equity securities to the public. The sale of equity to the public usually takes the form of a cash offer. The firm exchanges a share of the company's assets and voting rights in for cash. The very first time a firm issues shares to the general public, the offering is called an *initial public offering*, or IPO. The firm may also raise cash by selling additional shares to the public after its IPO. When an existing public firm sells equity to the public it is called a *secondary offering*. The money raised in a secondary offering is additional cash available for investment.

There are many steps involved with an IPO; including a vote of approval from the firm's board of directors, the filing of a registration statement with the government, the distribution of a preliminary prospectus to potential shareholders, and the determination of the offering price for the ultimate sale of the security to the public. We will look at each step in turn.

Once the board of directors for a firm has decided to take the company public, the management of the company will begin the necessary work to sell shares to the public. Before any public offering – IPO or secondary – the firm must comply with all federal laws enforced by the *Securities and Exchange Commission (SEC)*. The SEC is the branch of the federal government responsible for overseeing all sales of securities to the public. A registration statement, called an S-1, detailing the general facts of the company and the specific security issue is filed with the SEC. A summary of this registration statement, called a *prospectus*, is given to all interested investors. The prospectus tells investors most everything about the offering, but the amount of cash that the firm raises through the offering is not determined until the date of sales. In addition to the federal laws, each state has its own securities registration requirements, often called "blue-sky laws."

Every Monday, the Money and Investing Section in the *WSJ* includes reports on the upcoming IPOs for the week. This column is entitled IPO Outlook and includes a table called The Pipeline. The Pipeline lists the name of the issuer, their business, the expected price range for the stock, the number of shares to be sold, and the lead manager for the offer. To learn about any of these offers, an investor can either contact his or her brokerage firm, or order a prospectus from the lead manager's office.

Exercise 18-1

The Pipeline/*Securities Offering Calendar*

IPOs firmly scheduled for this week, in roughly the order expected. Despite the rocky stock market, underwriters continue to churn out IPOs. Two deals are expected this week.

ISSUER (SYMBOL)/HEADQUARTERS	BUSINESS	PRICE RANGE	SHARES EXPECTED (IN MILLIONS)	LEAD MANAGER(S)
Pacer International (PACR) Lafayette, Calif.	Transportation and logistics solutions	$15 – $17	14	Bear Stearns , Credit Suisse First Boston
Advantage Payroll Services (APAY) Auburn, Maine	Outsourced payroll processing and related services	$18 – $20	5.5	Lehman Brothers

Source: Dealogic CommScan   Note: As of noon Friday

Source: *The Wall Street Journal*, June 10, 2002. Reprinted by permission of Dow Jones & Company, Inc. (c) 2002 Dow Jones & Company, Inc. All Rights Reserved Worldwide.

1. According to this report, how many shares will Pacer International sell to the public in the upcoming week?

2. What type of business is Pacer International in?

3. If the stock is sold at the high price in the range, how much money is being raised through the offering?

Investment Banking

Before the IPO, an underwriter is hired by the firm for advice on how many going public.   The **underwriter** acts as a broker, buying the issue from the firm, and reselling the issue to the investor public. There are two basic types of underwriting agreements – the firm commitment and the best efforts.   Under a firm commitment, the underwriter guarantees a fixed price to the corporation for the stock it sells to the public. The difference between this fixed price received by the firm and the final price to the public is called the **spread**.   The spread may run anywhere from $1 to $2 per share and is the basic fee for bring a security to market. For example, a firm may agree with its underwriter to take $18 a share for its 10 million share offering. The underwriter would then sell the shares in the primary market for $20 a share, collecting the $2 per share as its fee. In many cases, it is too risky to offer a firm commitment. For firms with less history or operating in risky markets, the underwriter may just sell the stock for the firm at the best price available. This type of offering is called a best efforts underwriting. The underwriter will sell as much of the issue as possible, but will return any unsold shares to the issuer.

A group of underwriters, or a *syndicate*, is normally formed to share the risk of buying the issue from the corporation. The lead underwriter, or lead manager, is the direct contact for the corporation and normally contacts other investment bankers to organize a syndicate. Large syndicates are often formed to sell the issue quickly. The spread from the offering is split amongst the syndicate, with the lead manager taking a higher portion. For example, on June 6, 2002 the *WSJ* reported that an IPO for 13.5 million shares of Veridian Corporation, an Arlington, VA. provider of security systems and services to the U.S. government, was led by Credit Suisse First Boston (CSFB). CSFB was the lead manager of the syndicate that sold the Veridan shares. The lead manager will usually place an announcement in the *WSJ* about their public offerings. These announcements are called tombstone ads and include the members of the offering syndicate. Below is a Merrill Lynch & Company tombstone ad describing a common stock offering sold with CSFB and others.

April 29, 2002

5,750,000 Shares

IDEX

IDEX CORPORATION

Common Stock

Price $36 Per Share

Merrill Lynch & Co.   **Credit Suisse First Boston**

Robert W. Baird & Co.

Banc of America Securities LLC

Bear, Stearns & Co. Inc.

McDonald Investments Inc.   Barrington Research Associates, Inc.   The Shemano Group

Each day the *WSJ* reports on the new securities offerings in the U.S. and other markets. The New Securities Issues is a listing of all offerings in both the equity and debt markets for the previous trading day. For an equity offering, the listing will include the name of the company, the number of shares sold, the price per share, and the underwriter for the security. For example, on June 10, 2002, the WSJ reported that on Friday June 7, 2002, SciClone Pharmaceuticals sold 4.1 million shares of common stock at $2.60 per share through A.G. Edwards & Sons.

Exercise 18-2

New Securities Issues

The following were among yesterday's offerings and pricings in U.S. and non-U.S. capital markets, with terms and syndicate manager, based on information provided by Dow Jones Newswires and Factiva. (A basis point is one-hundredth of a percentage point; 100 basis points equals a percentage point.)

CORPORATE

Fannie Mae—$2.25 billion offering of callable reference notes was priced Thursday in two tranches: a new $1.5 billion five-year callable in two years and a $750 million re-opening of the 6% notes due Jan. 18, 2012, which are callable in 2005. The notes due 2007, which carry a 5% coupon, were priced at 99.239 to yield 5.175%, or 0.035 percentage point more than the Fannie Mae curve on an option adjusted spread, according to Fannie Mae. The 10-years were priced at 98.845 to yield 6.159%, or 0.03 percentage point above the OAS Fannie Mae curve. The deals were led by J.P. Morgan, Merrill Lynch & Co. and Morgan Stanley. The five-year will settle May 14, and the 10-year will settle May 10.

Freddie Mac—$500 million offering of 6.25% reference bonds due 2032 was reopened. The securities yielded 6.394%, or 0.725 percentage point above the 30-year Treasury, MCM CorporateWatch said. The transaction, which was led by Credit Suisse First Boston, Morgan Stanley and Salomon Smith Barney, will settle May 16.

EQUITY

Health Care REIT Inc.—Three million shares of common stock were priced in a public offering at $28 a share for gross proceeds totaling $84 million. The company will now have a total of 37 million shares outstanding. It is anticipated that closing and delivery will occur Tuesday. The underwriters for the offering were Deutsche Bank Securities, UBS Warburg, Legg Mason Wood Walker Incorporated and Raymond James. The company has granted the underwriters an option for 30 days to purchase as many as 450,000 additional shares of common stock to cover over-allotments, if any. The net proceeds of the offering will be used to repay borrowings under the company's revolving line of credit arrangements and to invest in additional health-care properties.

Regal Entertainment Group—18 million shares of common stock at $19 a share were priced in an initial public offering. In addition, the underwriters have been granted an option by certain of the company's stockholders to purchase as many as an additional 2.7 million shares of Class A common stock to cover over-allotments. The Class A common stock will trade on the New York Stock Exchange under the symbol "RGC". Credit Suisse First Boston, Lehman Brothers, Bear Stearns, and Salomon Smith Barney are the managers of the underwriting syndicate offering the shares to the public. Regal Entertainment Group is a motion-picture exhibitor operating Regal Cinemas Corp., United Artists Theatre Company and Edwards Theatres.

Source: *The Wall Street Journal*, May 10, 2002. Reprinted by permission of Dow Jones & Company, Inc. (c) 2002 Dow Jones & Company, Inc. All Rights Reserved Worldwide.

Use the above listing from the *WSJ* to answer the following questions.

1. How many shares of Regal Entertainment Group were offered with its IPO?

2. What was the price? What is the total amount of money raised from the public?

3. Which firms led the underwriting syndicate for this offering?

4. What other types of securities were offered for the given trading day?

Pricing IPOs

There are both implicit and explicit costs associated with selling stock to the public. The explicit costs include the spread (the underwriting costs) described earlier as well as legal and other administrative costs. Implicit costs are often harder to determine. One such implicit cost occurs when the issue is priced far below its market value. In order to sell a firm's quickly, ***underpricing***, or selling the securities below the true value of the security, is often practiced by the underwriters. This can be a significant cost of any equity issue. For example, if a corporation agrees with its underwriter to sell stock at $20 per share with a $2 spread but the same number of shares could have been sold at $30 per share, the firm has lost $10 per share in capital due to underpricing. The company is receiving only $18 per share when it could have taken in $28 per share. A possible reason why underpricing occurs is the potential backlash investment bankers (the underwriters) face if investors don't profit from IPOs. If investors don't receive above average profits from IPOs, the investment bankers may no longer be able to earn their fees from IPOs.

The potential for above average profits is what makes investing in IPOs so enticing. However, IPOs can be very risky. For example, eToys' May 1999 initial public offering was priced at $20 a share, but on the first day of trading, the stock's price was as high as $85 a share. The company has since filed for bankruptcy. Also, the performance of IPOs varies significantly from period to period. A June 3, 2002 article in the WSJ reported that during 2001, two months after the offering, the average IPO was up 9.9%, but in 2000, the price of IPOs were on average over 39.9% higher.

But even if the average return on IPOs was high, can the average investor get the average return on IPOs? The answer is no. This is known as the ***winner's curse***, and is due to how IPOs are distributed. To invest in an IPO, investors have to submit a request to the underwriter or member of the syndicate to get shares before they know if they will receive an allocation. If the offering is good, chances are that it is oversubscribed – more investors want shares at the offer price than there are shares to distribute. In this case the average investor may not receive any shares. If the offering is undesirable, then any request for shares is granted. This means that most investors receive more shares of poorly performing companies shares than shares of strong performers and receive below average returns. An investment banker is likely to know before IPO shares begin trading if they will perform well. If the IPO is significantly underpriced the banker is giving investors a gift. These gifts are likely to go only to important clients and institutional investors that generate other business for the investment bank.

As an example of the winner's curse, suppose the *WSJ* reports that two IPOs offered returns of 300% and –50%, an average return of 125%. An investor with $20,000 to invest, $10,000 in each IPO, could expect to earn $25,000. However, the investor is likely to receive only $5,000 worth of shares in the good IPO and all the shares in the poor IPO. The investor's earns $15,000 and loses $5,000 for a net gain of only $10,000. This 50% gain is still a nice return, but well below the average reported for the IPOs. Therefore, even if as a group IPOs were to have above average returns, the average investor will not see these profits.

Exercise 18-3

IPO Scorecard/*Update on Recent New Issues*

Online retailer Overstock.com could test the IPO waters for unprofitable companies as soon as today. It would be the first online company to go public since PayPal did earlier this year. PayPal stock is up 123% from its offer price.

COMPANY	SYMBOL	OFFER PRICE	YESTERDAY'S CLOSE	% CHANGE FROM OFFER PRICE	% CHANGE FROM FIRST-DAY CLOSE	IPO DATE*
SRA Intl.	SRX	$18.00	$21.50	+19%	-5%	May 24
AU Optronics	AUO	11.57	12.15	+5	-1	May 23
Eon Labs	ELAB	15.00	15.05	unch.	unch.	May 23
Netflix	NFLX	15.00	15.45	+3	-8	May 23
Altiris	ATRS	10.00	8.45	-16	-5	May 23
Liquidmetal Tech.	LQMT	15.00	15.11	+1	+1	May 22
MarkWest Energy	MWE	20.50	21.00	+2	+2	May 21
Computer Programs	CPSI	16.50	18.80	+14	+4	May 21
Kyphon	KYPH	15.00	17.00	+13	unch.	May 17
Verint Systems	VRNT	16.00	13.65	-15	-6	May 16
Aeropostale	ARO	18.00	26.21	+46	-6	May 16
Dickie Walker Marine	DWMA	5.00	5.27	+5	-1	May 16
Sabesp (Brazil)	SBS	11.22	11.20	unch.	-3	May 10
Regal Entertainment	RGC	19.00	23.53	+24	+8	May 9
Quinton Cardiology	QUIN	7.00	8.20	+17	+14	May 7

*First trading day

Sources: WSJ Market Data Group; Dow Jones Newswires

Source: *The Wall Street Journal*, May 30, 2002. Reprinted by permission of Dow Jones & Company, Inc. (c) 2002 Dow Jones & Company, Inc. All Rights Reserved Worldwide.

The performance of IPOs is followed regularly in the WSJ. The Deals & Deal Makers column regularly includes an IPO Scorecard which follows the performance of recent issues. Use the above IPO Scorecard to answer the following questions.

1. Which IPO had the greatest return since the close of the first trading day?

2. Which IPO had the greatest return based on its offer price?

3. What is the average return for all IPOs based on the offer price? In your opinion, is there any evidence of underpricing?

4. Base on the offer price, what return would an investor earn on average if he or she received an equal amount in all shares except the best performer?

Project 18-1

Locate a recent IPO Scorecard in the *WSJ* and repeat Exercise 3.

1. Which IPO has the greatest return since the close of the first trading day?

2. Which IPO has the greatest return based on its offer price?

3. What is the average return for all IPOs based on the offer price? Is there any evidence of underpricing?

4. Base on the offer price, what return would an investor earn on average if he or she received an equal amount in all shares except the best performer?

Project 18-2

The daily Deal & Deal Makers column in the *WSJ* is all about the business of Wall Street. The column reports activity of investment bankers including IPOs, new debt offerings, new investment products, and venture capital. In a recent edition of the *WSJ* find a Deal & Deal Makers column that reports on an upcoming or recent issue of either equity or debt. Use the report to answer the following questions.

Date of Report: _____

Title or Headline: _____

Debt or Equity Issue:

_____

Details of Offering:

Company Name: _____

Type of Business: _____

Lead Underwriter or Syndicate Manager(s): _____

_____

Size of Offering (number of shares x expected price, or amount of debt):

_____

Expected performance according to the article (what does the report say about this

issue?)

_____

_____

Discussion Questions

Overstock.com's Uncommon Debut Strikes Flat Note

By Raymond Hennessey
Dow Jones Newswires

NEW YORK—Internet-IPO nostalgia took a lackluster turn yesterday with **Overstock.com** Inc. shares nearly flat in their market debut.

The initial public offering of Overstock, an online retailer specializing in closeout merchandise, finished at $13.03, marginally above its offer price of $13, on the Nasdaq Stock Market. The three-million-share IPO, led by W.R. Hambrecht & Co. and Cantor Fitzgerald L.P., was priced toward the lower end of expectations of $12 to $16 a share.

That Overstock came to market at all this week was unusual for two reasons: First, dot-coms, once the bread and butter of the IPO market, just don't come to market like they used to. There have been exceptions—such as offerings this year from online-payment company **PayPal** Inc. and DVD-rental service **Netflix** Inc. But investors generally have been avoiding electronic retailers such as Overstock since late 1999. Many IPO hopefuls, including Netflix and last year's **Omnicell** Inc., shed the dot-com suffix from their names before coming public.

Also, Wall Street stock underwriters usually avoid bringing IPOs in holiday-shortened weeks such as this one, because trading volume tends to be light. Overstock's offering was the only IPO expected this week.

But the Salt Lake City company's offering wasn't conventional. Overstock became the seventh company to sell its shares through Hambrecht's OpenIPO method, a so-called Dutch auction wherein potential buyers bid on the offering price of the shares. This method decreases the chances that a deal will get a big first-day price "pop," though perhaps it leaves more money on the table for the issuing company itself.

Either way, OpenIPOs have been spotty. The last company to come public this way, restaurant company **Briazz** Inc., did so more than a year ago and has since lost more than 80% of its value. An OpenIPO "is typically not the preferred type of offering for IPO hopefuls that have a choice," said George Nichols, who tracks IPOs for Morningstar.com in Chicago.

1. What two reasons are given in the article for the 'lackluster' first-day performance of Overstock.com's IPO?

2. What is a Dutch auction? What is an OpenIPO?

3. What are the advantages and disadvantages of an OpenIPO to the firm?

4. What are the advantages and disadvantages of an OpenIPO to investors?

Chapter 19

Dividend Policy

Objectives

1. Describe the basic type of dividends paid by corporations.

2. Describe the effect of dividend payments on stock prices.

3. Review reasons why firms pay, or do not pay, dividends.

4. Use the *WSJ* to analyze the different dividend policies of firms.

Key Terms

Cash Dividends	Record Date	Stock Split
Declaration Date	Ex-dividend date	Dividend payout ratio
Regular Dividend	Stock Dividend	Dividend Yield

An important decision all corporations face is what to do with the earnings of the company – return them to shareholders or reinvest them in the company. In this chapter, we look at this issue by discussing dividends – payments by the corporation to its shareholders. First, the basic type of dividends paid by corporations and their effect on stock prices are described. Next, we will review reasons why firms pay, or do not pay, dividends and use the *WSJ* to analyze different dividend policies of firms.

Cash Dividends

The stock listings of the *WSJ* report any dividends paid by firms to their shareholders. The most common form of dividend payment is the cash dividend. **Cash dividends** are cash distributions from the corporation to its owners and are normally paid every quarter. To save costs, some firms have switched to annual dividend payments. The dividend amount reported with each stock listing in the *WSJ* is the latest amount per share that the company has indicated (declared) it will pay shareholders over the course of one year. Once declared, dividends become a liability of the company. This liability may be constrained if the company is not currently meeting its other liabilities. Creditors may limit, or prevent, the payment of dividends until the other debts are paid.

Cash dividend payments are decided by the firm's board of directors, and are usually expressed in dollars and cents per share. On the ***declaration date***, the board of directors declares the size and timing of the next dividend payment. A ***regular dividend*** is a level amount per share the board hopes to maintain in the future, but the board may also declare a special, one-time, dividend payment. Each day, the *WSJ* includes all dividend announcements from the previous day. The table includes all regular dividend announcements, as well as any announcements of increased dividends.

Dividends are payable to "holders-of-record" as of the ***record date***. Record dates generally fall two to three weeks prior to the payment dates. For example, on June 7, 2002, the *WSJ* reported the announcement by Wal-Mart Stores that their regular quarterly dividend of 7 and ½ cents per share would be paid on July 8, 2002 to shareholders of record on June 21, 2002. Even if shares change hands between June 21st and July 8th, dividend checks are mailed to holders-of-record on the payment date. Some firms have automatic reinvestment plans in which the shareholder elects that additional shares of stock be purchased with the cash.

Exercise 19-1

Corporate Dividend News

Dividends Reported May 31

COMPANY	PERIOD	AMT	PAYABLE DATE	RECORD DATE
REGULAR				
Dura Automotive pf	Q	.47	7-01-02	6-15
F.B. Cap 9.75%pf	Q	.24375	7-15-02	6-28
FleetCapl8%TOPrS	Q	.50	6-30-02	6-15
FleetCaprIIITOPrS	Q	.4406	6-30-02	6-28
FleetCapTrIVTOPrS	Q	.4481	6-30-02	6-28
FleetCapVITOPrS	Q	.55	6-30-02	6-28
FleetCapVII	Q	.45	6-15-02	6-14
Kellwood Co	Q	.16	6-21-02	6-10
Lakeland Capl pf	Q	.225	7-12-02	7-02
Marsh Supermkts A	Q	.11	8-02-02	7-19
Marsh Supermkts B	Q	.11	8-02-02	7-19
MidwestBancHldgsIl	Q	.15	7-05-02	6-14
NSD Bancorp	Q	.20	6-28-02	6-14
No Ind PS 4 1/4%pf	Q	1.0625	7-12-02	6-14
No Ind PS adjpfA	Q	.75	7-12-02	6-14
Peoples Bcp Auburn	Q	.15	7-18-02	7-01
Raymond J Finl	Q	.09	7-03-02	6-19
Simmons 1st Cap pf	Q	.285	7-01-02	6-14
UCBH Holdings Inc	Q	.05	7-11-02	6-30
United Secur Banc	Q	.30	7-01-02	6-11
World Fuel Service	Q	.075	7-02-02	6-14
FUNDS, REITS, INVESTMENT COS, LPS				
ColonialNYInsdMuni	M	.085	6-21-02	6-07
Eaton Vance CA MIT	M	.078252	6-17-02	6-10
Eaton Vance FI MIT	M	.08025	6-17-02	6-10
Eaton Vance MA MIT	M	.07825	6-17-02	6-10
Eaton Vance MI MIT	M	.08	6-17-02	6-10
Eaton Vance MIT	M	.086	6-17-02	6-10
Eaton Vance NJ MIT	M	.082	6-17-02	6-10
Eaton Vance NY MIT	M	.08225	6-17-02	6-10
Eaton Vance OH MIT	M	.080085	6-17-02	6-10
Eaton Vance PA MIT	M	.074583	6-17-02	6-10
Enerplus Res un	M	b.28	6-20-02	6-10
Equity Off Prp pfF	Q	.50	7-01-02	6-14
MerLyPharmHOLDRs	-	.077	7-03-02	6-07
Mkt2000+ HOLDRs	-	.0105	7-03-02	6-07
MinnMuniIncoPort	M	.073	6-26-02	6-05
MinnMuniTrmTrstIl	M	.0492	6-26-02	6-05
Taubman Centers		.255	7-22-02	7-01
TempletonGlobIInco	M	h.045	6-28-02	6-14
TrizecHahn Corp	S	b.0875	6-28-02	6-18
VK CA InsTxFrA	M	h.065	6-28-02	6-28
VK CA InsTxFrB	M	h.0545	6-28-02	6-28
VK CA InsTxFrC	M	h.0545	6-28-02	6-28
VK Corp Bd A	M	h.0327	6-28-02	6-28
VK Corp Bd B	M	h.0285	6-28-02	6-28
VK Corp Bd C	M	h.0285	6-28-02	6-28
VK Fla Ins TxFrA	M	h.056	6-28-02	6-28
VK Fla Ins TxFrB	M	h.0463	6-28-02	6-28
VK Fla Ins TxFrC	M	h.0463	6-28-02	6-28
VK GvtSecs A	M	h.038	6-28-02	6-28
VK GvtSecs B	M	h.0316	6-28-02	6-28
VK GvtSecs C	M	h.0316	6-28-02	6-28
VK HilncBd A	M	h.0334	6-28-02	6-28
VK HilncBd B	M	h.0311	6-28-02	6-28
VK HilncBd C	M	h.0311	6-28-02	6-28

COMPANY	PERIOD	AMT	PAYABLE DATE	RECORD DATE
VK HiYld MuniA	M	h.0532	6-28-02	6-28
VK HiYld MuniB	M	h.0465	6-28-02	6-28
VK HiYld MuniC	M	h.0465	6-28-02	6-28
VK HiYldA	M	h.053	6-28-02	6-28
VK HiYldB	M	h.0494	6-28-02	6-28
VK HiYldC	M	h.0494	6-28-02	6-28
VK InsTaxFrA	M	h.066	6-28-02	6-28
VK InsTaxFrB	M	h.0542	6-28-02	6-28
VK LM Govt A	M	h.04	6-28-02	6-28
VK LM Govt B	M	h.0353	6-28-02	6-28
VK Muni Inco A	M	h.0585	6-28-02	6-28
VK Muni Inco B	M	h.0496	-6-28-02	6-28
VK NY TaxFr B	M	h.0502	6-28-02	6-28
VK PA TaxFr A	M	h.072	6-28-02	6-28
VK PA TaxFr B	M	h.0612	6-28-02	6-28
VK TaxFrHilncA	M	h.059	6-28-02	6-28
VK TaxFrHilncB	M	h.0507	6-28-02	6-28
VK TaxFrHilncC	M	h.0507	6-28-02	6-28
VK US Govt A	M	h.06	6-28-02	6-28
VK US Govt B	M	h.0505	6-28-02	6-28
VK US Govt C	M	h.0505	6-28-02	6-28
VK USGovtIncA	M	h.0223	6-28-02	6-28
VK USGovtIncC	M	h.0223	6-28-02	6-28
VK WW HilncA	M	h.057	6-28-02	6-28
VK WW HilncB	M	h.0525	6-28-02	6-28
VK WW HilncC	M	h.0525	6-28-02	6-28

STOCKS

COMPANY	AMT	PAYABLE DATE	RECORD DATE
Expeditrs Intl WA	s	6-24-02	6-10
s-2-for-1 stock split.			
Student Advantage	s	-	-
s-1-for-10 reverse stock split pending shrhldr approval 06/28/02.			

FOREIGN

COMPANY	PERIOD	AMT	PAYABLE DATE	RECORD DATE
AmerMovilSA A	Q	t.0226	7-05-02	6-26

INCREASED

	AMOUNTS		PAYABLE DATE	RECORD DATE
	NEW	OLD		
Deb Shops Inc ... Q	.10	r.075	8-20-02	7-31

INITIAL

COMPANY	PERIOD	AMT	PAYABLE DATE	RECORD DATE
FedEx Corp	Q	.05	7-08-02	6-17

SPECIAL

COMPANY	PERIOD	AMT	PAYABLE DATE	RECORD DATE
Deb Shops Inc	Q	.05	8-20-02	7-31

A-Annual. M-Monthly. Q-Quarterly. S-Semi-annual.
b-Payable in Canadian funds. c-Corrected. h-From income. k-From capital gains. r-Revised. t-Approximate U.S. dollar amount per American Depositary Receipt/Share before adjustment for foreign taxes.

Stocks Ex-Dividend June 4

COMPANY	AMOUNT	COMPANY	AMOUNT
Alltrista Corp	s	Imperial Oil A	b.21
s-2-for-1 stock split.		Psychemedics	.01
BHP Billiton ADS	t.13	Royce Focus pfd	.465625
Brown-Forman A	.35	Royce Micro7.75%pf	.484375
Brown-Forman B	.35	RoyceValueTr	.39
ChemFirst Inc	.10	RoyceValuTaxAdvntg	.45625
Claire's Stores	.04	RoyceValuTr 8%pf	.4875
Falmouth Bancorp	.13		
Genl Amer Invst pf	.45	t-Approximate U.S. dollar amount per
Halliburton Co	.125	American Depositary Receipt/Share be-
Oil ServiceHOLDRs	.0275	fore adjustment for foreign taxes.

Source: *The Wall Street Journal*, June 3, 2002. Reprinted by permission of Dow Jones & Company, Inc. (c) 2002 Dow Jones & Company, Inc. All Rights Reserved Worldwide.

Use the above table from the *WSJ* to answer the following questions.

1. What was the amount of the dividend announced for Raymond James Financial (Raymond J Finl)?

2.   Was this an annual or quarterly dividend?

3.   What is the record date?

4.   What is the payment date?

Ex-dividend Date

Two business days prior to the record date is the ***ex-dividend date*** (stocks sales take two business days to settle). An investor that purchases the stock on or after this date will not receive the pending dividend. To alert investors to these pending ex-dividend dates, the *WSJ* reports all stocks that go ex-dividend the next trading day. For example, on June 10, 2002, the *WSJ* reported the ex-dividend date of June 11, 2002 for Home Depot for their regular quarterly dividend of 5 cents per share.   An investor who purchased Home depot on June 11, 2002 is considered a holder of record for the record date of June 13, 2002.

On the ex-dividend date the stock price must reflect the fact that any new investors do not have any rights to the dividends. On the day preceding the ex-dividend date any purchaser of the stock receives shares of the stock plus the future dividend. On the ex-dividend date, any purchaser receives only the stock. Therefore, the stock price should fall by about the amount of the pending dividend all else equal. Not surprisingly, all else is not equal and the supply and demand conditions for the stock on the ex-dividend date will prevail. That is, the stock may rise or fall on the ex-dividend date by more or less than the amount of dividend.

Exercise 19-2

Use the table in Exercise 1 to answer the following questions.

1.   According to the table, how many stocks were going "Ex-Dividend" on June 4?

2. What is the amount of the Halliburton Co. dividend? All else equal, what is the expected change in the price of Halliburton Co. stock on June 4?

Stock Dividends and Stock Splits

Firm's also declare other types of distributions to shareholders. A **stock dividend** is a distribution of additional shares of stock to existing shareholders. In this case, the firm holds its cash for investment opportunities. For example, on June 4, 2002, the *WSJ* reported that Business Bancorp announced a 5% stock dividend. A five percent stock dividend gives one share per twenty owned by stockholders. The additional shares of Business Bancorp were to be sent June 28 to shareholders of record on June 14. Thus, the ex-dividend date for the stock dividend is once again two business days prior, June 12.

Another form of distribution to shareholders is a stock split. Like a stock dividend, a **stock split** is also an issuance of added shares to shareholders. In a two-for-one split, each existing shareholder receives one additional share for each share currently held. This is identical to declaring and issuing a 100% stock dividend. For example, on June 4, 2002 J. Jill Group Inc. announced a 3-for-2 stock split. This is like a 50% percent stock dividend. Each shareholder of record on June 14 was to receive on June 28 three shares for every two held. An investor holding 100 shares of J. Jill Group Inc. would have 150 shares following the split.

Stock splits and stock dividends are accounting transactions only – no cash is exchanged. There is only a change in the number of shares issued and the par value. The total market value of the firm does not change, but the market value per share drops because more shares are outstanding. In many cases, however, the announcement of a stock split does result in a higher market value of the firm as investors perceive the announcement to indicate that management believes the company's prospects have improved.

Exercise 19-3

Use the table in Exercise 1 to answer the following questions.

1. What is the ratio for the stock split announced for Expeditors International of Washington (Expeditrs Intl WA)?

2. What is the record date? What is the payment date?

3. What do you expect to happen to the total market value of Expeditors International given this announcement?

Why Do Firms Pay Dividends?

As you can see from the *WSJ* reports in the previous exercises, many firms pay dividends. The reasons for declaring a dividend vary widely, but some recurring reasons are given by management. In theory, managers should continue to fund all their net income producing investments, and then distribute any funds remaining. In this manner, the dividend payment is a "residual" decision only. The fact that most younger, rapidly-growing firms retain their funds for investment, paying low (or zero) dividends, while mature firms with less investment opportunities have larger payouts is consistent with this theory.

Following this idea, increased dividends may suggest to investors that the firm's future cash flows will be higher. That is, dividend policy is a way for management to communicate to the market the future prospects of the company. A company that pays out all or much of their earnings is essentially telling its shareholders that they do not foresee a great deal of growth potential in their industry. For this reason, investors watch the dividend payout ratio. The ***dividend payout ratio*** is calculated by dividing the dividends per share by the firm's earnings per share. Earnings per share is calculated by dividing net income by the number of shares outstanding. Similarly, rapidly-growing firms have low (or zero) dividend yields, while mature firms have high dividend yields. The ***dividend yield*** is calculated by dividing the annual dividend amount by the last price at which the stock traded.

Many managers are likely to focus only on dividend changes and not dividend payout ratios. A constant payout ratio would mean that dividends would vary as earnings vary. This could send both positive and negative signals to investors. Just as dividend increases will increase the expectation of future earnings growth, a dividend cut may be taken as a signal of bad news to come. Companies will tend to raise dividends only in response to a sustainable increase in earnings. This is consistent with the fact that cash dividends per year for most companies are more stable than earnings.

Exercise 19-4

NASDAQ NATIONAL MARKET ISSUES

YTD %Chg	Hi	Lo	Stock	Sym	Div	Yld	PE	Vol 100s	Last	Chg
-55.5	35.44	2.35	CpStnTrbn	CPST		...	dd	4312	2.41	0.02
-21.4	3.98	1.70	Captaris	CAPA		...	dd	935	2.90	0.01
86.9	13.99	6.06	Carauster	CSAR	.12	.9	dd	752	12.95	0.21
-27.0	5.79	1.81	CardiacSci	DFIB		...	dd	3739	3.25	0.03
-17.1	3.09	0.60	CardioGen	CGCP		...	dd	1145	0.97	0.06
-49.3	7.62	2.72	CardioDynInt	CDIC		...	dd	787	3.35	-0.16
27.2	46.30	21.69	CareerEd	CECO s		...	45	4955	43.60	0.59
-8.0	1.95	0.89	CareScinc	CARE		...		5	1.15	-0.15
45.9	5.50	1.61	CarlsleHldg	CLHL		...	...	33	3.21	0.37
5.5	28.50	9.35	CrltnCm ADS	CCTVY	.66e	3.5	...	64	18.99	0.64
-5.3	30.19	28	CarmikeCnmas	CKEC n				232	28.52	0.02
67.5	21.90	3.30	Carreker	CANI				897	9.88	0.24
-7.5	7.80	1.96	CarrierAcc	CACS		...	dd	252	2.70	0.51
57.7	3.75	0.70	CaringtnLb	CARN				48	1.61	...
7.2	6.88	3.50	CarrizoOil	CRZO				79	4.75	0.01
-22.0	15.27	8.90	CaslaWste A	CWST		...		316	11.55	...
-20.1	15.47	10.73	CaseyGnStr	CASY	.10	.8	20	1440	11.90	-0.01
6.1	7.24	4.25	CastleEngy	CECX	.20	3.2	dd	178	6.30	0.10
-15.7	5.50	1.52	CatalystInt	CLYS		...	dd	34	2.25	-0.24
-16.8	24	2.96	CatEngySys wi			...	dd	489	3.80	0.05
-28.1	35.60	11.72	CatapulO	CATT		...	21	410	18.75	-0.19
33.0	48.30	22.83	CathayBcp	CATY s	.56	1.3	20	213	42.58	-0.32
42.9	27.75	13.55	CatoCp A	CACOA	.60f	2.2	15	921	27.01	0.66
13.9	13.25	9.75	CavalryBcp	CAVB	.20a	1.5	...	21	13.05	...
123.8	11.90	2.98	CeladonGp	CLDN		...	dd	541	11.19	-0.26
-38.1	16.91	7.65	Celeritek	CLTK		...	dd	283	8.29	-0.21
-43.6	38.88	17.55	Celgene	CELG		...	dd	4279	18	-0.26
-40.0	25.02	11.75	CellGenesys	CEGE		...	dd	2707	13.95	-0.57
-71.7	8.61	1.68	CellPathwy	CLPA		...	dd	2129	1.97	0.25
-70.5	34.70	7.02	CellThrp	CTIC				12829	7.12	-0.12
-73.4	9.15	2.02	Cellegy	CLGY				873	2.28	-0.02
-76.3	6.99	0.08	Cellpoint	CLPT		...	dd	1123	0.22	0.06
-3.1	13.50	2.75	Cellstar	CLST s		...	dd	19	4.07	0.06
19.2	30.18	14.27	Centene	CNTE n				531	26.16	-0.71
3.9	8.86	6.43	CntnlBcp	CEBC s	.13e	1.8	15	281	7.30	-0.11
-69.8	16.90	2.02	CntnlComm	CYCL		...	dd	71	3.09	-0.11
16.6	21.98	12	CtrBcp	CNBC	.68f	3.2	13	1	21.10	-0.30
-42.1	15.50	4.16	CtrspnComm	CSCC		...	dd	93	5.50	0.05
-9.0	28.10	4.30	CentIlmComm	CTLM		...	dd	2362	7.15	-0.08
-69.0	17.14	2.48	CntraSftwr	CTRA		...	dd	1479	2.48	-0.17
24.7	24.24	15.40	CntlCstbcp	CCBN s		...	21	58	21.95	0.31
24.6	19.43	3.45	CntlEuroDistr	CEDC		...	24	346	15.43	-0.57
73.8	15.56	5.94	CntlGarden	CENT		...	c	307	14.70	-0.39
21.6	22.08	7.40	CentAlu	CENX	.20	1.2	dd	1184	16.24	1.21
30.5	27.99	18.55	CentBcp A	CNBKA	.40	1.5	13	56	26.11	0.64
49.1	5.50	1.50	CentBusSvc	CBIZ		...	dd	1992	3.43	0.05
-29.1	78.88	43.40	Cephalon	CEPH		...	dd	17008	53.58	-1.98
21.9	11.48	1.48	Cepheid	CPHD		...	dd	2992	5.12	0.07
-29.0	12.80	6.31	Ceradyne	CRDN		...	20	58	8	-0.17
-51.2	4.80	1.88	Ceragon	CRNT		...	dd	120	2.18	-0.07
19.5	5.50	2.60	CeresGp	CERG		...	6	1013	4.41	0.02
9.0	60	37.31	CernerCp	CERN		...	dd	2912	54.40	0.16
-59.8	9.95	0.71	CrticmCp	CERT		...	dd	397	0.85	0.03
-5.5	76	39.55	Cerus	CERS		...	dd	1483	43.23	0.83
1.6	26.01	24.75	CFB	CFBXN n				80	25.50	...
-7.0	13.30	8.85	ChaloneWine	CHLN		...	39	7	9.02	...
0.3	3.54	1.65	ChampInd	CHMP	.20	6.9	dd	5	2.91	0.02
50.9	14.45	5.99	ChamppsEntn	CMPP		...	47	203	13.63	0.86
96.9	8.60	2.20	ChannlCmrcl	CHNL		...	dd	20	6.40	-0.10
194.2	6.09	0.80	Chris&Clvd	CTHR		...	42	312	4.59	-0.11
-28.6	22.29	11.62	CharlesRvr	CRAI		...	18	621	14.64	0.89
24.5	30.80	10.50	CharRusse	CHIC		...	26	2582	23.17	1.53
46.0	9.14	4.48	CharmShop	CHRS				7161	7.75	...
-57.6	24.45	6.92	ChrtrComm A	CHTR		...	dd	58317	6.97	-0.19
-15.3	30.36	16.06	ChrtSemi ADS	CHRT		...	dd	2523	22.40	-0.56

D E

YTD %Chg	Hi	Lo	Stock	Sym	Div	Yld	PE	Vol 100s	Last	Chg
-19.4	26	13.75	D&E Comm	DECC	.50	3.4	...	2345	14.51	0.10
17.6	36.30	13.13	DKHlthcr	DKWD s	.06f	.2	25	1951	33.48	0.48
256.0	1.60	0.13	DA Cnsltng	DACG				17	0.89	0.14
-72.1	23.47	2.09	DDiCp	DDIC		...	dd	4171	2.75	-0.07
-50.4	14.21	1	DECS TrVI	MFDE				2	1.19	...
-52.9	22.55	4.60	DECS	TWDE	1.39	26.8	...	1	5.18	0.38
-55.1	11.45	3.35	DMC Stratex	STXN		...	dd	2634	3.49	-0.12
-16.1	26.48	17.68	DSP Group	DSPG		...	28	1918	19.51	0.26
-67.8	4.40	0.26	DSET Cp	DSET s		...	dd	5	0.37	0.01
-33.6	6.30	2.64	DSG Int	DSGIF		...	dd	21	2.82	0.12
-50.8	1.49	0.14	DSL.net	DSLN		...	dd	1163	0.62	-0.01
-17.5	7.66	3.05	DT Ind	DTII	J	...	dd	76	4.54	0.29
-71.8	14.50	2.06	DUSA Pharm	DUSA		...	dd	143	2.27	0.04
8.0	18.41	9.64	DaisytekInt	DZTK		...	23	691	14.22	0.07
8.5	17.35	6	Daktronics	DAKT s		...	38	92	9.17	-0.05
-60.0	1.57	0.14	DaleenTch	DALN		...	dd	39	0.14	-0.02
-12.3	52.99	26.90	Dasaut ADS	DASTY	.56e	1.4	...	46	40.80	-0.24
-26.0	2.81	0.97	DanielO	DAIO		...	dd	1	1.14	...
-25.8	8.80	2.66	DataSysSftwr	DSSI		...	dd	52	3.60	0.20
-10.5	11.45	2.85	Datalink	DTLK		...	dd	87	5.44	-0.14
6.9	8.59	2.70	DataMirror	DMCX		...	dd	33	6.52	0.13
-31.1	12.25	5.25	Dataram	DRAM		...	dd	228	5.75	-0.27
-14.5	46.93	25.95	Datascope	DSCP x	.20	.7	23	456	29	0.30
6.2	10.11	2.20	Datastream	DSTM		...	...	480	6.55	0.46
-4.4	1.45	0.43	DatatcSys	DATC		...	dd	1016	0.87	0.01
9.4	4.99	1.21	DataTRAK	DATA		...	dd	22	2.90	0.01
-6.3	17.60	9.25	Datum	DATM		...	dd	703	12.99	0.14
-1.7	11.25	6.80	DawsnGeo	DWSN		...	dd	31	7.62	0.09
16.9	13.99	9.07	DerbrnBcp	DEAR	b	...	19	20	13.50	0.17
35.8	33.82	18	DebShop	DEBS	.30	.9	19	419	32.92	1.08
8.2	6.30	3.23	DeckrsOutdr	DECK		...	dd	174	4.60	-0.16
-51.9	15.15	4.44	deCodeGntcs	DCGN		...	dd	1855	4.71	-0.29
41.9	13.49	6.55	Dcomaint g	DECA	.20g		...	21	13.44	-0.05
-72.5	1.19	0.10	DelanoTch	DTEC		...	dd	5247	0.22	-0.01
-1.9	8.10	3.60	dELiAs A	DLIA		...	dd	2325	6.08	0.09
-1.2	30.52	16.01	DellCptr	DELL		...	58	155211	26.85	-0.17
-32.9	7.50	2.80	DelphaxTech	DLPX		...	17	1	4.05	0.08
8.9	23.08	18.67	DeltaNG	DGAS	1.16	5.3	15	17	22	0.53
-53.3	13.75	4.09	Deltagen	DGEN		...	dd	233	4.30	-0.21
-3.9	1.35	0.26	Delta3	DDDC		...	dd	9	0.78	0.03
61.1	7.12	4	DeltekSys	DLTK				22	7.12	...
-71.2	18	2.56	Dendreon	DNDN		...	dd	280	2.90	-0.09
-15.8	15.80	6.56	DendriteInt	DRTE		...	dd	876	11.81	-0.58
16.2	21.30	13.30	DenisnInt	DENHY		...	16	240	19.25	0.05
19.7	40.95	26.01	DENTSPLY	XRAY s	.18	.4	26	3463	40.06	-0.20
-54.4	19.55	2.87	Descartes	DSGX		...	dd	125	3.40	0.11
4.1	32.25	22.95	DsrtCmntyBk	DCBK	.22f	.8	...	26	29.16	-0.34
126.5	8.51	1.95	DesignsInc	DESI		...	dd	952	7.09	-0.23
14.2	23.65	13.51	Deswell	DSWL	1.29e	5.9	9	37	21.70	-0.10
6.6	7.28	5.50	DevcnInt	DEVC		...	8	77	6.82	0.32
-10.8	2.54	1.50	Diacrin	DCRN		...	dd	52	1.65	-0.07
-55.6	8.16	2.36	DialgSemi ADS	DLGS				4	3.09	0.10
-24.0	6.42	2.68	Diametrics	DMED		...	dd	136	4.30	0.05
-39.4	16.34	7.60	DiamondClstr A	DTPI		...	dd	5831	7.94	-0.08
6.1	72.05	33	DianonSys	DIAN		...	69	2275	64.50	-0.47
66.1	4.01	0.44	Dice	DICE		...	dd	72	2.99	0.04
48.7	14.55	8.40	DickClarkP	DCPI	stk	...	56	34	14.50	0.10
-21.2	41	20.50	DigeneCp	DIGE		...	dd	1493	23.26	0.06
-76.3	18.32	0.55	Digex	DIGX		...	dd	323	0.71	-0.07
-27.9	10.40	3.60	DIGI Intl	DGII		...	dd	1341	4.59	-0.16
-31.1	28.20	10.02	Digimarc	DMRC		...	dd	792	12.80	-0.97
-11.7	4.35	0.71	DgtlGenSys	DGIT		...	dd	492	0.98	-0.03

Use the Corporate Dividend News from Exercise 1 and the Stock Listings from previous page to answer the following questions.

1. For the given reporting date, what firm announced their first ever dividend? What signal may this give investors?

2. For the given reporting date, what firm announced an increase in their dividend? What signal may this give investors? According to the NASDAQ listing above, what was the stock price reaction for the company?

Project 19-1

Locate a Corporate Dividend News listing from a recent edition of the *WSJ* and answer the following questions.

1. Select a company paying a regular dividend.

Name of company_____

- What was the amount of the dividend announced?

- Was this an annual or quarterly dividend?

- What is the record date?

- What is the payment date?

2. For the given reporting date, how many stocks were going "Ex-Dividend"

3. For the given reporting date, what firm, if any, announced their first ever dividend? Check the stock listings. What was the market's reaction?

4. For the given reporting date, what firm, if any, announced an increase in their dividend? Check the stock listings. What was the market's reaction?

Project 19-2

Each Monday, the *WSJ* reports on the dividend yields for all stocks in the Dow Jones Averages. The listing "Yields on Dow Components" is found in the Money and Investing Section at the beginning of the NYSE stock listings. Find the Yields on Dow Components table in a recent edition of the *WSJ* and use it to answer the following questions.

1. What is the average Dividend Yield for the Dow Jones Industrial Average?

2. What is the average Dividend Yield for the Dow Jones Transportations Average?

3. What is the average Dividend Yield for the Dow Jones Utilities Average?

4. Compare and contrast each average yield. Why do you think one average is higher than the other?

Discussion Questions

Corporations Start to Shrink
Stock Buybacks

By SHAHEEN PASHA
Dow Jones Newswires

NEW YORK—Corporate buybacks aren't what they used to be.

In recent weeks, a number of well-known companies such as **International Business Machines** Corp. and **Aetna** Inc. initiated stock-repurchase plans. But data from the first quarter show the actual number of companies taking advantage of buyback programs has shrunk, as cash has become a luxury.

"If you go back into the late-1990s and 2000, we were averaging $40 billion per quarter in buybacks," said Richard Peterson, chief market strategist at Thomson Financial Securities Data. "That has significantly contracted in the first quarter of 2002 with less than $20 billion in repurchases." Mr. Peterson said the second quarter is shaping up to be even more sluggish for buybacks, with only about $12 billion to $13 billion of repurchasing activity anticipated.

The reason is simple. Buyback programs are reliant on companies having the extra cash to fund their repurchases. But during the last bear market, with disappointing earnings proving to be a headache for investors, corporations just don't have the extra money—or the inclination to use what funds they do have—to buy their own stock.

"When you buy back your stock, you're spending a lot of money, reducing your book value and decreasing your corporate net worth," said Alfred Goldman, chief market strategist at A.G. Edwards & Sons. "With the generally disappointing earnings we've had, money just isn't sloshing around the corporate coffers."

Mr. Goldman said with many corporations pinching their wallets a little bit tighter, there is a tendency to be more judicious about using extra funds to finance future growth.

With the recent weakness in the equities markets, and concerns that companies—particularly in the technology sector—are overleveraged, it would stand to reason corporations may find it in their better interest to focus excess cash on debt reduction.

Of those companies that have repurchased their own shares, traders said the most activity was seen in larger-cap, blue-chip names that were trying to offset dilution resulting from employee stock-option exercises.

Aetna, for example, resumed its share repurchases at the end of April after it had halted buybacks at the end of the first quarter 2001. Aetna said the primary reason for the renewed repurchase program was to mitigate dilution.

1. What is involved in a stock buyback? Why do companies make stock buybacks?

2. Other than stock repurchases, what other ways can companies disburse funds to shareholders?

3. According to the article, what is the reason for the decline in stock buybacks?

4. What alternatives do firms have for the use of cash generated from their operations?

Chapter 20

Mergers and Acquisitions

Objectives

1. Describe the market for corporate control.

2. Review the various ways that corporations are combined and acquired.

3. Discuss some of the motivations for mergers or acquisitions.

4. Use the *WSJ* to review recent merger and acquisition activity.

Key Terms

Corporate Control	Acquisition	Horizontal integration
Proxy Contest	Tender offer	Vertical integration
Merger	Leveraged buyout (LBO)	Economies of Scale

This chapter describes the market for corporate control – where corporations are bought and sold. The *WSJ* regularly reports on the various ways that corporations are combined, how shareholders vie for control of their businesses, and the ways that one corporation acquires another. We will use the *WSJ* to review recent merger and acquisition activity. In this chapter we will discuss some of the economic motivations for these mergers or acquisitions.

The Market for Corporate Control

Businesses change constantly. New firms are being created all the time through start-up ventures or through the exchange of ownership. The market place where ownership changes hands is called the market for corporate control. *Corporate control* refers to the ownership, and transfer of ownership, of corporations. We will look at the three main ways that the control, and therefore management, of a corporation can change: proxy contests, mergers and acquisitions, and leveraged buy-outs.

The existing management of a corporation may be replaced by the current board of directors, or by new directors elected by the shareholders. A ***proxy contest*** is an attempt by the firm's owners, and possibly other outside parties, to place new directors on the board, who later replace management. In this type of transaction, shareholders delegate, or proxy, their vote on issues to other shareholders or an outside group. That is, they give their right to vote to another party with which they are in agreement. Anyone may initiate a proxy fight. The idea is to elect directors that will act in accordance with their will. Ultimately, the control of the company is decided by the majority vote.

For example, on April 4, 2000, the *WSJ* reported on the plans of investor Carl Icahn to use a proxy contest for the purpose of changing the board of Nabisco Group Holding Corporation. Icahn planned to oust the company's board and replace them with his own people. Many proxy fights by outsiders fail because existing managers have advantages of control over the company's funding, and because many investors show little or no interest in the management of the company.

Corporate control may also change through a merger of companies, or the acquisition of one company by another. In a ***merger***, two firms combine their assets, liabilities, and all operations into one. In an ***acquisition***, the acquiring firm purchases the assets and liabilities of the target firm. The shareholders of the acquired firm receive cash or securities, perhaps in the acquiring firm, in exchange for their shares in the old firm.

For example, on October 11, 2001 the *WSJ* reported on the ongoing discussions between AT&T Corporation and BellSouth Corporation. The two companies were making plans to merge, but the articled pointed out that BellSouth was not interested in taking on AT&T's cable business. The article went on to say that if AT&T was to sell-off its cable business the merger would likely go through, but BellSouth was in discussion with other long-distance phone service providers as well. In this case, there are two potential deal. Before the two companies could merge (combining their operations) the BellSouth corporation wished for AT&T's cable business to be bought (acquired) by another company.

Exercise 20-1

Mergers Snapshot/*Billion-Dollar Deals*

As broad market mergers-and-acquisitions deals have plummeted, the marquee deals
that the big banks depend on to generate substantial portions of advisory fees have
virtually evaporated. Below, billion-dollar deals with U.S. targets.

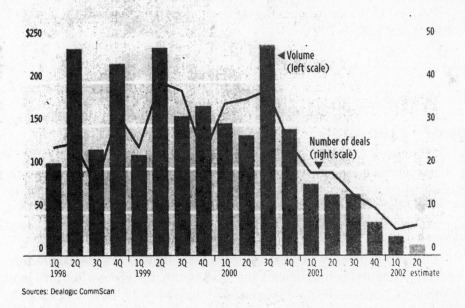

Sources: Dealogic CommScan

Source: *The Wall Street Journal*, May 15, 2002. Reprinted by permission of Dow Jones &
Company, Inc. (c) 2002 Dow Jones & Company, Inc. All Rights Reserved Worldwide.

Use the above chart from the *WSJ* to answer the following questions.

1. According to the chart, what has been the recent trend in the number of large
    mergers?

2. According to the chart, what has been the recent trend in the dollar value (volume) of large mergers?

3. According to the accompanying text, what industry depends on merger and acquisition activity?

Types of Takeovers

Firms also acquire other firms by purchasing the target company's stock. In this case, cash or securities are offered to stockholders, and corporate control is changed by changes to the board of directors and management. A ***tender offer*** is where an acquirer invites shareholders to offer, or tender, their shares at a specified price to the acquirer.

For example, on May 14, 2002, the *WSJ* reported an announcement from semiconductor firm Texas Instruments Inc. stating that its tender offer for German software maker Condat AG would be extended until May 29, 2002. Texas Instruments owned 93% of the company already, but was offering to purchase additional shares from remaining shareholders at 12 euros ($10.94) per share.

Not all tender offers are welcomed. Some corporations do not wish to be acquired, and often management feels that tender offers are too low. In many cases, defense mechanisms, or shareholder rights plans, are approved by shareholders or legislated by states to "protect" their businesses (managers) from unwanted takeovers. Two such actions are sometimes called shark repellent and poison pills. A shark repellent is an action where shareholders approve amendments to their corporate bylaws requiring that a large, rather than a simple 51%, majority of shareholders approve any merger. A poison pill involves contingency plans to distribute large numbers of common stock to friendly shareholders when an unwanted tender offer is made. The friendly shareholders will not tender their shares, keeping the existing board and management in place.

On March 4, 2002, the *WSJ* reported that defense company Northrop Grumman Corp. was launching a hostile takeover bid for the Cleveland, Ohio based TRW Inc. TRW's board of directors rejected an unsolicited bid from Northrop. The bid faced a tough law in the state of Ohio that prohibits shareholder from removing directors before the expiration of their terms. It would be difficult for Northrop to takeover the company without being able to replace the board of directors.

When a corporation's assets or stock is purchased by a private group using borrowed funds, the transaction is called a ***leveraged buyout,*** or ***LBO***. In most cases, the target company's assets are used as security for the loans acquired to finance the purchase. The group that takes control then repays the loans from the target company's profits, or by selling the company's assets. Many LBOs are financed through high yield, or junk, bonds. The buyers in an LBO are often current or former managers of the corporation.

For example, on May 8, 2002 the *WSJ* reported that more than a dozen firms that specialize in buying corporations through LBOs were interested in buying the telephone directories business of Qwest Communication Corporation. The articled said that the directories business was attractive to LBO firms since it produced steady cash flow. Steady cash flow is important when using debt to finance an acquisition since the buyer must meet regular interest and principal payments.

Exercise 20-2

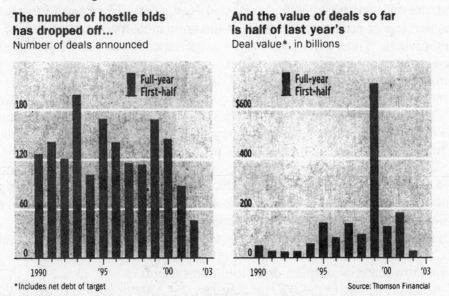

Mergers Snapshot/ *Hostile & Unsolicited Bids*

Overall the pace of hostile bids has remained tepid; however, the bids are becoming increasingly hostile in the mining sector, as underscored by Placer Dome's $1.1 billion hostile bid for Aurion Gold. That bid comes just four months after the end of a multi-billion dollar takeover battle between Newmont Mining and AngloGold for Australia's largest gold miner, Normandy Mining. Newmont won that battle. Below, hostile bids, charted according to the date and the value at which they were announced

The number of hostile bids has dropped off...
Number of deals announced

And the value of deals so far is half of last year's
Deal value*, in billions

*Includes net debt of target

Source: Thomson Financial

Source: *The Wall Street Journal*, May 29, 2002. Reprinted by permission of Dow Jones & Company, Inc. (c) 2002 Dow Jones & Company, Inc. All Rights Reserved Worldwide.

Use the chart on previous page from the *WSJ* to answer the following questions.

1. According to the chart, what has been the recent trend in the number of hostile takeover bids?

2. According to the chart, what has been the recent trend in the value of hostile takeover bids?

3. According to the accompanying text, in what industry has the level of hostility increased?

Motives for Mergers

Mergers can be described as horizontal, vertical, or conglomerate depending upon the nature of the business acquired. If a firm in a similar line of business is acquired, the transaction is called a horizontal acquisition. ***Horizontal integration*** involves mergers or acquisition of firms in the same industry, but often selling in different markets. Thus, the merger serves to increase the company's market share. Conversely, when a supplier or a customer is acquired, it is a vertical merger. ***Vertical integration*** is the merger of acquisition of firms vertical in the supply chain of the firms' industry. Firms may also purchase companies or assets in a line of business totally different from their own. In this transaction the firm becomes a conglomerate. In order to diversify its risk, a company may acquire an unrelated line of business. When one line of business is doing poorly, profits may be up in the other.

The predominant motives for acquiring another business are usually the desire to improve efficiency and/or produce product synergies. The value of the increased efficiency or synergy is dependent upon economies of scale. ***Economies of scale*** are cost efficiencies achieved through larger operations. In horizontal mergers, centralizing administrative functions, such as finance and accounting, will likely produce economies of scale. In a vertical integration, efficiencies arise from controlling raw material supplies or distribution systems.

A feature article in the *WSJ* on February 25, 2002 described in detail the economy of scale motive behind a surge in mergers during the 1990s. The article, entitled "Big Business: Why the Sudden Rise In the Urge to Merge and Form

Oligopolies?", reports on the increasing costs of production and delivery in many industries where there has been a significant number of mergers. Industries such as telecommunications, hospitals, and college textbooks, have higher fixed costs than before. When a company faces higher fixed costs it must increase its volume to keep prices competitively low.

Some mergers are motivated by both economies of scale and product synergy. For example, on September 4, 2001, the *WSJ* reported on the announcement that Hewlett Packard (HP) would buy Compaq in an $26 billion stock offer. The article cited both improved efficiency and product synergies as reasons for the merger. Management at HP and Compaq believed that the new combined company would have sufficient size to compete with Dell Computer in the large-computer market, and also believed that HP's expertise in the computer printer business is an excellent compliment to Compaq's strength in the PC market.

Exercise 20-3

Mergers Snapshot/*International Buyers*

It's not only the U.S. stock market that is hearing the running footsteps of departing foreign investors. The proportion of non-U.S. companies merging with or acquiring U.S. firms has shrunk to its lowest level in five years.

Foreign acquirers of U.S. companies stage a retreat ...

Value of U.S. M&A deals with foreign buyers and of all U.S. M&A deals, in billions[1]

And these merger deals fall to 11.5% of the U.S. total

Percentage of all U.S. M&A deals with foreign buyers

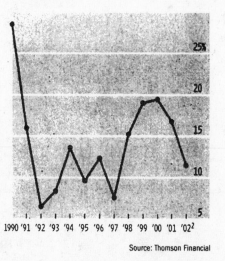

1990 '91 '92 '93 '94 '95 '96 '97 '98 '99 '00 '01 '02[2]

[1]Announced [2]Year-to-date

Source: Thomson Financial

Use the chart on previous page from the *WSJ* to answer the following questions.

1. According to the chart, what has been the recent trend in the percentage of merger deals from foreign firms?

2. According to the chart, what has been the recent trend in the value of all deals with foreign buyers?

3. What economic reasons may a non-U.S. firm have for purchasing a U.S. firm?

Project 20-1

Locate a recent Mergers Snapshot (located in the Deals & Deal Makers column) from the *WSJ* and use it to answer the following questions.

Date _____

Title _____

1. According to the chart or table, what has been the recent trend in mergers and/or acquisitions?

2. According to the accompanying text, what is the reason for this trend?

Project 20-2

The daily Deal & Deal Makers column in the *WSJ* reports activity of investment bankers including IPOs, new debt offerings, venture capital, and LBOs. In a recent edition of the *WSJ* find a Deal & Deal Makers column that reports on a upcoming or recent merger or acquisition. Use the report to answer the following questions.

Date of Report: _____

Title or Headline:_____

Merger or Acquisition:

_____

Company Name(s): _____

Type of Business(es):

_____

Merger Advisors if any: _____

_____

Size of Merger or Acquisition (cash paid or value of stock exchanged):

_____

According to the article, is this a friendly transaction or a hostile takeover?

_____

_____

_____

According to the article, what are the reasons for the transaction?

_____

_____

_____

Discussion Questions

Where Have the Masters of the Big Mergers Gone?

As Corporate Acquisitions Cede To Divestitures and Spinoffs, Epoch of Big Deals May Be Over

By ROBERT FRANK

THE DOG DAYS OF the deal market are likely to drag on well past summer.

Weak share prices, corporate scandals and a string of broken mergers from the 1990s all have conspired to create one of the worst slumps in history for corporate mergers. The number of mergers has fallen to its lowest level in a decade. As measured against U.S. gross domestic product, mergers have suffered their sharpest decline since the data were first compiled during the 1970s.

Most takeover experts say the slowdown is just another cycle, since mergers-and-acquisitions deals have historically followed the stock market in both good times and bad. They say the steep decline is due largely to artificially inflated prices in the late 1990s, where companies traded overpriced stock for richly priced assets.

HEARD ON THE STREET

Yet a number of deal specialists worry about an even bigger threat: that big mergers may be falling out of fashion and that the deal business may be in for fundamental change.

"The deal activity of the late '90s and 2000 was a bubble" says Ken Jacobs, head of Lazard LLC in the U.S. "I don't think we'll see a return to those levels and types of deals for years."

The merger meltdown marks a pronounced change from the days of $100-billion telecom deals and daily news conferences filled with back slapping and buzzwords such as "synergies" and "transformational deal." Deal activity topped $1.7 trillion in the U.S. in 2000, but it fell below $400 billion during this year's first six months.

The drop is likely to force painful changes on Wall Street. During the heyday of the 1990s, major securities firms earned between 10% to 25% of their profits from merger fees, which are some of the fattest on Wall Street. Now the decline in deals is a drag on business and a contributor to the swoon in shares of securities firms. **Morgan Stanley** and **Lehman Brothers Holdings** Inc. both reported double-digit earnings declines in the latest quarter due in large part to the drop in the merger business. Lehman's chief financial officer, David Goldfarb, doesn't expect the merger-advisory business to pick up until the fourth quarter at the earliest.

Although layoffs have helped reduce costs, securities firms are coming under increasing pressure to cut deeper. While deal activity has fallen to early 1990s levels, staffing levels have only slipped back to 1999 numbers. As a consequence, several firms have merged their merger departments into other industry groups, in part to better serve clients but also to reduce overhead.

"I think it feels worse this time compared to the last cycle because there are so many more bankers on the street," says James Neissa, co-head of U.S. mergers and acquisitions for UBS Warburg, a unit of **UBS** AG.

To keep busy, merger bankers are working on smaller deals and taking less traditional assign-

Mergers Switch to Minor From Mega Role

Slimming down...
U.S. merger-and-acquisition volume, in billions *(left axis)*, and the value of the average deal, in millions *(right axis)**

Losing weight
U.S. merger-and-acquisition activity* as a percentage of U.S. gross domestic product

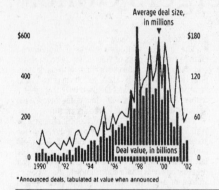

*Announced deals, tabulated at value when announced

Sources: Thomson Financial; Bureau of Economic Analysis

ments, such as bond offerings and capital raising. Some are working on "reverse M&A," that is, undoing some of the giant mergers-and-acquisitions combinations of the 1990s through divestitures, spinoffs and breakups. Bankers also are spending more time with clients, in hopes of gaining a better position for when the market returns.

Others are simply leaving the business. Herbert Lurie, 41 years old, ran Merrill's financial-institutions group for years and gained a reputation as a top deal maker. He stepped down in March and is now taking helicopter-flying lessons and attending Columbia University to get a master's degree in psychology.

"This was something I wanted to do for a while," Mr. Lurie says. "But looking back on the timing and subsequent events, I don't feel like I'm missing a lot on Wall Street right now."

The roots of the slowdown differ markedly from past cycles—and suggest the deal doldrums may continue for a while. The economy and stock market are partly to blame: Companies prefer to use their stocks as deal currency, but if their stock price is weak, they are less able to make acquisitions.

Yet an unusual series of economic currents is also beginning to roil the merger world, turning what began as a mild downturn into a more prolonged deal drought. "Serial acquirers" such as **Tyco International** Ltd., **AT&T** Corp., and **WorldCom** Inc. are struggling under the weight of their past deals, raising new questions about companies that grow through acquisitions. And the harsh reception for the **Hewlett-Packard** Corp. and Compaq Computer merger, which narrowly won shareholder approval, has made chief executives reluctant to announce major transactions that could be criticized by shareholders or board members.

In contrast to the "scale" that was touted a few years back, today's shareholders are demanding "organic" growth and "pure earnings"—free of deal-related write-offs and "special" charges. CEOs and boards are reluctant to commit to buying a company that may turn out to have hidden accounting troubles.

Charter Communications Inc. this month made a run at buying cable subscribers from **Adelphia Communications** Inc., whose stock has plummeted from an insider-dealing scandal. Yet Charter quickly backed down, in part because of the risks related to Adelphia's unfolding accounting, legal and financial troubles. During the fall, energy company **Dynegy** Inc.'s rescue bid for **Enron** Corp. collapsed, and now Dynegy itself is stumbling.

"Doing deals is all about having confidence in both your business and the business you're buying," says Steve Koch, co-chariman of global mergers and acquisitions at Credit Suisse First Boston, a unit of **Credit Suisse Group.** "Right now, we're in an unprecedented period where there is a meaningful crisis of confidence."

Some of the biggest mergers of the 1990s have also started unraveling. **AOL**

Time Warner Inc., **JDS Uniphase** Corp. and **Vivendi Universal** all have taken multibillion-dollar charges to reflect the fall in the value of assets they acquired during the bull market. While academic studies long have shown that a majority of acquisitions fail to deliver value for shareholders, the performances of recent mergers offer high-profile proof.

"The high-profile nature of the failures has made CEOs and boards cautious about driving their growth pans through acquisitions," says Mark Sirower, a mergers expert at Boston Consulting Group.

Granted, many investment bankers say the urge to merge is still strong in the U.S. economy and that companies are simply taking a breather until the scandals blow over. Plenty of companies are holding low-level discussions to merge, bankers say, even if they aren't closing any deals.

"This is just an occasional cleansing," and occasional cleansings are healthy," says Steve Wolitzer, co-head of mergers and acquisitions at Lehman Brothers. "I think there's a lot of pent-up demand for deals just waiting for the economy to turn around."

Whatever the case, the deal drop is one of the most severe since the modern merger-and-acquisition industry began in the early 1970s. Deal activity for the first six months of 2002 was about a quarter of the level in the late 1990s, and the lowest since 1994. Measured against gross domestic product, it has plunged from a high of more than 18% in 1997 to less than 4% so far this year—far more steep than the last significant drop during the late 1980s.

Bankers say several deals have broken down at the last minute. One large health-care merger fell apart because **Arthur Andersen** LLP, the auditor for collapsed Enron, was the auditor for the target and the buyer didn't want to reaudit the company. A multibillion-dollar technology deal recently fell apart because of the decline in the share price of the buyer. Other deals have hit the wall because of valuation, where sellers are reluctant to concede that their stock is worth a fraction of its price during the late 1990s.

"A lot of companies are having discussions," says Michael Schell, a takeover lawyer at Skadden, Arps, Slate, Meagher & Flom. "It's just a very difficult environment for getting deals completed."

1. According to the article, what is the preferred method of buying other companies?

2. What has been the historical relationship between stock market activity and merger and acquisition activity?

3. What is "reverse M&A"? Compare this term with the terms discussed in this chapter.

4. What is the difference between "scale" and "organic" growth? Explain.

Appendix

Answers to Selected Exercises

Note: In some cases, your answers may differ slightly due to rounding.

Chapter 1- Finance and Investments in The Wall Street Journal

Exercise 1-1

1. primary market: *"Treasury Plans Sale of $32 Billion in Short-Term Bills"*
2. secondary market: *"Wal-Mart, Target Slide on Gloomy Retail Data"*

Exercise 1-2

1. money-market: *"Treasury Plans Sale of $32 Billion in Short-Term Bills"*
2. capital market: *"Wal-Mart, Target Slide on Gloomy Retail Data"*

Exercise 1-3

1. The foreign exchange rates given are for trading in New York.
2. The foreign exchange rates given are for trades between banks.
3. This is an over-the-counter exchange since there is no central location.

Exercise 1-4

1. Financial asset information includes Stocks , Bonds and Currency (U.S. Dollar).
2. Real asset information includes Commodities such as Oil and Gold.

Chapter 2- Economics

Exercise 2-1

2. The unemployment rate increased; the number of unemployed rose; the size of the workforce rose.
3. The average weekly hours decreased by 0.1 hours; a decline suggests a weakening economy.

Exercise 2-2

1. Wholesale prices for finished goods decreased; Wholesale prices for crude goods decreased.
2. 1982
3. prices increased 39% since 1982: the average annual rate of change is 1.95% per year (39%/20 years).

Exercise 2-3

1. M1 increased 12.6 billion for the week and declined 11.5 billion for the month.
2. Total Reserves increased 526 billion over the two weeks; An increase in reserves suggests the Fed is trying to encourage economic activity.

Exercise 2-4

1. Receipts decreased 11%; Outlays increased 9%.
2. The deficit is higher (previous period is a surplus). Both, an 11% decrease in receipts and 9% increase in outlays.
3. Net interest decreased; Since receipts decreased while outlays rose the government must be borrowing more, but lower interest payments must mean they are borrowing at lower rates.

Chapter 3- Industry

Exercise 3-1
1. 26.27; 1.91%
2. 64; .08%
3. 51; 1.36%

Exercise 3-2
1. −0.87%; -8.14%
2. −0.45%; +0.40%
3. For the entire period the Russell 2000 is unchanged to slightly lower, while the DJ U.S. Total Market is down; Since the end of 2001 the Russell 2000 is higher while the DJ U.S. Total Market is down.

Exercise 3-3
1. Healthcare (+0.19%).
2. Technology (-2.23%).
3. Basic Materials: Dow Chemical and Newmont Mining - commodity products, high competition. Utilities: Duke Energy and AEP, low competition (regulated monopolies).

Exercise 3-4
1. Banks (+0.33%).
2. Technology (-1.99%).
3. Cyclical Goods: Fuji Photo and Sony Corp – consumer goods such as TVs and cameras, high level of competition.
   Noncyclical Goods; Phillip Morris and Tesco – food stuffs and oil and gas exploration, high level of competition.

Chapter 4- International

Exercise 4-1

2. increased 15.4%
3. exports decreased 0.09%, imports increased 3.63%; the increase in imports was the strongest influence on the deficit.
4. China (trade surplus of 6.86 billion); Canada's trade surplus with the U.S. declined by 1.45 billion (24%), the South/Central America trade surplus with the U.S. declined 41%

Exercise 4-2

1. Finland (+4.36%); Japan (-2.75%).
2. The 4.36% gain in Finland is more than twice the 2.07% gain in the DJ World Index.
3. Finland (622.88); Venezuela.

Exercise 4-3

1. 1.27%
2. 2.3%
3. Emerging (average gain of 15.3%).

Exercise 4-4

1. $15.35; 115,700 shares traded.
2. $34.25; 7,100 shares traded.
3. $8.00; 3,800 shares traded.

Chapter 5- Time Value of Money

Exercise 5-1

1. 3.20%, monthly compounding using actual days.
2. $FV = \$1000(1+(0.032/12))^{12} = \$1,032.47$

Exercise 5-2

1. 5.16%, daily compounding using actual days.
2. $PV = \$1000 / (1+(0.0516/365))^{1825} = \$772.61$

Exercise 5-3

1. $((1+(0.0516/365))^{365} - 1 = 0.05295$, or 5.30%.
2. $72/5.3 = 13.58$ years.

Chapter 6- Bond Valuations

Exercise 6-1

1. 110:31, or 110 and 31 32nds, or $1,109.69.
2. up 9 32nds.

Exercise 6-2

1. 95.75, or $957.50 per bond.
2. 522.

Exercise 6-3

1. July 1, 2033.
2. Below par, 99.08, or $990.80.

Exercise 6-4

Using the RATE function in Excel, the U.S. Treasury Note YTM is 3.61%, and the AT&T Bond YTM is 8.64%.

Exercise 6-5

1. The yield curve is upward sloping.
2. With no liquidity premium, investors expect rates to rise.

Chapter 7- Stock Valuations

Exercise 7-1

	KO	CL
1.	17.3%	-8.3%
2.	$55.30	$52.94
3.	$0.80, 1.4%	$0.72, 1.4%
4.	35	27

Exercise 7-2

	KO	CL
1.	$137,531	$29,529 (in millions)
2.	$4.57	$0.91
3.	12.1	58.46
4.	No, because different companies may use slightly different accounting rules, and since accounting rules change over time, the market-to-book value is hard to interpret.	

Exercise 7-3

	KO	CL
1.	1.4%	1.4%
2.	(1.4% + 8.5%) = 9.4%	

Chapter 8- Foreign Exchange

Exercise 8-1

1. 0.5569; up 0.0016.
2. Appreciate.
3. 49.455; up 0.13.
4. Depreciate.

Exercise 8-2

1. forward discount
2. forward premium
3. C$ depreciate –0.892%; SF appreciate 0.725%

Exercise 8-3

1. 114.22; (.9203/.008507 = 114.22).
2. fell 1.33 Yen, appreciated 1.15%.
3. the Euro depreciated, less Yen per Euro.

Exercise 8-4

1. The yields in Japan are much lower.
2. The Yen is selling at a forward premium (6-month forward rate is higher than the spot rate).

Chapter 9- Financial Statements

Exercise 9-1
1. The income statement.
2. Since Sales (Revenue) fell and Income was higher, expenses must have been lower.
3. No, the company may have used the cash for investment or to pay down debt.

Exercise 9-2
1. $345.8/$6,471 = 5.34%.
2. Revenue = $5,261 million; Net Income = $224.6 million.
3. $224.6/$5,261 = 4.27%; rising after-tax margin.
4. $0.08 annually; $0.02 quarterly.
5. $0.02/0.44 = 4.55%.

Exercise 9-3

	Lowe's	Limited	
# of shares	785.91	499	(in millions)
Sales per share	8.23	4.06	
1. PS =	46.8/8.23 = 5.68	21.5/4.06 = 5.29	
2. PE =	36	18	

3. Dividend is 0.30/4 = 0.075; payout = 0.075/ 0.10 = 75%; Based on current earnings, the Limited is not retaining a significant amount of earnings for growth.

Exercise 9-4

	Lowe's	Limited
1. Growth Rate:		
Revenue	0.23	-0.047
EPS	0.54	0.62
2.	5.68 x 8.23 x (1 + 0.23) = $57.56	5.29 x 4.06 x (1 +(-0.47)) = $20.49

Chapter 10- Technical Analysis

Exercise 10-1

1. Downward.
2. Upward
3. There are many secondary and/or reactionary trends.

Exercise 10-2

1. Below
2. Below
3. Below
4. Below
5. Downward

Exercise 10-3

1. Lower (1,691,439 v. 1,999,971).
2. 4.08, strongly negative.

Exercise 10-4

1. just slightly positive 16.2 (negative for block trades).
2. DJ US Total Mkt (621.2 million).
3. DJ US Total Mkt (106/100).

Chapter 11- Options

Exercise 11-1

1. $0.45; 1,160
2. $4.20; 107
3. $26.15

Exercise 11-2

1. $2.70; $1.20.
2. The call is in-the-money: the put is out-of-the-money.
3. The call premium is higher, the put premium is lower.

Exercise 11-3

1. Johnson & Johnson 15.66%, Applied Material 23.21%.
2. Percentage change necessary is greater for the stock with the higher premium.

Exercise 11-4

1. By 2 put options on IBM with a $75 strike price, total premium is 2 x $4.30 x 100 = $8,600.
2. By 1 call option on Oracle with a $10 strike price, total premium is $0.30 x 100 = $300
3. By both the call and the put (this strategy is called a straddle). Increased volatility will raise the premium on both options.

Chapter 12- Futures

Exercise 12-1

1. $326.20 x 100 = $32,620.00; $140.
2.   0.6562 x 100,000 = $65,620.00; $410.00
3. $92,462.50 - $87,937.50 = $4,525.00.

Exercise 12-2

1.   The spot price of gold is expected to rise.
2.   The spot price of unleaded gas is expected to fall.
3.   Supply has decreased; lower prices suggests this will reverse.

Exercise 12-3

1.   40 Sept Soybeans; 40 x 476.75 x 5,000 x .01 = $953,500.00
2.   December Treasury Bonds; 100 contracts; $10,293,750.00.

Exercise 12-4

1. $32,710.00 - $26,810.00 = $5,900.00; $35,800.00 - $32,710.00 = $3,090.00.
2. $82,775.00 - $82,137.50 = $637.50; $82,000.00 - $82,775.00 = -$775.00

Chapter 13 – Index Options and Index Futures

Exercise 13-1

1. $1.30; 930; 3,944.
2. $4.10; 84; not listed.

Exercise 13-2

1. 9755; 10705, 9230; 14,489 contracts
2. 9706.12, premium.

Exercise 13-3

1. $11.95
2. $38.00

Exercise 13-4

1. Gold/silver (XAU) on the Philadelphia Exchange.
2. Nikkei 225 Stock Average.
3. U.S. Dollar Index

Exercise 13-5

1. 30.1%.
2. Goldman Sachs, UBS Warburg, Morgan Stanley, RBC Dominion, Duetsche Bank Securities; 1,161.9 million shares.
3. RBC Dominion: 61.3 million shares.

Chapter 14 – Risk Management

Exercise 14-1

1.

Day	Price	Change	Daily Return
Friday	56.20	-0.49	-0.86%
Thursday	56.69	0.49	0.87%
Wednesday	56.20	0.74	1.33%
Tuesday	55.46	-0.74	-1.32%
Monday	56.20	-0.80	-1.40%

2.   -0.28%
3.   1.15%

Exercise 14-2

1. –0.58%
2. 0.52%
3. 0.72
4. 0.79%

Exercise 14-3

1.

Day	Price	Change	Daily Return
Friday	1083.82	-13.26	-1.21%
Thursday	1097.08	11.06	1.02%
Wednesday	1086.02	6.14	0.57%
Tuesday	1079.88	-12.00	-1.10%
Monday	1091.88	-14.71	-1.33%

2.   1.11
3.   0.49
4.   Coca Cola: 0.053%, Colgate Palmolive: 0.035%.

Chapter 15- Asset Allocation

Exercise 15-1

1.

Investment	Calculation	Return
U.S. Stocks (DJIA)	12-MONTH % CHG	-11.69%
Foreign Stocks (MSCI EAFE)	12-MONTH % CHG	-12.64%
Government Bonds (10 -year Treasury Note Yield		5.04%
U.S. Treasury Bills (3 month)	Yield	1.73%
Gold (Comex Spot)	% change in price v. one year ago.	18.96%

2. Gold
3. U.S. Stocks, Foreign Stocks, Government Bonds, U.S. Treasury Bills
4. The risk premium for both groups is currently negative.

Exercise 15-2

1. U.S. Small-Cap (-5.87%)
2. Value (-8.48%)

Exercise 15-3

1. 6.94%
2. Lower, 7.54%
3. Slightly Higher, 6.29%

Exercise 15-4

1. 10.87%
2. 10.60%

Chapter 16- Benchmarking

Exercise 16-1
1. $22.12
2. –0.6%
3. $25.76
4. 13.8%

Exercise 16-2
1. Value (average change of 2.24% for all sizes compared to –2.78% for Core and –9.98% for Growth).
2. Small-Cap (average change of –0.08% compared to –6.29% for Large, -5.93% for Multi, and –1.71 for Mid).

Exercise 16-3
1. (12.46% - 5%)/17.08% = 0.44
2. (12.46% - 5%)/1.01=.07
3. Compared to the Sharpe and Treynor ratios for the market discussed in the chapter, the Magellan fund has performed well on a risk-adjusted basis.

Exercise 17-1

1. $51.66; 51.66 x 5,400,000,000 = $278.964 Billion.
2. $278.964 Billion.
3. $254,340,000.00
4. $254,340,000.00 + $17,000,000.00 = $271,340,000.00

Exercise 17-2

1. 97.38, or 973.80 per bond.
2. Using Excel's rate function the YTM is 8.00%.
3. 8.00% x (1 – 0.35) = 5.20%.

Exercise 17-3

1. $22.75
2. $2.03
3. 2.03/ 22.75 = 8.92%

Exercise 17-4

1. $11.65, $0.15.
2. 0.15/11.65 + 0.05 = .0629, or 6.29%.

Exercise 17-5

WACC = (5.2% x 0.43) + (8.92% x 0.07) + (6.29% +0.50) = 5.99%

Chapter 18- Public Offerings

Exercise 18-1

1. 14 million.
2. Transportation and Logistics.
3. 14 million x $17 = $238 million.

Exercise 18-2

1. 18 million.
2. $19 per share; $19 x 18 million = $342 million.
3. CSFB, Lehman Brothers, Bear Sterns, and Salomon Smith Barney.
4. Corporate notes and bonds.

Exercise 18-3

1. Quinton Cardiology.
2. Aeropostale.
3. 7.87 %; this does not seem high, suggesting little if any underpricing.
4. Excluding Aeropostale, an investor would earn only 5.14% , significantly lower than 7.87%.

Exercise 19-1

1. $0.09.
2. Quarterly.
3. June 19, 2002.
4. July 3, 2002.

Exercise 19-2

1. 17 (including the stock split).
2. $0.125 ($0.50 annually); Halliburton's stock should decrease by at least $0.125.

Exercise 19-3

1. 2-for-1.
2. June 26, 2002; July 5, 2002.
3. The total market value should not change, but the announcement may give investors greater confidence in the prospects for the company.

Exercise 19-4

1. Fed Ex Corp.
2. Deb Shops Inc.; The stock (symbol DEBS) was up strongly (3.4%); the stock was up 6% the previous day, perhaps the market new the announcement was coming.

Chapter 20- Mergers and Acquisitions

Exercise 20-1
1. Significant downward trend.
2. Significant downward trend.
3. The banking industry depends on advisory fees from mergers and acquisitions.

Exercise 20-2
1. The number of hostile bids have fallen.
2. The value of hostile bids has fallen significantly.
3. The mining sector bids are becoming more hostile (more highly contested).

Exercise 20-3
1. The percentage of deals involving foreign firms has recently begun to fall.
2. After a strong run up in the late 90s, the value of foreign acquisitions has fallen dramatically.
3. Horizontal integration – expanding market share, or vertical integration with U.S. suppliers and distributors.